# BOSTON

**☒ INSIGHT** **CITY GUIDE**

**Discovery** CHANNEL

**L** **APA PUBLICATIONS**
Part of the Langenscheidt Publishing Group

# BOSTON

**Editor**
Brian Bell
**Updating Editors**
Bill and Kay Scheller
**Art Director**
Klaus Geisler
**Picture Editor**
Hilary Genin
**Production**
Kenneth Chan
**Cartography Editor**
Zoë Goodwin

### Distribution

*United States*
Langenscheidt Publishers, Inc.
36–36 33rd Street 4th Floor
Long Island City, NY 11106
Fax: (1) 718 784-0640

*UK & Ireland*
GeoCenter International Ltd
Meridian House, Churchill Way West
Basingstoke, Hampshire RG21 6YR
Fax: (44) 1256 817988

*Australia*
Universal Publishers
1 Waterloo Road
Macquarie Park, NSW 2113
Fax: (61) 2 9888 9074

*New Zealand*
Hema Maps New Zealand Ltd (HNZ)
Unit D, 24 Ra ORA Drive
East Tamaki, Auckland
Fax: (64) 9 273 6479

*Worldwide*
Apa Publications GmbH & Co.
Verlag KG (Singapore branch)
38 Joo Koon Road, Singapore 628990
Tel: (65) 6865-1600. Fax: (65) 6861-6438

*Printing*
Insight Print Services (Pte) Ltd
38 Joo Koon Road, Singapore 628990
Tel: (65) 6865-1600. Fax: (65) 6861-6438

*First Edition 1991*
*Third Edition 2005*
*Updated 2007*

# ABOUT THIS BOOK

■ nsight Guides pioneered the use of creative full-color photography in travel guides in 1970. Since then, we have expanded our range to cater for our readers' need for both reliable information about their chosen destination and a real understanding of the culture and workings of that destination. Now, when the internet can supply endless (but not always reliable) facts, our books marry text and pictures to provide those much more elusive qualities: knowledge and discernment. To achieve this, they rely heavily on the authority of locally based writers and photographers.

### How to use this book

The book is carefully structured to convey an understanding of the city:
◆ To understand Boston today, you need to know something of its past. The first section covers the city's people, history and culture in lively essays written by specialists.
◆ The main Places section provides a full run-down of all the attractions worth seeing. The main places of interest are coordinated by number with full-colour maps.
◆ Photographic features show readers around major attractions such as the Freedom Trail and the Museum of Fine Arts, and identify the highlights.
◆ Photographs are chosen not only to illustrate geography and buildings but also to convey the moods of the city and the life of its people.
◆ The Travel Tips listings section provides a point of reference for information on travel, hotels, shops and festivals. Information may be located quickly by using the index printed on the back cover flap – and the flaps are designed to serve as bookmarks.

**LEFT:** celebrating the American Revolution on Patriots' Day (April 29).

graphs used here) and **Alan Andres** (who has been an antiquarian bookseller and a magazine editor), and reflects the latest changes in the city. The most startling physical changes were wrought by the "Big Dig," the gigantic construction project that buried the main traffic artery of this chronically car-clogged town below ground. The cultural scene and sporting fortunes have changed too, and this book is carefully crafted to reflect the essence of today's Boston and convey the idiosyncracies of this self-styled "Hub of the Universe."

The text of writers who contributed to previous editions has been updated for this book. They include **John Gattuso**, who wrote some of the History and Places chapters; **Michael Wentworth**, curator of painting and sculpture at the Boston Athenaeum, who wrote the original chapter on the visual arts; **William Schofield**, who invented the concept of the Freedom Trail; **Ken Mallory**, who contributed to the chapter on the Harbor Islands; Cambridge-based urban planning writer **Peter Strupp**, who wrote on architecture; **Jon Marcus**, who supplied the profiles of educational institutions; and **Dana Berg**, an artist and art historian.

Local photographers **Kimberley Grant** and **Kindra Clineff** supplied many of the striking images. The book was indexed by **Penny Phenix**.

Given such a wealth of local expertise, Insight Guides can only commend their work and echo the telling words of Rudyard Kipling: "I have learned never to argue with a Bostonian."

## The contributors

This edition of *Insight City Guide: Boston* was produced by Insight's editorial director, **Brian Bell**, whose Irish roots help him relate to one major component of the city's ethnic mix, and by **Bill and Kay Scheller**, a Vermont-based travel-writing team with strong Boston connections. Kay, a Massachusetts native, is a graduate of Boston University and a former reporter for a Boston-area newspaper. Bill has lived on Beacon Hill, and taught at the Boston Center for Adult Education. As well as providing a wealth of fresh information for this edition, they wrote a new chapter on the city's literary heritage.

This edition builds on the success of earlier editions produced by **Marcus Brooke** (who once taught at Harvard and at MIT and also supplied many of the classic photo-

**CONTACTING THE EDITORS**
We would appreciate it if readers would alert us to errors or outdated information by writing to:
**Insight Guides, P.O. Box 7910, London SE1 1WE, England.
Fax: (44) 20 7403-0290.
insight@apaguide.co.uk**

**NO** part of this book may be reproduced, stored in a retrieval system or transmitted in any form or means electronic, mechanical, photocopying, recording or otherwise, without prior written permission of *Apa Publications*. Brief text quotations with use of photographs are exempted for book review purposes only. Information has been obtained from sources believed to be reliable, but its accuracy and completeness, and the opinions based thereon, are not guaranteed.

**www.insightguides.com**
*In North America:*
**www.insighttravelguides.com**

## Travel Tips

# THE BEST OF BOSTON

Setting priorities, saving money, unique attractions...
here, at a glance, are our recommendations, plus tips
and tricks even Bostonians won't always know

## BOSTON FOR FAMILIES

These attractions are popular with children,
though not all will suit every age group.

- **Boston by Little Feet** An hour-long walking tour of the Freedom Trail for ages 6–12. *Page 235.*
- **Boston Children's Theatre** Year-round productions, plus free outdoor performances in summer. *Page 235.*
- **Boston Duck Tours** Tours of Boston and the Charles River aboard World War II amphibious vehicles. *Page 232.*
- **Children's Museum** A rambling, laid-back, hands-on spot mixing educational and fun activities. *Page 106.*
- **Franklin Park Zoo** Exotic animals, a Tropical Rain Forest, and a petting zoo. *Page 150.*
- **Make Way for Ducklings Tour** Follows in the "steps" of the characters in Robert McCloskey's beloved book. *Page 125.*
- **Museum of Science, Hayden Planetarium and Mugar Omni Theatre** World-class, exciting and exhausting look-and-touch museum. *Page 170.*

- **New England Aquarium** Sea otters, penguins, dolphins, a 4-story tank, and live shows. *Page 104.*
- **Puppet Showplace Theatre** Classics such as *Cinderella*. 32 Station St., Brookline, tel: 731-6400.
- **USS Constitution** "Old Ironsides", the oldest commissioned ship in the US Navy, is a floating antidote to dry textbook history *Page 117.*
- **Whale Watch** Cruise lines set sail in the hope of sighting the mammals. *Page 112.*

**BELOW** aboard the USS *Constitution*; St Patrick's Day parade.

## BEST FESTIVALS AND EVENTS

- **New England Spring Flower Show** The nation's oldest annual flower exhibition lasts a week in March.
- **St. Patrick's Day Parade** Boston's Irish community hosts a big parade on the Sunday nearest to March 17.
- **Boston Marathon** A grueling, 26-mile route, run on the third Monday in April.

- **Battle of Lexington Reenactment** The Minutemen versus the British, each April on Patriot's Day.
- **Independence Day (Fourth of July)** The Boston Pops perform a free evening concert, culminating in a spectacular fireworks display, at the Hatch Shell on the banks of the Charles River *(see page 72)*.
- **North End Festivals** Streets are closed to traffic and the aroma of fried dough and grilled sausage and peppers permeate the air at this joyous series of saints' day feasts, weekends in July and August.
- **First Night** New Year's Eve art and entertainment events at venues throughout the city begin midday and continue into the wee hours of January 1.

## ONLY IN BOSTON...

- **Swan Boats** Since 1877, these swan-shaped boats have been plying the Public Garden lagoon. Fifteen-minute rides offered mid-April–Sept. *Page 125.*
- **Stroll through Harvard Yard** The walled, leafy campus of America's oldest college (1636) includes the 1726 Wadsworth House; impressive Widener Library. For guided tours, call 617-495-1573. *Pages 158–61.*

- **Filene's Basement** The atmosphere is chaotic at this entertaining discount merchandise mecca (dating to 1908) at 426 Washington St. Prices are cut automatically. *Page 77.*
- **Battle Road** Trace the route taken by the Minutemen and Redcoats on April 19, 1775, at the start of the American Revolution. *Page 180.*
- **Durgin Park** The legendary old dining hall (established 1826) is famed for communal tables, huge portions, and rude waitstaff. *Page 88.*
- **Harbor Islands** Several of the 30 islands that make up the Boston Harbor Islands National Recreation Area are served by a ferry from downtown Boston. *Pages 109–11.*

**ABOVE:** Freedom Trail actors as Abigail Adams, William Dawes.

**ABOVE:** swan boats.

## BEST MARKETS

- **Quincy Market**, packed with take-out eateries, souvenir vendors, and gift shops.
- **Chinatown**, a compact area near the Theater District, is packed with gift and antiques shops, and food markets.
- **Farmers' Markets** are held at Copley Square Plaza Tuesdays and Fridays from 11am–6pm, and at City Hall Plaza Mon

and Wed 11am–6pm, from late May until late Nov.
- **Haymarket Square** in the North End becomes a bustling open-air farmers' market Fri and Sat.
- **Formaggio Kitchen** 244 Huron Avenue (tel: 354-4750) and 268 Shawmut Ave (tel: 350-6996). More than 3,000 cheeses, artisanal oils, and delicacies.

## TOP WALKS

- **Freedom Trail** Sixteen locations that played a part in the city's Colonial and Revolutionary history are linked by a 3-mile (5 km) painted path. *Pages 54–57.*
- **Beacon Hill** Narrow, gaslit streets and tidy rows of Federal homes, haunts of Boston's elite, characterize this storied neighborhood bordering Boston Common. The Black Heritage Trail lies along the way. *Page 59.*
- **Back Bay** Amble along Commonwealth Avenue's grand mall, Newbury Street's fashionable shopping district, and quiet Marlborough Street, admiring Boston's finest residential architecture. *Page 126–29.*

- **Charles River Esplanade** Walkways along the banks of the Charles are popular with strollers, cyclists, and joggers, and offer splendid city views. *Page 71.*
- **Boston Common and the Public Garden** The 48-acre (19-hectare) Common is America's oldest public park (1634). Adjacent is the country's first public botanical garden, with rambling paths and formal flower beds. *Page 73.*

**RIGHT:** *Make Way for Ducklings* in the Public Garden.

# THE HUB OF THE UNIVERSE

### Life, liberty and the pursuit of happiness are all very well for most people, but what really counts in Boston is self-esteem

**B**oston is where the Mystic and the Charles rivers meet to form the Atlantic Ocean. It's an old joke, but it speaks volumes, like the line in William Dean Howells' *The Rise of Silas Lapham*: "The Bostonian who leaves Boston ought to be condemned to perpetual exile." There are still more than a few diehards who would agree.

Justifiable pride? Insufferable arrogance? Perhaps visitors' reactions to Boston and Bostonians reveal more about themselves than about the city and its inhabitants, but it is certain that no other American city has provoked so many polarized opinions. Writers in particular have always flocked to Boston, drawn by its strong literary tradition, so the quality of both praise and invective is of an uncommonly high standard.

Boston is "a state of mind," said Mark Twain (or perhaps Ralph Waldo Emerson, or possibly Thomas Appleton, for Bostonians can always find something to disagree about). It's "a moral and intellectual nursery," said (again, arguably) the Spanish philosopher George Santayana. "A museum piece," thought Frank Lloyd Wright. "A hole," wrote Robert Browning.

Maybe Boston simply oversold itself. Even today, when city halls all over America house marketing teams intent on promoting their "product" with the publicity tools once dedicated to breakfast cereals and suntan oils, no copywriter would dare claim for the city the status that Oliver Wendell Holmes, author, philosopher and professor of anatomy at Harvard, gave it in 1860: that "it is the thinking center of the continent, and therefore of the planet." Other 19th-century boosters went even further, extending Holmes's tongue-in-cheek description of the Massachusetts State House – "the hub of the solar system" – to the city itself, calling it "The Hub of the Universe."

The Hub hit harder times in the 20th century and, between 1950 and 1970, its population slumped from more than 800,000 to 563,000 as many abandoned the decaying inner city for the suburbs. Successive mayors and city planners campaigned to reverse the decline, and soaring modern architecture and a revived waterfront began to signal a new confidence. With the help of the research laboratories and high-tech industries of Cambridge, and the renewed vitality of the arts, Boston avoided relegation to the status of an outdoor museum of history and once again began to play a leading role in the nation's affairs. Self-esteem had been restored. ❑

---

**PRECEDING PAGES:** the thriving seaport of Boston, 1855; the Old State House *circa* 1801.
**LEFT:** today's soaring city – the Prudential Center in Back Bay.

# THE BOSTON CHARACTER

**Only Bostonians, they say, can understand Bostonians. That statement in itself says a lot about an enduringly singular psyche**

**B**oston's self-proclaimed status as the Hub of the Universe, though it wasn't meant to be taken entirely seriously, was a red rag that has infuriated many literary bulls. "Boston prides itself on virtue and ancient lineage – it doesn't impress me in either direction," wrote the philosopher Bertrand Russell in 1914. "It is musty, like the Faubourg St Germain. I often want to ask them what constitutes the amazing virtue they are so conscious of."

In the mid-19th century the valued virtue was culture, as the New World, rapidly approaching adulthood, sought to convey its maturity to the Old. Not that everyone worshipped it: "In Boston," wrote Charles Mackay in 1859, "the onus lies upon every respectable person to prove that he has not written a sonnet, preached a sermon, or delivered a lecture."

## Birth of the Brahmins

Self-esteem was certainly valued even more than sonnets, and the city's establishment readily approved Oliver Wendell Holmes's description of them as "Boston Brahmins." Not only was the alliteration attractive; the term also suggested an ancient lineage, a certain austerity, unquestioned wisdom. No matter that the 19th-century businessmen who ran Boston were often closer in their intellectual interests to Donald Trump than to an Indian ascetic: "Brahmin" was accepted. No Madison Avenue copywriter could have done a better job.

The tone had been set even earlier, in 1841, by George Combe, a phrenologist who, having studied the heads of the city's inhabitants

from 1838 to 1840, delivered the kind of prognosis that court physicians reserved for absolute monarchs: "The cerebral organization of this people, taking them all in all, appears really to have been enlarged in the moral and intellectual regions by long cultivation, added to the influence of a favorable stock."

But along with the superior stock came stock attitudes. The problem, for many, was that Boston, rather than creating its own distinctive culture, was slavishly imitating the discredited characteristics of its cast-off colonial parent. "The Bostonians are really, as a race, far inferior in point of anything beyond mere talent to any other set upon the continent of North America," wrote Edgar Allan Poe in 1849. "They are decidedly the most servile imitators of the English it is possible to conceive."

Even the Bostonians' speech patterns and accent came under fire as being slavish replicas of Oxford English. As an anonymous wit put it, if you hear an owl hoot "To whom" instead of "To who," you can be sure it was born and educated in Boston.

Many visitors brave enough to take a car into the chronically congested town remark that the locals' driving behavior sets Boston apart from other North American cities. The city center's roads, which remain more faithful in their patterns to 17th-century cow tracks

than to anything suggesting a grid, encourage local drivers to be aggressive: they race away from traffic lights, weave in and out of lanes, and tailgate alarmingly. Visitors from Europe are familiar with such behavior; people from other American cities, where driving is more sedate and courteous, think they're in a Hollywood movie. It's not just an impression either: insurers confirm that Boston's drivers are the nation's most accident-prone.

Ever adaptable, Bostonians have responded to the traffic chaos by regarding walking as a

**LEFT:** a modern Boston Brahmin.
**ABOVE:** Boston's finest on patrol.

virtue. Where New Yorkers would unhesitatingly flag down a cab, Bostonians, eschewing extravagance, will step smartly toward their destination. Given the jams, of course, that's sound common sense; as the joke has it: "Shall we walk or do we have time to take a cab?"

## Split personality

But if walking is sometimes a necessity, it is usually a pleasure. It enables one to savor the strange contradictions of this untypical town. The architecture expresses part of its split personality: the size, color and design of the carefully preserved older buildings convey class, heritage and a human scale, while the gleaming new skyscrapers and vast concrete bunkers radiate boldness, modernity and commercial confidence but can sometimes seem soulless. A spell of window-shopping will quickly indicate that Boston is an expensive place to live; yet here is Filene's Basement, where society matrons as well as secretaries boast of the bargains they unearth among the scheduled markdowns. The city is unquestionably America's medical capital; yet in its very center sits the vast Christian Science complex, whose occupants reject many of the tenets of modern medicine.

Academics adore such paradoxes and probably encourage them. Boston is a factory town whose product is college graduates and each new generation adds its own pinch of quirkiness to the cocktail, sustaining the legend. Also, many find jobs and stay on in the area after graduating, adding fresh blood to the population and keeping urban sclerosis at bay.

And so the debate goes on. For more than two centuries, the Boston character has delighted and infuriated, almost in equal measure, and has defeated most attempts to define it. Such attempts, Bostonians will tell you, are futile in any case, unless you had the good fortune to be born and brought up in the Hub of the Universe. It's an attitude summed up by the old story of the Bostonian who dies and, with due dignity, approaches St Peter at the Pearly Gates in order to present his credentials and seek permission to enter. St Peter asks him where he is from, and on being told "BOSTON," hesitates, then says, "Well, your record is spotless, and you may come in, but I don't think you will like it here." ❏

# THE MAKING OF BOSTON

**Boston is the cradle of American independence, where Samuel Adams, Paul Revere and John Hancock were transformed into players in a national mythology. Later, the energy generated by waves of immigrants ensured that modernity wasn't suffocated by tradition**

Although a solitude-seeking clergyman named William Blackstone had settled in 1625 on a spot now occupied by Boston Common, the history of the city really dates to 1630, when John Winthrop and a group of Puritans determined to create a new society – a "visible kingdom of God" – on the hilly Shawmut peninsula. While still aboard the *Arbella*, Winthrop had addressed his fellow colonists, clearly laying out for them the terms of the covenant with the Almighty that would form the foundation of their new enterprise.

"We must be knit together, in this work, as one man," he told them. "We must entertain each other in brotherly affection… We must delight in each other; make other's conditions our own; rejoice together; mourn together; labor and suffer together… For we must consider that we shall be as a City upon a Hill. The eyes of all people are upon us."

## The great adventure

The Puritan colonists were Calvinist reformers, seeking to purify the English Church and develop a "holy commonwealth." Winthrop, a Suffolk lawyer, had joined several other middle-class Puritans in purchasing a charter issued by the king and entitling the group, known as the Massachusetts Bay Company, to occupy a strip of land between the Charles and Merrimack rivers. They also arranged to "transfer the government of the plantation to those that

**LEFT:** British ships on the warpath in 1776.
**RIGHT:** eight-year-old Anne Pollard, the first white female to set foot in Boston (1630).

shall inhabit there," which effectively conferred independence on the company.

When Winthrop set out from England on March 29, 1630, with a fleet of 11 ships and about 750 colonists, there was some talk of joining a fledgling colony at Salem. Instead, they headed to the future site of Charlestown to build a settlement of their own. This first camp lacked reliable fresh water supplies, and several parties headed inland to where Watertown, Medford, Saugus, Dorchester, and Roxbury would arise. But John Winthrop took up the invitation of an eccentric minister, William Blackstone, who sold the newcomers his land at Shawmut. Some 150 settlers moved to the site and named it Boston, after their home town in Lincolnshire.

## An age of intolerance

The town grew quickly. There were about 300 people in 1632, 600 in 1635 and 1,200 in 1640 – most living in wood houses huddled around Town Cove or in the marketplace near present-day North Square. Although democratic in structure, the government was basically a theocracy. Only male church members could vote, and the ministers were consulted on all but administrative matters.

Though themselves religious dissenters, the Puritans showed little tolerance for non-

orthodox beliefs. Both Roger Williams and Anne Hutchinson tried to introduce theological innovations, and were banished from the colony. The Quakers who came to Boston were whipped or had an ear cut off, and were exiled. A few brave enough to return, including the heroic Mary Dyer, were hanged from the Great Elm on the Common.

Settlers nevertheless continued to pour into Boston – but many were more interested in the condition of their purses than the health of their souls. By the time John Winthrop died in 1649, Boston had become quite a different place, with an "aristocracy of saints" still commanding most of the political power through the churches, and the remainder of the community devoting itself increasingly to mammon. By the late 1630s, Boston ships were carrying loads of cod to England, Spain and Portugal, and were returning with much-needed manufactured goods. New England ships carried West Indies molasses to Boston distilleries, and brought slaves from Africa to the Caribbean.

## Interference from England

In its first 30 years the Massachusetts Bay Colony enjoyed virtual autonomy. But when, after England's Civil War and the republican rule of Oliver Cromwell, the monarchy was restored under Charles II in 1660, this age of benign neglect came suddenly to an end. Among the new king's first acts was to rein in the New England colonies, which were governing themselves like a sovereign nation and bringing little revenue to the Crown. First,

### WHAT THE PURITANS BELIEVED

To the Puritans, people were naturally sinful and required unrelenting discipline. Work, frugality and humility were valued, while "harmless" distractions such as dance, music and stylish clothes were scorned as frivolities. Education was deemed essential, and within six years of their arrival the Puritans established a public school for children and a college for ministers (later Harvard University).

The cornerstone of Puritan theology was the Calvinist doctrine of predestination, a belief that God preordained who was saved and who was damned. The key to acceptance in Puritan society was to demonstrate clearly through pious demeanor that you were, in fact, one of God's

chosen people. Because a saint was thought to despise sin in others, much effort was put into reforming those who didn't quite measure up.

Making a public display of just how much they detested sin was also believed to be a good way of protecting the town from divine retribution, and wayward members of the community were often cruelly punished. Even minor offenses like cursing or gossiping could lead to whipping, branding or being placed in the stocks. Ironically, the stock-maker, who gave the General Court an inflated bill, was the first to be locked in his contraption. A sailor just back from a long voyage was whipped for kissing his wife in public.

Charles used the Navigation Acts to force colonial merchants to do business exclusively with England. Then, in order to hamstring the Puritan leadership, he ordered voting rights in Massachusetts be granted to all men of "good estate" regardless of church membership.

Although the Puritans made a fuss over the change in suffrage, most merchants simply ignored the Navigation Acts and continued trading with whomever they wished. When Charles got wind of just how widespread smuggling had become, he answered the colonists' audacity by revoking the Massachusetts Bay charter in 1684 and transforming the whole of New England into a single royal colony.

Charles died before completing this work, but his brother, James II, picked up where he left off by appointing Sir Edmund Andros governor-general of the Dominion of New England in 1686. Bostonians, who regarded him as a contemptible man, chafed under Andros, who not only converted the Old South Meeting House into an Anglican church – sacrilege to the Puritan clergy – but also limited town meetings to one a year and forced all property-holders to make new payments on land titles.

The colonists were furious. When word reached them that the Catholic King James had been ousted during England's "Glorious Revolution" of 1689, they staged an insurrection of their own. Andros was thrown in jail and shipped back to England. Boston's most prominent minister, Increase Mather, was sent to England to ask William and Mary, the new Protestant monarchs, to restore the original Massachusetts charter. They offered a compromise: The colonists would be allowed to elect their own representatives, but suffrage would be extended to all property-holders, irrespective of religion, and the crown would appoint the governor. Puritan ideals would remain an integral part of everyday Boston life, but the old theocratic order was broken.

## The rise of the merchant class

With suffrage now open to all property-holders, a class of wealthy merchants emerged as an influential force in Boston's affairs. Ship-building, cod fishing, and the "triangle trade" (shipping fish and crafted goods to Europe and picking up molasses and slaves in the West Indies) enriched entrepreneurs, who built handsome homes, and financed civic projects such as Faneuil Hall. But, although a handful of merchants were doing well, the rest of the city was not. The economic slow-down was partly due to competition from other colonial towns, especially New York and Philadelphia. The French and Indian Wars, which flared again in 1740 and 1754, had also hit the town hard – hundreds of men were killed, ships were destroyed, and the city was overburdened with the care of widows and orphans. By the time

the French were defeated in 1763, Boston was in perilous economic condition. Just as it began to recover, the British renewed the old tug-of-war by trying to impose further taxes. In doing so, they lit the fuse of revolution.

## The road to rebellion

As always, England's aim was to get as much money out of the colonies as possible. In 1763, King George III launched the effort with a battery of legislation that prohibited colonial currency and cracked down on the lucrative sugar trade between Boston and the West Indies. Before New Englanders could mount an effective protest, Parliament also passed the

**LEFT:** the 1692 trial of George Jacobs for witchcraft.
**RIGHT:** Harvard College buildings in 1743.

# Paul Revere

I t was a lucky day for the Bay Colony when Paul's father, Apollos Rivoire, left his home in the Channel Islands, between Britain and France, and set sail for Boston. Apollos was a talented craftsman who produced goldware and silverware of exquisite design. And on January 1, 1735, he and Mrs Rivoire produced an extraordinary Boston baby who became Paul Revere.

Paul inherited the family business, improved on his father's craftsmanship, and, from his shop in the North End, quickly

won the reputation of being the best silversmith in colonial America. His career then broadened to embrace enough sidelines, specialties, diversions, adventures and excitements to satisfy a dozen men. He was an expert horseman, a skilled man-at-arms, and an authority on explosives. As a young man, he served as a worthy artillery lieutenant in the French and Indian Wars.

Through the years, Paul also excelled as an artist, inventor, merchant, mechanic, politician, engineer, orator, dispatch rider, leading bell-ringer for Old North Church, shareholder in the privateer *Speedwell*, operator of a gunpowder mill, maker of cop-

per sheathing for the USS *Constitution*, designer of whale-oil chandeliers for the Massachusetts State House, metallurgist skilled in casting cannon and bells, maker of false teeth for General Joseph Warren, participant in the Boston Tea Party, artillery colonel in defense of Boston Harbor, printer, publisher and propagandist. Meanwhile, he found time to marry and to sire eight children; when his first wife died, he re-married and fathered eight more.

This, then, was the man the Committee of Safety summoned on the night of April 18, 1775. There was a critical message to be delivered. Somebody must mount up and ride post-haste to Buckman's Tavern in Lexington to warn John Hancock and Sam Adams that 800 Redcoats would be moving out from Boston to arrest them, and would then march on to Concord to destroy a store of rebel guns and ammunition.

Revere galloped to Medford where he stopped at the home of Captain Isaac Hall, commanding officer of the local Minutemen as well as a well-known distiller of Medford rum and a most generous host. That might account for the unproven allegation that Revere hadn't bothered to wake up anybody between Charlestown and his stop-off at Isaac's. "After that," he wrote in his journal, "I alarmed almost every house till I got to Lexington." This was around 12.30am. Perhaps history owes a nod of recognition to Isaac Hall and his midnight rum.

At Buckman's Tavern, Revere joined with the alternate dispatch rider, William Dawes, who had made the run from Boston via another route. Neither Revere nor Dawes ever got to Concord that night. En route, they joined up with Dr Samuel Prescott of Concord, heading home from Lexington. The Redcoats ambushed all three horsemen, but Dawes and Prescott escaped, with Prescott managing to alert the colonial militia at Concord. The war was on.

As for Revere, the tireless old patriot was still handling enough tasks to keep 10 normal men busy when he died in 1818, aged 83. His much visited grave is in the Old Granary Burying Ground. ❑

**LEFT:** Paul Revere, a man of many talents.

Stamp Act (1765) requiring colonists to pay taxes on legal documents.

To Bostonians, these restrictions were worse than the old Navigation Acts. The rallying cry went out, "No taxation without representation," as mobs took the protest into the streets. At the heart of the uproar was an organization called the Sons of Liberty, which included Paul Revere, John Hancock, Dr Joseph Warren, and their leader, Samuel Adams. They were as unlikely a collection of conspirators as one could imagine. Sam Adams was a disheveled failed businessman who had squandered a sizable inheritance. John Hancock was the wealthiest man in New

his new chancellor of the exchequer, Charles Townshend, lashed out with a new tax on imported items such as paper, lead and tea. Again, the town reacted with predictable fervor. When the Massachusetts House of Representatives issued Sam Adams's "circular letters" denouncing the Townshend Acts, the governor closed it down – and Bostonians hit the streets. Four thousand British soldiers were sent to quell the unruly mobs. An ugly game of brinkmanship finally erupted into all-out violence on March 5, 1770, when a group of Redcoats fired into a threatening crowd. This "Boston Massacre" *(see page 83)* claimed the lives of five colonists. Ironically, the Town-

England, a dandy and bon vivant. Joseph Warren was a Harvard-trained physician. Paul Revere was a working-class Renaissance man – a gifted silversmith, a courageous patriot and indefatigable public servant *(see opposite page)*.

While the Sons of Liberty were raising hell in Boston, the hastily formed Stamp Act Congress called for an American boycott against British goods. By March 1766, the boycott had caused so much damage to British commerce that King George relented and lifted the tax.

George III didn't take defeat lightly. In 1767

**ABOVE:** a detail from Paul Revere's engraving showing British troops opening fire in King Street in 1770.

shend Acts were repealed in England on that very day. But a nominal tax on tea remained.

## The Boston Tea Party

The tea tax won no friends in Boston, and when the first loads arrived in Boston Harbor, the Sons of Liberty were ready. On December 16, 1773, about 50 townsmen disguised as Indians boarded the cargo ships and dumped the tea into Boston Harbor while a crowd of thousands cheered from the wharves.

The Boston Tea Party was more than the British could tolerate. They unveiled the Coercive Acts, closing Boston Harbor, dissolving the government of Massachusetts, installing

General Thomas Gage as military governor and providing for the use of private homes to quarter British troops. Thousands of people moved out of Boston, and business in the town ground to a halt.

In September 1774, the First Continental Congress met in Philadelphia and voted to form a colonial army. In and around Boston, citizens stockpiled guns and ammunition. When General Gage heard of a weapons cache in Concord, 20 miles (32 km) west of Boston, he sent 800 Redcoats to capture it. But as his troops prepared to move out, on the night of April 18, 1775, Paul Revere was already paddling across the Charles River to warn the countryside of the British march. When he reached Charlestown he borrowed a horse and rode into the countryside, warning villagers that the British were coming.

By the time the British regulars reached Lexington Green en route to Concord, 70 local "Minutemen" – armed civilians pledged to fight at a minute's notice – were assembled. The rebels were ordered to lay down their weapons, but refused. The British fired, the rebels scattered – and when the smoke finally cleared, eight Minutemen lay dead.

The British marched on to Concord, destroyed the few weapons they found there, and tried to return the same way they came. But by then rebels were hidden along the road and peppered the Redcoats with musket fire all the way back to Charlestown. By the time the troops returned to Boston, 73 Redcoats had been killed and 200 wounded.

### The Battle of Bunker Hill

As news of the confrontation at Lexington spread out from Boston, thousands of colonials poured into the area, forming an arching line of siege between Charlestown and Boston Neck. On June 17, 1775, more than 2,600 Redcoats tried to break the siege by storming a rebel position on Breed's Hill (adjacent to Bunker Hill). The colonials repelled two attacks and then, running out of ammunition, retreated on the third. It was a pyrrhic victory for the British, who sustained more than 1,300 casualties, and an enormous boost in American spirits.

Less than a month later General George Washington arrived in Cambridge and took command of the colonial forces. The siege of Boston continued through the bitter winter of 1775–76, until Washington forced out the British with a clandestine placement of artillery on Dorchester Heights. On March 17, 1776, nearly 9,000 Redcoats and 1,000 Tories sailed away while American militiamen re-occupied the town. The Revolution raged for seven more years and, although Boston was spared further combat, the population was reduced from 20,000 to 6,000 residents.

### Rise of the Brahmins

After the Revolution, Boston returned to business as usual. Wealthy merchants were still in

**JOHN ADAMS**

John Adams, who was to emerge as one of the most important American revolutionary figures and who would serve as the second US president from 1797 to 1801, was a rising attorney in the years before the rebellion. One of his most unusual cases – and one which earned him the temporary enmity of many of his fellow patriots – was his defense of the soldiers involved in the 1770 Boston Massacre. Adams and fellow lawyer Josiah Quincy, both ardent foes of British oppression but equally supportive of the right to fair trial, won acquittal for seven of the nine redcoats. The other two were branded on the hand for manslaughter.

control of local affairs, although their port city still largely resembled the colonial outpost of the century past. All that changed between 1795 and 1818, as the merchants' money, and the genius of a young architect named Charles Bulfinch *(see page 44)*, transformed an 18th-century town of wooden houses and crooked lanes into a 19th-century city of cobblestone and brick. Bulfinch spearheaded the development of Beacon Hill, and crowned it with the magnificent State House.

Politically, the merchant princes ensconced in their new Beacon Hill mansions were Federalists, favoring government by men of property. The egalitarian Thomas Jefferson's duced a river of cloth. The Lowells, Appletons, and others later labeled "Brahmins" by the doctor-poet Oliver Wendell Holmes showed impeccable timing. With European trade impaired by the war, Americans were clamoring for manufactured goods – and the old money was soon making new fortunes in the textile industry.

## Reform and abolitionism

From the days of the Puritans, Boston's ruling class acknowledged its obligation to improve the conditions of the less fortunate, if not by actual material assistance, then by the power of example. But in the early years of the new century

election as President in 1800 was bad enough news for them, but worse yet was his foreign policy. In 1807, hostilities with England led to the Embargo Act, which nearly strangled the lucrative China trade. The War of 1812, fought to stop England forcibly checking US vessels at sea, only made a bad situation worse, and Boston ships languished in the harbor while merchants scrambled to reinvest their capital.

They found their answer in New England's rivers, which soon powered mills that pro-

Brahmin paternalism took on a more ardent quality. The Unitarian Church grew popular. Unitarianism did away with the old Calvinist notions of predestination and original sin, stressing instead the benevolence of God and the potential for human perfectibility. The road to salvation, for Unitarians such as Ralph Waldo Emerson, was through the exercise of conscience, rationality and tolerance.

Causes such as temperance, prison reform, and women's rights were all taken up in the new spirit of the age. But the most significant new movement was William Lloyd Garrison's crusade against slavery. In 1831, Garrison began publishing an antislavery newspaper,

**LEFT:** Joseph Warren dies in the Battle of Bunker Hill.
**ABOVE:** this section of a painting by John White Allen Scott (1815–1907) shows Broad Street in 1853.

*The Liberator*, from a tiny office on Washington Street. Garrison's blistering diatribes naturally inflamed Southerners, but also unnerved Brahmins dependent on Southern cotton for their textile mills. Still, Boston became known as a hotbed of abolitionism, and even conservative Yankees joined the protest against slavery's expansion into western territories. When the Civil War began in 1861, Bostonians responded dutifully to Lincoln's call for volunteers.

## Expansion and Immigration

By the end of the Civil war, the balance of national economic power was shifting away

from New England to New York City. Nevertheless, Boston was growing, and changing physically. The city's population had not only increased (to 314,000, by 1875), but landfill projects such as the Back Bay *(see pages 123–4)* had swollen its dimensions from its original 780 acres (316 hectares) to 24,000 acres (9,700 hectares). Most important of all, Boston had undergone a huge increase in its immigrant population. Most newcomers were Irish, starved out of their homeland by the potato blight of 1845–50. Uneducated and desperately poor, they came by the thousands and huddled into tenements.

Shunned and vilified not only for their for-eignness but also for their Catholicism, the Irish began to break out of the slums and into at least partial respectability only in the 1880s. To some extent that was due to modernization of the city. The installation of electric wires, the construction of the country's first subway and the expansion of city bureaucracy created a demand for civil servants and utility workers. In 1884, Hugh O'Brien became the first Irish mayor of Boston.

Just as the Irish started to move up the economic ladder, a new wave of immigrants from southern and eastern Europe arrived at the bottom rung. By 1890 the Irish were sharing their neighborhoods with about 45,000 Italians, 4,000 East European Jews and a scattering of Poles, Portuguese and Greeks. Once again bigotry reared its head. In 1894, three Harvard graduates founded the Immigration Restriction League of Boston and even persuaded Congressman Henry Cabot Lodge to stand behind their cause. By then, however, the tide could not be stemmed. By 1910, 30,000 Italians and 40,000 Jews were firmly entrenched in the North and West Ends. Some of them – or at least their children – would themselves be Harvard graduates one day.

## The Curley years

Quintessential Boston Irish politicians like the blarney-dispensing but corrupt mayor John F. "Honey Fitz" Fitzgerald, grandfather of President John F. Kennedy, dominated city politics. Another celebrated example was James Michael Curley, who served at various times as mayor, governor and congressman and, in 1943, even won an election from a jail cell. A charming, witty, and ambitious man with poor immigrant parents and no formal education beyond grammar school, he devoured books on law, politics, literature and the fine arts and had a remarkable photographic memory. By the time he was a public figure, he dressed impeccably and could impress voters by quoting passages from Shakespeare and Tennyson.

Curley thumbed his nose at both Republicans and Democrats and created a city-wide patronage system, the "Curley Machine." He considered the bosses petty (the Democratic City Committee was a "collection of chowderheads") and the Brahmins "gabbing spinsters and dog-raising matrons in federation assembled." The day after his election he sent the Yankees into fits of apoplexy by proposing to sell the Public Garden for $10 million and put a water pumping station under the Common.

With a healthy cut of Franklin Roosevelt's New Deal and, after 1941, a piece of the war industry, Boston survived the Great Depression. But it was Curley's success at attracting federal projects that helped lead to his downfall. With the US government supplying jobs and money, the patronage system was destroyed. In addition, the Irish and the Brahmins were beginning to discover the advantages of cooperation. Why shouldn't they combine to work together in financial and political affairs? Curley, always hated by the Brahmins, no longer needed by his old constituency, was eased out.

### An era of urban renewal

Boston politics underwent a change after World War II. A younger electorate was more interested in economic progress than stale ethnic rivalries. Second- and third-generation immigrant families had now become part of the middle-classes, and they wanted leaders who represented mainstream values and clean government. In 1946, Bostonians elected a congressman who seemed to epitomize those qualities. John F. Kennedy, grandson of "Honey Fitz," was handsome, charming and idealistic, and he came to symbolize, both for Boston and the nation, the hope of progressive politics.

At the local level, John Hynes, an unassuming, soft-spoken bureaucrat, handed Curley a stunning defeat in 1949. "Whispering Johnny" showed remarkable ambition as mayor, launching in 1957 the Boston Redevelopment Authority which, over the next 15 years, would carry out urban renewal projects covering 11 percent of Boston's land. Public money went into a complex of government buildings, while private capital raised the Prudential Center, John Hancock Tower, and other landmark structures.

The urban renewal campaign was implemented mainly during the tenure of Mayor John F. Collins (1960–68). The program got

**LEFT:** the wharves in Boston Harbor were a major employer in the 19th century.
**RIGHT:** "Honey Fitz" hands out Christmas baskets.

off to a somewhat shaky start when, as the result of bureaucratic insensitivity, the West End – a well-established community of Italian, Irish and Russian Jewish immigrants – was razed, while a similar fate befell seedy but beloved old Scollay Square. But by the 1970s, under Mayor Kevin White, the thrust changed from mega-development to recycling. The star effort of the 1980s was Faneuil Hall Marketplace, a spectacular revival of the old Quincy Market along with adjacent Faneuil Hall.

But while resources were being lavished on the city center, trouble was brewing in the neglected outer neighborhoods. Since the war, middle-class families had been moving out to

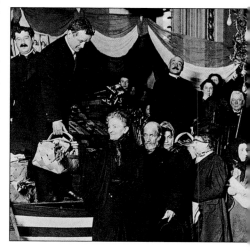

the suburbs, with the city losing nearly 250,000 residents between 1950 and 1980. Population then leveled off at today's figure of approximately 550,000, roughly where it had stood in 1900. The decline of the old neighborhoods was exacerbated by conflicts between entrenched ethnic groups and a new influx of blacks and Hispanics – conflicts brought to a head during the school busing crisis of the 1970s, begun when a federal court ordered that racial balance in Boston public schools be remedied by busing students out of their neighborhoods. The riots that surrounded the busing crisis shocked the nation and stained the reputation of its "cradle of liberty."

## The "Massachusetts Miracle"

After years of economic stagnation, Boston in the 1980s became the hub of the "Massachusetts Miracle," based largely on the high-tech know-how cultivated in the region's universities. Boston's long investment banking tradition helped get startup companies off the ground, and soon a thicket of new office towers radically transformed the downtown skyline. But what goes up must come down, and the end of the decade saw a marked reversal in the city's economic fortunes.

In less than 10 years' time, though, it was apparent that the "roaring 80s" would have a successor in the dot-com '90s. Again, Boston was poised to ride the crest of the boom — and to ride out the inevitable bust.

As the city celebrated its 375th anniversary in 2005, it had a lot more to boast than mere survival of so many cycles that have swung on codfish and rum, on sailing ships and computer chips. There were plenty of new things under the sun in the once self-styled "Hub of the Universe": in 2004, the city hosted its first major-party political convention, sending local favorite Senator John Kerry into the presidential fray and generating more than $160 million in local revenues. At long last, the "Big Dig" – America's most ambitious and expensive public works project – was completed, with a new tunnel under Boston Harbor and a much-despised elevated highway erased from the downtown landscape. Derelict piers and tired industrial blocks in South Boston had been transformed by hotels and exhibition space. The challenges of housing and schools, perennial bugbears for all older American cities, were met head-on; 10,000 new residential units are planned by 2007 and *Forbes* magazine praised Boston as offering the best public education of any large US city.

## City versus State

Controversy and political contentiousness, no strangers to this city through all of its 375 years, continue to arrive in new packages. Progressive Bostonians have welcomed the Massachusetts Supreme Court's sanctioning of gay marriage, while the conservative Republican state governor, Mitt Romney, strongly disapproves, as one might have expected of the Puritans and Irish Catholics who led the state long before him. And beyond such "hot button" issues, the old tussles between city and state go on: Boston, for decades led solidly by Democrats, bucks a recent Massachusetts trend for electing Republican governors, and fights for what it considers its fair share of state largesse.

About the only thing everyone can agree on is the decision of the new owners of the Red Sox – miracle of miracles, world champions at last – to fix up century-old Fenway Park, and keep it right where it is. There are some things you can't tamper with – especially when everyone's watching, and you are a City Upon a Hill.  ❑

### FANEUIL HALL'S WEATHERVANE

The weathervane in the shape of a grasshopper atop Faneuil Hall – sometimes called "Jiminy Cricket" and the symbol of Faneuil Hall Marketplace – is said to have been placed there by none other than Peter Faneuil, who donated the building to the city in 1742. Faneuil, who had been a member of the Royal Exchange, remembered a similar ornament atop the Exchange's London HQ. Sir Thomas Gresham, the Exchange's founder, was said to have been an abandoned baby, found in a field in 1519 by children chasing grasshoppers. As a successful financier, he supposedly erected the Exchange weathervane in memory of his humble origins.

**LEFT:** Senator Ted Kennedy, part of a political dynasty.

# The Big Dig

**B**ostonians have long worked wonders with their physical surroundings, drastically expanding the size of the peninsula and linking it to surrounding communities with a lacework of bridges and tunnels. In a colossal planning fiasco, however, the traffic engineers of the 1950s isolated the North End from downtown with the elevated beast called the Fitzgerald Expressway, or Central Artery.

The Central Artery cut an ugly swath through the city – and by the 1990s, it no longer did a good job of moving traffic. Designed for 75,000 cars a day, it now carried 190,000 vehicles daily between points south and the Charles and Mystic river crossings of Interstate 93 and Route 1. Another problem was getting to and from Logan Airport from the south and west.

Then a radical solution was proposed: if you can't beat the cars, bury them. This remarkable project became known as the "Big Dig," a drastic makeover involving 15 years of hellish traffic snarls for Boston drivers, a cacophony of cranes, excavators, and pile drivers that drove residents to distraction, and more than $14 billion dollars in public funds.

The elevated highway was replaced by a tunnel following the same route, a massive task that involved digging the new subterranean roadway – now the Thomas P. ("Tip") O'Neill Tunnel – while retaining the existing structure until traffic could be rerouted beneath it. Large sections of the granny knot of bridges and ramps crossing the Charles River were replaced with the dramatic Zakim-Bunker Hill Bridge, with its sleek tracery of cable stays.

Instead of the dreary green girders of the old Fitzgerald Expressway, the central city would now be bisected by a 27-acre swath of parkland officially named the Rose Kennedy Greenway, after the late matriarch of the city's foremost political clan. The North End, which spent nearly two generations isolated by traffic and water on either side, could now reclaim its position as a coveted place to live,

The Big Dig's other major component was the building of a third tunnel beneath Boston Harbor. The new Ted Williams Tunnel, named for the Red Sox great (1918–2002), veers away from expressways south of the central city and keeps airport traffic away from downtown.

Since most of the cost of the massive project was covered by federal funds, politicians in other parts of the country complained that taxpayer dollars from the

hinterlands were subsidizing roads, bridges, and tunnels that would never be used by most Americans – although they ignored the fact that, in similar fashion, tax monies generated in Boston often help pay for projects thousands of miles from Beacon Hill.

Unfortunately, the official completion of the Big Dig wasn't the end of the story. In July 2006, a concrete ceiling panel pulled loose and killed a car passenger in an underground roadway leading to the Ted Williams Tunnel. Portions of the system were closed, while engineers improved the bolt system anchoring the panels, and contractors braced for legal action. ❑

**RIGHT:** the Big Dig dramatically remodeled the area around South Station in the late 1990s.

# Decisive Dates

**1625** William Blackstone, 29, an Anglican clergyman and Boston's first European settler, builds a log cabin on what is now Boston Common.

**1630** John Winthrop, recently elected governor of the Massachusetts Bay Company, leads the Arbella and 10 other Puritan ships into Boston Harbor after a three-month trip from England.

**1631** Boston court officials create America's first police force by putting watchmen on duty from sunset to sunrise.

**1635** Boston Latin School, the nation's first public school, is founded.

**1636** The Puritans show their commitment to education by founding a college at New Towne, later Cambridge. It was subsequently to be named after its English-born benefactor, John Harvard, a young Charlestown minister.

**1640** Stephen Day, a locksmith and ironworker turned printer, publishes the first book produced in the colonies, *Bay Psalm Book*.

**1660** A Quaker, Mary Dyer, is hanged on the Boston Common. The Quakers were denounced by the Puritans as a "cursed sect."

**1684** The Massachusetts Bay Colony charter is revoked, bringing to an end Puritan independence from royal control.

**1690** The first American newspaper, *Publick Occurences: Both Foreign and Domestick*, is published in Boston.

**1692** The Salem Witch Trials begin.

**1717** Boston Light, the oldest lighthouse in the nation, is erected in the harbor.

**1761** Boston lawyer James Otis declares: "Taxation without representation is tyranny."

**1764** The Sugar Act and the Stamp Act arouse anti-royalist sentiments.

**1770** The Boston Massacre, in which British troops fire on a rock-throwing mob, killing five.

**1773** Phillis Wheatley, a young slave living with a wealthy Boston family, becomes the first published African-American poet. Boston Tea Party, in which a shipment of tea is thrown into the harbor in protest against a new three-pence tax on tea.

**1775** Paul Revere's ride and Battles of Lexington and Concord spark American Revolution. Battle of Bunker Hill. George Washington takes command of Continental Army at Cambridge.

**1776** British troops evacuate Boston. The Declaration of Independence is read from the State House balcony.

**1780** John Adams drafts the Massachusetts Constitution including a Bill of Rights; John Hancock becomes the first governor of the Commonwealth of Massachusetts.

**1795** On Beacon Hill, Paul Revere and Samuel Adams lay the cornerstone for the new State House designed by Charles Bulfinch, America's first professional architect.

**1812** War of 1812 against the British paralyzes the city's commerce.

**1814** American Industrial Revolution begins at Robert Cabot Lowell's first mill on the Charles River in Waltham.

**1815** The Handel & Haydn Society, now the nation's oldest continuously performing arts organization, gives its first concert.

**1822** Boston is incorporated as a city.

**1831** William Lloyd Garrison begins publishing an abolitionist journal, *The Liberator*. Mount Auburn Cemetery, the nation's first garden cemetery, opens in Cambridge.

**1845** Henry David Thoreau begins his three-year spell at Walden Pond.

**1846** First operation under general anesthesia is performed at Massachusetts General Hospital.

**1852** Boston Public Library, the first free city library supported by taxes, opens.

**1857** Filling of Back Bay begins, cleaning up a foul-smelling public dump.

**1861** Massachusetts Institute of Technology is granted its charter.

**1863** The 54th Massachusetts Voluntary Infantry, the first African-American regiment, is formed. The Oneida Club plays American-style football for the first time on Boston Common.

**1868** Louisa May Alcott of Concord publishes her novel *Little Women*.

**1872** Great Fire of Boston destroys downtown, killing 33 people and razing 776 buildings.

**1876** First words are spoken over a telephone by Alexander Graham Bell.

**1877** Swan boats launched at Public Garden.

**1879** Radcliffe College founded for women.

**1881** Boston Symphony Orchestra founded. Frederick Law Olmsted, landscape architect, begins work on Emerald Necklace park system.

**1886** Henry James publishes *The Bostonians*.

**1892** First Church of Christ, Scientist, established in Boston by Mary Baker Eddy.

**1897** First Boston Marathon. The first subway in America opens at Park Street.

**1903** Boston Pilgrims defeat Pittsburgh Pirates in first baseball World Series.

**1909** Filene's Automatic Bargain Basement opens in Washington Street.

**1919** Strike of 1,300 Boston police. Breaking it brings to national prominence Massachusetts Governor Calvin Coolidge.

**1920** Red Sox controversially sell Babe Ruth to New York Yankees for $125,000.

**1927** Italian immigrants Nicola Sacco and Bartolomeo Vanzetti are executed in a Charlestown prison for alleged killings and holdups. The case became a model for social injustice in the 1920s.

**1942** Fire in a Bay Village nightclub kills 490.

**1944** The computer age dawns in Cambridge laboratories as a 50-ft-long calculating machine gets its sums right.

**1945** James Michael Curley, although under indictment for fraud, wins fourth term as mayor.

**1946** John Fitzgerald Kennedy, 29, elected to US Congress from Charlestown and Cambridge.

**1947** Polaroid founder Edwin Land demonstrates his first instant camera in Cambridge.

**1950** A Brinks armored car is robbed in North End. Thieves net $2.7 million. Eight men are convicted six years later.

**LEFT:** the Pilgrims come ashore in the New World.
**RIGHT:** detail from the Café du Barry mural by Josh Viner on Newbury Street, Back Bay.

**1953** The world's first kidney transplant is performed at Brigham Hospital.

**1959** The Boston Redevelopment Authority begins razing the old West End, long a center for gambling dens, burlesque halls and brothels but home to 7,000 people, and starts building Government Center and luxury apartments.

**1962** The "Boston Strangler" begins a 21-month rape and murder spree, killing 13 women.

**1972** After 75 years as a men-only race, the Boston Marathon acknowledges the first women's winner.

**1990** In the largest art heist in history, thieves remove $200 million in paintings from Isabella Stewart Gardner Museum.

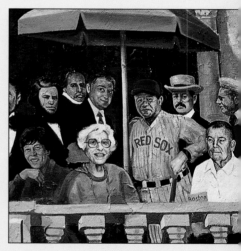

**1993** The TV series *Cheers*, set in a fictional Boston bar, ends after 275 episodes.

**1996** The Harbor Islands are designated a national park area.

**2001** Two planes are hijacked after taking off from Logan Airport and crashed into New York's World Trade Center, killing nearly 3,000 people.

**2004** Boston hosts the national convention of the Democratic Party; nominee Massachusetts Senator John F. Kerry wages an unsuccessful presidential campaign. Boston Red Sox win first World Series in 86 years.

**2005** The 14-year "Big Dig," replacing downtown's elevated highway with underground route and creating third harbor tunnel, is completed. ❑

# TREASURE TROVES OF ART

**The founding fathers had little time for frivolities
such as painting and sculpture, but their descendants
determined to turn Boston into the Athens of America**

Eighteenth-century Boston, like any self-respecting English provincial capital, delighted in status symbols and luxury goods – portraits and tombstone carvings, silver teapots and coats of arms on carriage panels. There was no artistic past; even if there had been, nobody would have cared. Boston was a thoroughly modern town: everything was fashion and the latest style. The cult of the past would arrive only later.

Monumental sculpture and history painting, the touchstones of the visual arts on the continent, would not be appreciated to any real degree – and then only in a limited manner – until the early 1800s and the Federal era. Landscape painting would not truly flourish before the coming of the Victorians. Genre painting appeared with the Edwardians and the "Boston School" of 1900.

### Copley and Revere

In artistic terms, however, great strides were made in the 18th century by Bostonians as gifted as John Singleton Copley and Paul Revere, and the general level of artistic achievement was unsurpassed, and quite probably unmatched, in the American colonies. Copley's portrait of Revere, now in the Museum of Fine Arts (MFA), is the result of a fortuitous meeting of artist and sitter, and worth careful study for what it tells of 18th-century Boston – practical, proud and unafraid of a dignified opulence.

The message is writ large in Copley's great portraits of Boston's mercantile aristocracy, which are also seen at their best in the MFA.

Keeping these faces in mind gives added meaning to a visit to King's Chapel, where it is easiest to find the 18th century in the modern city. The air is chill and sweet with an unmistakable New England tang.

The Revolution changed many of the players, but the game remained the same as Boston entered its 19th-century era of greatness. Even so, the arts remained more than a little suspect. John Adams, with a whiff of brimstone, still pondered whether the arts, those suspicious handmaidens of luxury and aristocracy, had any place in a democracy. "Are we not," he cautioned with fretful anxiety, "in too great a hurry in our zeal for the fine arts?"

Federal Boston, unlike earlier periods, remains very much in evidence, with Charles Bulfinch's gold dome of the State House – it was originally gray – dominating Beacon Hill. Esthetically, the city today is its own greatest asset, with the carefully preserved Federal townscape of the Hill blending seamlessly with the Victorian sweep of the Back Bay.

Nineteenth-century Boston took pride in its transformation of the "howling wilderness" into the "American Athens" – no mean feat in a scant 200 years when the odds are against you. Educational, charitable and cultural institutions (with "fair" Harvard generally given pride of place) were carefully nurtured as the proper

tions and with kind words. In a few notable cases – Copley and William Morris Hunt, for example – a handsomely dowered daughter tempered the force of artistic fury.

## The French influence

The terrible social and political catharsis of the Civil War (1861–65) brought forth a rich artistic flowering in New England. Culturally, Boston tended to define itself in terms of education and morality, but this would always be challenged, after the 1850s, by a bold and unexpected interest in modern French art. Its earliest champion was the painter William Morris Hunt, a New Englander who had

sphere for a "Brahmin" aristocracy, rich beyond the wildest dreams of their immigrant ancestors and heavy with intellectual pretension.

Artists were admired and assimilated as the ornaments of that society. This high regard is sometimes said to account for the decorative rather than incisive character of much of this Brahmin culture, where the unpredictable tendency of artists to comment and to criticize was curbed with the flattery of dinner invita-

**PRECEDING PAGES:** *West Church*, Maurice Prendergast.
**LEFT:** *Mrs Fiske Warren and her Daughter* by the influential John Singer Sargent.
**ABOVE:** *Boston Common at Twilight* by Childe Hassam.

### THE ATHENAEUM

No cultural institution was as central to the arts in Federal Boston as the Boston Athenaeum. In a series of increasingly grand homes, it mounted the city's first public exhibitions of painting and sculpture and assembled its first generally accessible public collection of art. By 1850, it had taken up residence in the Italianate palazzo on Beacon Street where it remains. Some of its collection also remains, and some has gone to enrich the holdings of the MFA, whose parent the Athenaeum became in 1870 when it divided its responsibilities between literature and the visual arts. The Athenaeum represents the penetrating taste that marked Federal America's neoclassicism.

studied in France with Couture and Millet, and who married so well that Bostonians paid more attention to his taste than they might otherwise have done. They patronized his French friends and acquired fine collections of French pictures into the bargain. Hunt is responsible for many of the Millets and Monets that found their way to the MFA.

Most private collections formed in 19th-century Boston were smaller and generally less showy than their counterparts in New York. They were, however, often more discerning, and ranged through the entire history of taste with a remarkable lack of prejudice. The MFA has been heir to quite a few of these

collections, and its galleries on Huntington Avenue are unsurpassed in areas as diverse as Asian and classical art and 19th-century French painting.

In plastic arts, the MFA's Egyptian Old Kingdom collection, unrivaled except at the Cairo Museum, is the result of joint Harvard-MFA expeditions, which began in 1905 under the direction of Dr George A. Reisner. The glorious sculpture and the architectural pieces in the Indian Art Section owe much to joint MFA-University of Pennsylvania expeditions.

A number of other institutions, mainly educational, have also assumed the role of the private collector, and well repay the trouble of a visit. The Fogg Art Museum at Harvard in Cambridge houses outstanding collections. Also noteworthy are the Rose Art Museum at Brandeis University in Waltham, with its remarkable contemporary American art, and the Wellesley College Museum in Wellesley, with its distinguished historical collection (the superb ancient marble known as the "Wellesley youth" is alone worth the trip).

Collecting as a cultural pursuit began rather later than it did elsewhere in America, and the few early local collections of importance have long since been dispersed, as have those of early institutions such as the Athenaeum. Several important collections from the second half of the 19th century were embedded more or less intact in various local museums, but one – the finest of them all – has been preserved as it

**LEFT:** *The New Necklace* (1910) by William Paxton.
**RIGHT:** *My Family* (1914) by William Tarbell.

## THE BOSTON SCHOOL

Painting would flourish once again around 1900 with the emergence of the "Boston School." Encouraged by the vital example of John Singer Sargent, who indulged the contemporary taste for mural painting in the Boston Public Library, MFA and Harvard's Widener Library, the work of William Paxton and Edmund Tarbell clearly also grew out of the esthetic shock administered by Mrs Gardner's superb Vermeer at Fenway Court. (This Vermeer and several other treasures were stolen in 1990's $200 million art heist.)

The Boston School summarized everything that Boston had come to admire in the arts: technical skill, languid sentiment, and an often maddening refinement brought to the

study of a narrow, genteel world. Looks can be deceiving, because the style took root with the rude health of a roadside weed and its practitioners are still numerous and popular. Their work, in fact, fuels the success of today's Newbury Street art market.

Newbury Street, long the center of the art market and the luxury trades in Boston, has always suffered because of its proximity to New York. Madison Avenue is too close for comfort, and collectors, no less than artists, regularly fall subject to its variety and charm. Nonetheless, artists both serious and admirable remain, and the graduates of the art schools and universities continually swell the ranks.

was created, a few hundred yards from the MFA. For many, the MFA with all its masterpieces takes emotional second place to the Isabella Stewart Gardner Museum, for where it is great, the Gardner is unique.

## The Gardner Museum

Although the collection built up by Isabella Stewart Gardner *(see panel below and page 135)* is uneven, its highlights are remarkable. They include Giotto and Piero della Francesca, Degas and Sargent, and the Titian Room is stunning. But even Titian gives pride of place to the ensemble she lovingly created. In an age when museums have almost totally decontextualized their works of art, Mrs Gardner's context makes her Titian sing with an added resonance. There is really nothing more wonderful, or more of a piece with Boston, than the Gardner.

Fenway Court is often said to have inspired a revival of interest in local artists and revived a long tradition of local patronage, but in truth Boston, like most American cities, was (and, alas, is) conspicuously unenthusiastic about the home-grown product. Boston patronage of American sculptors followed the same downward curve, from brisk interest to benign neglect, although a taste for public monuments made Boston a marvelous place in which to stroll and to look at statues.  ❏

### HOW ISABELLA STEWART GARDNER BUILT AN INSTITUTION

Isabella Stewart, born in New York in 1840, became a Bostonian when she married the financier Jack Lowell Gardner. The Brahmin and his vivacious wife, whose actions were often frowned upon by proper Bostonians, became enthusiastic art collectors and filled their Commonwealth Avenue home with treasures from Europe.

When Gardner died in 1889, "Mrs Jack" set about building the Venetian palazzo of her dreams and embellishing it with her collection of spectacular paintings, sculpture, furniture and textiles. Fenway Court opened with a private party on New Year's Day, 1903. Mrs Gardner received her guests at the head of the double staircase while 50 members of the Boston Symphony Orchestra entertained. Logs burned in each room as guests indulged in two of her delights: doughnuts and champagne.

Mrs Gardner lived on the top floor of Fenway Court until her death in 1924, and she still presides there in the shape of her controversial portrait painted by Sargent in 1888. It caused a Boston scandal because Mrs Gardner appeared in what was then considered to be a revealing low-cut gown. Fenway Court's surfeit of masterpieces has less to do with its glory than one might expect, for although masterpieces are not in short supply, most museums would consign a good part of the collection to the storeroom.

# LITERARY BOSTON

**From Puritan times to the present, Boston authors have put the distinctive stamp of the New England character on American literature**

The Puritans who founded Massachusetts placed great value on literacy. The colony's first printing press arrived in 1640, and promptly turned out *The Bay Psalm Book*. Puritan authors soon began producing original material, much of it theological. Increase Mather, in *An Essay for the Recording of Illustrious Providences* (1684) chronicled the Devil's work in Massachusetts; his son, Cotton Mather, was author of more than 400 works, including *Memorable Providences, Relating to Witchcrafts and Possessions* (1689). Puritans also penned biographies and histories: Governor John Winthrop himself wrote a chronicle of the Massachusetts Bay Colony.

Remarkably, for such a patriarchal society, 17th-century Boston produced a competent female poet. Anne Bradstreet, who arrived with the first settlers, collected her early work in *The Tenth Muse Lately Sprung Up in America* (1650).

## Political polemic

Although early 18th-century New England writers still frequently mined a religious vein – this was the era of Jonathan Edwards and his 1741 sermon "Sinners in the Hands of an Angry God" – the era marked the beginning of a secular turn of mind. In Boston, James Franklin (brother of Benjamin) launched one of New England's first successful newspapers, the *New England Courant*, in 1721, introducing America to the urbane style of Addison and Steele.

As tensions with Britain heightened,

Boston was more concerned with politics than literature. The city retained a reputation for political polemic in the mid-19th century, when William Lloyd Garrison made it the base for his abolitionist newspaper *The Liberator*. The true center of New England literary activity in those years was Concord *(see box opposite)*, while Boston itself was renowned as a publishing capital. Periodicals such as *The North American Review* and *The Atlantic Monthly*, and the publishing firm of Ticknor and Fields, helped secure its reputation.

**ABOVE:** the young Henry James.
**RIGHT:** Ralph Waldo Emerson.

## The Fireside Poets

The post-Civil War "Indian Summer" of New England literature was the era of William Dean Howells, who made Boston the setting of *A Modern Instance* (1882) and *The Rise of Silas Lapham* (1885), both about men on the make. Henry James set many of his short stories in Boston upper-class society, and satirized the city's radical and reformist circles in *The Bostonians* (1886).

On a gentler note, Boston and environs nurtured the "fireside poets" of the late 1800s. Working in genres such as the pastoral (John Greenleaf Whittier's 1866 "Snow-Bound") and historical narrative (Henry Wadsworth

Longfellow's "Evangeline" and "The Song of Hiawatha," published respectively in 1847 and 1855), these poets were often read aloud. This genteel tradition was shared by writers such as poet and essayist Oliver Wendell Holmes, Sr. (*The Autocrat of the Breakfast-Table*, 1858), and poet James Russell Lowell. (The poetic tradition ran strong in later generations of Boston's Lowell family. Amy Lowell was a leader of the early 20th-century Imagists, and Robert Lowell's *For the Union Dead* and *The Public Garden* take up Boston themes.)

## Contemporary concerns

The critical view of Boston society resounded in John P. Marquand's skewering of the Brahmins in *The Late George Apley* (1937), and in George Santayana's *The Last Puritan* (1936). John Updike presented the quandaries of his characters in early novels and stories set in the Boston suburbs. Archibald MacLeish, a onetime Boston lawyer, struck a remonstrative note in his 1976 poem *Night Watch in the City of Boston*, written amidst the school busing crisis and the American bicentennial celebrations.

Edwin O'Connor offered an insightful portrayal of a James Michael Curley-based Boston politician in *The Last Hurrah* (1956), and Boston lawyer George V. Higgins gave us the rough side of his city's life and language via *The Friends of Eddie Coyle* (1972). Dennis Lehane's *Mystic River* (2001), made into an acclaimed film by Clint Eastwood, is set in a grim, working-class Charlestown. ❑

### CONCORD'S RENAISSANCE

In 1836, a Unitarian clergyman living in Concord published *Nature*, an essay emphasizing the unity of the individual soul with all creation and the divine. Ralph Waldo Emerson became the outstanding voice not only of the Transcendentalist movement the essay helped inspire, but of a famous coterie of Concord writers.

The "Concord Renaissance" included Emerson's friend Henry David Thoreau. The two men became the focus of New England Transcendentalism, a literary movement that emphasized emotion, intuition and nature, and above all valued the individual above society. Striving for self-sufficiency, the 27-year-old Thoreau built his own home on the shores of Walden Pond, on land owned by Emerson. He lived there from 1845 to 1847, growing his own food, fishing and meditating. He later documented these two years of solitude in 18 essays called *Walden; or, Life in the Woods* (1854). His most influential essay was *Civil Disobedience*, published in 1849.

Another prominent member of the circle was Bronson Alcott, father of Louisa May Alcott (*Little Women*). A Concord school superintendent, Alcott was an educational reformer and philosopher. Nathaniel Hawthorne, too, was close to the Concord Transcendentalists. All of these authors lie in Concord's Sleepy Hollow Cemetery.

# FOOD

**Seafood remains one of the New England classics, but the influence of immigrants and new traditions are making their mark**

Stereotypically, Boston is thought of as the home of the baked bean, traditionally cooked with molasses, brown sugar, or maple syrup. Yet one will have to search a score or more restaurant menus – offering everything from *crème de cailles au genièvre* to *pla rad pik* – before finding a side order of Boston brick-oven baked beans.

Not so with seafood. The Pilgrims might have been a bit confounded by today's mania for lobster. They considered the crustaceans fit only for pig food, or bait; well into the 19th century, boatloads of lobsters sold for pennies, and prisoners rioted at the prospect of yet another lobster dinner. Today New England's lobster harvest is a $150 million-a-year enterprise. And, while creative preparations abound, menus still feature traditional boiled lobsters and "lobster rolls" – toasted hot dog buns filled with chunks of lobster meat, tossed with celery and mayonnaise.

The settlers weren't quite so blind to the appeal of oysters, however. As early as 1601, Samuel de Champlain had singled out the area now known as Wellfleet, on Cape Cod for its exceptional beds of oysters.

## Clam chowder

Boston's fabled clam chowder got its name from the Breton French settlers of Quebec, who simmered their soups in a *chaudière* (cauldron). Such long, slow cooking is needed to render the hard shell quahogs (pronounced "co-hogs") palatable. The small and medium-size versions – cherrystones and littlenecks – are delectable served raw, on the half shell. Soft-shell, long

neck clams – commonly known as "steamers" – are a favored food all along the coast, dipped first in brine (to wash off the grit), then in melted butter. Outside of the city, clam shacks fire up their fry-o-lators to prepare another favorite: clams batter-coated and fried.

Clambakes were once a New England tradition, especially on Cape Cod. The customary procedure was to lay out a stone pit on the beach, build a driftwood fire, cover the hot stones with seaweed, add clams and their accompaniments (typically lobsters, potatoes

**ABOVE:** fresh lobsters, tastefully presented.
**RIGHT:** eating out by Faneuil Hall Marketplace.

and corn on the cob), and then top it all off with more seaweed, a sailcloth tarp, and plenty of sand, leaving the whole to bake for about an hour. Most coastal resort restaurants these days dispense with clambake *per se*, and just serve what's called a "shore dinner" – steamed.

It was the abundant cod, however, that initially lured English fishermen, and eventually settlers, to the Boston area. Fillet of young cod, called scrod (from the Dutch *schrood*, for "a piece cut off"), still graces traditional menus.

Exposure to European traditions has introduced two relatively new seafood treats. Mussels, long ignored by Boston restaurants, are now very nearly ubiquitous, usually served

marinière, or poached in white wine. Bay scallops are now available all year round, and the more adventurous fine restaurants serve them whole, whether on the half-shell or cooked.

Cranberries – so named by Dutch settlers who thought the flowers resembled cranes – are one of the few fruits that are native to North America. Native Americans used sassamanesh – "bitter berries" – as a dye, a poultice, and as food, pounded with venison to make "pemmican" (meat cakes) or sweetened with maple sap. Long before Vitamin C was recognized, whalers would set off to sea with a barrel of cranberries to prevent scurvy.

Today, visitors can tour Massachusetts cranberry bogs and celebrate fall festivals from Plymouth to Nantucket.

## Beer and cider

With no access to safe drinking water, the Pilgrims – adults and children alike – had no choice but to drink beer (the alcohol content kept the microbes in check). Today they could travel north to visit Boston's many microbreweries, and perhaps join a Brew Pub Tour.

Apple seeds, which came to New England with the Pilgrims in 1620, contributed another popular beverage: apple cider. This fresh pressed apple juice, a favorite drink in colonial times, was also converted into "hard" or alcoholic cider. President John Adams claimed that a tankard of hard cider every morning calmed his stomach and alleviated gas. Hard cider has enjoyed a trendy revival, led by a number of New England brands that even offer exotic raspberry and cinnamon varieties.    ❏

### THE IMMIGRANT INFLUENCE

In Boston, flavors that would previously have been considered "exotic" have entered the mainstream food vocabulary, in part due to the waves of immigration that have brought new culinary traditions to the city. The Italian immigrants who settled in the city in the late 1800s and early 1900s have left an indelible stamp on the city's food, and the many North End restaurants are always popular.

Since 1960, almost 80 percent of immigrants to the US have come from Asia, Latin America, and the Caribbean. Boston now has Chinese, Japanese, Thai, Vietnamese, Cambodian, Malaysian, Puerto Rican, Mexican, Haitian, and many other ethnic eateries, where clams in black bean sauce and lobster sautéed with ginger and scallions blend local ingredients into the classic cuisines of their home countries. The possibilities are endless.

This melting pot of flavors has also turned into more upscale fusion cuisine, where celebrity chefs are transforming Boston restaurant menus. Adventurous eaters can indulge in salad of Maine rock crab with lobster knuckles and fried taro, crispy squash risotto cakes, pumpkin ravioli with mussels marinière, lightly fried lobster with lemongrass and Thai basil, ginger barbecued skate wing served over spicy jalapeño slaw with Boston baked beans, or seared scallops in cider sauce.

# A PASSION FOR SPORT

Baseball, basketball, hockey and football all have their fanatical followers. And few participatory activities can outpace the Boston Marathon

On the morning after, the banner headline on the *Boston Globe* said it all: "On Top of the World." It was October 28, 2004, and for the first time in 86 years, the Red Sox were the champions of baseball. Who was on top of the world? The Sox, of course. But so were most Bostonians.

Bostonians are sports fanatics. The Red Sox, the New England Patriots (football), the Celtics (basketball), and the Bruins (ice hockey) all inspire desperate allegiance. To put it simply, Bostonians love their teams because they consider them to be their patrimony. How many times it must have been repeated during that ebullient autumn of 2004: "If only my dad and my granddad were around to see this."

### The Sox

Before their 2004 redemption the Red Sox were considered to be not merely unlucky, but the victims of a curse — specifically, the "Curse of the Bambino," brought down on their heads when the team's owner sold Babe Ruth to the Yankees in 1920. It wasn't that the Sox were perennially awful. It was worse: they were often quite good, with a roster that at various times boasted all-stars like Ted Williams, Carl Yasztremski, and Roger Clemens. But they would either get into the Series and lose, as in 1946, '67, '75, and '86, or else collapse (usually at the hands of the Yankees) before season's end. Some philosophers even looked beyond the curse, portraying the team as a paradigm of Calvinist mortification in Puritanism's hometown. Still the faithful came, sinners in the hands of an angry God, to their Fenway Park shrine. And eventually their prayers were answered.

### The Celtics

The Boston Celtics followed a far different script, chalking up 16 National Basketball Association (NBA) championships. Unlike the Sox, who began at the top and went into decline, the Celtics started disastrously when the 11-team NBA was founded in 1946. Then, coached by Arnold (Red) Auerbach and fielding such immortals as Bob Cousy, Dave

**ABOVE:** the Boston Celtics in action.
**RIGHT:** the Patriots keep football's flag flying.

Cowens, John Havlicek, Tom Heinsohn, K.C. Jones, Sam Jones, Bill Russell, and Larry Bird, they started winning until the rafters at Boston Garden (since replaced by the T. D. Banknorth Garden, formerly the Fleet Center) had scarcely space for another banner. Since the mid-1980s, though, the Celtics have been eclipsed by powerhouse teams such as the Chicago Bulls and Los Angeles Lakers.

## The Bruins

Next to the Celtics. Boston's winningest team has been the Bruins of the National Hockey League (NHL). The Bruins logged a winning record for 23 years in a row – the longest of

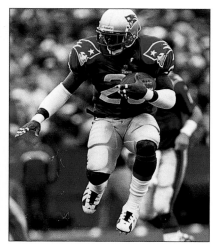

*any* professional team in any sport. Greatest of all Bruins was Bobby Orr, who joined the club when only 18 and who revolutionized hockey by showing that defensemen could attack and score goals. Other greats have included Eddie Shore, Phil Esposito, and Ray Borque. Scarcely a season passes when the Bruins fail to reach the playoffs – but the most recent of their Stanley Cup victories was in 1972. And, like the rest of the North American professional hockey world, they languished in limbo throughout the 2004–2005 season as a labor impasse kept NHL teams off the ice.

## The Patriots

The National Football League (NFL) team now called the New England Patriots debuted in 1965, originally as part of the now-defunct American Football League. In 1971, they moved to suburban Foxboro and dropped "Boston" from their name in favor of "New England." Like the Red Sox, the Pats for many years never seemed more futile than when playing for the championship. Super Bowl appearances in both 1986 and 1996 ended in successive maulings by the Chicago Bears and Green Bay Packers. But, like the Sox, the Patriots made it to the promised land — big time. Thanks to the coaching of master defensive tactician Bill Belichick, the arm of quarterback Tom Brady, and the deadly accuracy of kicker Adam Vinatieri, the Pats won the Super Bowl in 2002, 2004, and 2005.

But for Boston fans, last year was last year. Let's see what the teams can do this season. ❏

## THE BOSTON MARATHON

It all began in 1897 when 15 runners lined up in Ashland and, when the gun was fired, started to run to Boston. Thus began the world's oldest annual marathon, held on Patriot's Day (in mid-April), and drawing its inspiration from the marathon at the first modern Olympics in 1896. Since 1907 the race has started at Hopkinton rather than Ashland and, since 1927, has been run over the official Olympic distance of 26 miles, 365 yards. The race passes through eight municipalities and is watched by 1½ million spectators.

Apart from 10 years between 1973 and 1983 when the laurel wreath crowned an American entrant seven times, foreigners have dominated since World War II. The first wheelchair competitor raced unofficially in 1970, completing the course in about seven

hours. Visually impaired runners also compete. Women first began to run in 1966 but official entries weren't accepted until 1972.

In the early 1980s the marathon – which remained an amateur event in which athletes ran for prestige and fun – ran into cash problems. The John Hancock financial company came up with a sponsorship deal, and prize money at Boston, the only marathon to offer equal prize money in all classes to both men and women, is now the same as that awarded at other major marathons.

Today, about 15,000 runners who have met pre-entry time qualifications line up for the starter's gun, but thousands more manage to find their way to Hopkinton and then jog, walk or limp across the finish line as unofficial entrants.

# ARCHITECTURE

**Boston is like a museum of architecture – but it's a living museum, still setting standards for the rest of the United States**

**B**oston has been called the "most European city in America," thanks primarily to its compact urban scale. Arguably, Chicago is its only rival as a living study of American architecture and urban planning, though due to the latter's relative youth and the catastrophic fire of 1871, Chicago can't claim a comparably rich legacy – something quite evident when one walks Boston's Beacon Hill, the North End, or Back Bay.

Like most East Coast cities, Boston has been too short on space to have preserved its earliest buildings. One exception – the Paul Revere House – survives more because of history than aesthetics. Other 17th-century structures must have been similarly utilitarian, until expanding prosperity allowed grander statements.

British-inspired, early 18th-century Georgian architecture is best represented in Boston by the Old State House, step-gabled and gracefully steepled, at the head of State Street; and by a pair of churches – Old North, on Salem Street in the North End; and Old South Meeting House on Washington Street. Elegantly simple, these churches have, like the Revere House, survived as much as historical icons as architectural artifacts.

Boston's Federal period of the late 18th and early 19th centuries belongs to Charles Bulfinch. Bulfinch brought the chaste, restrained Federal aesthetic to the three Harrison Gray Otis houses on Beacon Hill and in the West End, and to smaller row houses on the Hill. His masterpiece is the 1795 State House, whose dome caps Beacon Hill as it once did the entire Boston skyline.

### CHARLES BULFINCH

Boston-born Charles Bulfinch (1763–1844), America's first professional architect, took much of his inspiration from the classical and neoclassical traditions of Europe. After graduating from Harvard University, he traveled widely in Europe, seeking the advice of Thomas Jefferson, whom he met in Paris, and being strongly influenced in London by the style of Robert Adam. As head of Boston's local government for many years, he played a central role in upgrading the street system and improving Boston Common. In 1818 he became the fourth architect to take responsibility for designing the US Capitol in Washington, DC.

The Greek Revival "Granite Age" survives in the three buildings of Quincy Market (1826), designed by Alexander Parris. Parris was also responsible for a Greek Revival successor to the Federal hegemony on Beacon Hill, the 1819 Somerset Club (originally the Sears mansion) at 42 Beacon Street. And Ammi Young's 1847 Custom House – the original part, beneath the 1915 tower – is a splendid coda to the Greek era in Boston.

Little more than two decades later, the weighty extravagances of the French Empire style arrived in the shape of Old City Hall (Bryant and Gilman, 1869). The period of Victorian eclecticism it helped usher in is best represented in the Back Bay, where historicism ran riot. The most inspired of the architects who mined the past in this era was Henry Hobson Richardson, whose 1877 Trinity Church in Copley Square is regarded as the masterwork of the man who gave his name to "Richardsonian Romanesque." McKim, Mead and White finished the century of historical eclecticism with their Boston Public Library, exemplifying the Renaissance Revival.

Economic doldrums kept Boston architecture in an undistinguished state in the early 20th century. But a number of non-native architectural titans soon put their stamp on the area, particularly in Cambridge. Walter Gropius, Eero Saarinen, Le Corbusier, and Alvar Aalto all designed notable structures for Harvard and MIT. On the Boston side of the Charles, no survey of modern architects can omit I.M. Pei, whose work in the 1970s and '80s included the Christian Science Center and the West Wing of the Museum of Fine Arts.

## Renewal, reuse and originality

Boston's massive redevelopment projects of the 1960s were frequently disregardful of human scale. Government Center Plaza is a prime example, centered on Kallman, McKinnell, and Knowles's City Hall (1969), a stark inverted ziggurat. But in the 1970s, adaptive reuse became the byword, with the Rouse Company's rejuvenation of Faneuil Hall Marketplace. Lewis and Mercantile wharves have been converted into condominiums. Graham Gund's Church Court condominium transforms the shell of a 19th-century Gothic revival church into a structure that blends seamlessly with the surrounding Back Bay.

None of this is to say that original designs have been lacking. Goody, Clancy & Associates created the splendid multi-use State Transportation Building close to the Theater District, and the landmark Tent City residential complex in the South End. Philip Johnson designed stylish high rises at 500 Boylston and International Place. And Skidmore, Owings & Merrill's 1987 Rowes Wharf, with its Boston Harbor Hotel, finally gave Boston the majestic waterside portal it deserved. ❏

### THE JOHN HANCOCK TOWER

A photographer's favorite because of the mirrored images it provides of its more classical neighbors, New England's tallest building was designed by I.M. Pei & Partners for the John Hancock Mutual Life Insurance Co. and was completed in 1976. Its 60 stories of gray-tinted glass framed in black aluminum reach 740 ft (226 meters) into the sky. Built over eight years, the tower was plagued with problems after its 10,000 panes of glass were installed. Unanticipated torquing of the structure caused some of the panes to pop out (remarkably, there were no casualties among passing pedestrians) until the building's core was stiffened.

**FAR LEFT:** the Old State House, built in 1748.
**LEFT:** the John Hancock Tower, opened in 1976.

# PLACES

A detailed guide to the city and its
surroundings, with the principal sites clearly
cross-referenced by number to the maps

**B**y American standards, Boston is old. There are cobbled streets still lit by gas-lamps, and the city has dozens of National Historic Landmarks as well as more than 7,000 individual buildings locally designated as historic landmarks. Yet, because of the hundreds of thousands of students who flock here (and the many who remain after graduation), Boston is a young city well endowed with comedy clubs and restaurants and a vibrant musical and theatrical life. It also has superb museums and outstanding modern architecture. It is also a small city. Its population is 580,000 and its area 40 sq. miles (105 sq. km); and the central, most historic quarter is compact enough to be easily walkable. Greater or Metropolitan Boston, with nearly 100 towns, encompasses 3 million people and covers 1,100 sq. miles (2,850 sq. km).

The city proper consists of 14 tight little neighborhoods, each embracing its territorial imperative. Thus, those who reside in Dorchester, Charlestown or South Boston (all part of the city) scarcely admit to being from Boston: rather, they belong to Dorchester, Charlestown or South Boston. On the other hand, those who live in Newton or Quincy, separate cities within the metropolitan area, are perfectly content to be called Bostonians.

The city's two major attractions are the Freedom Trail and Faneuil Hall Marketplace. The former consists of 16 sites, many of which played a seminal part in the history of the nation and all of which played a major role in the development of Boston. The Marketplace, revived in the 1970s, is the prototype for all such enterprises in and beyond the United States.

The harbor – always Boston's and Massachusetts' greatest natural asset – has been resurrected and the waterfront is now a joy. Then there is the river. Paris may have the Seine and Cairo the Nile, but locals exalt the glorious Charles River, which separates Boston and Cambridge. The latter, home of both Harvard University and the Massachusetts Institute of Technology, is not part of Boston but is a city in its own right with a population of about 100,000 and more than a dozen National Historic Landmarks.

Boston is also an excellent base for excursions. Head south to historic Plymouth, and the inviting beaches and dunelands of Cape Cod; to the north, discover the old seafaring towns that dot Cape Ann and points beyond. Westward lie Lexington and Concord, crucibles of the American Revolution. All of these places and more are covered in the following pages. ❏

---

**PRECEDING PAGES:** Copley Square's Trinity Church reflected in the John Hancock Tower; swan boats in the Public Garden. **LEFT:** cobblestoned Acorn Street in Beacon Hill.

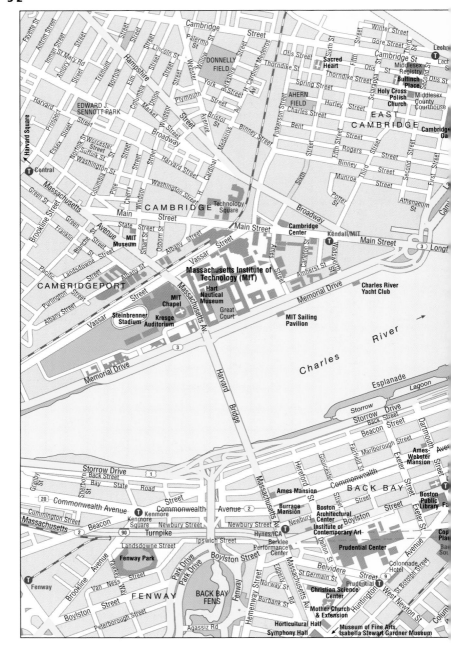

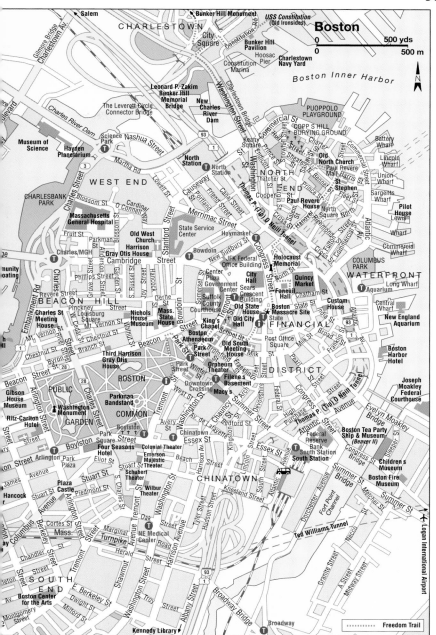

Boston

# BOSTON'S FREEDOM TRAIL

**Boston is both rich in history and small enough to navigate on foot. The Freedom Trail is a handy way for visitors to take in the most important sites**

The Freedom Trail, which is a 3-mile (5-km) painted path linking 16 historic locations that all played a part in Boston's Colonial and Revolutionary history, was born in 1951 and, in 1974, part of it became Boston's National Historical Park.

Although its individual attractions are several centuries old, it was only in 1951 that newspaperman William Greenough Schofield suggested that the sites be linked in a numbered sequence. Until then, according to Schofield, "tourists were going berserk, bumbling around and frothing at the mouth because they couldn't find what they were looking for."

## A leisurely pace

It may be tempting to see the city by tour bus, sightseeing trolley or the amphibious vehicles called duck boats. All provide quick introductions to some of the major sites, but only by walking can you choose your own pace, decide when to eat, or explore that interesting-looking building around the corner that isn't on the tour guide's itinerary. Good walking shoes and a map are a necessity. (Free Freedom Trail maps are available at the National Park Visitor Center at 15 State Street next to the Old State House.) The entire trail can be walked in one day, but it's probably wiser to do it more leisurely over two days.

These four pages give a broad overview of the Freedom Trail. The individual attractions are covered in detail in the various chapters of the Places section; cross-references are given.

**RIGHT:** A red line of paint or brick runs from the Boston Common to the Bunker Hill monument in Charlestown. In some locations – leaving the Old South Meeting House, navigating the streets of the North End or crossing over into Charlestown – it's fairly easy to lose the trail if you aren't watching it carefully. So be sure to have a map handy.

**BELOW:** Charles Bulfinch designed the magnificent red brick and domed **State House** ("the hub of the solar system") when he was only 24. A guided tour is available. *See page 61.*

**ABOVE:** Reliving the past. An actor impersonates Benjamin Franklin at Faneuil Hall *(page 83)*, adjacent to Quincy Market's shops and restaurants. Franklin (1706–90) was born in Boston, although he ran away to Philadelphia when he was 17.

**LEFT:** King's Chapel Burying Ground *(page 79)* became the town's first cemetery in 1630. A chapel joined it in 1689. Many colonists are buried here, including John Winthrop, the colony's governor; Hezekiah Usher, its first printer; and Mary Chilton, the first women to step off the *Mayflower* in 1620.

**BELOW:** Books by Stowe, Emerson, Hawthorne and Thoreau were edited and first printed in the **Old Corner Bookstore** *(page 80)*, originally built in 1712 as an apothecary shop, office and home.

**BELOW: Park Street Church** *(page 62)* dates from 1810 and is known for its architecture and its place in abolitionist history. The hymn *America* was first sung here on July 4, 1831.

**BELOW:** The infant Benjamin Franklin was baptized at **Old South Meeting House** *(page 81)*, which was also the site of many incendiary debates, including a famous rally against the hated tea tax.

**BELOW:** John Hancock, Paul Revere, Samuel Adams, and James Otis are all interred in the **Old Granary Burying Ground** *(page 63)*. Many headstones have been moved so often that they no longer correspond with the original graves.

**LEFT:** The **Old State House** *(page 82)* contains many historic artifacts, from ship models to a vial from the Boston Tea Party. Outside, a star within a circle of cobblestones marks the site of the Boston Massacre of March 5, 1770, when British soldiers fired into a hostile crowd. Now a history museum, it was the center of political life and debate in colonial Boston. On July 18, 1776, citizens gathered in the street to hear the Declaration of Independence read from the building's balcony. The Royal Governor presided here until the new State House was built on Beacon Hill in 1798.

**BELOW:** **Old North Church** *(page 95)* is Boston's oldest place of worship, dating from 1723. The Episcopal church housed the signal lanterns that told Paul Revere the British were heading for Concord. The interior high box pews and brass chandeliers are original.

**ABOVE:** The **USS** *Constitution* *(page 117)*, familiarly known as "Old Ironsides," is the oldest commissioned ship in the United States Navy and is consistently the most visited site on the Freedom Trail. An adjacent museum details the navy's early history.

**BELOW:** Expect during the tourist season to encounter actors on the Freedom Trail. This one is filling in some of the background to the Boston Tea Party *(pages 23 and 105–6)*, which is re-enacted in the Old South Meeting House on December 16.

**ABOVE:** The first floor of the magnificent **Faneuil Hall** *(page 83)* is a lively marketplace, and the second-floor assembly room is still used for debates, lectures and readings.

**ABOVE:** The **Paul Revere House** *(page 94)*, built around 1680, is the oldest house in downtown Boston. Its frame is mostly authentic, but the interior is a recreation of a colonial household. Revere and his family lived here from 1770 to 1800 and he left from here for his renowned "midnight ride" in 1775 *(page 22)*.

**LEFT:** Copp's Hill Burying Ground *(page 97)*, once a Native American cemetery, offers an eclectic assortment of old colonial gravestones and great views. Thousands of blacks who lived in the "New Guinea" community at the base of Copp's Hill are buried in unmarked graves.

## PAUL REVERE RIDES AGAIN

Boston misses few opportunities to relive its stirring history. On March 5, Boston Massacre Day, the Charlestown Militia leads a parade from the Old State House to City Hall Plaza. Patriots' Day, on the third Monday in April, is the year's biggest celebration. Paul Revere's and William Dawes' rides are re-enacted the previous evening. On the day itself, after a parade in Back Bay, the first two battles of the Revolution are staged with gusto at Lexington Green and Concord *(pages 179–81)*. The Boston Marathon *(page 43)* is also run on that day.

● On the first Monday in June, the Ancient and Honorable Artillery Company gathers at Faneuil Hall and parades to Copley Square.

● On June 17, following a parade from Charlestown, the Battle of Bunker Hill *(page 24)* is re-enacted at the Monument.

● On July 4, the Declaration of Independence is read from the balcony of the Old State House.

● On December 16, the Boston Tea Party of 1773 is re-enacted *(pages 105–6)*.

**ABOVE:** Although the 1775 Battle of Bunker Hill is remembered primarily for the costliness of the British victory, the engagement – actually fought on Breed's Hill – was accompanied by a British naval bombardment that reduced a good part of Charlestown to ashes. This explains the neighborhood's lack of pre-Revolutionary structures; most buildings standing today were erected after 1800.

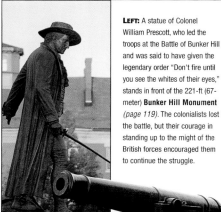

**LEFT:** A statue of Colonel William Prescott, who led the troops at the Battle of Bunker Hill and was said to have given the legendary order "Don't fire until you see the whites of their eyes," stands in front of the 221-ft (67-meter) **Bunker Hill Monument** *(page 119)*. The colonists lost the battle, but their courage in standing up to the might of the British forces encouraged them to continue the struggle.

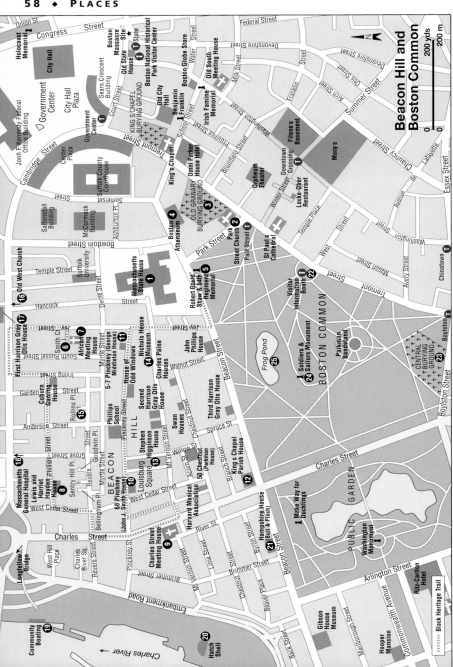

# Beacon Hill and Boston Common

N

0        200 yds
0        200 m

Union St
Congress Street
Holocaust Memorial
City Hall
Jonh F. Kennedy Federal Office Building
Government Center
City Hall Plaza
Center Street
Cambridge Street
Center Plaza
Government Center
Court Street
Sears Crescent Building
Boston Massacre Site
Old State House
Boston National Historical Park Visitor Center
State
Federal Street
Devonshire Street
Boston Globe Store
Water Street
Old South Meeting House
Milk Street
Franklin
Arch Street
Otis Street
Summer Street
Devonshire Street
Filene's Basement
Macy's
Chauncy Street
Chancy Street
Essex Street
Lafayette Avenue
Washington Street
de
Chinatown
Mason Street
Avery Street
West Street
Temple Place
Winter Street
Downtown Crossing
Locke-Ober Restaurant
Opheum Theater
Bromfield Street
Province Street
School Street
Benjamin Franklin
Old City Hall
Irish Famine Memorial
King's Chapel
Tremont Street
KING'S CHAPEL BURYING GROUND
Omni Parker House Hotel
Park Street Church
Park Street
St Paul's Cathedral
OLD GRANARY BURYING GROUND
Boston Athenaeum
Park Street
Washington Street
Suffolk County Courthouse
Somerset
Ashburton Pl.
Saltonstall Building
McCormack Building
Bowdoin Street
Suffolk University
Derne Street
Massachusetts State House
Robert Gould Shaw & 54th Regiment Memorial
Beacon Street
Visitor Information Booth
Soldiers & Sailors Monument
Parkman Bandstand
BOSTON COMMON
CENTRAL BURYING GROUND
Boylston Street
Tremont Street
Hancock Street
Temple Street
Old West Church
First Harrison Gray Otis House
Joy Street
Smith Ct.
African Meeting House
South Russel Street
Irving Street
Myrtle Street
5-7 Pinckney (George Middleton House)
House of Odd Windows
Nichols House Museum
Charles Paine Houses
Walnut Street
John Phillips House
Frog Pond
Garden Street
Coburn Gaming House
Anderson Street
Rollins Pl.
Phillips School
Pinckney Street
BEACON HILL
Second Harrison Gray Otis House
Mt Vernon Street
Third Harrison Gray Otis House
Spruce St
Swan Houses
Massachusetts General Hospital
Lewis and Harriet Hayden House
Grove Street
Phillips Street
Sentry Hill Pl.
Revere Street
Myrtle Street
Goodwin Pl.
Stephen Higginson House
Louisburg Square
Willow Street
Acorn Street
King's Chapel Parish House
50 Chestnut (Perkman House)
Branch Street
Charles Street
Harvard Musical Association
Bellingham Pl.
68 Pinckney (John J. Smith House)
West Cedar Street
Chestnut Street
Beaver Place
Make Way for Ducklings
West Cedar Street
Charles Street Meeting House
Pinckney St.
Charles River Sq.
Revere Street
Mt Vernon Street
Brimmer Street
River St
Lime Street
Byron St
Hampshire House (Bull & Finch)
Beacon Street
Byron Pl.
PUBLIC GARDEN
Washington Monument
West Hill Place
Longfellow Bridge
Embankment Road
Chestnut Street
Brimmer Street
Beaver Street
Back Street
Marlborough Street
Gibson House Museum
Commonwealth Avenue
Hooper Mansion
Arlington Street
Ritz-Carlton Hotel
Charles River
Community Boating
Hatch Shell
Black Heritage Trail

# BEACON HILL AND BOSTON COMMMON

Here the Freedom Trail links with the
Black Heritage Trail. Architectural gems
include the State House, Park Street
Church and many of Charles
Bulfinch's finest houses

**B**ack in the 1970s, when American television executives had been blindsided by the success of *Upstairs, Downstairs*, the British import depicting life among Edwardian nabobs and their servants, they did what television executives always do: they quickly cobbled together an imitation. Of course, they had to set their creation in an American neighborhood more ineradicably associated with old money, exclusivity, and propriety than any other. That neighborhood – and the name of the short-lived program – was Beacon Hill.

The Americanized *Upstairs, Downstairs* failed, no doubt in part because no one could believe that a rich Irish family could have inhabited these precincts in the 1920s, when the show was set (even the Kennedys didn't live there then, although Joseph Sr. could have bought and sold most of the inhabitants). Beacon Hill was *ur*-Yankeedom, and it still is, at least in the cultural imagination.

Today, an up-and-coming investment banker of whatever ethnicity one cares to name can buy a million-dollar condominium on "The Hill." But its bricks and its gas lamps, its narrow side-lanes and secret gardens, are forever associated with the close-knit tribe that created them.

Beacon Hill isn't the oldest neighborhood in Boston, nor is it the wealthiest or liveliest. Its importance to the city is based on that tribe, and what they came to represent. From 1800 to about 1870, Beacon Hill was the home of Boston's oldest, wealthiest and most distinguished families – those whom Oliver Wendell Holmes Sr. called "the Brahmin caste of New England… the harmless, inoffensive, untitled aristocracy." Appleton, Cabot, Lodge, Lowell – the list includes several hundred, all of them related to early Boston settlers and many of them enriched by the

Map
on page
58

**BELOW:**
stained-glass window
in the State House.

*Joy Street bikers.*

China trade. It was a class, said social historian Cleveland Amory in *The Proper Bostonians* , that had "grandfather on the brain."

In many ways, Beacon Hill and Boston Common make an unlikely pair. Beacon Hill is a residential neighborhood, quiet and reserved; the Common is loud and lively, with all kinds of characters passing through. It's the nation's first public park and the democratic heart of Boston, a place where anyone with a soapbox is welcome to hold forth. Together, the two areas have a dynamic but balanced relationship, and it's safe to say that neither would be the same without the other.

### A little world all its own

**BELOW:** Christmas comes to a Beacon Street townhouse.

Beacon Hill rises from the northern border of the Common at Beacon Street, peaks at the crest of old Mt Vernon, and then slopes down to the Charles River and the West End. The streets are relatively long and narrow, and the tidy rows of Federal-style houses make this one of Boston's loveliest and most architecturally homogenous quarters.

By accidents of history and geography, Beacon Hill is divided into three distinct sections. The **South Slope**, generally recognized as classic Beacon Hill, is bordered by Beacon, Pinckney, Bowdoin and Charles streets. The less exclusive **North Slope** runs down the opposite side of the Hill from Pinckney to Cambridge Street. This is where, in the early 1800s, a community of free blacks gathered around Joy Street; many of its members were leaders in the anti-slavery movement preceding the Civil War. And the **Flat Side**, which is built entirely on landfill, occupies the broad area of level ground west of Charles Street and bordering the Charles River.

The relatively modest homes of Beacon Hill were perfectly suited to the Brahmins' peculiar blend of wealth and self-restraint. But, by about 1870, many of the old families began leaving Beacon Hill for more spacious homes in the Back Bay, which was then being developed. The Hill was considered quaint and a bit déclassé for some years, until its charms were re-discovered by a new

### Famous Residents

**B**eacon Hill's illustrious residents include Henry James, Louisa May Alcott, Charles Sumner and Oliver Wendell Holmes, and there are plenty of stories about Charles Dickens hanging around with Henry Wadsworth Longfellow and publisher "Jamie" Fields, and about Edgar Allen Poe getting kicked out of parties for drunkenness.

In 1849, an upper level Brahmin, George Parkman, was killed and dismembered by Dr John Webster, a Harvard Medical School professor who owed him money, and then shoved down the privy in his laboratory. Brahmin society, always mortified by excessive attention, was doubly mortified by the sordid nature of the crime.

generation of residents in the mid-1900s. Today, many single-family homes have been made into condos and apartments, but externally the Hill still represents a remarkably complete picture of early 19th-century architecture and urban planning.

## A sense of separation

But there's more to Beacon Hill than its past. Of all the neighborhoods in Boston, this is the most insulated and self-contained. It's as if the architects designed it as an answer to the old Puritan dilemma – how to be in the world but not of it – because Beacon Hill is both a part of, and apart from, the surrounding city.

The first thing you notice on entering Beacon Hill is exactly this sense of separation. It feels as if you've left modern Boston behind and stepped into a 19th-century village. Traffic thins out, the streets narrow and city noises begin to fade. This is the Boston of another age. It's a town of red brick and cobblestone, of walled gardens and graceful bay windows. Flower boxes brim with color. Trees shade the sidewalk. Aside from a few other tourists, there's almost no one on the street.

The effect is created by a number of factors, but the most important element is stylistic homogeneity. Except for the parked cars (resident sticker required), the modern world intrudes little, and thanks to aggressive historic preservation, many of the original details survive. But, above all, Beacon Hill owes its special ambiance to its original developers and to the native talents of the untrained housewrights who designed and built most of the homes.

## The State House

The first European resident of Beacon Hill was the Rev. William Blackstone, an English hermit who settled on the Shawmut Peninsula several years before the Puritans.

After selling most of his land to John Winthrop, Blackstone retired to a small, 6-acre (2.4-hectare) estate at the foot of the South Slope. At the time, the area was called Tri-mount after the three distinct peaks (Sentry Hill, Mt Vernon and Cotton Hill) that rose above the Common. Between the 1790s and 1830s, all three summits were gradually flattened by as much as 60 ft (18 meters) and the excess soil and rock were used to fill in the North Cove, between modern-day Beacon Hill and the North End, and tidal flats where Charles Street is today.

In 1737 Beacon Hill got its first building of any true substance and Boston got its finest "mansion-house." The house was built by Thomas Hancock, a wealthy merchant and the uncle of revolutionary figure and Massachusetts governor John Hancock, who inherited both house and fortune after his uncle's death. The landmark stood on Beacon Street overlooking the northeast corner of the Common until 1863. The site is marked by a plaque – a poor substitute for what today

Map on page 58

*Beacon Hill charm.*

**BELOW:**
the State House.

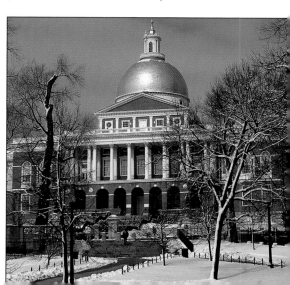

*John F. Kennedy statue outside the State House.*

would have been one of Boston's premier historic attractions.

In 1798, the Hancock mansion was joined by a building that continues to dominate Beacon Hill: the **Massachusetts State House** ❶ (Mon–Fri 8.45am–5pm; tours 10am–3.30pm; tel: 727-3676). It is the masterpiece of Charles Bulfinch, the most important American architect of his day *(see page 44)*, and the building Oliver Wendell Holmes Sr. called "the hub of the solar system," thereby giving the city itself its nickname, "The Hub." (Of course, Holmes also wryly remarked that "the axis of the earth sticks visibly through the center of each and every town or city."

Today, the State House's appearance is the result of several significant changes. The original red brick structure is now backed by an ungainly rear extension and flanked on either side by marble wings. Although clumsy, the side additions innocuously frame Bulfinch's dignified facade, whose grand two-story portico is surmounted by the famous gold dome. In Bulfinch's original design the dome was covered with white shingles. Paul Revere sheathed it in copper and later, in 1861, it was gilded with gold leaf. It was also changed during World War II, when it was painted gray to keep it from shining as a beacon of the wrong sort in case of a nighttime air raid.

Inside the State House, the most impressive rooms are the few that survived the building's alterations. Especially notable are the Senate Chamber, the Reception Room, the House of Representatives (home of the beloved Sacred Cod, a carved wooden fish memorializing Massachusetts' original source of wealth) and Doric Hall, a vaulted, columned, marble chamber that rises beneath the dome.

From the front steps of the State House one can cross Beacon Street and stroll the short length of Park Street, which terminates below the sturdy Georgian steeple of the **Park Street Church** ❷ (mid-June–late Aug, Tues–Sat 8.30am–3pm; Sept–June by appointment; tel: 523-3383). The church was designed by Peter Banner and completed in 1810. The

renowned abolitionist William Lloyd Garrison launched his public crusade against slavery from the pulpit in 1829, and Henry James described the church as "the most interesting mass of brick and mortar in America." That may be true from a historian's point of view, but architecturally the interior is not especially interesting. A film recounting its history is shown in the basement.

## The Old Granary Burying Ground

Although it's now surrounded by modern buildings, the **Old Granary Burying Ground** ❸ (spring–fall, daily 9am–5pm, winter daily 9am–3pm; tel: 536-4100), located near the corner of Park and Tremont streets, was originally a part of the Common and took its name from an old granary that once stood where the Park Street Church is now located. The first body was committed in 1660, making it one of the oldest cemeteries in Boston. Among the historic figures buried here are Samuel Adams, Peter Faneuil, Paul Revere, John Hancock, and the victims of the Boston Massacre. An obelisk in the middle of the graveyard marks the resting place of Benjamin Franklin's parents. Unfortunately, the headstones have been moved so many times, they no longer correspond to the actual graves, some of which are four bodies deep. Believe it or not, the neat rows we see today are an accommodation to the lawnmower. Still, the icons and inscriptions carved into the stones tell much about the deceased and the era they lived in.

Taking the longer route back to the State House, walk down Tremont away from the Common and take a left on Beacon Street. The unobtrusive entrance at 10½ Beacon Street is that of the **Boston Athenaeum** ❹ (tel: 227-0270), a private library and Brahmin stronghold. Casual visitors are only allowed limited access to the first and second floors. Founded in 1807, the Athenaeum, whose barrel-vaulted fifth floor is nirvana for the book lover, contains the library of George Washington and also houses a notable collection of American portrait paintings. (So impressive is the Athenaeum's superb Italian palazzo-inspired interior that Hollywood movie crews have used it to double for Harvard's libraries.) From here it is a very short walk up Beacon Street back to the State House.

## The Black Heritage Trail

Begin exploring Beacon Hill history with the short **Black Heritage Trail**, a sort of "second Freedom Trail" overseen by the National Park Service. Guided tours begin at the Robert Gould Shaw Memorial on Boston Common (Memorial Day–Labor Day 10am, noon, and 2 pm; Labor Day–Memorial Day, reservations needed; tel: 742-5415.) When Massachusetts declared slavery illegal in 1783, the migration of runaway slaves to Boston grew enormously. Free blacks settled in the North End but later moved to the North Slope of Beacon Hill.

Map on page 58

*Park Street Church.*

**BELOW:**
Paul Revere's tomb in the Old Granary Burying Ground.

*The New England Anti-Slavery Society started here in 1832.*

The **Robert Gould Shaw Memorial** , on Beacon Street directly across from the State House, is one of the most moving pieces of public art in America and, to many, the finest work of sculptor Augustus Saint-Gaudens. It is a bronze bas-relief honoring the Massachusetts 54th Regiment, the first black regiment recruited in the North during the Civil War, and Shaw, a young white Bostonian who volunteered for its command. He and many members of the company were killed during the assault on Fort Wagner, South Carolina, an event recreated in the 1989 movie *Glory*. Although the bas relief is only a few inches front to back, Saint-Gaudens created a sense of great visual depth, and gave the face of each of the marchers tremendous dignity and individuality. The memorial was celebrated by Robert Lowell in his poem "For the Union Dead."

Just off Joy Street, three blocks from the Common, is tiny **Smith Court** ❻, where, at one time, all the houses were occupied by blacks. Facing these is the **African Meeting House** ❼, the oldest black church in the nation still standing. Dedicated in 1806, it was called "the haven from the loft" because of the practice in Old North Church of relegating black worshippers to its loft. It was also known as "Black Faneuil Hall" because of its fiery anti-slave meetings. These culminated in 1832 when William Lloyd Garrison founded the New England Anti-Slavery Society here.

Next door, at the corner of Joy Street, stood the Abiel Smith School, dedicated in 1834 to the education of the city's black children. Yet voices of integration were already being heard, for, although the black community had fought hard for this school, some were opposed, arguing that it would crystallize segregation. Led by William C. Neill, who lived in Smith Court and who was the first published black historian, they formed the Equal Schools Association, which called for the school to be boycotted.

In 1850 the state's highest court ruled that the school provided an education equal to that of other public schools in the city and so blacks

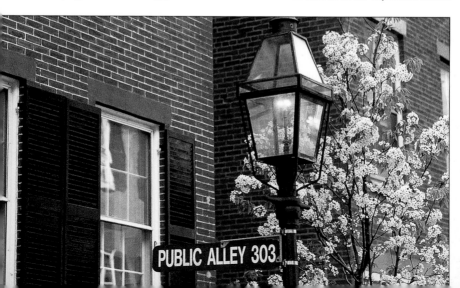

PUBLIC ALLEY 303

need not be admitted to the public system. However, in 1855 the State Legislature outlawed segregation and the Smith School was closed.

A few blocks away at the corner of Phillips and Irving streets was the Coburn Gaming House, a "private palace… the resort of the upper ten who had acquired a taste for gambling." Also on Phillips Street (No. 66) is the **Lewis and Harriet Hayden House ❽**. This was one of the most important of the many "underground railway" stops on the Hill that sheltered fugitive slaves on their way to freedom in Canada. In 1853 the Haydens were visited by Harriet Beecher Stowe, who was researching for her book *A Key to Uncle Tom's Cabin*. She was astonished that the house was a haven for 13 slaves. It is said that Hayden kept two kegs of gunpowder in the basement so that the house could be blown up if searched.

The Black History Trail continues on to Charles Street, where the **Charles Street Meeting House ❾** was built in 1807 for the Third Baptist Church. In the mid-1830s the Church's segregationist traditions were challenged by Timothy Gilbert, who invited black friends to his pew. He was expelled and, with other white abolitionist Baptists, founded the First Baptist Free Church. It became Tremont Temple, "the first integrated church in America." In 1876 the Meeting House was bought by the African Methodist Episcopalian Church and, in 1939, was the last black institution to leave the Hill.

Further up the Hill, at **68 Pinckney ❿**, is a fine house that belonged to John J. Smith, a distinguished black statesman who migrated to Boston from Virginia in 1848. Stationed in Washington during the Civil War, he was a recruiting officer for the all-black Fifth Cavalry. Later, he was appointed three times to the Massachusetts House of Rep-

resentatives, and to the Boston Common Council.

The large red-brick building at the corner of Pinckney and Anderson streets is the **Phillips School**, which, when opened to blacks in 1855, became the city's first inter-racial school. The clapboard house at **Nos. 5–7 Pinckney ⓫** is the oldest (1791) existing home on the Hill built by a black person. The lot was bought by G. Middleton, a black equestrian, and Lewis Glapion, a mulatto barber. Middleton, a colonel in the Revolutionary War, led the all-black company "Bucks of America."

## The South Slope

At about the same time that the State House was being completed, Charles Bulfinch became involved in another large-scale project on Beacon Hill. Together with other enterprising townsmen (including Harrison Gray Otis, Joseph Woodward, Jonathan Mason and William Scollay), Bulfinch became a member of the Mt Vernon Proprietors, which bought about 19 acres (7.7 hectares) of pasture on the South Slope. Plans were drawn to level

Map on page 58

*Harriet Beecher Stowe, author of* Uncle Tom's Cabin *, wrote the lesser-known* A Key to Uncle Tom's Cabin *– a compilation of material culled from court records, press accounts, and private correspondence – to defend herself from charges of inaccuracy in the earlier book.*

**BELOW:** pooches meet up in Pinckney Street.

*Harrison Gray Otis, a US Congressman and mayor of Boston, played a central role in buying land to facilitate the development of Beacon Hill. Bulfinch designed a succession of three homes for him on Cambridge Street (1796), Mt Vernon Street (1800) and Beacon Street (1804), all of which survive.*

**BELOW:**
fine houses grace
Louisburg Square.

the summit, lay out streets and subdivide house lots.

The Proprietors originally intended to build free-standing homes surrounded by gardens, but the economics of development soon dictated a more efficient plan – joining homes at a common wall. At first, two or three houses were built together, and then, as the pace of development quickened, entire streets were lined with single unbroken rows. Although Bulfinch designed several of Beacon Hill's grandest estates – and a few more modest row houses – most of the buildings were erected by untrained artisans. Their instincts for proportion, sturdiness and modest ornamentation still define the neighborhood's essential character.

A tour of the old Mt Vernon properties is limited entirely to the South Slope. The best place to start is on the northeast corner of the Common, directly in front of the State House. From here, proceed straight down Beacon Street until you reach the corner of Charles Street.

Fronting the Common along its northern border, **Beacon Street** is the

Hill's public face. This is Oliver Wendell Holmes's "sunny street that holds the sifted few." The buildings here are among the oldest on Beacon Hill, and boast a level of grandeur and ornamentation largely unmatched by the rest of the neighborhood.

As you stroll down the hill, be sure to take note of the **John Phillips House** (1 Walnut St.) and the **Third Harrison Gray Otis House** (45 Beacon St.), both designed by Bulfinch between 1804 and 1808. "Purple panes" still hang in the window frames of **King's Chapel Parish House ⓬** (63–64 Beacon St.) and of 39 and 40 Beacon Street. The unusual color is caused by a chemical defect, and the purple panes, installed in the early 1800s, have become a part of Beacon Hill folklore.

Take a right at the corner of Charles Street and then turn right again at one of the narrow cross streets that lead up the slope. The first and most intimate one is **Chestnut Street**. The combination of simple structures, modest scale and artful detailing make this one of the most pleasing streets on the Hill. The buildings are especially notable for the del-

icate use of ornamentation, including wrought-iron balconies, bootscrapers, Greek Revival porticos and fan lights, all of which tend to vary and lighten the plain brick facades.

Again, there are far too many distinguished homes to list, but highlights include the **Charles Paine Houses** (6–8 Chestnut St.), the **Swan Houses** (13, 15 and 17) and No. 29, all attributed to Bulfinch. The home of historian **Francis Parkman** is located at No. 50 , and the **Harvard Musical Association**, the country's oldest music library, is at No. 57A.

Take time to explore the narrow lanes that intersect Chestnut Street. Many of the smaller houses on Willow, West Cedar and Acorn streets were originally servants' quarters and kitchens that serviced the wealthier households. Today, these slender byways are among the most private locations on the Hill. **Acorn Street**, the steep cobbled alley lined with gas lamps and flower boxes, is not to be missed.

Following Willow Street uphill, you immediately come to **Mt Vernon Street**. Here the houses are larger and the street wider; and the original families were more distinguished. In one of his more snobbish moments, Henry James called it "the only respectable street in America."

## Louisburg Square

The highlight of Mt Vernon Street, and the crown of Beacon Hill, is **Louisburg Square** ⓭, a small rectangle of grass and trees surrounded by a cobblestone plaza and stately homes built in the 1840s. The gently rippling bowfront houses on the west side of the square (numbers 8 to 22) have been called the finest row houses in Boston, and possibly in the United States.

Louisa May Alcott lived at No. 10; William Dean Howells at Nos. 4 and 16; and, at No. 20, the singer Jenny Lind married her accompanist Otto

Goldschmidt. The little park at the center of the square, graced by the statues of Christopher Columbus and Aristides the Just, is owned collectively by the square's householders – although perhaps condominium holders might be a more apt description today. One of the remaining single-family homes is owned by Massachusetts Senator John Kerry, the 2004 presidential candidate, and his wife Teresa Heinz Kerry.

Just beyond Louisburg Square, in the direction of the State House (to the southeast), is an impressive series of freestanding mansions. The **Stephen Higginson House** at No. 87 and its much-altered neighbor at No. 89 were both designed by Charles Bulfinch between 1804 and 1809. The **Second Harrison Gray Otis House**, next door at No. 85, is a Bulfinch design of 1800.

The brownstone mansions across the street were constructed in 1850; their Gothic touches are a striking counterpoint to the other buildings on the street. The 1804 **Nichols House Museum** ⓮ at 55 Mt Vernon Street is also a Bulfinch creation, and guided

Map on page 58

*Traditional knocker.*

**BELOW:** winter in Louisburg Square.

*Hanging out on Pinckney Street.*

**BELOW:**
a bust of Paul Revere catches the eye in an antiques store.

tours are offered (noon–5pm Thur–Sat, on the half-hour; tel: 227 6993). Like the Back Bay's Gibson House *(see page 126)*, the lifelong home of the philanthropist Rose Standish Nichols is a true period piece; few of its furnishings are more recent than the mid-Victorian era.

At the opposite end of Louisburg Square, **Pinckney Street** runs along the crest of Beacon Hill, separating the South Slope from the less affluent North Slope.

Noteworthy homes in this area include No. 24, the "**House of Odd Windows**," which has the most eccentric design on the Hill.

### The North Slope

Beyond Pinckney, the North Slope pitches toward Cambridge Street and the West End. Until not so long ago, this was the bohemian half of Beacon Hill, one of the few places where artists, writers and students could find tiny yet affordable apartments. From the very beginning, it was considered the "bad side" of the Hill, but that would be a relative term indeed given today's rental costs. Gentrifi-

cation has certainly found the North Slope of Beacon Hill.

Still, the North Slope retains a different feel than "classic" Beacon Hill. It doesn't share the same architectural pedigree, and even has a number of buildings built frankly as apartment houses. There are neighborhood businesses here – corner groceries, cafés, pizzerias, and barber shops. The students bustling up and down Temple Street near **Suffolk University** further animate the district, and you are far more likely, as you get down near Cambridge Street, to hear music blasting from an apartment window or car horns honking. That sort of thing simply wouldn't do on Mt Vernon.

While walking the North Slope, be sure to poke into the four quiet, charming cul-de-sacs that run off Revere Street. **Rollins Place** ⑮ is especially interesting because the classical two-story portico at the end is a mere facade. There's nothing behind it but a 20-ft (6-meter) cliff dropping down to Phillips Street. The other alleyways – **Goodwin Place**, **Sentry Hill Place** and

Bellingham Place – are equally enchanting, each paved with red brick and lined with compact row houses. Branching off from opposite sides of Phillips Street (near the corner of West Cedar) are **Primus Avenue** and a very narrow passage known as **Flower Lane**, two other alleyways worth investigating.

The North side of the Hill ends in wide, busy **Cambridge Street**, on whose far side are several interesting buildings. At the west end of this street is the **Old West Church** , a handsome red-brick Federal-style building from 1806. The original church was razed in 1775 when the British thought that the Americans were using it as a steeple from which to signal to their compatriots in Cambridge. The current building, a Methodist church, is an oblong meeting house fronted by a rectangular block rising in several stages to a square cupola beneath which are swag-ornamented clocks. The large, empty interior has a balcony, supported by delicate columns with attenuated acanthus-leaf capitals, running around three sides.

Next door is the **First Harrison Gray Otis House** ❶ (Wed–Sun 11am–4.30pm; tel: 227-3956; tours on the hour and half-hour), designed by Bulfinch in 1796 and now the headquarters of Historic New England (formerly the Society for the Preservation of New England Antiquities). Otis, whose later Bulfinch houses we've seen on the South Slope of the Hill, was a Boston mayor, congressman, and real estate developer. This, the most distinguished old mansion still standing in Boston, is a completely symmetrical three-story rectangular block of red brick, with each story defined by a brownstone string course. The interior has been meticulously restored with furniture and portraits, bright replica wallpapers and carpets, and mirror-paneled doors that would reflect candlelight. The basement contains an architectural museum.

*The First Harrison Gray Otis House.*

Map on page 58

## Massachusetts General Hospital

Farther to the east on Cambridge Street is the sprawling **Massachusetts General Hospital** ❶, possibly

**BELOW:**
Old West Church.

### The Unsavory Slope

Soon after its founding around 1725, the North Slope Village began to take on an unsavory character. Its proximity to the river and its detachment from town made it a perfect spot for sailors looking for taverns and bordellos. North Slope entrepreneurs were only too glad to oblige them, and within a few years Boston had its first red-light district. Among sailors, the village became known as Mount Whoredom, and for nearly 100 years it rankled the morals of god-fearing citizens.

In the early 1820s, though, a crackdown forced the last of Mount Whoredom's bawdy houses to shut down, and the area began to change as the city's black population began to move in.

# Medical Trailblazers

I n 1846, Dr John Collins Warren delivered his verdict to those who had observed Mr Gilbert Abbot undergoing surgery at the Massachusetts General Hospital: "Gentlemen, this is no humbug." Mr Abbot, who was operated on for a tumor, had just told the entranced gathering that he had "suffered no pain." This was because here in Boston, for the first time in the world, ether had been used to anesthetize the patient. Today, at the hospital (usually known as the MGH, Mass General, "Man's Greatest Hospital" or, to medical students, the "massive genital"), the visitor can see the Ether Dome, the work of Bulfinch, and the operating theater where ether was first used. (Public tours Tues and Thur at 2pm.)

Just as Boston is top in education, so it is America's leader in medicine. Today, the hub has 17 major hospitals and Greater Boston has nearly 100 facilities. Harvard, Boston University and Tufts each has its medical school and the Massachusetts Institute of Technology has a medical program with Harvard. In the past 50 years more than a score of doctors and scientists working at Boston's hospitals and medical schools have won Nobel prizes in physiology and/or medicine.

Among these is John Enders who, with Frederick Robbins and Thomas Weller, won this award in 1954 for their work in developing the poliomyelitis vaccine, which effectively eliminated this scourge. Almost 150 years before this, Dr Benjamin Waterhouse of Harvard Medical School (HMS) had been the first to introduce smallpox vaccination in the country.

A more recent Nobel laureate in medicine (1990) is Joseph Murray who, in 1954, at the Peter Bent Brigham Hospital, was part of a team that successfully performed the first human kidney transplant. And open-heart surgery was first performed at the Boston Children's Hospital by Professor Robert Gross in 1967. Then there was 12-year-old Danny Everett who, in 1962, while hitching a ride home on a train after pitching in a Little League baseball game, had his arm shorn off. Dr Ronald Malt and his emergency room team at the MGH performed the first successful replantation of a human limb.

The list of firsts is long: abdominal surgery (1886); creation of the Drinker respirator (iron lung) in 1928; artificial kidney (1945); clinical reports on efficacy of birth control pills (1959); techniques for freezing and thawing blood (1964); abdominal electrocardiography for monitoring the fetus during labor (1973), and creating artificial skin for burn victims (1981).

Less dramatic, but just as important, Boston national medical firsts include Linda Richards, the first trained nurse; the first medical school to admit women (Boston University); the first city to establish a municipal water supply; and the first Board of Health. On an international level, the much respected, oft-quoted *New England Journal of Medicine*, founded in 1812 by Dr John Collins Warren and James Jackson, is the oldest continuously published medical journal in the world.

With the ratio of doctors to residents nearly 50 percent above the national average, is Boston a good place to fall ill? Not necessarily: many physicians are more interested in research than in everyday caring.

The greatest concentration of hospitals is in the Longwood area in Brookline – almost a mini-city, with five major hospitals. ❏

**LEFT:** history is made at Massachusetts General Hospital when ether is used for the first time.

America's greatest hospital. Its very first building, the Bulfinch Pavilion and Ether Dome, was designed by Bulfinch just before he departed for Washington to work on the United States Capitol. Ask at the hospital's main entrance for directions to this building, an historic landmark twice over: once because of its architecture and once because here ether was used as an anesthetic for the first time *(see opposite page)*. The Federal-style building stands on a high podium, and the main entrance is approached by two stairways that lead to the sides of a portico formed by 10 unfluted Ionic columns.

## The Flat Side and Charles Street

The remaining part of Beacon Hill, a broad area of level ground built entirely on landfill, is known as the **Flat Side**. Its outstanding feature is **Charles Street**, Beacon Hill's only commercial street, while its most distinguished building is the **Charles Street Meeting House**, on the corner of Mt Vernon Street.

Relative to the other two sections of Beacon Hill, the Flat Side occupies a neutral position. It has few of the grand associations boasted by the South Slope and almost none of the negative ones once tagged on the North. As a result, people tend to overlook the residential areas, although here, as elsewhere on the Hill, the overall effect is of a quaint 19th-century town located in the middle of a modern city.

Most people come to the Flat Side to shop on Charles Street, which tends to be less hectic than downtown and more casual than the boutiques on Newbury Street. Antiques are a local specialty and there are several good restaurants and cafés where one can buy Italian pastries, gelato and a stiff cup of espresso.

The finest homes tend to be gathered on Brimmer, Lime and Mt Ver-non streets between Charles Street and the river. There are also two very interesting courtyards tucked into the block immediately off Embankment Road. **Charles River Square** is a hidden enclave of tidy row houses surrounding a rectangular plaza.

About a half-block away, the row houses at **West Hill Place** use concave facades to define a circular courtyard; there's a tunnel in the back that opens to Charles Street. With the intersection of three major highways only a few hundred feet away, the sound of traffic often penetrates the superb isolation these lovely courtyards must have enjoyed in the past.

## Along the Charles and its Esplanade

Just downstream from Charles River Square is the **Longfellow Bridge**, completed in 1900 and the oldest and most ornate bridge across the river. Its four readily recognizable towers have led to the nickname Salt and Pepper Bridge. Originally called the Cambridge Bridge, it was renamed in honor of the poet Henry Wadsworth Longfellow (1807–82).

**Map on page 58**

**TIP**

Rock star and one-time Bostonian Steven Tyler is the narrator of "Boston: City of Rebels and Dreamers," a taped tour accessible via cell phone. For details, call 617- 262 8687; www.talkingstreet.com

**BELOW:** the Salt and Pepper Bridge.

*Bust of conductor
Arthur Fiedler near
the Hatch Shell.*

**BELOW:**
the Hatch Shell.

Tucked into the southwest corner of the bridge is the clubhouse of **Community Boating** ⑲, which is believed to organize the world's oldest and largest public sailing program. Many an Olympic and America's Cup sailor first put to sea here on the embankment of the Charles River.

However, not all the scudding white sails of traditional centerboards and psychedelic sails of windsurfers have set off from the Community Boating quay. Some belong to the Massachusetts Institute of Technology Sailing Club whose clubhouse is somewhat upriver and across from the Community Boating. Others belong to the Emerson College Sailing Club, whose headquarters building is just a few yards upstream from the Community Boating quay.

Immediately beyond this is the boathouse of the Union Boat Club, founded in 1851 by gentlemen interested in rowing who were also admirers of Daniel Webster's Union Forever speeches. In order to maintain the integrity of the riparian banks, they built their clubhouse, not on the river, but diagonally across Embankment Road, at the foot of Chestnut Street.

Along the Esplanade just beyond the end of Chestnut Street is the **Hatch Shell** ⑳, an outdoor concert venue that is home to the Boston Pops and other performers during summer (the annual Fourth of July concert, followed by fireworks, is a favorite tradition). It's accessible by a pedestrian bridge across Storrow Drive, at the corner of Beacon and Arlington streets.

Near the Shell is a large **bust of Arthur Fiedler** (1894–1979), who founded the Boston Sinfonietta in 1924 and went on to conduct its successor, the Pops, for 49 years from 1930 until his death. The atmosphere is informal: many concertgoers come equipped with blanket and picnic basket.

## Stately homes and a famous saloon

Although the architecture of the Flat Side isn't as old or interesting as the rest of the Hill, there is an excep-

tionally handsome row of granite houses on Beacon Street directly across from the Public Garden. When they were built in 1828, most of the Flat Side was still under water. The houses actually stood on the Mill Dam, which started at the edge of the Common and arched across the Back Bay. The dam later became the extension of Beacon Street which proceeds through Back Bay.

Probably the most popular attraction on the Flat Side is still the **Hampshire House ㉑** restaurant, with its street-level Bull & Finch pub. In the early 1980s this cozy watering hole, on the corner of Beacon and Brimmer streets, was scouted by television producers looking for inspiration for a situation comedy revolving around the characters frequenting a Boston bar. The show became *Cheers*, and its subsequent popularity transformed the place into a major tourist attraction. The crowds have thinned somewhat, but if it's just a couple of cold ones you're after, walk midway up Charles Street to the Sevens Ale House, where you can still belly up to the bar without having to breathe in quite so much self-promotion.

## Boston Common

**Boston Common** is such an integral part of Beacon Hill that it's impossible to talk about one without mentioning the other. Although the two areas represent different aspects of Boston, they are linked by history and should be thought of as elements of a larger whole.

The Common, a pentagon covering about 50 acres (20 hectares), is bounded by Beacon, Boylston, Charles, Park and Tremont streets. It is both a geographical and social crossroads: the people one sees on the Common represent a broad sampling of the city. Chinese women practice tai chi in the shade of an ancient elm tree; Italian men stroll with their grandchildren; rappers and break-dancers show off their skills; kids play ball; and office workers soak up the sun while enjoying their lunch.

For those unfamiliar with the city, the Common is probably the best place to start a visit. There is a **Visitor Information Booth ㉒** (tel: 536-4100) located just south of the Park Street subway station (corner Park and Tremont streets), where you can pick up free maps and which also serves as the beginning of the Freedom Trail *(see pages 54–57)*.

Most activity occurs on the fringe of the Common, near Park Street station. Here, vendors sell ice-cream, hot-dogs, T-shirts and other souvenirs, and, on occasions, religious fanatics vent their wrath. Opened in 1897, "Park Street Under" was the first subway station in the nation and is now a Historic Landmark.

### Taking a trolley

Several privately operated sightseeing "trolleys" (in reality, conventional wheeled vehicles with trolley-like bodywork) that run every 10 or 15 minutes set off on

Map on page 58

*Boston Common was described in 1674 by John Josselyn as "a small, but pleasant Common, where the Gallants a little before Sun-set walk with their Marmalet-Madams… till the nine o'clock bells rings them home to their habitations [and] the Constables walk their rounds to see good order kept, and to take up loose people."*

**BELOW:**
a sightseeing trolley.

Map on page 58

*The Soldiers and Sailors Monument.*

**BELOW:** skating on Frog Pond.

their city tours from here. Although some guides seem to be more interested in auditioning for comedy clubs than giving useful information, a trolley ride is an excellent way to become acquainted with the city, especially if time is limited. Best of all, one can hop off the trolley wherever one likes, explore on foot for a while and then re-board a later trolley. There's hot competition between lookalike trolley companies; take care to re-board a trolley of the company whose ticket you hold.

Most people don't realize that the Common is probably the oldest and least changed section of Boston. It was established more than 350 years ago, when John Winthrop and his neighbors bought the site from the Rev. William Blackstone. In 1640, the townsmen agreed to preserve the land as a "Comon Field" *(sic)* on which sheep and cattle were to be grazed, and it soon became a popular spot for sermons, promenades and, in the years before the Revolution, political protest. Militias used the land as a mustering ground, and public hangings were conducted at

the Great Elm, which stood on the Common until 1876. Among the heretics who met a cruel end here was Mary Dyer, the heroic Quaker who insisted on the right to worship freely. A statue in her memory, and another commemorating exiled religious dissenter Anne Hutchinson, stand near one of John F. Kennedy on the grounds of the State House.

During the American Revolution, the Common was transformed into a British military center. As many as 2,000 Redcoats were quartered here during the occupation of Boston, and several dozen British soldiers killed at the Battle of Bunker Hill were interred at the **Central Burying Ground** ㉓ in the southeast corner. It is the fourth oldest cemetery in Boston, but few of note are buried here. One exception is Gilbert Stuart, the painter who gave us the classic portrait of George Washington.

The west part of the common is devoted to athletic endeavor – baseball, tennis, volley ball and frisbee are all popular – and to large public meetings.

Elsewhere on the Common are several works of public art. Outstanding is the 70-ft (21-meter) **Soldiers and Sailors Monument** ㉔, which is located atop Telegraph Hill on the western side of the park. It is dedicated to the Union forces killed in the Civil War.

### From sheep to skaters

Close by is the **Frog Pond** ㉕, which is a children's wading pool in summer and an ice rink in winter. In colonial times sheep and cows slaked their thirst at the pond. Later, proper Bostonians fished in it for minnows in the summer and ice-skated on it in the winter, and here they celebrated the first arrival of piped-in municipal water from a suburban reservoir in 1848. There are no minnows, nor frogs, in the pond today. It is lined with concrete. ❑

# RESTAURANTS & BARS

## Restaurants

### American

**75 Chestnut**
75 Chestnut St.; Tel: 227-2175. Open: D nightly; Sun. brunch. $$$–$$$$
www.75chestnut.com
"The hidden jewel of Beacon Hill" is a romantic hideaway with dark wood panels and comfy banquettes. Specialties include truffled lobster hash and coquilles St. Jacques. A three-course dinner is $30, and there's a fine Sunday jazz brunch Sept–June.

### French

**Beacon Hill Bistro**
Beacon Hill Hotel, 25 Charles St.; Tel: 723-1133. Open: B, L & D daily. $$
www.beaconhillbistro.com
French food with a New England influence in a long, narrow room lined with leather banquettes and mirrors. Weekend brunch is popular.

**Spire at the Nine Zero Hotel**
90 Tremont St.; Tel: 772-0202. Open: B, L, D daily. $$$$
www.spirerestaurant.com
A luxurious boutique hotel, across from Park Street Church, houses this ultra-sophisticated dining room. Dishes aim to integrate the flavors of France, Italy, Spain and Portugal with seasonal New England ingredients.

**No. 9 Park**
9 Park St.; Tel: 742-9991. Open: L Mon–Fri, D Mon–Sat. $$$$
www.no9park.com
Award-winning chef/owner Barbara Lynch prepares European country cuisine in a Bulfinch-designed 19th-century mansion overlooking the Common. Seven- and nine-course tasting menus change daily, and an à la carte menu is available.

### Italian

**Antonio's Cucina Italiana**
288 Cambridge St.; Tel: 367-3310. Open: L & D Mon–Sat. $$
Good value and terrific red-sauce cooking. The fusilli is homemade, the veal is tender, and the cannoli with an espresso is a great conclusion.

**Avila**
1 Charles St.; Tel: 267-4810. Open L & D daily, Sun brunch. $$$$
www.avilarestaurant.com
The flavors of the Mediterranean are presented at this chic, new upscale spot. Highlights include a serano ham, manchego cheese, and fresh figs appetizer; kobe beef pizza, and hand-rolled gnocci.

**Figs**
42 Charles St.; Tel: 742-3447. Open: L Mon–Fri, L & D (serving dinner menu only) Sat & Sun. $$–$$$
(also 67 Main St., Charlestown, Tel: 242-2229; 92 Central St., Wellesley, Tel: 237-5788). Call for hours)
www.toddenglish.com
Todd English, Boston's one-man restaurant consortium, offers pizzas and panini, along with more elaborate dishes such as such as garganelli (pasta with broccoli sauce, Parmesan, and confit veal ragu).

**Ristorante Toscano**
47 Charles St.; Tel: 723-4090. Open: L & D Mon–Sat. $$$
www.ristorantetoscano.com
For more than 20 years Florence-born Vinicio Paoli has been serving classic Italian dishes in his recreated Tuscan retreat. Nothing nouvelle, just simplicity and freshness.

**Upper Crust**
20 Charles St: Tel: 723-9600 (also at 286 Harvard St., Brookline, Tel: 739-8518. Open: L & D daily. $
www.theuppercrustpizzeria.com
The pies at this popular eatery are Neopolitan-style (thin crust, chunky sauce), and available by the slice, with a wide selection of toppings.

### Persian

**Lala Rokh**
97 Mt. Vernon St.; Tel: 720-5511. Open: L Mon–Fri, D nightly. $$–$$$
www.lalarokh.com
Sophisticated Persian cuisine with elements of Indian, Turkish and Armenian flavors in a romantic townhouse.

### Thai

**The King & I**
145 Charles St.; Tel: 227-3320. Open: L Mon–Sat, D nightly. $$
A large selection of authentic Thai specialties served in cozy, elegant surroundings.

## Bars

The happening place for singles on the Hill, **Harvard Gardens** (316 Cambridge St. Tel: 523-2727) also serves decent pub grub. The **21st Amendment** (150 Bowdoin St. Tel: 227-7100), an historic tavern near the State House, is named for the amendment repealing prohibition (it's open until 2am daily). Serves sandwiches and signature Baked Potato Soup. **Cheers** (84 Beacon St. Tel: 227-9605), inspiration for the TV series, serves food (the burgers are terrific) until midnight, drinks until 2am.

### PRICE CATEGORIES

Prices for three-course dinner per person with a half-bottle of house wine, tax and tip:
**$** = under $25
**$$** = $25–$40
**$$$** = $40–$50
**$$$$** = more than $50

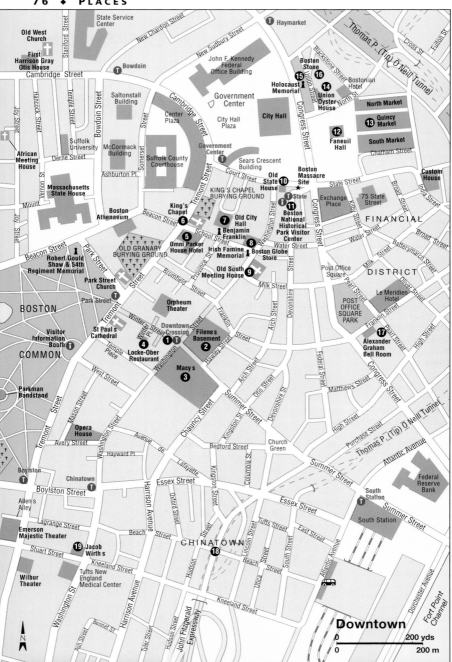

Downtown

0        200 yds

0        200 m

# DOWNTOWN

Old City Hall, Old South Meeting House, Ye Olde
Oyster House – everything seems ancient. But
then there's Quincy Market and Chinatown

To walk the streets of Downtown Boston today is to walk with the ghosts of colonial settlers upon ground now shadowed by modern skyscrapers. As the centuries have passed, many street names have changed. But the streets themselves follow much the same design as they did back in the 1630s when Anne Hutchinson, the feminist leader of her day, was ousted from her home on what is now School Street, or in October 1746, when the Rev. Thomas Prince of Old South Meeting House "prayed up" a hurricane that wrecked an invading force of French warships.

There's nowhere more appropriate for starting such a walk than at **Downtown Crossing ❶**, where Summer and Washington streets intersect. At this spot, you are standing at the very center of Downtown Boston – a huge bronze disc embedded in the sidewalk assures you of the fact. What the plaque doesn't tell you is that South Boston is east of Downtown Boston, that East Boston is north of where you stand, and that the North End just north of Downtown Boston is south of East Boston. Also, as you stand at the center of Downtown Boston, if you move your feet a few paces to the west, Summer Street becomes Winter Street without changing its face or its direction.

## Bargain basement

As for other things unique – well, right there at Downtown Crossing, just at your elbow, is the entrance to the internationally popular **Filene's Basement ❷**. Its clientele has ranged from royalty to bag ladies, from presidents to punks, all drawn by its system of bargain-slashing, each hoping to outwit, outwait or outgrab the other at the correct instant for a sensational bargain. An $800 Brooks Brothers suit goes on sale in the Basement at, say, $400;

Map
on page
76

**BELOW:**
Downtown Crossing.

*They're not joking.*

if unsold after 14 days, it's $300; after 21 days, $200; after 28 days, $100. (At that point, of course, It helps if you are a 36 short or a 50 long.) Find one unsold for 35 days and your check goes to charity. Fun shopping? Sometimes it's a riot. Filene's landmark regular-price store, once located directly above, had less commercial success and closed in 2006.

Sharing Summer Street with Filene's Basement is **Macy's ❸**, formerly the flagship store of the Jordan Marsh chain. This outfit had its beginning on a frosty morning in 1851 when young Eben Dyer Jordan made his first sale in his newly opened shop – one yard of red silk ribbon, sold to a little girl for two cents. This was a big deal for a man who had sailed down from Maine five years earlier with just $1.25 in his pocket.

By contrast with that commercial coup, Boston's financiers today handle transactions of mega-millions. Although not nearly as important as New York in general financial transactions, Boston has carved out for itself some special niches. Mutual funds, in which it still leads the field, began here in 1925 and, nearly a century earlier, the concept of venture capital, which still thrives here, was introduced in Boston. Many families and institutions throughout the nation depend on conservative Boston firms, hidden in unobtrusive offices, to handle their trust funds.

## Frenzied construction

Financial success here, as elsewhere, invariably translates into bricks and mortar. Two generations ago, the gold dome of the Massachusetts State House was surpassed on the skyline only by similarly gilded summit of the United Shoe Machinery Building and the Custom House Tower *(see panel, page 86)*. Today, all three of those edifices are lost in the vertical tumult of downtown Boston's architecture. The 1970s, '80s, and '90s were a frenzied period of construction, with architects proceeding from the sleek but bland International style to various excesses of postmodernism.

Brown-bagging drones aside,

much business is still conducted over lunch or dinner. Just off Winter Street lies **Winter Place**, a narrow alley leading to the elegant and perennially popular **Locke-Ober Restaurant** ❹, traditionally a stronghold of lamb chops, scrod and lobster *(review: page 88)*. Its menu has been updated by the celebrated chef Lydia Shire, but time cannot improve on a bowl of oyster stew in the downstairs bar.

Head toward Boston Common on Winter and take a right on Tremont Street, passing the Park Street Church and the Old Granary Burial Ground to arrive at School Street. At the corner of School and Tremont is the venerable **Omni Parker House Hotel** ❺. This is the oldest continuously operating hotel in the US, although the present building is not the original. Charles Dickens conducted literary seminars at an earlier Parker House, and here Ho Chi Minh waited on tables and Malcolm X toiled in the kitchen.

Across from the Parker House on School and Tremont is **King's Chapel** ❻ (Mon–Sat 10am–4pm; winter Sat 10am–3pm; services Wed 12.15pm and Sun 11am; tel: 227-2155), an early stop on Boston's Freedom Trail. The Chapel had its origins in the 1680s when Britain's King James II made a colossal political blunder by sending to Boston a clergyman whose job was to install in the town the very thing the Puritans had hated and fled: a branch of the Church of England.

The Rev. Robert Ratcliffe's arrival in Boston was greeted with a roar of protest. This bothered him not one whit, and since he had no church in which to hold services he teamed with the royal colonial governor, Sir Edmund Andros, to usurp a church the Puritan-Congregationalists were using, the Old South Meeting House. Finally in 1688, Andros seized a piece of land belonging to a Sir Isaac Johnson, and there the original King's Chapel, a wooden structure, was built in 1689. This was replaced in 1754 by the present structure, built of granite blocks ferried from Quincy, 8 miles (13 km) to the south. The dedication was attended by hundreds of crown-

*Paul Revere's largest bell is housed in King's Chapel. He called it "the sweetest bell we ever made."*

**BELOW:** the perennially popular Locke-Ober Restaurant.

hating locals who hurled garbage, manure and dead animals at the presiding Anglicans.

Next to the Chapel, on Tremont Street, is Boston's first cemetery, **King's Chapel Burying Ground** (daily 9am–5pm; winter to 3pm), long predating the Anglican edifice whose name it later assumed. It was in use from 1630 to 1796. The Bay Colony's first Governor, John Winthrop, was buried here in 1649. The monument at the corner of the burying ground honors a French naval adjutant, the Chevalier de St Sauveur, killed by a Boston mob in September 1778 during an altercation over bread. The French, who had come to help the colonials, were baking bread using their own stores of wheat; Bostonians, who were enduring a severe shortage of flour, were incensed when told that they could not buy the French Navy's bread. The Chevalier's funeral service is said to have been the first Catholic Mass said in Boston.

A few yards down School Street, on the left, is the site of America's first school. This was the original

*At King's Chapel Burying Ground, look for the 1704 grave of Elizabeth Pain, said to have been the model for Hester Prynne in Nathaniel Hawthorne's classic The Scarlet Letter.*

**BELOW:** the Old Corner Bookstore, probably the city's oldest brick building, as it looked in 1909.

**Boston Latin School**, which opened in 1635, and accounts for the naming of School Street when it was laid out in 1640. (Boston Latin still exists, in a different part of town; although part of the municipal school system, it accepts only students who pass an entrance exam).

## Old City Hall

**Old City Hall** ❼ rises in the immediate background here, a massive pile of Second Empire granite architecture. The city government decamped from here in 1969, when the new City Hall *(see page 85)* was built; the old mansarded structure now features a restaurant and office space. In its forecourt is a bronze statue of Benjamin Franklin, with pedestal tablets chronicling the important events of his life.

A few more yards down the slope is the intersection of School and Washington streets, where stand two sets of bronze figures that constitute the **Irish Famine Memorial** commemorating The Great Hunger of the 1840s that resulted in many Irish emigrating to Boston.

And here on the left is one of Downtown Boston's most loved and best preserved colonial structures, the former site of the **Old Corner Bookstore** ❽. Until 2004 the Boston Globe Company kept it going as a souvenir store selling such items as replica front pages with accounts of historic events. But they found it more profitable to move that business online, and the building is currently a jeweler's store.

Originally on this site stood the home of the celebrated and courageous Anne Hutchinson. She lived here from 1634 to 1638, when she was banished from town by colonials who objected to her principles of free speech. In exile, she was killed during an Indian attack in what is now the Bronx, New York.

The big Boston fire of October 3,

1711, destroyed Anne's cottage. It was replaced in 1712 by the present structure, which over the years has served as an apothecary shop, a dry goods store, and private residence; in 1828 it became the home of a book store and the eminent Ticknor and Fields publishing firm. In the Golden Age of American literature, this was a popular browsing and meeting place for Whittier, Emerson, Stowe, Alcott and other distinguished writers. By the 1960s it had become a pizza parlor, a fate it was rescued from by its present owners, the *Boston Globe* newspaper.

## Old South Meeting House

At this point we cross Washington Street to the juncture of Spring Lane and turn right. A walk of only a few yards brings us to one of the most important forum locations in the growth of American independence, **Old South Meeting House** ❾ (Apr–Oct daily 9.30am–5pm; Nov–Mar 10am–4pm; tel: 482-6439). The land on which Old South was built was originally a sloping cornfield and potato patch, owned and

tilled by Governor Winthrop. When he died, it was taken over by a preacher, John Norton, whose widow Mary offered it to her neighbors in 1663 as a church site. The grateful parishioners quickly built themselves a Meeting House of oak and cedar-board, which served them for more than 60 years.

In March, 1727, the old wooden structure was replaced by a beautiful new church of brick and mortar, styled after the graceful London churches of Sir Christopher Wren. "New" Old South, dedicated on April 26, 1730, figured in American annals as the most important Meeting House in American colonial history. It was the scene of scores of protest meetings denouncing British taxation, the Stamp Act, the presence of British troops, and the Townshend Acts. Ultimately, on December 16, 1773, it was the launching pad for a band of Bostonians who – inflamed by the oratory of Samuel Adams, then more famous for patriotism than beer – converged on Griffin's Wharf to stage the Boston Tea Party. Early in the Revolution, the Red-

*The firm of Ticknor and Fields, once located in the Old Corner Book Store, was founded in 1832 by George Ticknor, who partnered with James Fields in 1854. In addition to releasing works by many of the greatest literary lights of 19th-century New England, the firm published* The Atlantic Monthly, *still one of America's most respected periodicals.*

**BELOW:** Old South Meeting House.

coats turned Old South into a stable and riding school for the horses of the Queen's Light Dragoons. George Washington corrected that situation in March 1776.

When new Old South was new no more, it was replaced by the 1877 structure now known as New Old South, in the Back Bay *(see page 130)*. The proposed demolition of the 1727 church was the occasion of perhaps the first Boston campaign – at least, the first successful one – to save an historic structure.

One of the more important events that took place at Old South occurred on a bitterly cold, blizzardy, midwinter morning. This was the baptism of a squawking baby named Benjamin Franklin, born just around the corner at No.1 Milk Street. As a parish pastor later described it: "This little quivering mass of flesh, hardly a day old, was carried across the wintry street to be baptized on January 6, 1706, the parents evidently thinking that the midwinter climate here was less to be dreaded than the climate in the other world." Unfazed by the cold –

*Although born a Bostonian, Benjamin Franklin made his name in Philadelphia. He ran off to the Pennsylvania city at the age of 17 after a quarrel with his brother, a printer, to whom he had been apprenticed. The tale of the penniless youth's migration is engagingly told in his autobiography.*

**BELOW:** the Old State House, from whose balcony the Declaration of Independence was read.

or by much else in this world – Franklin lived until 1790.

## The Old State House

Turning back now on Washington Street, we pass Spring Lane and Water Street on the right and arrive at the intersection with State Street. There stands the **Old State House** ❿ (daily 9am–5pm; until 6pm June– late Aug; tel: 720-1713), the seat of colonial government.

Since l632, in the Pudding Lane– King Street–Crooked Lane area (now Congress Street) there had been stocks and pillory, a whipping post and a thatched-roof church of sorts. And here in l658 the Bostonians built their first official Town House, headquarters for royal rulings and for demonstrations for and against hanging Captain Kidd for piracy. The great fire of 1711 burned the place flat, but within two years the colonists rebuilt with the present brick structure at the head of State Street. Then, on December 9, 1747, another great fire gutted the building and destroyed valuable town records but left the brick walls standing, as they are today. The walls even survived the horrendous conflagration of 1872, which leveled most of downtown Boston's center.

Bostonians are very fond of this old building. It still displays the Lion and Unicorn symbols of British dominion (replicas, as the originals were cheerfully burnt during the Revolution), and still features the white balcony where the Declaration of Independence was first read to the citizens of Boston. Inside is a small museum run by the Bostonian Society, formed in 1879 for the purpose of keeping the structure from being removed to Chicago. The museum (hours and tel. no. same as for Old State House, above) contains items relating to maritime, military, and business history; also paintings and prints. It's

recommended mainly for those with a more than passing interest in the city itself, and not simply its place in American history,

The area beneath the balcony was the site of the famed Boston Massacre on March 5, 1770, when a handful of British soldiers fired into a crowd that was jeering them and pelting them with snowballs; five men were killed *(see panel below)*. A circle of paving stones marks the spot of the Massacre.

Across the road at 15 State Street is the **Boston National Historical Park Visitor Center ⓫** (tel: 242-5642), from which Rangers lead walking tours of the Freedom Trail from April through November.

From the Massacre site marker, head north on Congress Street and turn right to reach the Faneuil Hall–Quincy Market complex. Here, fronted by a statue of Sam Adams, stands **Faneuil Hall ⓬** (daily 9.30am–4.30pm; tel: 242-5642), designated by patriot orator James Otis as "The Cradle of Liberty."

Faneuil Hall, built for the commercial benefit of Boston's merchants, was personally financed by young Peter Faneuil, whom John Hancock labeled "the topmost merchant in all the town." Designed by the Scottish-born portrait painter John Smibert, it was dedicated on September 10, 1742, and soon served as a forum for the raw opinions of rebels and patriots. In 1806 the hall was expanded by Charles Bulfinch. It is still in demand as a forum for oratory and opinion.

### Quincy Market

Adjacent to Faneuil Hall is the "festival marketplace" variously known as Faneuil Hall Marketplace or simply **Quincy Market ⓭**. This is a vibrant, contemporary urban spot redolent with history. Quincy Market was constructed by order of Mayor Josiah Quincy in 1826, and served for almost 150 years as a retail and wholesale distribution center for meat and produce. By the early 1970s the market and its surroundings, though still housing a number of old-fashioned food shops, had become extremely seedy and plans were afoot for its demoli-

Map on page 76

*Faneuil Hall Marketplace lights up for Christmas.*

**BELOW:** the rotunda at Quincy Market.

## The Boston Massacre

Just outside the Old State House on the night of March 5, 1770, a group of citizens got into a hostile shouting match with British soldiers. Rocks and snowballs filled the air, bayonets clanged, then somebody fired a shot. Five colonists were killed. The only one widely remembered was the first to die, Crispus Attucks, a black sailor and former slave, aged around 47. His body lay in state for three days in Faneuil Hall. Samuel Adams, the leading advocate for independence from Britain, turned the incident, the most serious of a number of such brawls, into effective propaganda, presenting it as a battle for American liberty. From that moment, revolution became inevitable.

*Clowning around at Quincy Market.*

tion. Fortunately, "adaptive reuse" was just then coming into vogue, and Quincy Market became the template for renovated urban spaces throughout the nation.

The market consists of three long Greek Revival buildings. The center one is of granite with a Doric colonnade at either end and a dome and rotunda in the center. Tree-lined malls separate this building from two longitudinal side buildings, which are built mainly of brick. The first floor of the main building bulges with more than 40 foodstalls while the upper floor has a few somewhat more formal restaurants. More than 50 retail stores compete for your money in the lateral buildings, which also house a number of restaurants. These include **Durgin Park** *(review: page 88),* here since 1826. Its waitresses are famed for harassing and insulting patrons, who appear to love the treatment.

A lively flower market adds further color, as do many colorful wooden push-carts from which peddlers sell their wares, most of which are geared to tourists. Entertainers perform regularly. Little wonder that Faneuil Hall Market is now one of the major tourist attractions, not only in Boston but throughout the entire nation, attracting more than 10 million visitors a year.

## The Union Oyster House

North from here, on Union Street, stands the **Union Oyster House ⑭** *(review: page 88).* The building was specifically mentioned in a plan of 1708, and has housed the restaurant since 1826; this would secure it a tie with Durgin-Park for honors as Boston's oldest eatery. Oysters have long been its forte. Legend has it that the place sometimes served up 35 barrels of Cape Cod oysters a day, with Daniel Webster regularly downing six of the bivalves per glass of brandy – and he drank several of the latter.

The building housed the *Massachusetts Spy* newspaper from 1771 to 1775. It then became the headquarters for Ebenezer Hancock, brother of John Hancock and paymaster for the Continental Army, who lived in a neighboring house

just a few steps along and to the right, on Salt Lane. The city's oldest brick house, it dates to 1660, when it was owned by Boston's first Town Crier, William Courser.

Later, the Oyster House building was briefly home to Louis Philippe, later ruler of France (1830–48). He eked out his exile in Boston by teaching French to students in his second-floor bedroom. Nearby is a slender line of six glass and steel towers that form the **Holocaust Memorial** ⓯. The solemnity and severe design of the Memorial are juxtaposed by two nearby life-size bronzes – one seated, one standing – of former mayor James Michael Curley *(see page 26)*. The shine on the seated statue's knee suggests that many visitors like to perch there.

### The Boston Stone

Behind the Oyster House, Marsh Lane, Salt Lane and Creek Square meet at the Blackstone Block, where three centuries of architecture can be found. And here, at Salt Lane corner, sits the **Boston Stone** ⓰, a huge stone ball and a stone trough,

shipped from England in 1700 to serve as a paint mill. While grinding out oil and pigment, it was also established for more lasting use as the Zero Stone – that point from which all distances from Boston were measured. The Downtown Crossing marker notwithstanding, this humble but historic monument still stands as the hub of "The Hub."

### Burlesque to bureaucracy

Return to Congress Street and climb the many stairs leading up to the new **City Hall** (1969), a charmless inverted ziggurat once described in the Boston press as "the ugliest pigeon coop in the world."

This area was Scollay Square, a slightly disreputable entertainments area *(see panel)*. Then, in 1960, along came urban renewal in the form of the new Boston Redevelopment Authority. In rumbled the bulldozers to level not only Scollay Square but the entire West End, a tenement quarter that has been replaced by the luxury apartments of Charles River Park. Scollay Square suddenly became the new squeaky-clean Gov-

Map on page 76

*All distances from Boston are measured from this point.*

**BELOW:** the Holocaust Memorial.

### Scollay Square

**W**here City Hall now stands used to be Scollay Square. Here was the Old Howard burlesque theater, the stage-home of such show-stoppers as Ann Corio, Jimmy Durante and Sliding Billy Watson, and the Crawford House, in which dancer Sally Keith nightly twirled her two top tassels in opposite directions, openly defying the laws of physics. Here were tattoo parlors, fortune tellers, gypsy palmists, cheap gin mills, snap-photo joints, hash houses – just about anything a lad on leave from the Charlestown Navy Yard could desire. The nostalgia surrounding Scollay Square is such that it is fondly remembered even by people too young to have yielded to its temptations.

The sterile plaza surrounding City Hall is enlivened during summer weekday lunch hours by occasional live music concerts. Check the entertainment pages of the *Boston Phoenix* or the *Boston Globe*'s weekly calendar section for schedules.

**BELOW:** the Financial District viewed from the waterfront.

**ernment Center**, as the planners wiped out almost every physical vestige of the past. They created an emptiness fanning out from Court Street and called it **City Hall Plaza** – a delightful place for those who like acres of dull bricks unrelieved by shrubbery or trees.

## Temples of finance

Boston's Financial District reaches roughly from Federal and High streets near the waterfront to Franklin and State streets near Post Office Square on the north. This part of Downtown, especially State Street, is a superb architectural sampler, encompassing a wide variety of styles. Step into Exchange Place, Church Green Building, One International Place and 75 State Street to gawk at their glorious marble halls.

Visit, in this part of town, the **Alexander Graham Bell Room** 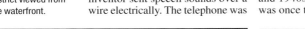 at 185 Franklin Street (open during regular business hours) to view the reassembled attic from nearby Court Street where, on June 3, 1875, the inventor sent speech sounds over a wire electrically. The telephone was

born. On display are the world's first telephone switchboard – it connected six lines in 1877 – and the world's first commercial telephone.

Elsewhere, much of downtown Boston has changed or disappeared during the past half-century. The famed Boston Wool District, liaison between Australia and New England's voracious textile mills, now exists in name only. The same is true of the Leather District, crippled by the disappearance of the New England shoe industry but recently revived by chic stores and eateries. (So far, the district has no leather bars.)

Returning to Downtown Crossing, walking south along Washington Street toward Kneeland, you soon pass on the right the site of the old Adams House and restaurant of the same name. This was once a terminal stop on the early Boston–Hartford–New York stage coach route. This section of the city has been in limbo for years. On Washington you can see the remains of what were once the movie palaces of the 1930s and 1940s. Little remains of what was once the Combat Zone, one of

## Vanished Glories

In the early 1900s, the architectural symbol of the Financial District was the new 495-ft (151-meter) Custom House Tower. Some style-conscious financiers applauded the obelisk-like tower, some loathed it. The original Custom House, at its base, had been a thing of true beauty, a superlative example of Greek Revival architecture. But then, in 1913–15, the old Greek temple was encumbered with an extra 30 floors of office (now hotel) space, crowned by decorations that included winged beasts, scrolls and a huge clock face. The top of the tower is now a nesting place for peregrine falcons, which swoop over the deep canyons between the counting houses.

the sleaziest and most notorious enclaves of commercial vice on the East Coast. Thanks to prolonged public outrage and the demands of civic leaders, it has been politically garroted to extinction. The topless bars and sex pockets have been virtually wiped out, with only a few stubborn traces remaining.

With Emerson College's purchase of many buildings on **Tremont Street** in the 1990s this area began to transform itself. Pride of place on Emerson's urban campus goes to the College's glorious 800-seat **Majestic Theater** in Boston's Theater District.

Nearby is **Allen's Alley**, honoring Boston's wry comedian Fred Allen, who left his imprint on most aspects of show business, from burlesque to musical revue, and from New York radio to Hollywood television. Allen loved his Boston. As he once remarked: "California is a great place to live – if you're an orange."

## Chinatown

Alongside the former Combat Zone (and gradually absorbing its streets and alleys) is Boston's colorful

**Chinatown ⓲**, guarded at its eastern gateway, diagonally across Atlantic Avenue from South Station, by a looping arch and an ornate pair of stone dragon dogs. Chinatown, whose main drag is Beach Street, is not very large but is packed with Asian restaurants and exotic stores that draw thousands of tourists and regulars nightly from the nearby Theater District on Tremont Street and the hotels to the west. It's great fun to visit.

On leaving Chinatown and turning right on Kneeland, look for **Jacob Wirth's ⓳** old-time restaurant on the right *(review: page 89)*. Since 1868, generations of newsmen, theater people and students from Tufts University's nearby Medical Center have relished the dark brew and bratwurst (plated, oddly enough, not only with sauerkraut but with a stewed tomato), served by white-aproned waiters. It's a place that never changes.

Just up Stuart on Tremont Street are the **Wilbur** and **Shubert** theaters, where for years many Broadway-bound productions have had their first performances. ❏

Map on page 76

*Jacob Wirth's old-time restaurant.*

**LEFT:** Chinatown.
**BELOW:** detail from a Chinatown mural.

# RESTAURANTS & BARS

## Restaurants

### American

**Avenue One**
Hyatt Regency Boston, One Ave. de Lafayette; Tel: 912-1234. Open B, L, & D daily. $$$
www.avenueoneboston.com
Contemporary cuisine, with a new take on favorites such as short ribs and roast chicken, in the third floor restaurant of this Financial District hotel. Fondues served for one to four people, and the Ultimate Chocolate is to die for.

**Durgin Park**
340 Faneuil Hall Marketplace. Tel: 227-2038. Open: L & D daily. $$
www.durgin-park.com
Yankee cooking attracts flocks of tourists to this legendary old dining hall (established 1826), famed for communal tables (smaller tables available on request), and huge portions.

**Milk Street Café**
50 Milk St.: Tel: 542-3663 (also Post Office Square, Tel: 350-7275. Open B & L Mon–Fri. $
www.milkstreetcafe.com
Kosher cafeteria with a vegetarian slant, with dishes such as roasted salmon salad, and good selection of nutritious, homemade soups.

**South Street Diner**
178 Kneeland St., Tel: 350-0028. Open: B, L, D daily. $
Class diner fare and atmosphere, right down to the jukebox and all-day breakfasts. Funky, fun, and open 24/7.

**Spire**
90 Tremont Street; Tel: 617-772 0202. Open: B Mon-Fri, L Mon-Sat, D Mon-Sat, Brunch Sat & Sun. $$$$
www.SpireRestaurant.com
Seafood is the star here, with local fluke sashimi, fried Wellfleet oysters, and a take on the classic clambake that includes chorizo sausage. Extremely unusual desserts.

**Union Oyster House**
41 Union Street. Tel: 227-2750. Open: L & D daily. $$
www.unionoysterhouse.com
Daniel Webster dined here, where steaks and seafoods are served in atmospheric rooms with creaky floors, low ceilings, and wooden booths. A popular raw bar. Good clam chowder.

### Chinese

**Chau Chow City**
83 Essex St.; Tel: 338-8158. Open: L & D daily. $–$$
One of Chinatown's best destinations for dim sum, the glitzy three-story neon palace serves Hong Kong-style fare until 4am.

**Cindy's Planet**
70 Tyler St. Tel: 338-8837. Open: Mon–Fri 9am–6pm., Sat & Sun 11am–5pm. $
Serving homemade desserts, snacks, and pearl tea (Chinatown's newest drink trend, a mix of flavored teas and coffees, milk and tapioca pearls).

**East Ocean City**
27 Beach St.; Tel: 542-2504. Open: L & D daily. $
Marble floors, table cloths and exotic seafood raise this Chinatown restaurant a notch above the competition.

**Empire Garden**
690 Washington St; Tel: 482-8898. Open: L & D daily. $
Waitresses circle this large room with carts filled with dim sum – snack-size treats such as steamed dumplings and barbecue pork buns. Diners are charged by the number of plates stacked up at the end of the meal.

### European

**Locke-Ober**
3 Winter Place: Tel: 542-1340. Open: L Mon–Fri, D Mon–Sat. $$$$
www.locke-ober.com
Renowned Boston restaurateur Lydia Shire has kept many of the traditional favorites, such as JFK's lobster stew and calves' liver with bacon, but she has added contemporary touches that breathe new life into what was

### PRICE CATEGORIES

Prices for three-course dinner per person with a half-bottle of house wine, tax and tip:
**$** = under $25
**$$** = $25–$40
**$$$** = $40–$50
**$$$$** = more than $50

becoming a stuffy institution. Power dinners take place in small dining rooms upstairs.

### German

**Jacob Wirth**
31 Stuart St.; Tel: 338-8586. Open: L & D Tues–Sun. $–$$
www.jacobwirthrestaurant.com
This time-warp in the Theater District has served wurst, sauerkraut and beer since 1868. Sawdust on floor.

### French

**Café Fleuri**
Langham Hotel, 250 Franklin St.; Tel: 451-1900. Open: B, L, & D. $$$
www.langhamhotels.com
Sunday jazz brunch (11am–1pm) and the Saturday noon–3pm (last seating at 2pm.) and chocolate buffet (served Sept–May) are major draws at this upscale hotel cafe.

**Pigalle**
75 S. Charles St.; Tel: 423-4944. Open: D Tues–Sun. $$$–$$$$
A sophisticated and romantic French bistro in the heart of the Theater District, where the chef gets creative with classic dishes, and makes it all work.

### Fusion

**Mantra**
52 Temple Pl.; Tel: 542-8111; Open: L Mon–Fri, D Mon–Sat. $$$$
www.mantrarestaurant.com

A blending of French flavors and techniques enhanced with subtle Indian "accents" in a renovated, turn-of-the-century bank building.

### Italian

**Café Marliave**
10 Bosworth St.; Tel: 423-6340. Open: L & D daily $$–$$$
A downtown Italian-American institution which oozes ambiance and red sauce in large portions. Delightful outdoor patio.

### Japanese

**Beard Papa's**
Faneuil Hall Marketplace; Tel: 570-9090. Open: daily. $
www.muginohousa.com
It's cream puffs all the way at this Japanese-owned franchise. They're filled with whipped cream custard studded with fresh vanilla beans, and prepared fresh throughout the day.

**Ginza**
16 Hudson St.; Tel: 338-2261 (also at 1002 Beacon St., Brookline, Tel: 566-9688). Open: L & D daily. $$
One of the finest Japanese restaurants in the city. Waitresses in kimonos serve elegantly-prepared sushi and 20 brands of sake.

### Seafood

**McCormick and Schmick's**
North Market Building, Faneuil Hall Marketplace.

Tel: 720-5522. Open: L & D daily. $$–$$$ (also: Boston Park Plaza Hotel, 34 Columbus Ave. Tel: 482-3999)
www.mccormickandschmicks.com
This chain, decorated like an upscale steak house, serves 40 varieties of seafood, and prints a new menu daily. Offerings might include wild king salmon, Dungeness crab, lobster, and Massachusetts scrod. Outdoor patio, and a happy hour Mon–Fri 3:30pm–6:30pm; and Mon–Thurs 10pm–midnight.

### Vietnamese

**Buddha's Delight**
3 Beach St., Chinatown; Tel: 451-2395 (and 404 Harvard St., Tel: 739-8830). Open: L & D daily. $
Asian fare especially recommended to vegetarians who like make-believe meat. The dish-

es made with tofu taste reasonably like the real thing; the fresh vegetable dishes are excellent. But the setting is lackluster, and service can be a bit slow.

### Bars

Single Boston professionals gather at **Aqua** (120 Water St.; Tel: 720-4900) after work. The retro **Good Life**, 28 Kington St., Tel: 451-2622) is a fine place for jazz, martinis, and a decent burger. **Peking Tom's** (25 Kingston St., Tel: 482-6282) serves up exotic libations, pupu platters, sushi, and other Pan-Asian snacks. The snazzy Lobby Bar in **Hyatt Regency Hotel** (One Ave. de Lafayette, Tel: 912-1234) is open 2pm–midnight. Dancing upstairs Fri/Sat, with panoramic views.

**LEFT:** communal tables at legendary Durgin Park.
**RIGHT:** Union Oyster House, where Daniel Webster ate.

# THE NORTH END

**Paul Revere lived here, and so did successive waves of European immigrants. Old North, Boston's oldest church, is a major stop on the Freedom Trail**

There is a bust of Dante Alighieri in the central court of the little branch library on Parmenter Street, in Boston's North End. Perhaps this doesn't seem so unusual – after all, great literary figures are often so commemorated, and in fact there are dozens of such luminaries whose names are inscribed in the exterior walls of the central library in Copley Square. But the wise visage of Dante has a special meaning on Parmenter Street. Dante is the national poet of Italy, the first writer to create great art out of the nascent Italian language. And it is here, in the North End, that Italian was first commonly spoken on the streets of Boston.

## An ethnic progression

Much of the North End looks and sounds like an Italian *quartiere*. Many streets are narrow and crooked, laundry flaps on outdoor clotheslines, and produce is sold at open-air stands. Children play in the street, young couples talk in cafés, old women dressed in black head for early morning Mass at St Leonard's Church, and slick young immigrants argue about soccer in the middle of Hanover Street. At a social club tucked away in a quiet alley, old men sip wine while they play a few hands of cards. But the Mediterranean cast of these old streets, somewhat faded now but still very much apparent to even the casual visitor, is only the most recent face of what is, aside from Charlestown, the oldest neighborhood in Boston.

Three hundred years ago, the North End was known as the "island of North Boston." On colonial maps it looks like an irregular thumb jutting into the Atlantic Ocean with a canal, called the Mill Stream, cutting it off from the larger Shawmut

Map on page 92

**LEFT AND BELOW:** traditional Italian festivals are held in the North End.

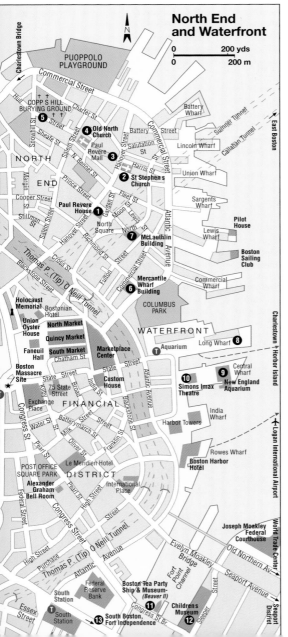

**North End and Waterfront**

0        200 yds
0        200 m

Charlestown Bridge
Commercial Street
PUOPPOLO PLAYGROUND
COPP'S HILL BURYING GROUND
Hull
Snowhill St
Sheafe St
Street
Charter St
Old North Church
Paul Revere Mall
Battery Street
Salutation St
N. Bennet St
Hanover Street
St Stephen's Church
Harris St
Prince Street
NORTH END
Margin
Cooper Street
Paul Revere House
Garden Ct
Fleet St
Moon St
Lewis
North Square
McLaulhin Building
Stillman St
Salem St
Hanover St
Richmond Street
North St
Cross St
Thomas P. (Tip) O'Neill Tunnel
Blackstone Street
Fulton
Commercial Street
Atlantic Avenue
Mercantile Wharf Building
Holocaust Memorial
Bostonian Hotel
Union Oyster House
North Market
Quincy Market
Faneuil Hall
South Market
Chatham St
Marketplace Center
COLUMBUS PARK
WATERFRONT
Boston Massacre Site
State Street
75 State Street
Custom House
State Street
Broad St
India St
Atlantic Avenue
Blackstone St
Aquarium
Long Wharf
Central Wharf
Simons Imax Theatre
New England Aquarium
Exchange Place
FINANCIAL
Battery
Street
March St
India Wharf
Harbor Towers
Congress St
Water St
Milk St
Oliver St.
Franklin Street
Pearl St
Rowes Wharf
Boston Harbor Hotel
POST OFFICE SQUARE PARK
DISTRICT
Le Meridien Hotel
Alexander Graham Bell Room
Federal Street
Pearl Street
International Place
Congress Street
High Street
Thomas P. (Tip) O'Neill Tunnel
Atlantic Avenue
Joseph Moakley Federal Courthouse
Evelyn Moakley Bridge
Old Northern Av.
Seaport Avenue
Federal Reserve Bank
Boston Tea Party Ship & Museum (Beaver II)
South Station
Childrens Museum
South Boston, Fort Independence
Essex Street
Purchase Street
High Street
Congress St Br
Fort Point Channel
Sleeper Street
Battery Wharf
Sumner Tunnel
Callahan Tunnel
East Boston
Lincoln Wharf
Union Wharf
Sargents Wharf
Pilot House
Lewis Wharf
Boston Sailing Club
Commercial Wharf
Charlestown ▸ Harbor Island
Harbor International Airport
Logan International Airport
World Trade Center
Seaport District

Peninsula. Until recently the Fitzgerald Expressway (also known as the Central Artery) followed the same course as the old canal, and cut off the neighborhood even more abruptly. While water no longer surrounds the North End, it is still set apart from the rest of the city that grew out of and away from it. Now that the expressway has been rerouted underground, it remains to be seen whether a thin strip of green parkland will now serve as a physical and psychological barrier.

When the Puritans arrived in 1630, the North End was a marshy finger of land with few apparent virtues. But by the late colonial period, the small cluster of wooden houses had become one of Boston's most fashionable quarters, with several fine brick homes and some of the richest families in town.

Unfortunately, many of the prominent residents were Tories who, when the British evacuated in 1776, hightailed it to Canada and took their money with them. Rich Yankees pulled out too, preferring the more genteel atmosphere of Beacon Hill, then being developed. Artisans, sailors and tradesmen filled the empty houses, and throughout the 19th century the North End was a workingman's quarter dominated by the shipping industry.

## Irish domination

In the mid-1800s, the North End was overrun by European immigrants, and the neighborhood became a slum notorious for its bordellos, street crime and squalid conditions. The Irish were the first to settle in any great numbers. They poured into the neighborhood after the Irish Potato Famine of the 1840s and soon dominating the area politically. A latter-day reminder of the old Irish days was the 1995 funeral of Rose Fitzgerald Kennedy, mother of President John F. Kennedy, conducted at

St Stephen's Church on Hanover Street. Rose Kennedy had been born in that neighborhood, 105 years earlier, when there were no cannolis in the local cafés.

East European Jews followed the Irish, and by 1890 had established a thriving residential and business district along Salem Street. The Italians – mostly from Sicily and the southern provinces of the mainland – were the last group to arrive in substantial numbers; but by the 1920s they had established an overwhelming majority and have dominated the neighborhood ever since.

## Good food, colorful history

Most people come to the North End for one of two reasons. During the day they visit historic sites, and at night they come to eat. Both activities are certainly worthwhile, but there's much more here than the Freedom Trail and veal scallopini.

By and large, the North End isn't much to look at. Unlike Beacon Hill or the Back Bay, it isn't a planned community. There isn't a uniform architectural style or much interest in large-scale historical preservation: in fact, quite the opposite. The North End has an improvisational quality, as if the neighborhood was built piecemeal without the benefit of an overall plan. What evolved is a hodgepodge of buildings, some quite attractive, others downright ugly. Many were built in the late 1800s as tenement houses for European immigrants. The concern at that time wasn't how pretty a building looked but how many people could be crammed inside.

The archaic street plan makes things even more confusing. The North End is one of those places where it's easy to get lost and probably best that you do. With alleyways and side streets running off in every direction, all kinds of unconventional spaces can be discovered in the neighborhood's less-traveled areas. Turn a corner, and you're likely to bump into anything from a vegetable garden to a colonial graveyard. When you tire of walking around the neighborhood, you can always head for one of the cafés on Hanover Street and watch the

Map on page 92

*The speed of tenement building can be gauged by the fact that, between 1850 and 1855, the number of Irish in Boston soared from 35,000 to 50,000. Most of them settled in the North End.*

**BELOW:** an outdoor market in Blackstone Street, near the Haymarket subway stop, sells fresh fruit and vegetables from area farms on Fridays and Saturdays.

## The Gentrifiers Arrive

In recent years, the North End's well-earned reputation for neighborliness has made it a prime target for gentrification, especially along the waterfront. Rents have skyrocketed, condo conversions have run rampant, and some old-time residents are getting priced right out of their homes. With the old guard aging and the new generation moving out, some dyed-in-the-wool North Enders worry that the old neighborhood is slipping away. But, although it's true that the Italian population isn't as large as it used to be, the spirit of the community persists. And more than a few of the clubs and cafés are patronized by suburban Italians who enjoy coming back to the streets where they grew up.

neighborhood walk around you *(see panel below)*.

From Hanover Street, turn right on Richmond Street and then left to enter North Square, where the Pierce-Hichborn and Paul Revere houses stand side by side. The **Pierce-Hichborn House**, which belonged to Nathaniel Hichborn, Paul Revere's cousin, is an asymmetrical, three-story brick building built between 1711 and 1715 in the new English Renaissance style. This was a radical departure from the Tudor-style wooden dwellings built in the previous century. It was restored in 1949.

### Paul Revere's home

The **Paul Revere House** ❶ at 19 North Square (open daily mid-Apr–Oct 9.30am–5.15pm, Nov–mid-Apr 9.30am–4.15pm; tel: 523-2338) is a two-story dwelling with an overhanging second floor. It was built in 1676 and is the oldest house in downtown Boston. When the 35-year-old Revere, then a silversmith, purchased the house in 1770, the third floor had been added, but in the early 20th century this was removed to "restore" the building to its original appearance. It is furnished today much as it was when it was home to Paul and the first Mrs Revere, who bore him eight children, and then, when she died, to the second Mrs Revere, who produced a similar brood *(see profile of Paul Revere, page 22)*.

One of the upstairs rooms is covered with wallpaper that is a reproduction of paper made in Boston toward the end of the 18th century. The room also contains several pieces of furniture that belonged to the Reveres. A cabinet displays attractive silver, some made by Revere. Outside, in the courtyard, is a 931-pound (422-kg) bronze bell cast by Revere, generally acknowledged to have been the best bell-maker of his time.

Nowadays, when historic preservation is much more of a research-informed science than it was when the Revere House was rescued from near-dereliction, architectural historians argue with some of the restoration work done back then. But this

*Not long after Paul Revere bought his North Square House in 1770, he built an adjacent barn – only to learn that the new structure stood partly upon a neighbor's land. The neighbor, Manasseh Marston, graciously let the oversight stand.*

**BELOW:**
Paul Revere House.

## Hanover Street

The best place for people-watching is Hanover Street, the neighborhood's central thoroughfare and the heart of its business district. Restaurants and cafés stretch from one end to the other, and a steady stream of tourists walk the Freedom Trail. If you're looking for a place to eat, you can't go far wrong here, or for that matter, anywhere else in the neighborhood. Making a selection is more a question of style than of quality: are you looking for traditional, pasta-and-tomato-based southern Italian fare, or are you more interested in the more imaginative offerings of the trend-setter chefs that have been colonizing the district? There's a wide choice.

structure provides as good a look as you are going to get anywhere in Boston at what domestic arrangements were like in the prerevolutionary town.

Return to Hanover Street via Fleet Street and, after 150 yards, reach **St Stephen's Church** ❷ with its white steeple. Built in 1804 as a Congregationalist Meeting House, this simple, dignified structure is the only one of five Boston churches designed by Charles Bulfinch that still stands. It has had a checkered history. In 1813 it became a Unitarian church and in 1862 it was acquired by the Roman Catholic archbishopric. Eight years later, when Hanover Street had to be widened to accommodate traffic, the church was moved back 12 ft (3.7 meters) and raised 6 ft (1.8 meters); then, in 1965, it was restored to its original level and to its Bulfinch stark simplicity.

The **Paul Revere Mall** ❸, known locally as the Prado, faces St Stephen's Church. Built in 1933, this generous brick courtyard is one of the liveliest public spaces in the North End – a sort of Americanized piazza where kids run around, old folks play cards, and footsore tourists take a breather from the Freedom Trail. In addition to the traditional Italian fountain, the Prado features a magnificent equestrian statue of Paul Revere, modeled in 1885 by Cyrus Dallin and cast in 1940. On the south (left) wall, bronze panels recall the history of Boston and its people.

## Old North Church

At the far end of the Prado a small gate opens to the rear of Christ Church, more often known as **Old North** ❹ (June–Oct daily 9am–6pm; Nov–May Mon–Sat 9am–5pm, Sun 9am–9.45am, 10.45am–12.15pm; tel: 523-6676). To the left of the gate is the three-story (origi-nally it was two) brick home of Ebenezer Clough, built in 1712.

The Old North, Boston's oldest church, is one of its most treasured historical monuments. Built in 1723 to house the town's second Anglican parish, the Old North is most famous for its part in Paul Revere's ride to Lexington. On April 18, 1775, sexton Robert Newman snuck out of his home and placed two lanterns in the belfry as a signal to Revere – "one, if by land, and two, if by sea" – that the British army was advancing to Concord. Ironically, British General Thomas Gage is said to have watched the Battle of Bunker Hill from the very same belfry only a few months later.

Old North's steeple, 191 ft (58 meters) high, has always been Boston's tallest and a major landmark. Twice, in 1804 and again in 1954, it was blown over by hurricanes and subsequently restored. America's first peal of eight bells hangs in the belfry; it was first rung in 1745 and has tolled for every departed President of the nation since George Washington died in

Map on page 92

*The four 18th-century Belgian baroque cherubim with trumpets that stand in front of the organ in Old North Church were booty captured by a privateer owned by members of the congregation. They were probably destined for a French church in Canada.*

**BELOW:** re-enacting Paul Revere's ride past Old North Church.

*Paul Revere statue at Old North Church.*

**BELOW:** the box pews in Old North Chuch are laid out as in colonial times, although they are not as tall.

1799. The bells were cast in England and range in weight from 620 to 2,545 pounds (281–1,155 kg), with a total mass of 7,272 pounds (3,300 kg). They are a "maiden peal" (because each bell has a perfect tone without having been filed down or machined). Reputed to be the sweetest in the nation, they bear the inscription "We are the first ring of bells cast for the British Empire in North America." Paul Revere, at 15, came to this church and, with some other young men, signed a contract to ring the peal.

Enter the church, whose interior has been painted white since 1912. High pew boxes, designed to keep in the warmth of braziers filled with hot coal or bricks, which were placed on the floor on wintery days, are still intact, with the names of the family owners engraved on bronze plates. The clock at the rear of the church and the four baroque Belgian cherubs that surround it date back to the opening of the church. So does the organ case, although the actual instrument dates only from 1759. The chandeliers are brass, made in

Holland in 1700. The bust of George Washington, in a niche to the left of the apse, was the first public memorial to the great man and was said by General Lafayette in 1824 to be "more like him than any other portrait." Another historical artifact is the "third" steeple lantern, lit by President Gerald Ford during the American bicentennial observance at the church in 1775. The church has 37 crypts, containing, it is claimed, 1,100 bodies.

Immediately to the north of the church is a small garden with markers recounting historic events and distinguished persons of the parish. One of these informs that "Here on 13 Sept. 1757, John Childs, who had given public notice of his intention to fly from the steeple of Dr Cutler's church, performed it to the satisfaction of a great number of spectators." Childs made three flights, once firing a pistol in mid-air: alas, nobody knows how he flew.

## Copp's Hill Burying Ground

On exiting from the church, walk up Hull Street for about 150 yards to

## Museum Oddities

**N**ext to Old North Church is a gift shop selling more than a few tacky items but worth visiting for the tiny museum at the rear. Its major treasure is the Vinegar Bible, sent by King George II to Christ Church in 1733. One of only several still in existence, it derives its name because of a typographical error on a page heading in which "Parable of the Vinegar" appears instead of "Parable of the Vineyard." The oddest exhibit is a vial purportedly containing water stained brown by tea during the Boston Tea Party and decanted from the boots of one of the participants. This is the only tea conventionally taken not with milk and sugar, but with a grain of salt.

**Copp's Hill Burying Ground** ❺ (summer daily 9am–5pm; in other months 9am–3pm), Boston's second-oldest cemetery (after King's Chapel; *see page 79*) and the North End's quietest corner. Its present name comes from that of William Copp, who farmed on the hill's southeast slope in the mid-17th century. In the colonial period, the base of the hill, known pejoratively as New Guinea (after the African country of Guinea), was occupied by the city's first black community, and about 1,000 blacks are buried in the cemetery's northwest corner.

A tall black monument commemorates Prince Hall, who helped found Boston's first school for black children. However, his main claim to fame is that he was the founder, in 1784, of the African Grand Lodge of Massachusetts, the world's first black Masonic Lodge.

Near here is the tombstone of "Capt. Daniel Malcolm, Mercht," who is remembered for smuggling 60 casks of wine into port without paying the duty. He asked to be buried "in a Stone Grave 10 feet deep," secure from desecration. His body may have been safe, but his tombstone was not: on it are scars made by the Redcoats who singled out this patriot's gravemarker for their target practice.

In the southeast corner of the cemetery is the Mathers' family tomb, where the Puritan divines Increase, Cotton and Samuel Mather may be buried. Another Copp's Hill grave was left deliberately unmarked, and no one knows where it is. It holds the remains of Dr John Webster, murderer of George Parkman *(see page 117)*, who was hanged for his 1849 crime and promptly interred here.

## Weekend processions

If you visit the North End in summer, be sure to catch one of the local feasts or *festas*, celebrated in honor of saints' days. They are held almost every weekend in July and August, with Sunday being by far the more exciting day, and usually involve street fairs, brass bands, singers, raffles, food stalls selling sausage and peppers and *zeppole* (fried dough), and processions in which saints' statues are carried, often festooned with contributions of paper money.

If the feast is that of the Madonna del Soccorso (Our Lady of Succor), celebrated in mid-August, the star of the show is the famous flying angel. The angel is the messenger of the Madonna, protector of the fishing fleet and patron saint of Sicilian immigrants. Portrayed by a little girl on a pulley, she floats above North Street, her arms outstretched to the crowd, and is lowered to the statue and the procession below.

"Viva la Madonna!" shout the men bearing the statue, and the throng echoes, "Viva la Madonna!" It is the language of Dante, and to this day the authentic language of Boston's North End. ❑

**TIP**

While strolling through the North End, one of the best places to stop for an authentic Italian pastry – a cannoli, zuppa inglese, or flaky sfogliatella – is the Modern Pastry Shop, at 257 Hanover Street. Just look for the vintage neon sign.

**BELOW:** Copp's Hill Burying Ground.

# RESTAURANTS & BARS

## Restaurants

### Fusion

#### Sage Restaurant
69 Prince St., Tel: 248-8814. Open: D Mon–Sat. $$$–$$$$
www.sagerestaurant.com
Chef/owner Anthony Susi uses classic Old World recipes to create innovative New World masterpieces, offering regional Italian and New American dishes such as pan-fried lobster fritters, and braised rabbit lasagna. The candlelit bistro seats only 28, so booking is a must.

#### Taranta
210 Hanover St.; tel: 720-0052. Open: D nightly. $$$–$$$$
www.tarantarist.com
Pastas, antipasti and traditional dishes such as osso buco and saltimbocca share the menu with offerings such as grilled cotechino sausage with dried Peruvian potato stew, Venezuelian Bucare chocolate and Panca chili. The combination of Italian and Peruvian ingredients is creative.

### Italian

#### Antico Forno
93 Salem St.; Tel: 723-6733. Open: L & D daily. $$–$$$
www.anticofornoboston.com
A large, beehive-shaped, wood burning brick oven and sawdust-covered floors set the mood for this cozy spot decorated to resemble a rustic Neapolitan trattoria. Just about everything is cooked in the oven

#### Bacco
107 Salem Street; Tel: 617-624 0454. Open: D nightly. $$$$
www.baccoboston.com
Have a drink in the handsome first-floor bar, with French doors opening onto Salem Street, then head upstairs to an upscale Italian menu. Hearty entrées include sweet potato gnocchi with braised short ribs; lobster with fettucini, laced with a tarragon-flavored cherry tomato mascarpone cream; or osso bucco with saffron risotto. Standout dessert: the orange and saffron panna cotta. The wine is moderately priced.

#### Bricco Enoteca & Lounge
241 Hanover St.; Tel: 248-6800. Open: D nightly. $$$$
www.bricco.com
In this chic, upscale boutique restaurant, executive chef Marisa Iocco prepares regional treats such as wild mushroom Napoleon, homemade gnocchi stuffed with buffalo mozzarella and mushrooms, and wild Alaskan salmon with wild boar prosciutto carpaccio. Free valet parking.

#### Caffé Paradiso
255 Hanover St.; Tel: 742-1768. Open: 6:30 A.M.–2 A.M. daily (also: 1 Eliot Sq., Cambridge, Tel: 868-3240; Lowell, Tel: 978-454-6073: call for hrs.). $
www.caffeparadiso.com
For more than 40 years the premier North End hangout for espresso, cannoli, and chit-chat. The panini and calzones are particularly delicious. The TV beams in soccer games from Italy via satellite.

#### Cantina Italiana
346 Hanover St., Tel: 723-4577. Open: L Thurs–Sun, D nightly. $$$
www.cantinaitaliana.com
That large neon sign of a bottle pouring wine directs diners to one of the North Ends's oldest (established 1931) and most traditional restaurants. The booths are black and red, the wine of choice is Chianti, the house antipasto is a classic, and the pastas are homemade.

#### The Daily Catch
323 Hanover St., Tel: 523-8567. Open: L daily, D Mon–Sat (also at Fan Pier, Two Northern Ave., Tel: 772-4400; call for opening hours). $
www.dailycatch.com
It's calamari all the way at this tiny, hole-in-the-wall institution which specializes in Sicilian seafood. If you're not in the mood for heaping platters of fried calamari, calamari meatballs, or calamari scampi, other choices might include black pasta Putanesca, caramelized monkfish, or mussels marinara.

#### Davide Restaurant
326 Commercial St. Tel: 227-5745. Open: D nightly. $$$
www.davideerestaurante.com
Old-world ambiance, handmade pasta, and well-prepared, traditional dishes have been hallmarks of this basement-level establishment since 1982. Among the house specials: veal scallopini in a marsala wine sauce with hazelnuts and mushrooms, tableside Caesar salad, and pan-roasted whole lobster with a basil cream sauce. For privacy, request one of the high-backed banquettes. Award-winning wine list.

#### Dino's
141 Salem St.; Tel: 227-1991. Open: L & D daily. $
www.dinosboston.com
"No frills, fast feasts", is the promise of this tiny spot whose special-

### PRICE CATEGORIES
Prices for three-course dinner per person with a half-bottle of house wine, tax and tip:
$ = under $25
$$ = $25–$40
$$$ = $40–$50
$$$$ = more than $50

THE NORTH END ◆ 99

ty 16-inch hot and cold subs, for just $6.50, are one of the area's greatest bargains. Homemade pastas in a variety of permutations are also on the menu, as are gnocchi, salads and more elaborate entrées.

### Joe Tecce's Ristorante & Cafe
61 North Washington St., Tel: 742-6210. $$
Frank Sinatra is on the jukebox, the veal parmesan is exactly the way grandma made it, the chianti is flowing... it's been this way since 1948 at this family-owned restaurant with many small rooms and muraled walls.

### Lucca
226 Hanover Street; Tel: 617-742 9200. Open: D nightly. $$$$
www.luccaboston.com
Elegant, quiet, and dimly lit. The sophisticated ambiance resonates in the menu, with appetizers such as a rustic duck torta, warm potato and wild mushroom lasagna with balsamic glaze, and homemade rigatoni with wild boar in a sweet/sour tomato sauce. For dessert, a splendid flourless chocolate cake. Extensive wine list.

### Monica's Trattoria
67 Prince Street; Tel: 720-5472.
The Mendoza family, Argentine expats, know their pasta and pizza. Hence the sometimes long lines in front of this

tiny, casual spot. On the menu: build-your-own pizzettas (individual pizzas), soups and salads, and house specialties such as gnocchi Bolognese and fettucine Parma. No reservations on weekends; cash only. D nightly. (The family also operates the more upscale Monica's at 143 Richmond Street). $

### Pizzeria Regina
11½ Thatcher St. Tel: 227-0765. Open: L, D daily. $
Since 1926, this classic North End pizzeria has been the place to go for thin-crust Neapolitan pie. Waits for booths can be long. There are numerous branches throughout the area, but the original is still best.

### Prezza
24 Fleet St. Tel: 227-1577. Open: D Mon–Sat. $$$$
www.prezza.com
Named after a village in Northern Italy, Prezza incorporates the peasant fare there with that of other regions of the Mediterranean. Dishes include chestnut ravioli topped with pulled duck, butter, and parmigiano; wild mushroom soup; and an elaborate fish stew. The pastas are homemade, and the extensive wine list – almost 500 selections – is outstanding.

### Ricardo's
175 North Street, Tel: 720-3994
Ricardo Travaglione and his son, Richie, combine

their talents to create dishes such as Risotto Ricardo, and pork loin stuffed with prosciutto, fontina cheese and spinach at their cozy, two-story restaurant overooking North Street. Lighter dishes are also featured. L & D daily. $$–$$$

### Villa Francesca
150 Richmond Street; Tel: 617-367 2948. Open: L Tues–Sun; D nightly. $$$
www.ristorantevillafrancesca.com
Located right along the Freedom Trail near Paul Revere's house, this is a great place for summer people-watching if you can get one of the street-side seats by an open window. Starters run from rustic to elegant, from dry salami with black olives to salmon carpaccio. For an entrée, try fettucini with artichokes, ravioli with

butter and sage, or a grilled lamb cutlet. The copious Italian wine collection is right out in view. Busy on weekends, but be warned there's street parking only – in other words, none.

## Bars

**Goody Glover's** (48 Salem St., Tel: 367-6444), is a popular tavern that adds a touch of Irish blarney to the heart of the Italian North End.
Near North Station, **The Grand Canal** (57 Canal St., Tel: 523-1112), an Irish bar, has a large-screen (72") TV and hosts live entertainment nightly. Just up the street is **Boston and Salem Beer Works** (112 Canal St., Tel: 896-2309), the city's oldest brewery-restaurant.

**RIGHT:** tempting fare in a North End pastry shop.

# THE WATERFRONT

**The handsomely renovated wharf district conjures memories of the great days of maritime trade, and of the brash protest known as the Boston Tea Party. Here are a world-class aquarium, an engaging Children's Museum, and access to the fascinating Harbor Islands**

From its earliest days Boston was a busy seaport. Until the second half of the 19th century, it was the busiest port in the nation, reaching its apogee in the 1850s when, it was said, 15 vessels entered and left the harbor every day of the year. Then, warehouses and counting houses occupied a dozen wharves at which clippers, "the highest creation of artistic genius in the Commonwealth," unloaded and loaded their cargoes.

In the second half of the 19th century the port went into decline, a process hastened when, in 1878, the construction of Atlantic Avenue severed the finger-like piers from the rest of the city. With the building in the 1950s of the Fitzgerald Expressway, which, mile for mile, was then the most expensive stretch of road ever built in the country (and which has since been relocated underground as part of a new superlative in highway spending), Boston finally turned its back on its patrimony.

Then, in the 1970s, with the restoration of Quincy Market and Faneuil Hall, the resurrection began. Abandoned warehouses on dilapidated, rickety wharves were transformed into condominiums. Berths once occupied by barques and brigantines became home to elegant cabin cruisers and sleek sloops, many belonging to the condo dwellers. Offices and hotels, restaurants and museums were also built and the population of longshoremen, truckers and Irish laborers was replaced with realtors, lawyers and tourists. The waterfront regained its prominence, if not its old rough bustle.

## Columbus Park

If you leave the Quincy-Faneuil carnival and head toward the water, crossing busy Atlantic Avenue, you

Map on page 92

Map on page 92

**LEFT:** under a giant lobster at the Children's Museum.
**BELOW:** boat watching at Long Wharf.

*The view from Columbus Park.*

**BELOW:**
the condos come with a berth for your boat.

will immediately encounter **Columbus Park**, a small grassy sward with the Rose Kennedy Rose Garden and a children's playground. A trellised walkway leads to the waterfront which, at this point, has been landscaped into a romantic area of cobblestones, bollards and anchor chains.

On the left stretches **Commercial Wharf** with its granite warehouse. This massive structure, in which the second set of sails for the USS *Constitution* was made, has been recycled into a condominium complex. But the best example of a recycled warehouse stands inland (remember, the contours of the waterfront have been altered many times) behind you on the far side of Atlantic Avenue. The **Mercantile Wharf Building ❻**, originally twice its present length, is constructed of rough Quincy granite ashlar blocks and is the masterpiece of what has been called Boston's "Granite Age," part of the early 19th-century Greek Revival. Those interested in architecture will wish to continue along Richmond Street, at the north side of this building, and then

immediately turn right onto Fulton Street to see the **McLauthlin Building ❼**, the first cast-iron building in New England. This five-story 19th-century jewel has delicate rounded arched windows separated by subtle pilasters, and each level is separated by a string course. Its perfect, repetitive rhythm is marred only by the uppermost level.

From here, a right turn on Lewis leads back to Atlantic Avenue, which – if you turn to the left – soon becomes Commercial Street. Proceed northward past Lewis and Union wharves, both of which support gentrified granite warehouses. Granite is replaced by red brick to **Lincoln Wharf**, where a massive red building with magnificent rounded, arched windows covering five stories has been recycled into apartments.

The north side of Lincoln Wharf is bounded by **Battery Street**, whose name gives the clue to the fact that here, in 1646, the North Battery was built in order to command the entrance to the inner harbor and the Charles River. It was from here that, in 1775, British troops were ferried

to Charlestown to take up their positions in the Battle of Bunker Hill. Immediately beyond this, on the site now occupied by the Coast Guard, once stood Hartt's Naval Yard, where the USS *Constitution* was built and launched in 1797.

The Mirabella Swimming Pool in **Puoppolo Park** (fee), just beyond, awaits those who are hot and tired. Others might wish to proceed on an immaculate waterfront esplanade to the Charlestown Bridge, which, after about a mile, leads to Charlestown and the USS *Constitution* and the Bunker Hill monument *(see page 119)*. But to go on exploring the waterfront, return to Columbus Park.

## Long Wharf

Immediately to the south of Columbus Park is **Long Wharf ❽**. When built in 1710, it was, if not one of the wonders of the world, at least the wonder of the region. The wharf, which had roots near where the Custom House now stands, stretched out into the harbor for almost 2,000 ft (600 meters). It was here, in 1790, that the *Columbia Rediviva*, the first

American ship to sail around the world and the first to participate in the China trade, berthed after a 35-month, almost 50,000-mile (80,000-km) voyage. From here, in 1819, the first missionaries for Hawaii departed and, in 1895, Joshua Slocum set off aboard the *Spray* on the first one-man voyage around the world – an adventure that lasted more than three years.

Gaze out from the beautiful esplanade at the end of the wharf to East Boston and to the planes taking off from **Logan Airport**. These are the successors to the swift clippers that Donald McKay built on land now occupied by the airport. McKay's clippers, epitomized by the *Flying Cloud* , were the fastest and most beautiful sailing ships ever to fly the stars and stripes. "The *Flying Cloud* was our Rheims, the *Sovereign of the Seas* our Parthenon, the *Lightning* our Amiens," wrote maritime historian Samuel Eliot Morison, "but they were monuments made of snow. For a brief moment of time they flashed their splendor around the world, then disappeared

Map on page 92

*Christopher Columbus gazes stonily over the park named after him.*

**BELOW:** seeing the city from a cruise boat.

*The Aquarium's logo.*

with the sudden completeness of the wild pigeon." Mountains of sail gave the clippers remarkable speed, which made them ideal for tea, silks, and other high-value cargoes; but they were all too soon eclipsed by steamships that could carry far more than the clippers' narrow holds would allow.

At Long Wharf, you can still fantasize that you are on a clipper setting sail for the East Indies or China, even if you're only taking brief passage on one of the boats for Provincetown, the Charlestown Navy Yard, or the Harbor Islands *(see page 109)*. All of these depart from Long Wharf.

### New England Aquarium

Long Wharf on its south side joins with the vestigial remains of **Central Wharf**, built according to Charles Bulfinch's plans in order to accommodate the overflow of the China trade. The wharf is now home to one of Boston's most fascinating attractions, the **New England Aquarium** ❾ (July 1–Labor Day Mon–Thur 9am– 6pm; Fri, weekends and holidays 9am–7pm; day after Labor

**BELOW:** New England Aquarium.

Day–June 30 Mon–Fri 9am–5pm, weekends and holidays 9am–6pm; tel: 973-5200). It's impossible to miss the Aquarium: high above it a bright red sculpture, "Echo of the Waves", slowly rotates. In the center of the plaza water flows through a large basin, at the bottom of which stands a bronze sculpture, "Dolphins of the Sea." To the left of the aquarium entrance, harbor seals frolic and provide free entertainment.

Nobody has told the rockhopper penguins in the enormous Ocean Tray, which covers most of the first floor of the Aquarium, that the cold water section is their territory and that the warmer water is for the jackass penguins – and so they swim from island to island and the two groups freely intermingle.

Soaring skyward from the floor of the Ocean Tray is the giant ocean tank, the world's largest cylindrical salt-water habitat, in which giant turtles, sharks, moray eels and a multitude of other fish swim in and out of a spectacular man-made coral reef. At set times, a diver enters to feed the tank's occupants. A ramp gradu-

ally winds around the tank, ascending for four stories and providing a view of more than 70 small tanks containing thousands of fish from all over the world. A hands-on tidal pool enables small fry to become acquainted with the marine realm.

The *Discovery*, a floating pavilion whose design is evocative of a Mississippi river steamer, is moored alongside the main building and contains a large theater where dolphins demonstrate their remarkable intelligence. The Aquarium-owned *Voyager II* makes whale-watching cruises *(see pages 112–3)* with a naturalist aboard who also lectures on the harbor and its islands; rain checks are given if whales not seen.

Located just across the plaza from the Aquarium is the six-story-high **Simons IMAX Theatre ⑩**, which shows spectacular IMAX and IMAX 3D films of the natural world's wonders (tel: 1-866-815-4629 for program information).

Immediately south of the Aquarium, on the stump of **India Wharf**, two bland 40-story towers, designed by I.M. Pei and built in 1971, soar

skyward. These are **Harbor Towers**, originally comprising rental units but now converted to some of the choicest condominiums in Boston.

Next comes **Rowes Wharf**, entered through a monumental, gold and russett postmodern six-story arch penetrating the **Boston Harbor Hotel**. The lavish hotel stands on the site of the South Battery, built in 1666. The wharf, no longer busy with clippers and barques, is now the terminal for sleek commuter craft that serve the South Shore and Logan Airport. Some harbor cruises also depart from here.

## Tea Party Ship and Museum

Fort Point Channel now intersects the waterfront. This area was the bustling transfer point for many New England industries during the latter years of the 19th century. On a short wharf in the Channel at Congress Street Bridge stands the **Boston Tea Party Ships and Museum ⑪**, currently being rebuilt following a fire (check www.bostonteaparty.com for progress). When it reopens in 2008, it will have added new replicas of

Map on page 92

*In addition to being incensed over the tax on tea, colonial Bostonians were also upset that Britain had awarded the East India Company a monopoly on sales of the popular commodity in America. To add to the insult, the British had cut out local retailers by assigning "consignees" sole right to sell the tea.*

**LEFT:** Rowes Wharf.
**BELOW:** re-enacting the Boston Tea Party.

two traditional tall ships, the *Dartmouth* and the *Eleanor*, to the existing *Beaver II*, a Danish brig built in 1908. Exploring the ships and checking out a new interpretive facility should give visitors a reasonably authentic feel for life on board 18th-century sailing ships.

The three tea ships were moored at Griffins Wharf on a December evening in 1773 when patriots disguised as Mohawk Indians boarded the ships and threw all their tea – 340 chests of it – into the harbor. This was the most flamboyant act of defiance against the British Parliament for its manipulation of taxes, such as that on tea, to favor British interests. It was "the spark that ignited the American revolution."

## The Children's Museum

On leaving the Tea Party Exhibit, turn left and make for a giant, 40-ft (12-meter) milk bottle, a vintage lunch stand from the 1930s. It marks the entrance to the **Children's Museum** ⓬ at 300 Congress Street (Mon–Thur 10am–5pm, Fri 10am–9pm; tel: 426-8855). There's noth-

ing elegant about this museum; occupying a former warehouse, it is a place where, apart from some dolls and their houses in glass display cases, the visitor is encouraged to touch, push, twist and shove the exhibits, to blow bubbles and to clamber on suspended sculpture.

The museum also attempts to instill visitors with social conscience. A major exhibit is the Kids' Bridge, which helps children learn about other cultures and racial diversity. This learning process is furthered by a complete two-story Japanese silk merchant's home, a gift from Kyoto, Boston's sister city. A full-size wigwam and contemporary American Indian house show the past lifestyles and present traditions of the region's Native Americans, and a Grandparents' House recreates home life *circa* 1959, complete with old board games and black-and-white TV programs.

Kids learn about Latin-American food and culture at Supermercado, based on a real Latino supermarket in Boston. New England's maritime traditions are reflected in hands-on

Map on page 92

boating exhibits and an environmental display, "Under the Dock," which simulates the underwater landscape of Fort Point Channel and includes a 14-ft (4-meter) fiberglass lobster. Youngsters are given easy-to-digest information about bodily functions in a popular section of the museum, and toddlers have their own safe play space.

Engaging as it is, the Children's Museum will likely represent a fair outlay of time and energy for youngsters, so it is best set aside as a separate destination, or at least one that follows lunch or a rest period – especially if kids have spent a busy morning at the Aquarium.

Leaving the museum, turn right to cross Seaport Boulevard and reach Northern Avenue. The recently designated **Seaport District**, which begins here, is the locus for some of Boston's most ambitious 21st-century revitalization projects. Between Old Northern Avenue and the water is **Fan Pier**, site of a new Federal Courthouse named after the late beloved Congressman Joseph Moakley, and the site of a dramatic new

glass-sheated structure, just under construction, that will be the home of the **Institute of Contemporary Art**, currently located in Back Bay *(see page 133)*. Proceed westward along this avenue for the **World Trade Center**, a vast exposition facility; just inland from here new hotels and a convention center are rising.

Nearby on Northern Avenue are two of Boston's most popular seafood restaurants, Anthony's (Pier 4) and the No-Name (Fish Pier) *(see listings, page 108)*. Early risers might like to show up on Pier 4 around 6.30am, for the daily fish auction.

## South Boston

South and east of the Seaport District is **South Boston**, a peninsular neighborhood that has long been a special province of Boston's Irish community. Of course, the Irish presence is strong throughout the Boston area, and has been ever since the great migrations of the 1840s and '50s; but here in "Southie" the bonds of ethnicity, culture, politics and religion remained especially strong. One reason for its insularity was

*Boys' club in South Boston.*

**BELOW:**
the Irish influence remains strong in South Boston.

**Map on page 92**

*Studying outside Fort Independence.*

geographical: South Boston was long separated from the city proper by vast gray industrial blocks, by Fort Point Channel, and by a tangle of highways and railroad tracks.

Now, the rehabilitation of the warehouse and industrial zones, coupled with the influx of young professionals drawn not only by the proximity of new businesses but by real estate prices substantially below those in Beacon Hill, Back Bay, and the South End, have begun to crack the old Irish hegemony. While no one expects the world of lattes, bistro dining and gourmet delicatessens to completely supplant a realm of Catholic school uniforms, corner taverns, and neighbors waving at neighbors from the porches of double-decker houses, change is no doubt in the air.

South Boston's top attraction is **Fort Independence** ⓭, built in 1801 on what was then an island just offshore; since 1891 the fort has been connected to the mainland. There have been fortresses on this site since 1634, but its only military involvement was during the last days of the siege of Boston in 1776, when

British artillery unsuccessfully bombarded the Americans on Dorchester Heights. A young Edgar Allen Poe was stationed here during his brief military career; supposedly, he heard a story about a soldier who had been sealed up alive in a dungeon at the fort by his enemies. This may have been the source for Poe's tale *A Cask of Amontillado*.

A promenade encircles the massive stone fort, and continues around landlocked **Pleasure Bay**. Here are splendid views of the outer harbor and islands, a fishing pier, and ample grounds for picnicking. An obelisk commemorates Donald McKay, the East Boston clipper builder, whose ships once sailed past this point on their way to the ends of the earth.

Because Fort Independence isn't near any "T" stops, and since most visitors won't be driving, it's best suited for those who enjoy a long walk – roughly 2½ miles (4 km) from the Children's Museum by way of Summer and East First streets to Day Boulevard. If harbor views are the object, less ambitious perambulators should instead consider a boat ride out to the Harbor Islands.                      ❑

---

### Restaurants

#### American

**Aura**
Seaport Hotel, 1 Seaport Lane. Tel: 385-4300. Open: B & L Mon–Fri, D Mon–Sat. $$$–$$$$
www.seaportboston.com
The menu, which changes with the seasons, is varied, from hot dogs (lunch) to fois gras, and the breakfast buffet is excellent. Gratuity is included in the bill, and there is complimentary under-

ground parking. Note: there are no water views from the restaurant.

**Meritage**
Boston Harbor Hotel, 70 Rowes Wharf. Tel: 439-3995. Open: D Tues–Sat., Sun. brunch. $$$$
www.bhh.com
Each New American dish is available in a small ($15) or large ($29) portion and is linked to one of six wine categories. Thus diners know that crisp veal sweetbreads are best with a full-bodied white wine, and a spicy/earthy red goes

best with zinfandel-braised beef short ribs. Award-winning 15,000-bottle cellar. Sunday brunch costs $45.

#### Seafood

**Anthony's Pier 4**
140 Northern Ave. Tel: 423-6363. Open: L & D daily. $$$
www.pier4.com
Directly on the waterfront, Anthony's has long reigned as the city's premier tourist destination for traditional New England seafood. The dining room is huge, the fare is solid, and

the service courteous if brisk. For a mainstream American spot, the wine list is extraordinary.

**No-Name**
15½ Fish Pier (just off Northern Avenue). Tel: 338-7539. Open: L & D daily. $–$$
Very popular, no-frills operation with fresh-off-the-boat seafood and terrific chowder. No reservations and lots of free parking.

● ● ● ● ● ● ● ● ● ● ● ● ● ● ● ● ●
*Prices for three-course meal for one, with half-bottle of house wine, tax and tip.*
**$** *under $25.* **$$** *$25–40.*
**$$$** *$40–50.* **$$$$** *$50-plus.*

# THE HARBOR ISLANDS

After years of being largely ignored, the islands have been designated as a national park area and recreational facilities are being expanded

The 30 Boston Harbor Islands were added to the National Park system by the federal government in 1996. Their designation as the **Boston Harbor Islands National Recreation Area** follows a nearly four-century history of use, abuse, and neglect of what is one of the most interesting, yet little-known, parts of metropolitan Boston.

Some of the islands, created by retreating glaciers 16,000 years ago, are now connected by bridges or causeways to the mainland, and three (Governor's, Apple and the aptly named Bird) have become one and are now Logan Airport.

The farthest Boston Harbor island is The Graves, a rocky outcrop with a lighthouse, 10 miles (16 km) from downtown Boston, and the biggest is 214-acre (87-hectare) Long Island, linked by bridge to Moon Island, Quincy, and the south shore.

## A checkered past

The islands' first visitors, Native Americans (the Massachuset and others) used them for hunting. But, as their strategic importance as guardians of the harbor roads and the city itself was appreciated, forts were constructed on Peddock's (Fort Andrews), Lovell's (Fort Standish) and George's (Fort Warren), which remained active from King Philip's War

of 1675 to the 20th century. Some of the islands served as hospitals, almshouses, quarantine facilities, prisons, and reformatory schools.

In the 18th century, they were popular with Bostonians who would visit to enjoy not only the sea air but also the illicit pleasures of gambling and boxing matches. Others hosted summer homes for the wealthy, lighthouses, and makeshift encampments for fishermen, while some islands were later used for the disposal of sewage, trash, and deceased horses.

Map on page 110

**BELOW:**
George's Island.

And as one would expect of any decent archipelago, the Islands are said to harbor buried pirate treasure (Lovell's) and ghosts (George's). Although much of the islands' future remains to be defined, seven are currently the focus of visitor activity.

## George's, Lovell's, Gallop's and Peddock's Islands

**George's Island ❶**, the main gateway to the other Harbor Islands, is a 45-minute boat ride (7 miles/11 km) from downtown Boston. Its amenities include recreational fishing along its shores for bluefish and striped bass, and a chance to learn about the harbor's military history through its Fort Warren (built in 1833), a training ground for Union soldiers and a prison for Confederate captives. Georges has a refreshment stand, picnic areas, guided tours, and magnificent views of the Boston skyline, Boston Light, and nearby Gallop's and Lovell's islands.

*Fort Warren on Georges Island.*

From June to October there is a daily ferryboat service from George's to Gallop's, Lovell's, Peddock's, Grape, and Bumpkin islands, with a weekend service in spring and fall.

**Lovell's Island ❷** was runner-up to New York as the site for the Statue of Liberty. It offers the opportunity for overnight camping by special permit near the ruins of Fort Standish, built in 1900, and has one of the islands' few inviting beaches.

The adjacent **Gallop's Island ❸** is dominated by the remains of a large drumlin, surrounded by trails. During World War II, Gallop's was the site of a US Maritime Radio Training School and a hospital. Its main inhabitants these days are rabbits.

A little more than a mile south of George's lies **Peddock's Island ❹**, which consists of four drumlins connected by sand or gravel bars. On it were discovered 4,100-year-old human bones, the oldest archeological find in New England. This third-

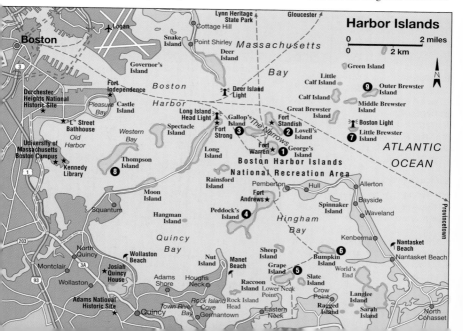

largest harbor island has a brackish pond, a marsh, many walking trails, and the remains of Fort Andrews built under the shadow of the Spanish American War and garrisoned during World Wars I and II.

## Grape, Bumpkin, and Little Brewster Islands

These are the final three islands accessible by daily ferryboat in the spring and summer. Grape and Bumpkin are located in Hingham Bay and are protected by the long arm of Nantasket Beach and the town of Hull; Little Brewster lies farther out, beyond the crook of the peninsula. **Grape Island** ❺ is one of the finest camping islands in the harbor, offering a wealth of trails for inquisitive visitors who may encounter skunks, rabbits, and lots of birds among the wild berry trees. **Bumpkin** ❻ lies close to the Hull peninsula, and hosts the remains of a children's hospital and a farmhouse now overgrown with local vegetation including bayberries and wild raspberries. There is a choice of campsites among its walking trails.

**Little Brewster** ❼ offers magnificent panoramas of the inner harbor and the open Atlantic, but its chief attraction is Boston Light. Its original beacon, built in 1716, was the first in the nation, but the present building was constructed in 1782 after the British had blown up the original before departing Boston in 1776. The lighthouse, a National Historic Landmark, is the only one in the nation still manned (except in winter) by resident keepers. Near here, during the War of 1812, the British ship *Shannon* engaged the American frigate *Chesapeake*. The British won the battle but not immortality: that went to Captain James Lawrence of the *Chesapeake* with his command: "Don't give up the ship!"

Access to many of the other harbor islands is possible by private boat or from tours arranged by organizations including the Friends of Boston Harbor and the New England Aquarium. The Friends take visitors to **Thompson Island** ❽, owned and managed by private, non-profit Thompson Island Outward Bound Education Center. The island has a large salt marsh and rolling fields.

In addition to hiking and camping, the islands are often used for a variety of other activities: there are apple festivals, cruises to experience nature in winter, Civil War reenactments on George's Island, and an Edgar Rowe Snow Day to celebrate the memory and works of Boston Harbor's consummate Harbor Islands storyteller.

For the more adventurous, the outlying **Outer Brewster Island** ❾ offers some of the best scuba diving in New England; and wildlife cruises to the islands offer a chance to view sea ducks, barn owls, redwing blackbirds, double crested cormorants, harbor seals, and a variety of seashore life in easily accessible tidepools. There is recreational fishing throughout the islands for striped bass, winter flounder and bluefish. ❑

Map on page 110

### TIPS

● Trips to the islands embark from Long Wharf, as well as from Lynn Heritage State Park north of the city, and from the John F. Kennedy Library in Dorchester and Hewitt's Cove in Hingham to the south.

● For more information on visiting the islands, log on to www. boston islands.com or call 617-223 8666.

**BELOW:** Boston Light on Little Brewster.

# WATCHING FOR WHALES

**One of the world's greatest gatherings of humpback whales takes place every summer off the coast of Massachusetts. Today their hunters take aim with cameras rather than guns**

**ABOVE:** It's fairly rare for a visitor not to see at least one whale during a trip. More often than not, the whale-watching boats are able to approach within 50 ft (15 meters) of at least half a dozen humpbacks.

Pegasus and Pepper, Batik and Gemini, Petrel and Ishtar make a great spectacle as they lunge, breach and flipper. You can see them by boarding one of the large whale-watching boats which, daily from Easter until early October, leave Boston and Province-town on three-hour sightseeing trips.

Their destination is Stellwagen Bank, a shallow underwater deposit of sand and gravel, to which these humpbacked whales return after spending the winter in their Caribbean breeding grounds. Experts recognize the different humpbacks, which often reach lengths of 40–50 feet (15 meters) and weights of 30 tons, by their distinctive body markings, especially those on their tail flukes.

Huge quantities of plankton and an infinite number of small sand eels are the magnets that attract to Stellwagen Bank the world's largest concentration of whales. The vast majority of the 500 or so who visit each year are humpbacks, but there are minkes, finbacks and a few right whales.

The humpback is basically a bulk feeder who dives deep below the schools of sand eels and then lunges upward through the school with its mouth open to engulf large quantities of fish and water. These voracious eating machines are capable of capturing hundreds, if not thousands, of small fish with every lunge they make.

**BELOW:** The waters can be rough, so it's a good idea to carry anti-seasickness tablets. Rainwear is useful in April and May. A versatile SLR is more effective than an automatic camera.

**LEFT:** When to see them: the season lasts about six months; humpbacks and minkes begin arriving in April and May and the numbers peak from June to October.

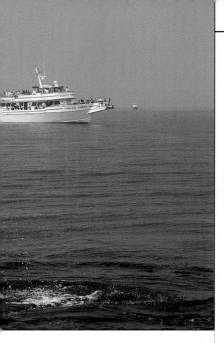

## THE HEYDAY OF YANKEE WHALING

The dramatic painting *(left)* by Robert Walker Weir, Jr., on show at the Kendall Whaling Museum in Sharon, Massachusetts, is a reminder that whales as a source of income are not new to New England. Nor is their annual visit to Stellwagen Bank. In the 1770s local fishermen hunted the right whales that populated Stellwagen and started the decline in their numbers from 50,000 to the 250 or so which now survive. (Right whales are so-called because they were the right whales to hunt: they swim slowly, enabling the hunters to keep abreast of them in row-boats. Once harpooned, right whales float on the surface rather than sink.)

Whale oil lit the lamps of the world, and New England vessels – 735 of them at their peak – prowled the globe. Then petroleum-based kerosene was discovered in Pennsylvania in 1859. Whaling began to decline and soon the opening up of the West offered more alluring opportunities to the adventurous than a hazardous life at sea.

**LEFT:** Because they offer rain checks if whales are not spotted on a trip, some whale-watching operators feed gulls, hoping that their presence, usually a good indicator that there are fish close by, will help attract whales to the area.

**BELOW:** Visitors are often fortunate enough to be entertained by scores of frolicking dolphins, which seem to be more curious than fearful of their human observers.

**RIGHT:** A humpback pokes its head out of the water (spyhopping, as it's called), and reveals its pleated throat. These folds of skin balloon up and, during feeding, probably double the capacity of the mouth.

# CHARLESTOWN

The USS *Constitution* and the Bunker Hill
Monument attract the Freedom Trail trekkers,
and the Warren Tavern allows you to combine
historical research with having a drink

harlestown, which today is a northern neighborhood of Boston, was founded in 1629, one year before Boston, when 10 men with their families and servants were sent by the Massachusetts Bay Company to occupy the company's New England holdings. One year later this scant band was joined by John Winthrop, who would become the colony's first governor, and his shipload of 800 Puritans.

Conditions were difficult, disease was rife, the water was foul and fear of Indians was ever-present. In 1631 Winthrop and many of his followers headed south across the Charles River estuary and settled on the Shawmut peninsula, today's Boston proper. However, the doughty few who remained on the Charlestown side prospered and by the end of the 17th century had established a democratic town meeting, founded a church and school, built a mill and even hanged Massachusetts' first witch.

## Total destruction

The town thrived and became the fourth busiest port in the country. However, in 1775 it was razed by the British and consequently none of the buildings bordering its tree-lined streets pre-dates 1800.

Charlestown is usually reached via the Charlestown Bridge, an extension of Washington Street in Boston's North End, although a more pleasant and exciting approach is to board the ferry at Long Wharf for a short voyage to the USS *Constitution* National Park. (Alternatively, take the Orange Line of the "T" to the Community College stop; if you choose this option, the route described below will have to be taken more or less in reverse.) A forerunner of today's Charlestown Bridge was the very first span across the river, which opened in 1786 with

**LEFT:** housing
in Charlestown.
**BELOW:** the new
Leonard P. Zakim
Bunker Hill Bridge
across the Charles,
the world's widest
cable-stayed bridge.

**TIP**

If you feel inclined to join the scullers, Charles River Canoe & Kayak (617-965 5110) rents single and two-person kayaks. Duck Tours (617-267 3825) offers a less strenuous ride on the river in military-surplus amphibious vehicles.

**BELOW:** dragon boat on the Charles River.

mighty cannon salutes and shouts of:

*You Charlestown pigs,*
*Put on your wigs,*
*And come over to Boston town.*

That original Charlestown Bridge, with an enormous span of 1,053 ft (321 meters) and a width of 423 ft (129 meters), was considered the greatest feat of engineering yet undertaken in America. Within 15 years a further three privately funded bridges had firmly linked Boston to the mainland; until then, the city had been a peninsula with something of the character of a tight little island.

Immediately upstream from the bridge, the **New Charles River Dam** controls the water level in the river basin. There's a Charles River Information Center here, and an observation window overlooks three locks. The two for pleasure boats can be extremely busy, with more than 1,000 craft passing through on a summer day; only a rare commercial vessel ventures into the basin via the

third lock. Beyond, on the Cambridge (north) side, is the Charlesgate Yacht Club, one of four power-boat marinas on the river.

The Charlestown Bridge leads directly into Charlestown's **City Square ❶**. Immediately to the northwest is small, leafy **John Harvard Mall**, in the center of which stands a granite memorial to this Charlestown man who "was sometimes minister of God's word" and who, when he died in 1638 aged 27, bequeathed his library of 300 books and half his estate to the struggling Newtowne College, which thereupon assumed his name. Harvard Mall is where the first settlers built their fort. Eight plaques embedded in the walls recount the subsequent early history of the settlement.

Immediately to the right of the mall is tiny **Harvard Square**, where No. 27, built around 1800, is one of the very few stone houses in Charlestown. It originally served as

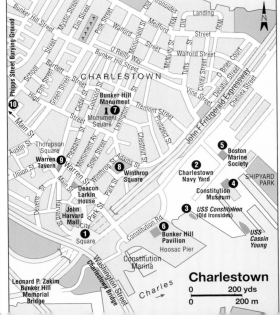

**Charlestown**

| 0 | 200 yds |
| 0 | 200 m |

the town dispensary. Above the mall is **Harvard Street**, a dignified curving street where many notables lived in still-standing, handsome mid-19th-century houses with mansards and bow windows. Turn left and return to City Square, passing No. 16, once occupied by Edward Everett (1794–1865), governor of Massachusetts and president of Harvard.

## Old Ironsides

Turn right after crossing the bridge into City Square to reach the decommissioned **Charlestown Navy Yard** ❷ which, during its heyday (1825–68 and World War II) employed thousands of men. Largely abandoned during the postwar era, it is enjoying a resurrection not only because of the **USS Constitution** ❸ and other tourist attractions but because many buildings have been recycled into handsome apartments and hi-tech laboratories.

The towering masts of the *Constitution*, which can be seen from afar, dominate the yard and are the magnet that attracts visitors to the Park (Apr–Oct Tues– Sun 10am–4pm;

Nov–Mar Thur–Sun 10am–4pm; expect long lines; tel: 242-5670).

"Old Ironsides," whose copper sheathing, bolts and fittings were made by Paul Revere, was built in Boston and first sailed from the harbor in 1778 in a shakedown cruise. Thirty years later she was retired after being involved in 40 victorious engagements, including the sinking of the British warship *Guerrière* in 1812. During this battle the Constitution earned the nickname "Old Ironsides" when a British sailor, on seeing cannon balls apparently bouncing off her side, exclaimed "Her sides are made of iron!" The *Constitution* had been constructed of "live oak," from the Sea Islands of Georgia, which is said to have five times the durability of common white oak. The ship's imperviousness to cannon fire was also due to her ribs being placed closer together than was the usual custom, and the extra thickness of her planking.

The fact that the *Constitution* is moored in Boston and has not long since been scrapped is the result of several land battles. In 1830 she

Map on page 116

*USS Constitution, launched in 1778.*

**BELOW:**
aboard Old Ironsides.

*The wheel of the USS Constitution.*

earned a reprieve from the ship-breaker's yard when the young Oliver Wendell Holmes Sr. penned a poem with the lines "Ay! pull her tattered ensign down,/Long has it waved on high," which touched the nation's heartstrings.

Holmes, portrayed by an actor, can be seen in stovepipe hat wandering about the Navy Yard, often accompanied by Captain Isaac Hull, who commanded the *Constitution* in her engagement with the *Guerrière*. The actor playing Hull, by the way, will likely be a mere shadow of the original – the captain was an immensely fat man. As for the period-costumed tars who escort visitors around the great vessel, they, like she, are very much on the official rolls. Each is an active-duty sailor in the US Navy.

In 1905, the venerable ship again faced destruction. This time she was to be used for target practice by the Navy. A group of concerned citizens intervened, and finally, in the 1920s, when she was in need of restoration, Boston schoolchildren contributed their pennies to a drive that spread throughout the land. In 1954, legislation was enacted making Boston the permanent home port of the *Constitution*, and here she proudly sits, the oldest commissioned warship in the world and liable – in theory, anyway – to be called into active service. It's unlikely, though: since 1897, apart from a 22,000-mile (35,000-km) voyage in 1921 and a short overnight trip – once again, under her own sail – to Marblehead in 1997, she has left her berth only on each July 4, when tugs pull her into the harbor for her annual "turn-around." Then she fires her cannons in joy rather than in anger.

A tour of the *Constitution* is a must for anyone even remotely interested in naval history, let alone rabid devotees of Patrick O'Brian's Aubrey-Maturin novels. Along with Lord Nelson's *Victory* at her berth in Portsmouth, England, "Old Ironsides" offers one of the few opportunities in the world to walk the decks of one of the great wooden fighting ships of two centuries ago. Regardless of whether the fascination lies in imagining the cacophony of the great guns and the impact of enemy fire, or simply wondering what it would be like for hundreds of sailors to share such close quarters, she is a ship to conjure with.

### Naval insights

Further insight into the *Constitution* and life aboard her can be gained by visiting the **Constitution Museum** ❹, about 600 yards east of the mooring. Between the two, and a couple of hundred yards to the south, the sleek, gray World War II destroyer USS *Cassin Young* DD-793 also welcomes visitors. Although she was built in California, she represents 14 sister-ships launched in the Charlestown Yard during World War II; at that time, the yard employed 50,000 workers who constructed 141 ships and serviced 5,000 others.

You can rest your feet in the wardroom of the **Boston Marine Society** ❺, just beyond the Constitution Museum. The two main purposes of this Society, formed in 1742 by Boston sea captains, was to start a collection box – it can still be seen and still functions – to provide assistance to members and their families in times of distress, and "to make navigations more safe." Even today, the Society appoints the Pilot Commissioners who, in turn, appoint the Boston Harbor pilots.

The Museum's two rooms are rich in paintings, models of ships (including those great clippers built across the harbor in East Boston at the yard of Donald McKay) and much nautical memorabilia.

Follow the Freedom Trail markers inland from the Navy Yard to the **Bunker Hill Pavilion** ❻. It presents an excellent wrap-around show, "The Whites of Their Eyes," which owes its title to the command given by Colonel William Prescott to the American militia at the battle of Bunker Hill not to shoot "'til you see the whites of their eyes."

## The Bunker Hill Monument

And so to Breed's Hill where, in Monument Square, a 221-ft (67-meter) high granite obelisk, the **Bunker Hill Monument** ❼ (daily 9am–5pm; tel: 242-5641), soars from the heart of an immaculate sward the size of three or four football fields, which is surrounded by iron rails and pierced by four gates. This is where, on an area probably twice as large, was fought the Battle of Bunker Hill. (The designation is a misnomer; Bunker Hill itself actually lies about 300 yards to the north.)

The cornerstone for the Monument was laid by the Marquis de Lafayette on the 50th anniversary of the battle and the finished obelisk was dedicated in 1842 with a speech by Daniel Webster. Its construction resulted in the first commercial railroad (horse-drawn) in the nation. This was required to haul the massive granite blocks from their Quincy quarry to the Neponset River, from where they were floated on barges to Charlestown.

Alongside the Monument is a small museum with several exhibits

Map on page 116

*After taking Bunker and Breed's hills from American forces in the costly battle of June 17, 1775, the British fortified this commanding section of Charlestown. A strategic component of the stalemated siege of Boston for the next nine months, it was abandoned by the Redcoats as part of their evacuation of the area under threat of George Washington's guns on Dorchester Heights.*

**BELOW:** the Bunker Hill Monument.

## The Battle of Bunker Hill

On the hot afternoon of June 17, 1775, the Americans inflicted more than 1,100 casualties on the approaching British regulars. The British seized the hill, but the colonists took heart from their own stubborn stand, which left 440 of them dead or wounded. Both sides lost notable officers. Major Pitcairn had led British troops at the Battle of Lexington two months earlier; American Dr. Joseph Warren, a valued revolutionary activist and close friend of Paul Revere, died fighting as a private although he had just been commissioned a major general. Several months later, Revere – once a dentist – identified his friend's remains from dental work he had done.

including an excellent diorama of the battle. A strenuous climb of 294 stone stairs leads the visitor to the top of the Monument. The views were the most breathtaking in Boston when the structure was new; today, the downtown skyline, rather than the open sea, offers the most dramatic vista.

At the park's south end, between the obelisk and the main entrance gate, the Massachusetts Gate, stands a bronze statue of Colonel Prescott, who uttered the famous "whites of their eyes" command.

Leave Monument Square by heading south on Winthrop Street and you immediately enter **Winthrop Square ❽** which, for a century, was the training field where Charlestown boys learned the art of war. From here, soldiers were sent to fight in the Revolution, the War of 1812 and the Civil War. Monuments and plaques at the north of the Square remember those who did not return. The Old Training Field School from 1827 at the south border of the square is now a handsome private residence.

Charlestown, like many Boston neighborhoods, has lured professionals seeking homes with plenty of character, within a short distance of downtown. Historically a working-class Irish community, Charlestown in recent decades has not only acquired this more affluent social component, but has attracted lower-income citizens to public housing projects modeled on traditional rowhouse design. The ethnic and racial diversity is welcome – but some worry that Charlestown risks becoming a quarter of rich and poor, with little middle ground.

Descend Winthrop Street for a couple of hundred yards and turn right onto Main Street. At Nos. 55–61 is the post-revolutionary home of Deacon Larkin, who lent Paul Revere a horse for his famous ride to Lexington. Incidentally, the horse was not returned.

### Warren Tavern

Continue along Main Street. The immaculately restored three-story **Warren Tavern ❾** (2 Pleasant Street, tel: 241-8142) was one of the first buildings erected, in 1780, after

*St Patrick's Day is not forgotten in this traditionally Irish community.*

**BELOW:** remembering Bunker Hill.

the burning of Charlestown by the British during the Revolution and is the oldest tavern in continuous use in Boston. It is also probably the oldest extant building in Charlestown. It was named after General Joseph Warren, who died at Bunker Hill and had been described by a British prime minister "the greatest incendiary in North America." The low-ceiling beamed timbers and wall sconces evoke a colonial atmosphere, but the food, served until 10.30pm, is nothing special.

Further along Main Street, past handsome three-decker clapboard houses painted in a variety of hues, there's an incongruously imposing French château, which was formerly the Charlestown Savings Bank.

Beyond this and across the road is the **Phipps Street Burying Ground** ❿, Charlestown's first cemetery (1630). At least 100 graves are pre-1700 burials and about 10 times that number date to before 1800. It provides the best historical record of pre-revolutionary Charlestown. This is because of a unique layout: families were buried in rectangular plots that were arranged to correspond to the locations of their homes. A granite obelisk commemorates preacher John Harvard, who died in 1638; it was erected by Harvard graduates in 1828 because his original gravestone had been lost.

From here, it is just a couple of hundred yards to the Community College stop of the "T". ❏

---

## Restaurants

### American

**Ironside Grill**
25 Park St., Tel: 242-1384. Open: L & D Mon–Fri, D Sat & Sun. $$
A good spot for lunch after a visit to the USS *Constitution*.

**Warren Tavern**
2 Pleasant St. Tel: 241-8142. Open: L & D daily. $
Paul Revere may not have slept here, but he certainly quaffed a few brews here. This has been a popular watering hole since 1780, and a popular destination for great burgers, terrific clam chowder, and one of Revere's favorites: lobster ravioli.

### Italian

**Figs**
67 Main St., Charleston. Tel: 242-2229. Open: L Mon–Fri, L & D (serving dinner menu only) Sat & Sun. $$–$$$
www.toddenglish.com
Popular restaurateur Todd English's Charlestown outpost serves pizzas, panini, and more elaborate dishes such as garganelli (pasta with broccoli sauce, Parmesan, and confit veal ragu).

**Paolo's Trattoria**
251 Main St., Tel: 242-7229. Open: D nightly. $$
Wood-oven pizza and traditional dishes, along with a few Greek specialties in a laid-back, family-friendly trattoria.

**Santarpio's Pizza**
111 Chelsea St., East Boston. Tel: 567-9871. L & D daily. $
Serving crispy-crust pizza and grilled sausage sandwiches in "modest" surroundings since 1930.

### Greek

**Meze Estiatorio**
100 City Sq. Tel: 242-6393. Open: D nightly. $$$
www.mezeboston.com
Traditional fare with a contemporary twist in classic surroundings, plus live Greek music. A fine selection of small plate choices (mezes), as well as entrées prepared in the wood-burning stove. Complete the meal with a cup of stone-ground coffee.

### Mediterranean

**Olives**
10 City Square, Charlestown. Tel: 242-1999. Open: D Mon–Sat. $$–$$$
www.toddenglish.com
The original establishment of celebrity chef Todd English specializes in rustic Mediterranean bistro fare in "casual elegant" surroundings. Among the specialties: intricate hand-crafted dishes such as rabbit cacciatore with crispy polenta filled with farmhouse ricotta, roasted tomato, and roasted pine nut cream.

### Moroccan/North African

**Tangierino Restaurant & Lounge**
83 Main St., Tel: 242-6014. Open: D nightly. $$$
www.tangierino.com
Plush red tapestries, chandeliers, and red velvet seats set the mood in this romantic spot whose specialties include braised lamb with honey and toasted almonds, and Moroccan duck confit. Intimate lounge and a hookah den. Valet parking.

● ● ● ● ● ● ● ● ● ● ● ● ● ● ● ● ●

*Prices for three-course meal for one, with half-bottle of house wine, tax and tip.*
**$** *under $25.* **$$** *$25–40.*
**$$$** *$40–50.* **$$$$** *$50-plus.*

# Back Bay

Third Harrison Gray Otis House
King's Chapel Parish House
Bull & Finch (Hampshire House)
Soldiers & Sailors Monument
Boylston St
South Charles Street
Charles Street Playhouse

BOSTON COMMON

Branch Street
River St
Byron St
Beaver Place
Chestnut Street
Brimmer Street

Make Way for Ducklings
Washington Monument
Lagoon
PUBLIC GARDEN

Charles Street
Beacon Street
Back Street

Park Square
Eliot Street
Park Plaza
Four Seasons Hotel

BAY VILLAGE

Piedmont Street
Stuart Street
Winchester Street

Tremont Street
Herald
Marginal Rd
Turnpike

Shawmut Av
Paul
Dwight St
E. Berkeley Street

Arlington Street
Arlington

Arlington
Street
Ritz-Carlton Hotel
Arlington St Church
Emmanuel Church
Louis Boston
Teddy Bear
FAO Schwarz

Plaza Castle
Cortes Street
Isabella Street
Massachusetts

Columbus
Berkeley Street

Boston Center for the Arts (Cyclorama Building)
Warren
Appleton

Gibson House Museum
Hooper Mansion
Berkeley Street

Church of the Covenant
New England Life Building
500 Boylston
John Hancock Tower
Boylston Street

Newbury Street
Clarendon Street
Trinity Church
Copley Square
Trinity Place

Back Bay/South End
Back Bay Station

Dartmouth
Columbus
Yarmouth
W. Canton St
Holyoke St
Carleton St

Marlborough Street
Clarendon Street
First Baptist Church
Hunnewell Mansion
Commonwealth

Fairmont Copley Plaza Hotel
Westin Hotel
Copley Place
Colonnade Hotel

New Old South Church
Boston Public Library
Blagden Street
Stuart Street

Cushing-Endicott Mansion
Ames-Webster Mansion
Dartmouth Street
Exeter Street

Lenox Hotel
Lord & Taylor
Saks Fifth Avenue

Huntington Avenue
St Botolph Street
West Newton St

Algonquin Club
St Botolph Club
BACK BAY

Former Exeter St Theater

Prudential Center
Prudential Tower
Sheraton Boston Hotel
Hynes Convention Center
Prudential

Boylston Street
Gloucester Street
Fairfield Street
Exeter Street
Dartmouth Street

John F. Andrew House
Charles Francis Adams House
Boston Architectural Center
Institute of Contemporary Art

Broadcasting Center
Administration Building
Christian Science Center

Dalton St
Scotia St
Cambria St
Back Bay Hilton Hotel

Burrage Mansion
Tower Records
Hynes/ICA

Ames Mansion
Church Court

Hereford Street
Gloucester Street
Beacon Street

St Cecilia Street
St Germain Street
Belvidere Street
Clearway
Cleveland
Norway Street

Mother Church & Extension
Publishing Society Building
Horticultural Hall

Massachusetts Avenue
Commonwealth Avenue
Marlborough Street
Newbury Street

Massachusetts Historical Society
Boylston Street Performance Center
Berklee
Haviland St
Hemenway Street
Edgerley Road

BACK BAY FENS

Esplanade
Storrow Drive
Storrow Drive
Charles River

Lagoon

Harvard Bridge
Charlesgate East
Charlesgate West
Fenway
Boylston Street
Ipswich Street

0    200 yds
0    200 m

N

# BACK BAY AND FENWAY

**This varied area encompasses grand houses, the Public Garden, the Boston Public Library, the Christian Science complex, and the Museum of Fine Arts**

Time and again, visitors from more carefully planned cities have suggested that Boston's streets were laid out by colonial cows allowed to wander whatever routes they chose. The **Back Bay** is the Hub's answer to those wags. It was laid out very carefully by mid-Victorian true believers in the urban grid pattern, anxious to make expansive use of what they called "made land" and eager to put downtown's tortuous alleys and the narrow streets of Beacon Hill behind them.

The French formal influence – the Back Bay was built in the era when Baron Hausmann was creating the grand boulevards of Paris – is more evident here than in any other part of Boston, and the cool logic of the layout is reflected even in the alphabetical progression of the cross streets from Arlington to Hereford.

But two things have kept the Back Bay from being severe and unimaginative. The first is the progression of architectural styles characterizing the row houses that dominate its streets – walking from the Public Garden to the Fenway is like taking a seminar in the evolution of 19th-century taste, from Italianate through beaux arts to Colonial Revival. The second is the progression of time: succeeding generations have made the Back Bay their own, creating

sleek shopping districts along Newbury and Boylston streets and turning a once-staid quarter of single-family homes into a chic warren of condominiums and apartments.

## Taming the tide

Originally the Back Bay was exactly that – a shallow estuary that reached well beyond Columbus Avenue. In 1814, a developer, Uriah Cotting, built a dam across the bay from the Boston Common to Sewall's Point, near today's Kenmore Square. His

Map on page 122

**BELOW:** the magnolias bloom in the Back Bay.

*Filling in the stagnant estuary was a major undertaking. The first trainload of gravel from West Needham was dumped into the fetid water in 1857, and for more than 30 years a new load arrived every 45 minutes, 24 hours a day. (Contrary to common belief, the fill was not taken from the top of Beacon Hill, which had been lowered more than a half century earlier). The project created 450 acres (180 hectares) of new land.*

**BELOW:** Back Bay with, in background, the Charles River Basin and Cambridge.

plan was to harness the bay's tidal currents in order to power some 80 mills. Cotting died before his mill dam was finished, but in any event there was far less tidal power than his grand scheme would have required.

With its outlet now obstructed by the dam, the estuary became stagnant, and the sewage that, until then, had been channeled into the bay and flushed out with the tides began to present a problem, especially when the wind shifted east. In 1849 the mayor declared the Back Bay "offensive and injurious to the large and growing population," and after eight years of political wrangling a plan was finally approved to fill it in.

The rush of speculation that accompanied the project was tempered with public concern. Most people accepted that the city needed more space for parks and civic institutions, and a remarkable 40 percent of the new land was reserved specifically for these purposes. Generous though it was, there were definite limits to public beneficence. With so much at stake, there was never any question about who was in control.

The Back Bay would ultimately bear the stamp of society's upper crust.

By the mid-19th century, Boston's upper class was beginning to pull away from its Puritan moorings. The Brahmins' inclination for thrift was being challenged by a new spirit of self-indulgence and the rise of the *nouveaux riches*.

By 1900, construction of the Back Bay was virtually complete, and apart from a few isolated structures, it remains essentially unchanged. Today, its homes and churches comprise perhaps the finest cache of Victorian architecture in the US.

## Mapping out the territory

Geographically, today's Back Bay falls into two distinct areas. North of Boylston Street, the old Back Bay proper is criss-crossed by the perfect grid ordained by its original planners. Other than Newbury and Boylston streets, this area is almost exclusively residential. The northern border is marked by the busy traffic of Storrow Drive, although footbridges provide access to the riverside greenspace beyond.

South of Boylston, the tidy grid gives way to the logic of public spaces. This is where the Back Bay gets "lumpy," each lump defined by a large, self-contained development: Copley Square, Copley Place, the Prudential Center and the Christian Science Headquarters. Although several large apartment buildings stand here, the area is predominantly occupied by department stores, hotels, shops and offices.

## The Public Garden

One other section of the Back Bay stands alone: the **Public Garden**. Adjacent to the Common, it was built on landfill in 1859, some 200 years after the Common was established. Its designer was George Meacham. This lush 24-acre (10-hectare) rectangle, probably Boston's prettiest, most relaxing park and a perfect spot to begin a Back Bay tour, has flower beds, exotic trees and several splendid works of sculpture, including the magnificent equestrian statue of George Washington facing the Arlington Street gate at Commonwealth Avenue.

The Garden's central attraction is the **Lagoon ❶**, surrounded by enormous willow trees. Inspired by *Lohengrin*, the swan boats that make lazy figure eights in the water have been operated by the same family, the Pagets, for three generations, and have given as many generations of young swan pilots the opportunity to develop heroic quadriceps: the boats are pedal-powered. A suspension bridge, supposedly the world's shortest, crosses the pond at its center.

Just inside the park's entrance at the corner of Charles and Beacon streets is a set of bronze statues depicting the Mallard family of *Make Way For Ducklings ❷*, Robert McCloskey's classic children's book set along the Charles River and on the Public Garden Lagoon. Small children adore clambering over the eight ducklings or riding on Mrs Mallard's back. Elsewhere in the park, statues of interest include that of Edward Everett Hale, author of *The Man Without a Country* (at the Charles Street entrance opposite the Boston Common), and Charles Sumner, who led abolitionist forces

Map on page 122

*The Public Garden.*

**BELOW:** *Make Way for Ducklings* in the Public Garden.

*Commonwealth Avenue Mall.*

**BELOW:** swan boats have been operated by the same family for three generations.

in the US Senate before the Civil War (on the Public Garden's Boylston Street perimeter).

The Public Garden is fronted by an impressive line of buildings, including the **Arlington Street Church** ❸ and the **Ritz-Carlton Hotel** ❹. The Arlington Street Church was the first building to rise in the Back Bay, and its elaborate spire and brownstone facade are a departure from the chaste Georgian meeting houses favored by the previous generation. Built in 1927 and burdened with a graceless new wing in the 1980s, the Ritz was for years the city's most prestigious hotel; now, it shares that honor with the nearby Four Seasons and a second Ritz-Carlton, on Tremont Street facing the Common. The old Ritz's sedate bar still commands a peerless view of the Garden, but, sadly, its grand formal dining room is closed except for holidays (by reservation) and private parties. We suspect the mania for hip new dining spots helped do in the most splendidly unhip room in Boston.

The Back Bay grid is immediately west of the Public Garden and connected to it by the **Commonwealth Avenue Mall**. Although Commonwealth Avenue is one of the most pleasant strolls in the city, it is the smart shops on **Newbury Street** that grab most attention. Unfortunately, **Beacon Street** attracts too much auto traffic to carry off its traditional reserve. **Marlborough Street**, on the other hand, in spite of a lively contingent of students, is still quiet and shady. In spite of excellent stores and sidewalk cafés, **Boylston Street** lacks the quiet ambience of the rest of the Back Bay.

A long but rewarding stroll through Back Bay requires moving up and down the grid of streets. Start on Beacon Street near the Garden and finish at the corner of Boylston Street and Massachusetts Avenue. Fortunately – as this walk will take several hours if done at the proper leisurely pace – those Newbury Street cafés will intervene at just the right time.

The 1860 **Gibson House Museum** ❺ at 137 Beacon Street (tours Wed–Sun 1pm, 2pm, 3pm; tel: 267

Map on page 122

6338) is a brick home from the first period of Back Bay construction complete with original Victorian furnishings, preserved intact through the tenure of the last owner, a scion of the Gibson family who died in the 1950s. The sumptuously furnished dining room is set with a Rockingham service and English Regency chairs; downstairs, the kitchen and laundry room are much as they were when maintaining even a modest row house like this one required a corps of servants. A tour of the the Gibson House is highly recommended for anyone interested in social history as well as architecture and decor; it offers a rare encounter with a place and time frozen in amber.

## Commonwealth Avenue

The Back Bay comes gloriously into its own on **Commonwealth Avenue**. A shady mall containing several interesting statues runs down the middle of this nearly 100-yard-wide boulevard, whose openness would have been impossible in the tight quarters of old Boston. Although the houses tend to be uniform in propor-

tion and ambience, the play of styles on "Comm Ave" covers more architectural ground than elsewhere in the Back Bay and gives the street an almost whimsical quality. Exemplifying this is No. 176–178; built in 1883, it has a Romanesque rusticated stone porch that supports a bay window and a bowfront tower topped by a conical roof. The mansard on the top floor is Flemish in style.

The parade of spectacular buildings continues on Newbury Street, but for most visitors, the architecture is secondary to the galleries and stores that make this a haven for Boston's "beautiful people." Outdoor cafés add a Continental élan to Newbury Street and provide the best vantage for the chic to see and be seen.

Between Arlington and Berkeley streets on Newbury can be seen the first Gothic Revival Church in the Back Bay, **Emmanuel Church**. Since 1970 it has been dedicated to "a special ministry through art," and is famed for its cycle of Bach cantatas performed Sundays at 10am between September and May (tel: 536-3355).

*The attractions of the Back Bay were not appreciated by some conservatives. Even in the 20th century, one Beacon Hill gentleman told his prospective son-in-law, who was hoping to build a house in the Back Bay, that he could not allow his daughter to live on "made land." He got his way: the couple elected to settle on Beacon Hill.*

**BELOW:** topiary in the Public Garden.

## Back Bay's Social Mix

Originally, the wealthiest old families resided on Beacon Street, the less affluent old families on Marlborough, the *nouveaux riches* on Commonwealth Avenue and the social climbers on Newbury Street. After the 1930s Great Depression, many houses were subdivided into apartments or rooming houses. In the 1970s and 1980s, condominium conversions gutted the interiors even further. Recently, with a new generation of wealth moving in, more care is being taken to preserve historic details. A very few single-family homes remain – reflecting, one suspects, clever exits from the stock market before the dot.com bust as well as a burning desire to climb stairs.

Nearby on Newbury is Ralph Adams Cram's **New England Life Building** ❻, built on the original site of MIT. Evoking both corporate power and a mausoleum, the insurance firm's building, begun in 1939, inspired poet David McCord to write: *Ralph Adams Cram / One morning said damn, / And designed an Urn Burial / For a concern actuarial.* (Cram, incongruously enough, had been a Gothic Revivalist earlier in his career.)

Some of the chill has disappeared as the first floor has been converted into stores on Newbury and Boylston. Its plain granite face is offset by the 236-ft (72-meter) spire of the **Church of the Covenant**, a stirring Gothic structure with original Tiffany windows and a bristling crown of peaks and gables.

The magisterial structure across the street, which now houses **Louis Boston** was completed in 1864 as the Museum of Natural History, the forerunner of Boston's Museum of Science. Its serene classical design is by William Gibbons Preston. Inside, you'll find Boston's finest men's clothing and accessories, albeit at stratospheric prices; but gentlemen of physical as well as financial substance might feel thwarted by the emphasis on styles for young, slim physiques.

Across the street at 500 Boylston is the imaginatively named **500 Boylston** ❼, designed by Philip Johnson and John Burgee in 1988. The designers apparently took an ironic approach to the problem of relating a modern skyscraper to its old neighbors. They transformed the simple elegance of a Palladian window – a common feature in old Boston houses – into an enormous, looming black-glass facade. The building is fronted by an equally monstrous colonnade which, again, gives it a certain ironic continuity with the classical 19th-century revival. When it first appeared, it was compared to a 1930s parlor radio and called the Philco Building.

Soaring above Commonwealth Avenue (at Clarendon) is the tower of Richardson's Romanesque **First Baptist Church**. The tower's frieze was modeled by Bartholdi (sculptor of the Statue of Liberty) in Paris and was carved by Italian craftsmen. The faces in it are said to be likenesses of noted Bostonians, including Longfellow, Emerson, Hawthorne and Sumner. The trumpeting angels on the corners looking down on the Back Bay have earned the building the sobriquet of "Church of the Holy Bean Blowers."

### John Hancock Tower

Between the east and west sections of Boylston is **Copley Square**, one of America's most celebrated public spaces. Its appeal derives not from the sterile square itself – if you want to sit and relax, you'd be better off in the Public Garden or even on a bench along the Commonwealth Avenue mall – but from the structures that flank it on three sides.

The eastern side of the square is dominated by the bold juxtaposition of **Trinity Church ❽** and the 1976 **John Hancock Tower ❾**. When I.M. Pei's plan for the Hancock Tower was unveiled, there was a fear that the giant, rhombus-shaped skyscraper would overpower Trinity Church. At 790 ft (241 meters), it is the tallest building in New England, but Pei's design has an intriguing twist. Because the building is sheathed with reflective glass, it acts like an enormous mirror. In a sense, it is both conspicuous and invisible. It steals Trinity's glory but reflects it right back.

The Hancock Tower is an eyecatcher, but Copley Square belongs to Trinity. With this 1877 masterwork, Henry Hobson Richardson's adaptation of the Romanesque style

came into full blossom. The ingenious arrangement of large-scale masses, coupled with an artful use of polychrome masonry and ornamentation, make this one of the great ecclesiastical buildings in the US. Richardson continually altered the plans while the church was being constructed, and said of his winning design: "I really don't see why the Trinity people liked them, or, if they liked them, why they let me do what I afterwards did."

Visit the interior, resplendent with intricate woodwork and with stainedglass and frescoes by John La Farge, William Morris, and Edward Burne-Jones; this lavishly decorated space is a dramatic Pre-Raphaelite / Artsand-Crafts reversal of the old New England ecclesiastical aesthetic that produced all those stark Puritan meeting houses. A bronze statue of the Rev. Phillips Brooks – author of the Christmas carol "O Little Town of Bethlehem" – stands outside the north transept of the church. It's inscribed with the Bostonian's concept of the cardinal virtues: "Preacher of the Word of

Map on page 122

*The massive New England Life headquarters on Newbury Street, built between 1939 and 1942.*

**LEFT:** the John Hancock Tower.
**BELOW:** Trinity Church.

God/Lover of Mankind/Born in Boston/Died in Boston."

## Boston Public Library

Across the Square from Trinity Church is the **Boston Public Library** , a Renaissance Revival palace designed by Charles Follen McKim, and built between 1887 and 1895. A 1971 addition by Philip Johnson, quoting the original in shape and size but devoid of its magnificent beaux arts detail, fronts Boylston Street.

Explore the sumptuous interior of the old library. The **John Singer Sargent Gallery** features a series of murals on the subjects of Judaism and Christianity that some critics rank among his most powerful work. At the head of the main staircase, murals by Puvis de Chavannes depict the nine muses; in an adjacent room is Edwin Abbey's treatment of the Holy Grail legend. **Bates Hall** is a 218-ft-long, barrel-vaulted reading room wrapped in marble, oak and sandstone. And the lovely Italian cloistered courtyard in the center of the building is one of the city's most peaceful retreats and a joy for those who enjoy thumbing through a book in the open air – although, now that it serves as a chic open-air café at lunchtime, scholars and researchers who once enjoyed toting their peanut butter sandwiches to this quiet retreat resent their displacement.

On the south side of Copley Square stands the **Fairmont Copley Plaza Hotel** , an elegant 1912 Renaissance-style palace with a theatrical lobby worth a peek. Designed by Henry Hardenbergh, who is famed for both the Plaza Hotel and Dakota apartments in New York and the Willard Hotel in Washington DC, the Copley Plaza serves as a sedate and subtle foil to the showstopper architecture of Trinity Church and the Library.

Poised at the southwest corner of Copley Square is a starkly modern and frankly commercial counterpoint to all of these grand old piles. **Copley Place** is a sprawling, 9-acre (3.6-hectare) development that combines shops, offices, hotels (Westin and Marriott) and parking facilities. The exterior is neither especially offensive nor attractive, although as far as shopping malls go, the interior is quite plush. The gleaming glass canopies and crisscrossing superstructure are visually exciting, and there's an interesting stone waterfall in the central atrium that adds a surprisingly restful quality. The stores – including Tiffany, Gucci, Sharper Image, and Neiman Marcus – are clearly targeted for the high end of the market. A glass-sided footbridge connects Copley Place with the Prudential Center.

## New Old South Church

The beautifully ornamented, polychromatic **New Old South Church** is an 1875 Gothic gem that sits across from the Boston Public Library on Boylston Street. Anywhere else, it would be the center of attention, but here it is something of an afterthought. The tower, dating

**BELOW:**
Boston Public Library.

from 1938, is not the original but retains much of its predecessor's stones. That tower turned out to be Boston's Leaning Tower of Pisa, tilting at the rate of about an inch a year; when dismantled in 1931, it had already tilted almost 3 ft (1 meter).

Back on Commonwealth Avenue observe the former **Hotel Vendôme** (No. 160), designed in the French Second Empire style in 1871. Once the most prestigious hotel in the Back Bay, the Vendôme hosted Presidents Grant, Harrison, Cleveland and McKinley. Diagonally across from the hotel on the Commonwealth Mall is a memorial to firefighters who died battling a blaze at the Vendôme while it was undergoing conversion to condominiums in 1973.

## Myriad mansions

Facing Commonwealth with an entrance on Dartmouth is the **Ames-Webster Mansion**  (306 Dartmouth Street), built in 1872 for the railroad tycoon and congressman Frederick L. Ames. Now converted into a handsome office building, this is home to the most palatial space in all of the Back Bay mansions and features stained-glass windows by John La Farge.

Around the corner, Marlborough Street has a number of charming Queen Anne houses including numbers 276, 257 and 245, all built between 1883 and 1884. Although Marlborough is generally more modest than the rest of the neighborhood, there are a few exceptions. The 1878 **Hunnewell Mansion** (303 Dartmouth Street) and the mansarded 1871 **Cushing-Endicott House** (165 Marlborough Street) represent two very different styles but are equally grand in size and bearing. Bainbridge Bunting, in his authoritative book *Houses of Boston's Back Bay*, suggests that the latter is perhaps the most handsome house in the district.

Back on Commonwealth, note the **statue of Samuel Eliot Morison** (1887–1976), a sailor, historian, and lifelong Bostonian, shown here dressed in foul weather gear and seated on a rock. His 1962 book *One Boy's Boston* recalls life in the city at the end of the 19th century. The statue sits outside the **St Botolph Club**, of which Morison was a member. (Boston is named after Boston, England, whose name is an abbreviation of St Botolph's Town.)

On Newbury, the old **Exeter Street Theater**  dominates its corner like a medieval fortress. The massive Romanesque structure was built in 1884 for a group of psychics known as the Working Union of Progressive Spiritualists. An account of the temple's dedication informs that an astral spirit materialized for the occasion, appearing out of nowhere in the darkened auditorium "like a column of phosphorescent light." The Temple was converted into a movie theater in 1913 and in recent years has served as a furniture store and bookstore.

Moving west, the **Algonquin**

Map on page 122

*The Copley Plaza Hotel.*

**BELOW:** New Old South Church.

*The Algonquin Club.*

**BELOW:** the Christian Science complex.

**Club** (217 Commonwealth Avenue) has a self-important Italian Renaissance Revival facade and dates from 1887.

Looking south, one sees Back Bay's skyline dominated by the 52-story **Prudential Tower** ⓰, a monument to 1960s urban renewal and the international style. Below the tower, set somewhat back from the south side of Boylston Street is the **Prudential Center**, or "Pru," a mixed project completed in the early 1960s. At the time, the *Boston Globe* hyperventilated that "All the daring and imagination in this country today is not being spent on launching space missiles. Boston and Prudential are shooting for their own moon."

The **Tower Skywalk** (daily 10am–10pm; tel: 859-0648) has stunning views, and the central shopping core was renovated in the 1990s, with notoriously drafty mall areas now enclosed. Back on Boylston and merging with the Prudential is the spacious **Hynes Convention Center**. Rounding out the Pru are a pair of apartment buildings and the Sheraton Boston Hotel, none distinguished.

## Christian Science complex

Adjacent to the Pru is Boston's most monumental space, the **Christian Science Center** ⓱. Designed by I.M. Pei, it was created in the early 1970s by the Christian Science Church, a worldwide movement founded by Mary Baker Eddy and headquartered in Boston since 1882. The centerpiece is a 670-ft (204-meter) long reflecting pool – a welcome venue for Bostonians on hot summer days. It also serves as part of the center's air-conditioning system, and beneath it is a garage. Its south side in summer is ablaze with flowers that border a stately row of linden trees. Dominating the other long side of the pool is a domed 1906 Renaissance-style basilica and a modern, five-story colonnaded building.

Tucked in between the two and engulfed by the basilica is the original Mother Church, built in 1893–94 as a Romanesque affair with a square bell-tower and a rough granite facade. A five-story elliptical Sunday school at the southwest corner of the pool and a 28-story administrative building at the southeast com-

plete the ensemble. The interior of the basilica – the church annex, entered through a handsome portico of 10 limestone columns – is a glorious column-free affair which can seat 5,000 people on three levels. The impressive organ is the largest pipe-organ in the Western hemisphere.

The Christian Science media organization is housed in the classically inspired **Publishing Society Building**, which contains a comfortably appointed reading room and the **Mapparium**, a remarkable walk-in stained-glass globe of the world with fascinating acoustic properties. Entry to the reading room and Mapparium is free (Tues–Sun 10am–5pm; Thur and Fri until 9 pm; tel: 450-7000). Close by, at the corner of Massachusetts Avenue and Huntington Avenue, is **Horticultural Hall**, a handsome baroque building dating from 1900–01 and housing the venerable Massachusetts Horticultural Society, founded in 1829.

## New art, old mansions

Back on Boylston Street and across the road from the Hynes Convention Center is the **Institute of Contemporary Art (ICA)** ⑱ (Tues, Wed, Fri noon–5pm; Thur noon–9pm; Sat, Sun 11am–5pm; tel: 266-5152), housed in a 19th-century Romanesque former police station. The ICA, a laboratory for new ideas in the visual arts, hosts many new exhibitions each year, but it has no permanent collection. It is, however, planning a spacious new home at downtown's Fan Pier.

Nearby are the turreted, medieval-looking **Charles Francis Adams House** (1886), at 20 Gloucester Street; and the Italian Renaissance **John F. Andrew House** (1884), at 32 Hereford Street. (Not unexpectedly, some of the grandest houses occupy the corners of blocks.)

Further toward the river are some other unusual houses that shouldn't be missed. The 1882 **Ames Mansion** (No. 355) on Commonwealth Avenue and Massachusetts Avenue, now occupied by offices, informally welcomes visitors. A few blocks away, at the corner of Massachusetts Avenue and Beacon, Graham Gund's 1980s **Church Court** devel-

Map on page 122

*Mary Baker Eddy, founder of the Mother Church.*

**BELOW:** inside the Mapparium.

## Mary Baker Eddy's Empire

Mary Baker Eddy (1821–1910) opened her first church in 1894. Today Christian Science has more than 2,600 churches in 67 countries and reaches millions more people through print, radio, television and the internet.

Eddy believed that numbers are not a measure of spiritual vitality and kept the Mother Church's statistics secret. That attitude remains, but it is known that this very wealthy church is an aging organization that has failed to attract enough new members and that its media activities have sustained some heavy losses. Its newspaper, the *Christian Science Monitor*, does not have a religious bias and is highly respected.

**BELOW:**
Burrage Mansion.

opment integrates the facade of a 19th-century church into a lively condominium complex. And, if living in a church is too elevated, the 1899 **Burrage Mansion** (314 Commonwealth Avenue) bristles with turrets, towers and Gothic ornamentation, suggesting a French château.

The modern concrete structure at the corner of Hereford Street and Newbury is the **Boston Architectural Center**. The Richard Haas *trompe-l'oeil* mural on its rear wall is a cross-section of a Renaissance duomo. The two-story buildings on the rest of the block are converted stables where Back Bay families originally kept their horses and carriages. Be sure to take a look at the surrealist "Tramount" mural near the end of the block. Beyond this, **Tower Records** and the Hynes/ICA subway station at 360 Newbury are housed in a dramatic modern recycled building designed by Frank Gehry (prior to his titanium period).

Just across Massachusetts Avenue from the Horticultural Society (corner of Huntington Avenue), **Symphony Hall** ❶ puts the finishing touches to the Back Bay. The modest 1900 McKim, Mead, and White brick Renaissance exterior isn't as impressive as the interior. A young professor of physics, Wallace Sabine, was hired to guarantee that the hall would be acoustically perfect, and there isn't a bad seat in the house. The Boston Symphony play Oct–Apr; the Boston Pops May–June.

## Fenway

Beyond Massachusetts Avenue, the densely packed Back Bay yields to the **Fenway**, a loose collection of institutions and apartment buildings joined by the meandering path of the Back Bay Fens. These islands of activity form an urban archipelago that drifts out to Brookline without any real focus or organizing theme.

The Fenway first became fashionable in the early 1900s, when the Back Bay was nearing completion. The area was especially attractive to civic and to educational institutions that had outgrown downtown quarters and were looking for a place to expand. The **Massachusetts Historical Society** (founded in 1791) moved into a grand new mansion at 1154 Boylston Street in 1899 and **Harvard Medical School** followed its lead in 1906. Today, the Fenway is home to several important museums and theaters, a number of major hospitals and 14 colleges, including part of the sprawling campus of Northeastern University.

The geographical focus of the area is the **Back Bay Fens** ❷, a reedy marshland along the Muddy River (a creek, actually) and a major link in Frederick Law Olmsted's Emerald Necklace. Unfortunately, a busy road encircles the Fens and isolates it from the neighborhood. Joggers and community gardeners still make good use of the area, but it could do with more attention – not from tourists after dark, however.

Moving away from the Christian

Science Church and Symphony Hall on Huntington Avenue are some of Boston's most beloved arts institutions. **The Boston University Theater** is home to the Huntington Theater Company, a professional resident company noted for its classic and contemporary drama. Nearby is **Jordan Hall** at the **New England Conservatory of Music ㉑**, internationally renowned for both its acoustics and the music performed.

## Two major galleries

Huntington Avenue opens up somewhat with the buildings of the **Northeastern University** campus, but what attracts most visitors to the Fenway are the **Museum of Fine Arts (MFA) ㉒** (tel: 267-9300) and the Isabella Stewart Gardner Museum. The former's collection, one of the world's greatest, is housed in a massive classical structure completed in 1909 and in I.M. Pei's West Wing, built in 1981. Visitors pressed

for time might concentrate on the Old Kingdom Egyptian treasures; the Asiatic collection, especially the Japanese items; Impressionist paintings, especially those of Monet; the Boston school of painters (Stuart, Sargent and Copley); and the early American silver collection. In the **Japanese Garden**, an attempt has been made to recapture the spirit of the 18th-century New England coastline *(see also pages 140–1)*.

The **Isabella Stewart Gardner Museum ㉓** (tel: 566-1401) is within easy walking distance of the Museum of Fine Arts. The Venetian palace in which the museum is housed was built by Gardner for the specific purpose of displaying her art collection. A native New Yorker of clearly extravagant means, Isabella Stewart married John Lowell Gardner of an equally wealthy Boston family in 1860. Until her death in 1924, "Mrs Jack" cultivated a reputation for unconventional behavior

**Maps: pages 122, 135**

*Isabella Stewart Gardner engaged many performers, such as Paderewski and Nellie Melba, for private concerts, and her museum still presents more than 125 concerts a year.*

**BELOW:** a student conducts at the New England Conservatory of Music.

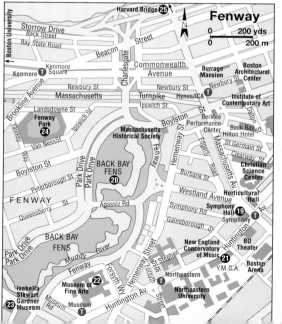

Map
on page
135

*Red Sox fans in
search of autographs
at Fenway Park.*

in the primly conventional society of Victorian Boston. Although she apparently did not keep lions in her cellar or walk them on a leash down Beacon Street (as legend has it), Mrs Gardner had wide-ranging interests, from Oriental philosophy to the Boston Red Sox.

Her will stipulated that everything be preserved exactly as she left it – and so it was until March 1990, when thieves disguised as policemen made off with works of art valued at $300 million, including Vermeer's *The Concert*, three Rembrandts, five works by Degas and a Manet. To date, they're still missing.

But the museum still has plenty of eclectic European and American items. Exceptional works include paintings and drawings by Titian, Bellini, Matisse, Botticelli, Whistler and Sargent. In the center of the palace is a glorious courtyard with a Roman mosaic pavement, a skylight and an abundance of flowers.

## Fenway Park

North of the Fens is an institution closer to the hearts of most Bosto-nians: **Fenway Park** ㉔. Built in 1912, this is the smallest and oldest stadium in the major leagues. Baseball legends like Ted Williams and Carl Yastrzemski played their entire careers at Fenway, which novelist John Updike called a "lyrical band-box." Red Sox fans, heartbroken since 1918, the last year Boston won a World Series, rejoiced when the team brought home the trophy in 2004.

**Kenmore Square** is two blocks away from Fenway Park. The inter-section is a major link for commuter lines and is usually choked with traf-fic and pedestrians. Most of the square is devoted to fast-food joints and convenience stores.

**Boston University** stretches along Commonwealth Avenue at the western end of the square and also spills into Bay State Road, a quiet strip of ivy-covered townhouses.

Kenmore Square's real claim to fame is the giant "**Citgo**" sign flash-ing from a nearby rooftop. It's Boston's unlikeliest landmark, but local devotees convinced the city to give the sign protected status.

## River vistas

Perhaps the best way to conclude a Back Bay tour is to be reminded that, after all, this is really the waterside neighborhood that its name implies. Head back to Massachusetts Avenue and walk north to the **Harvard Bridge** ㉕, also called the Massa-chusetts Avenue Bridge but referred to, more often than not, as the MIT Bridge because its northern end leads directly to that institute's cam-pus. This is where the Charles River is at its widest. Look eastward from here; the vista is magnificent.

The river is vibrant with sailing boats and shells, and the pathways along the **Esplanade** teem with strollers, joggers, cyclists, roller-bladers, and, in winter, cross-country skiers. This is Boston at its best. ❑

# RESTAURANTS & BARS

## Restaurants

### American

#### Abe & Louie's
793 Boylston St. Tel: 536-6300. Open: L & D daily. $$$$
www.abeandlouies.com
The place to tuck into a dozen chilled oysters, a corn-fed, Midwestern USDA prime porterhouse steak, or the two-pound lobster Savannah.

#### Azure
Lenox Hotel, 61 Exeter St. Tel: 933-4800. Open: B & D daily. $$$$
www.azureboston.com
The decor of this seven-time winner of the AAA Four Diamond Award is inspired by the rich blue hues of the ocean. The contemporary American menu, with an emphasis on fresh seafood, draws inspiration from French, Asian, Latin and Mediterranean flavors. Landlubbers will be delighted to spy offerings such as grilled rib eye and "humanely raised veal scaloppini."

#### B. Good
131 Dartmouth St., Tel: 424-5252. $
www.bgood.com
"Fast food" with a healthy twist served up cafeteria-style. The burgers, served with a huge selection of toppings and oven baked french fries, are a standout, along with numerous vegetarian options and a good selection of salads.

#### Boston Public Library
700 Boylston St., Tel: 385-5660. $
www.bpl.com
There are two restaurants on the first floor of the BPL: Novel, in the Italianate courtyard, serves an elaborate luncheon buffet with home-made soups, hot and cold entrées, and luscious desserts from 11am until 2pm. Mon–Fri, followed by tea from 2:30–4:30pm; Sebastian's Map Room, in the original 1895 map room, serves breakfast, lunch, and snacks Mon–Sat 9am–5pm.

#### The Café & Lobby Lounge
The Ritz-Carlton Boston, 15 Arlington St., Tel: 536-5700. Open: B, L & D daily. $$$
www.ritzcarlton.com
The café, with its wall of windows overlooking Newbury Street, is one of the nicest places in town to relax and enjoy gracious service and fine American fare. For a true taste of Ritz-Carlton elegance, however, opt for afternoon tea in the Lobby Lounge. Silver-tiered service includes baked scones, clotted cream, raspberries, cucumber sandwiches, and mini-pastries, and a harpist plays Wed–Sun.

#### Excelsior
The Heritage on the Green, 272 Boylston St; Tel: 426-7878; Open: D nightly. $$$$
www.excelsiorrestaurant.com
Boston's only all-glass elevator whisks patrons up through a three-story wine tower to renowned Boston restaurateur Lydia Shire's newest creation, a sleek, leather-and-wood dining room overlooking the Public Garden. The cuisine is contemporary American, the service is superb, and Lydia's famous lobster pizza is still on the menu. A pub menu is available on the second floor Crystal Bar.

#### Gardner Museum Café
Isabella Stuart Gardner Museum, 280 Fenway. Tel: 566-1088. Open: L Tues–Sun (until 4pm). $
www.gardnermuseum.org
What could be more elegant than a glass of wine, a poached shrimp cobb salad, and pumpkin bread pudding in this Venetian palazzo's courtyard café? Perhaps the roasted peach and arugula salad, chocolate mousse torte, and coffee in the outdoor garden. Museum admission not required.

#### Grill 23 & Bar
161 Berkeley St., Tel: 542-2255. Open: D nightly. $$$$
www.grill23.com
Since 1983 a premier destination for prime, dry-aged beef, fresh seafood, and fabulous desserts. Built in the former Salada Tea building, the independently-owned restaurant, with its mahogany panels, Corinthian columns, and marble floors, sets the standard for steakhouse dining.

#### Smith & Wollensky at Boston
Park Plaza Castle, 101 Columbus Ave. Tel: 423-1112. Open: L Mon–Fri, D nightly. $$$$
www.smithandwollensky.com/Boston.asp
The renowned steak chain has a branch in the renovated castle-like armory built in 1891 to headquarter the First Corp of Cadets. The specialties include dry-aged steaks, enormous lobsters, split pea soup, and creamed spinach.

#### Top of the Hub
Prudential Center, 800 Boylston St. Tel: 536-1775. Open: L Mon–Sat, D nightly, Sun brunch. $$$$
www.selectrestaurants.com/tophub
One of the most romantic spots in Boston is

### PRICE CATEGORIES

Prices for three-course dinner per person with a half-bottle of house wine, tax and tip:
$ = under $25
$$ = $25–$40
$$$ = $40–$50
$$$$ = more than $50

high atop the Pru on the 52nd floor. The ambiance is classic, with candlelight and linen; the food, New American, features dishes such as spicy lobster soup, macadamia nut crusted tuna, and braised lamb shank. For the undecided, $70 per person and $90 per person tasting menus are offered. There's a lively bar, live jazz, and dancing. Sunday brunch (fixed price $37) is a treat.

### Asian

#### Betty's Wok and Noodle Diner

250 Huntington Ave. Tel: 424-1950. Open: L daily; closed Sun in August. $
www.bettyswokandnoodle.com
Fusion at its finest, where Asian meets Cuban, and jasmine noodles and Cabana Juan-Tons can be washed down with sake or sangria. Surprisingly, it all comes together. So do the leather banquettes, abundant mirrors, and funky, laid-back ambiance.

#### Island Hopper

91 Massachusetts Ave. Tel: 266-1618. Open L & D. $
www.islandhopperrestaurant.com

#### PRICE CATEGORIES

Prices for three-course dinner per person with a half-bottle of house wine, tax and tip:
$ = under $25
$$ = $25–$40
$$$ = $40–$50
$$$$ = more than $50

Who can resist a restaurant whose mission is to fuse recipes of the Far East with American comfort food? We're not certain where the meatloaf and potatoes come in, but sure winners include calamari in a spicy red pepper chutney, and eggplant in black bean sauce.

### French

#### Aujourd'hui

Four Seasons Hotel, 200 Boyston St. Tel: 351-2071. Open: D nightly, Sun brunch. $$$$
www.fourseasons.com/boston
One of few restaurants in the state to be awarded the AAA Five Diamond Award, the restaurant overlooking the Public Garden recently completed a $2 million renovation to assure its rating as the special place for a night out. The menu accent is on modern French cuisine, with specialties such as Maine lobster with corn galette, and cured king salmon with artichoke. Jacket and tie are required.

#### Clio

Eliot Suite Hotel, 370A Commonwealth Ave. Tel: 536-7200. Open: B daily, D Tues–Sun. $$$$
www.cliorestaurant.com
At one of Boston's most sophisticated restaurants, award-winning chef/owner Ken Oringer prepares New French-New American dishes such as toasted bread soup with reblochon

cheese and black truffle; glazed kobe beef short ribs; and caramelized croissant bread pudding. More casual dining is offered at the sleek Umi Sashimi Bar.

#### L'Espalier

30 Gloucester St. Tel: 262-3023. Open: D Mon–Sat. $$$$
www.lespalier.com
The classic, housed in an opulent 1880 townhouse, has topped epicures' lists for more than 20 years. The New England-French cuisine includes appetizers such as a ragout of frogs' legs; among entrées is roasted Vermont rabbit with a confit of ugly ripe tomatoes with pan-fried artichokes, polenta, chestnut mushroom, and eggplant caviar. Among the special offerings: a Degustian of Caviar ($165); a cheese tasting ($25), and a Fantasy Tea Party ($23) Sat 2–3pm.

### Global Latin

#### Bomboa

35 Stanhope St. Tel: 236-6363. D Mon–Sat; bar open 5:30 PM–2AM. $$$
www.bomboa.com
The place to see and be seen in the Back Bay. The setting is minimalist, the bar rocking, and the food – a fusion of French and Nuevo Latino cuisines – is superb. There's often a wait between courses, so order one of those colorful, fruit-flavored drinks, sit back, and enjoy the

scene. A prix-fixe special ($30), which might include an appetizer of steamed mussels with black beans, Romesco Chicharron and lime, and an entrée of wild striped bass over gigande beans, is offered Sun– Thur, except holidays.

### Indian

#### Kashmir

279 Newbury St. Tel: 536-1695. Open: L & D daily. $$
www.kashmirindianrestaurant.com
A large selection of tandoori dishes, traditional favorites including samosas and curries, and selections that offer combination plates for one or two people. The weekday luncheon and weekend brunch buffets are a great bargain.

### Italian

#### Crazy Dough's

1124 Boylston St. Tel: 266-5656. Open: L & D daily. $
When you're in the mood for a slice of pizza topped with pesto tortellini, or even a pedestrian slice with pepperoni, this is the place. Add a salad, maybe a second slice topped with pastrami and sauerkraut, a glass of wine, and you've got a unique Boston treat.

#### Sorellina

1 Huntington Ave. Tel: 412-4600. Open: D nightly. $$$$
One of the city's newest and most gracious dining destinations offers high-concept Italian fare

prepared with a hint of the Asian. Look for treats such as kobe beef meatballs and homemade cannoli.

### Middle Eastern

**Cafe Jaffa**
48 Gloucester St. Tel: 536-0230. Open: L & D daily. $
Very little ambiance but huge servings of well-prepared treats such as tabouli, stuffed grape leaves, and falafel.

### Seafood

**Jasper White's Summer Shack**
50 Dalton St (also 149 Alewife Brook Parkway, Cambridge. Tel: 520-9500). Tel: 867-9955. Open L Mon–Fri, D nightly. Late night menu Fri & Sat. $$$
www.summershackrestaurant.com
If "food is love," as proclaimed on the restaurant's marquee, there's a whole lot of love to be had at the city's 4,000-piece raw bar, designed by the owner, a master chef and local food legend. Although the word "shack" is rather a stretch, few will quibble as they tuck into pan-roasted lobster, steamers, fresh seafood chowder, and, for land-lubbers, fried chicken and meatloaf.

**Legal Sea Foods**
Copley Place, 100 Huntington Avenue. Tel: 266-7775. (also at 26 Park Square, Tel. 426-4444; 5 Cambridge Center, Kendall

**RIGHT:** Legal Sea Foods is a reliable chain.

Square, Cambridge Tel: 864-3400; 255 State St, Tel: 227-3115; Prudential Center, Tel: 266-6800). Open: L & D daily. $$–$$$
A once-small Cambridge fish store has grown into a small industry, having earned a reputation as the best place around for flopping-fresh seafood. No reservations; waits can be long.

### Thai

**Bangkok City**
167 Massachusetts Ave. Tel: 266-8884. Open: L & D. $$
www.bkkcity.com
Classic Thai fare in an intimate, candlelit setting with both Western and traditional (low tabled) seating. Among the favorites: pad Thai and crispy duck. For those who like it hot, there's a special menu, and imported beer to quench the fire.

### Tea Rooms & Coffee Houses

**Tealuxe**
108 Newbury St; Tel: 927-0400 (also at 0 Brattle St., Harvard Square, Cambridge, Tel: 441-0077. Open: L & D daily. $
www.tealuxe.com
More than 100 loose teas from around the world, along with a creative selection of sandwiches and sweets (including an excellent shortcake). Seating, both in the main room and downstairs, is intimate.

### Bars

The **Renaissance Revival** piano bar at Julien, in the Langham Hotel (250 Franklin St) is an elegant spot for cocktails.
The martinis at **The**

**Lounge** in the Ritz-Carlton Hotel (15 Arlington St) are legendary, the setting overlooking the Public Garden is magnificent, and the ambiance is pure Boston Brahmin.
The view from the 52nd-floor bar at the **Top of the Hub Restaurant & Skywalk** (Prudential Center, 800 Boylston St.; Tel: 536-1775) will even make teetotalers giddy. There's live entertainment Tues–Sat. Locals and tourists share beers, burgers, and loud conversation at the gritty **Bukowski Tavern** (50 Dalton St., Tel: 437-9999; 1281 Cambridge St., Cambridge. Tel: 497-7077).
**Daisy Buchanan's** (240A Newbury St) has no cover, a great rock jukebox, and a rollicking thirty-something crowd.

# THE MUSEUM OF FINE ARTS

**Few museums in the world rival this one for the quality and scope of its decorative and fine art collections as well as its acclaimed "super shows"**

**ABOVE:** Edward Hopper's watercolor *Lighthouse and Buildings, Portland Head, Cape Elizabeth* (1927). The varied New England landscape is also captured in the museum's collection by other well-known American artists such as Winslow Homer.

One of the first museums in America, the Museum of Fine Arts opened in 1870 and in 1909 moved into the present building. Cyrus Edwin Dallin's bronze equestrian statue *Appeal to the Great Spirit* (left) was placed in the forecourt in 1913.

The highly cultured citizens of 19th-century Boston were keen collectors. Many were passionate about all things Asian, and their treasures in due course came to the MFA, forming the nucleus of an outstanding collection. Others traveled to Europe, and the museum acquired one of the foremost holdings outside Paris of Impressionist painting, in particular works by Monet, Pissaro, Sisley, Renoir and Manet. It has nearly 70 works by Jean-François Millet. The American art collection is one of the best in the US; the European and American decorative arts rooms display superb silver, porcelain, furniture and musical instruments. The Nubian and Egyptian collections are unrivaled in the world.

There is so much to see, the first-time visitor would be well advised either to pick out just one collection, or take a (free) tour that highlights the best from all the collections.

● *For contact details, see page 135.*

**RIGHT:** The museum is strong in decorative arts from pre-Civil War New England, such as this Paul Revere teapot, *circa* 1760–5.

**ABOVE:** The Japanese Garden, Tenshin-en, "The Garden of the Heart of Heaven" (beside the West Wing; open spring through early fall) is one of three gardens in which visitors may draw breath.

**BELOW:** The Impressionists: Renoir's *Dance at Bougival* (1883) shares wall space with equally important works by such European painters as Van Gogh, Degas, and Gauguin.

## TREASURES OF THE ANCIENT WORLD

For 40 years from 1905, Harvard University and the Museum of Fine Arts collaborated on an archeological excavation in Egypt, based at the Great Pyramids at Giza. From this, the museum acquired a world-famous collection of Egyptian treasures. Among many Old Kingdom sculptures is a beautiful statue of King Mycerinus *(above)*, who built the Third Pyramid at Giza, and his queen, dated to around 2548–2530BC.

Other treasures include gilded and painted mummy masks, and some remarkably well-preserved hieroglyphic inscriptions.

The Giza expedition's director, Dr George A. Reisner, also worked in the Sudan and brought home a dazzling collection of Nubian artifacts, the best in the world outside Khartoum. Particularly awe-inspiring is the exquisite gold jewelry, inlaid with enamel and precious stones, and the sculptures, varying in size from huge statues of Nubian kings to tiny shawabtis (funerary figurines).

**BELOW:** One of the many highlights of the excellent Asian Collection is this little 12th-century AD (Jin Dynasty) Chinese buddha, made of lacquered wood with painting and gilding.

**ABOVE:** *The Letter* by Mary Cassatt (1890). More formal exhibits are the portraits by colonial painters Gilbert Stuart and John Singleton Copley, and society portraitist John Singer Sargent.

# THE SOUTH END

This area, an ethnic cocktail of more than 40 nationalities, includes the massive Cathedral of the Holy Cross and some of Boston's most distinguished residential areas

'Thunderation, there is a man in shirt sleeves on those steps." That was the reaction of the Brahmin father of the title character in John P. Marquand's famous satire on upper-class Boston, *The Late George Apley*. Observing the construction of stately row houses in the recently developed district in the 1870s, Apley Senior concluded that here was another Back Bay, and promptly bought in. But he just as promptly left when he saw that already, the South End was taking a middle-class turn away from frock-coat propriety.

If Marquand's character could (with the immortality one supposes fictional entities possess) come back and see everything that has transpired in the South End since that famous decampment, he might wish he had made a long-term investment in the place – even if shirtsleeves, in the 21st century, would be the least of his sartorial worries. Perhaps no Boston neighborhood has gone on such a roller-coaster ride of respectability and real estate values, not to mention diversity of residents, as the South End.

The South End – not to be confused with South Boston – is that area adjacent to, and to the south of, the Back Bay. It is delineated by the Southwest Corridor, Berkeley Street and Harrison and Massachusetts avenues. This area, where landfill and building began in the 1830s, was originally called Shawmut Neck. By the middle of the 19th century its layout was very similar to that seen today, and by the 1870s the area was fully developed into a grid pattern with blocks of homogeneous red-brick three- and four-story stooped row houses. These lined short, often discontinuous, streets running perpendicular to the main thoroughfares. It has often been said that, if

Map on page 144

**LEFT:** on parade in the South End.
**BELOW:** garden in Union Street, South End.

*During the early part of the 20th century, many of the African-American owners of South End homes were porters working on the railroads' Pullman sleeping cars. Pullman porters were relatively well-paid by the standards of the black working class of that era, and ownership of a South End row house was a clear mark of upward mobility.*

**BELOW:**
the leafy residential
squares attract
professionals.

the Back Bay is French-inspired, the South End is English, with more park-centered squares and a rather more florid style of architecture.

Some of the new houses had mansard roofs. Indeed, the first such roof – now so much part of the Boston architectural scene – appeared in the South End in the free-standing Deacon House, which was acclaimed as "one of the wonders of the mid-century."

The South End enjoyed a fleeting decade of prosperity. But when its wealthier residents abandoned it for the new and fashionable Back Bay, it became home to the nouveaux riches (in shirtsleeves, no less), and then the working class and the latest immigrants. True, some Yankee stalwarts, such as Walbridge A. Field, who had been Chief Justice of Massachusetts, remained loyal and still resided in the South End at the turn of the 20th century. But by this time, many private homes had been turned

into rooming houses, and only seven of the 53 houses in elegant Union Park *(see page 146)* remained private. Desuetude engulfed the district.

## A phoenix and a polyglot

As recently as the 1950s, when the Massachusetts Turnpike cut a swath along the edge of the South End, the run-down rooming houses in its path were scarcely lamented; their owners were compensated as little as $5,000 for each building when they were taken by eminent domain and demolished. But in the late 1960s and early '70s, the old brick row structures began to appeal to "urban pioneers" who saw their intrinsic value and were willing to restore them – even at the end of the 1970s, it was still possible to buy an old rooming house for just $40,000.

New buyers with a taste for city life but without the means for Back Bay or Beacon Hill began the task of turning one South End block after

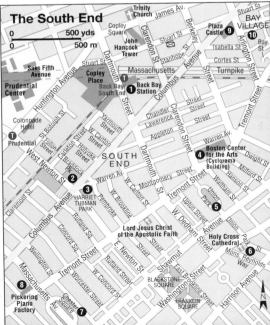

another back into single-family homes. Often, these gentrified sections rubbed shoulders with quarters that were still inhabited by poor black and Hispanic families; the trend towards gentrification produced some friction as values climbed and rental units became more scarce, but an impressive racial and ethnic diversity still characterizes much of the district. Today, more than 40 nationalities reside here, and there is a substantial gay community.

In the late 1980s the South End entered yet another phase of its evolution. As property values skyrocketed and the original pioneers of restoration saw their children grow up and move out, many of the row houses were again partitioned – this time, into attractive condominiums rather than seedy rooms for rent. It's possible, in this compact quarter, to encounter not only just about every type of Bostonian, but every type of Boston housing.

## Leafy little squares

Leave Copley Square and stroll south on Dartmouth Street for about 300 yards to **Back Bay Station ❶**. Facing the Station is the Southwest Corridor, a landscaped 50-yard wide park under which the railroad tracks run. This park, built in the 1980s, links the Back Bay and the South End: formerly, the railway track was a barrier that separated the two.

Enter the Southwest Corridor and immediately turn left onto Yarmouth Street and appreciate the attempts that have been made to retain the integrity of the South End. The right side of the street is lined with 19th-century red-brick row houses; the left side consists of modern, low-rent, red-brick apartments. The rounded bows, so characteristic of the older South End houses, are echoed in the new apartments by much more linear bays.

Return to the Southwest Corridor and, before turning into Braddock Park, three blocks beyond Yarmouth Street, make a brief diversion via Follon Street, on the right side of the park, into St Botolph Street. This street is named after the monk for whom England's Boston was named. **Braddock Park ❷** is typical – but the least known – of half a dozen leafy residential squares that pepper the South End.

These areas all have a long, narrow garden, enclosed by wrought-iron railings. Each red-brick, three- or four-story row house that lines the long axes of the square is entered by a steep stoop which often rises a full story to the second floor (in which case a door beneath the stairway enters directly into the lower first floor). All have a regular cornice line; some are topped by a mansard roof. Adding attraction is wrought-iron ornamentation in the form of balustrades and railings around small gardens and sometimes over windows and balconies.

Leave Braddock Park and turn right on Columbus Avenue, immediately reaching the sharp-angled

Map on page 144

*While a doctoral student at Boston University's School of Divinity, the Rev. Martin Luther King Jr. lived on St Botolph Street.*

**BELOW:** gentrification adds primary colors.

intersection of that street and Warren Avenue. Here stands the red-brick Concord Baptist Church, readily recognizable by its large octagonal clerestory. It was built in the 1870s, when many Baptist congregations moved to the South End, but most of its members now live in other parts of metropolitan Boston.

Tiny **Harriet Tubman Park** ❸, which stands in the lee of the church, remembers the "Moses of the South," a runaway slave who organized the "underground railway," a network of abolitionists who helped thousands of slaves escape to freedom. They built secret passageways in their homes and held huge parties to cover the flight of their transient guests who were en route to freedom in Canada. But many escaped slaves remained in Boston.

Continue on Warren Avenue for about 500 yards, turn left onto Clarendon Street, and enter an enclave known as Clarendon Park. Its streets carry the names – Appleton, Warren, Chandler, Lawrence – of prominent Beacon Hill residents. These streets are lined by attractive small versions of Beacon Hill houses, which were built, it has been suggested, to accommodate the servants of those whose names they bear.

## Cyclorama to arts center

A right turn from Warren onto Clarendon takes the visitor to the unusual **Cyclorama Building** ❹, recognizable by the kiosk, a salvaged lantern, which stands outside it. The Cyclorama was built in 1884 to house a gigantic circular painting (400 by 50 ft/122 by 15 metres) of the Battle of Gettysburg by Paul Philippoteaux. Subsequently, it was used for revivalist meetings and sporting events. It was here in 1907, when it was used as a garage, that Alfred Champion pioneered the spark plug. Since 1970 the building has been part of the Boston Center for the Arts, which has attracted some excellent restaurants to the neighborhood. The lively complex encompasses artists' studios, galleries and small experimental theaters.

Proceed southwest on Tremont Street for a couple of hundred yards and turn left into **Union Park** ❺, since 1859 the South End's most distinguished residential area. Facing one another and separated by a garden with two splashing fountains are rows of red-brick houses with swells (not the occupants but the bays that protrude from the facades), oriel windows and steep stoops.

## A great cathedral

Exit from Union Park, cross Shawmut Avenue and continue to Washington Street. Here is the imposing towering facade of the **Cathedral of the Holy Cross** ❻. This, one of the world's largest Gothic cathedrals, can seat 3,500 and accommodate double that number. The puddingstone exterior with granite and sandstone trim has an asymmetrical facade. (Even if the spires had been added, it would still be asymmetrical.) Since the

*The Lebanese poet, essayist, novelist and artist Khalil Gibran (1883–1931) came to Boston in 1885 with his parents and grew up in the South End.*

**BELOW:** the Cathedral of the Holy Cross.

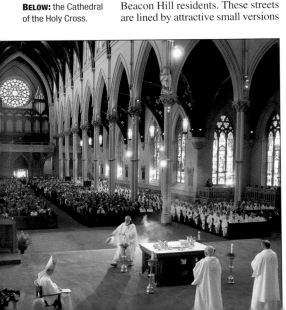

Map on page 144

Catholic population of Boston is no longer heavily concentrated in this area, the cathedral is now used largely on special occasions.

The exterior belies a truly Gothic interior, which has a vast clear space interrupted only by two rows of columns extending along the nave and supporting the central roof. Light enters through innumerable undistinguished stained-glass windows. The largest of these line the transept and tell the story of the exaltation of the cross by the Emperor Heraclitus and the miracle by which the cross was verified.

Until the 1980s the Washington Street "El," the elevated train line built in the early 20th century, passed close to the Cathedral's entrance. The noise was deafening, and it is claimed that the Yankees routed the line this way in order to disturb the Irish congregants.

## Elegant squares

Proceed southwest on Washington Street for three blocks. There, side by side, are Blackstone and Franklin squares, two geometrical, flat, grassy areas, each the size of four football fields and each with a splashing fountain as a centerpiece. Although not built until the 1860s, the squares had already been planned by Bulfinch at the start of that century.

Each square, on its south side, is backed by a stately building. One can readily believe that the elaborate French Second Empire edifice that graces Franklin Square was formerly one of the city's most elegant hotels, the St James, where General Grant once lodged when he was president. The building, which became familiar to many through the television series *St Elsewhere*, now serves as elderly housing. The Blackstone building, less flamboyant and more severe, consists of brownstone row houses with handsome pedimented formal windows and doors enclosed by pilasters.

Continue on Washington Street for half a dozen blocks. Turn right onto Massachusetts Avenue and enter **Chester Square ⓬**, which, until 40 years ago, was the most expansive – though faded – residential square in all Boston, and indeed could begin to be compared to the great London squares. Then Mass Ave was re-aligned. It now pierces the heart of the oval park which separates the two crescents of 70 opulent row houses.

Chester Square debouches into Tremont Street. A left turn immediately leads to the **Pickering Piano Factory ⓭**, which, when opened in 1850, was the largest building in the nation, other than the Capitol. It was saved from extinction by being converted into artists' studios and apartments. The dominating feature of this handsome six-story building is an octagonal tower.

A right, rather than a left, turn onto Tremont leads first to **Concord Square** and then to **Rutland Square**, two more handsome residential squares. Further down Tremont Street, on the right, rises the square-campanile red-brick Romanesque

*The St James, on Franklin Square, had a short life as a hotel. It opened in 1868 with more than 400 rooms but was taken over in 1882 by the New England Conservatory of Music.*

**BELOW:** a Holy Cross congregation at the installation of a new Archbishop of Boston.

Map on page 144

*The name Bay Village is a relatively modern one, conjured up by real-estate developers. Many of the painters, housewrights and cabinetmakers who created the grand homes on Beacon Hill built and lived in these much more modest homes, and a number of these houses have been sensitively renovated by people who can't quite afford a Beacon Hill property.*

**BELOW:**
the 19th century
lives on in Bay Village.

revival tower of the Church of the Lord Jesus Christ of the Apostolic Faith. It is now part of the very successful Villa Victoria Housing Project, most of whose inhabitants are Puerto Rican, and most of whose architecture is somewhat at odds with the rest of the South End.

If, at the Cyclorama, instead of continuing your explorations of the South End you had turned left onto Berkeley Street, proceeded for 400 yards and then turned right onto Columbus Avenue and proceeded a further 200 yards, you would have arrived at Bay Village, a tiny, delightful oasis that makes the South Slope of Beacon Hill look like a bustling metropolis.

(An alternative way to enter this haven is from the intersection of Columbus, Arlington and Stuart streets, which is dominated by a massive rusticated granite Italian Renaissance fortress whose hexagonal tower is a landmark. This building, now the **Plaza Castle** ❾, was once an armory; today, it's an annex of the nearby Park Plaza Hotel and houses Smith and Wollensky's restaurant.)

## Village in a city

**Bay Village** ❿, where Edgar Allan Poe once lived, has been described as Beacon Hill on mud-flats. It was developed in the 1820s when the Back Bay was still a tidal basin and a quarter of a century would elapse before the first buildings appeared in the South End. Today, the neighborhood, consisting of half a dozen short, gas-lit streets lined by uniform, almost toylike red-brick row houses, still has a 19th-century ambiance.

Enter the Village by **Piedmont Street**, which faces the Plaza Castle's Arlington Street facade. There's nothing special here, but at No. 52 stood the "Napoleon Club," reputed to have been America's first gay bar. It owes its location to the fact that Bay Village is near the city's Theater District and, during Prohibition, was filled with speakeasies.

A half-block down Piedmont is a plaque in the sidewalk commemorating one of Boston's – and America's – worst disasters. Here stood the Coconut Grove nightclub where on the evening of November 28, 1942, 492 people died when a fire spread throughout the building.

Turn right onto Church Street and, proceeding along it, wander into Winchester and Melrose streets before arriving at **Fayette Street**, the oldest street in the district. It is all quite lovely, with immaculate window-boxes filled with colorful blooms. Near the end of Fayette Street is **Bay Street**, Boston's shortest street; it contains just one house – the smallest house in Boston.

These streets and homes you admire were originally 12–18 ft (3.7–5.5 meters) lower. When Back Bay was filled in, Bay Village (then called the Church Street district) flooded and, in a mammoth undertaking, about 500 buildings were raised. From Fayette Street, turn onto Arlington Street and resume the hurly-burly of life in Boston. ❑

# RESTAURANTS & BARS

## Restaurants

### American

**Charlie's Sandwich Shoppe**
429 Columbus Ave. Tel: 536-7669. Open: B & L Mon–Sat. $
The landmark diner (since 1927) serves breakfast all day, terrific pancakes, and signature turkey hash. Cash only.

**Icarus**
3 Appleton St. Tel: 426-1790. Open: D nightly. $$$
www.icarusrestaurant.com
Original New American fare includes dishes such as polenta with braised exotic mushrooms and grilled shrimp with mango and jalapeno sorbet. Jazz pianist Friday nights.

**Quiet Man Pub**
11 W. Broadway. Tel: 269-9878. Open: L & D daily. $
An informal spot featuring solid comfort food, including the John Wayne Platter for two, with steak tips, chicken, sausage, ribs, rice pilaf, and salad. Cash only.

### PRICE CATEGORIES

Prices for three-course dinner per person with a half-bottle of house wine, tax and tip:
$ = under $25
$$ = $25–$40
$$$ = $40–$50
$$$$ = more than $50

**Tremont 647**
647 Tremont St. Tel: 266-4600. Open: D nightly; brunch Sat & Sun. $$$
www.tremont647.com
Dishes prepared with big, layered flavors include specialties such as pumpkin and ricotta ravioli, BBQ chicken pizza, and Too Stinky Cheeses. Pleasantly funky environment. Weekend pajama party brunches.

### Ethiopian

**Addis Red Sea**
544 Tremont St., Tel: 426-8727. Open: L Sat & Sun, D nightly. $–$$
www.addisredsea.com
Dishes include tantalizing vegetarian options, many eaten in the traditional method – scooped up with bread by hand. For a true sampling, choose one of the combination platters.

### French

**Hamersley's Bistro**
553 Tremont St. Tel: 423-2700. Open: D nightly. $$$$
www.hamersleysbistro.com
Simple, hearty fare in a comfortable, banquette-lined room. The house special is roast chicken with garlic, lemon and parsley, but the contemporary menu includes pan roasted lobster with leeks, roast chestnuts, and black truffles.

### Italian

**Giacomo's**
431 Columbus Ave. Tel: 536-5723 (also 355 Hanover St. Tel: 523-9026). Open: D nightly. $$
Small, busy, and worth the wait: terrific seafood and classic Italian dishes, including fine homemade pastas.

### Polish

**Cafe Polonia**
611 Dorchester Ave. Tel: 269-0110. Open: L, D daily, breakfast weekends only. $
Polka music and bread served with lard set the mood at this small, informal eatery whose specialties include stuffed cabbage, pierogis, kielbasa, and homemade desserts. Breakfasts (from 10am weekdays and 8am weekends) are also hefty.

### Seafood

**The Fish Pier Restaurant and Market**
667 E. Broadway. Tel: 269-2111. Open: L & D daily. $
No atmosphere, just great fish and chips (and squid and chips), seafood platters, and a good selection of meat and poultry entrées.

### Southern/Soul

**Bob the Chef's**
604 Columbus Ave. Tel: 536-6204. Open: L Sat only, Sun brunch, D Tues–Sun. $
www.bobthechefs.com
Since the late 1950s

the place to go for barbecue, sweet potato pie, macaroni and cheese, fried chicken, and pecan pie. Thur–Sun specialties include ham hocks, pig's feet and chitterlings. Cajun dishes include creole jambalaya. There's a popular Sunday jazz/gospel brunch buffet ($18.95), and live jazz Thur–Sat.

### Vietnamese

**Pho République**
1415 Washington St. Tel: 262-0005. Open: D nightly. $–$$
Hip, upscale spot with the ambiance of a Saigon brothel and decent ethnic cuisine. Serves dim sum and pho, the national noodle soup dish of Vietnam.

## Bars

Fans of the 1997 movie Good Will Hunting will want to make a pilgrimage to L Street Tavern (58 E. 8th St. Tel: 268-4335), the Southie bar hangout of Matt Damon, who played a mixed-up mathematics genius working at MIT and trying to survive in South Boston. Sister Sorel (645 Tremont St. Tel: 266-4600), shares its kitchen with Tremont 647, but also offers snacks and a more lounge-like setting.

# The Streetcar Suburbs

**U**rban historian Sam Bass Warner, Jr. coined the term "streetcar suburbs" for neighborhoods outside of Boston's core made easily accessible by late 19th-century advances in transportation. Some lie within the city limits; Brookline and Watertown are separate municipalities. Many of these areas were beautified as part of the great landscape architect Frederick Law Olmsted's "Emerald Necklace", a 6-mile (10-km) skein of green spaces that gave a growing city much-needed breathing room.

The Emerald Necklace begins at the Public Garden, extends along the Commonwealth Avenue Mall and continues through the Back Bay Fens *(see page 134)*, and ends at Franklin Park in Roxbury. If you're starting from the Back Bay, it's fairly easy to walk as far as the Fens or a bit beyond; to head farther, consider public transportation (call the MBTA for bus information, including details on reaching sites via bus from "T" stops mentioned below).

The marshy Fens begin at the intersection of Boylston Street and the Fenway, just west of Massachusetts Avenue. Beyond the Fenway loops into the Riverway, which soon becomes the Jamaicaway, passing on the right **Olmsted Park**. Just ahead lies **Jamaica Pond**, a small jewel ringed by tree-lined paths. Sailboats and rowboats can be rented at a half-timbered boathouse.

Follow the Jamaicaway to the Arborway and the entrance to Harvard University's 260-acre (105-hectare) **Arnold Arboretum** ("T" Orange Line Forest Hills stop), designed by Olmsted and Charles Sprague Sargent. Open during daylight hours throughout the year (tel: 617-524 1718), the Arboretum is home to many rare trees and shrubs, including 300-year-old bonsai trees and the world's largest collection of lilacs, in glorious bloom during Lilac Week each June.

**Franklin Park**, a couple of miles farther along the Arborway (the Forest Hills terminus of the "T" Orange Line is within a mile of the park's entrance) was intended to be the crown jewel of the Emerald Necklace. Years of neglect left the park a hostile wilderness, but recent efforts have returned it to something of its intended beauty.

The **Franklin Park Zoo** (Apr–Sept Mon–Fri 10am–5pm; 10am–6pm weekends; Oct–Mar 10am–4pm daily; tel: 617-541 5466) has been revived, and a handsome addition is the African Tropical Forest, a 3-acre (1.2-hectare) environmental building where more than 100 free-flying birds dart among gorillas, hippos and thousands of plants. Other attractions include the aviary (Birds' World), the Children's Zoo, and the 18-hole public golf course.

## Memories of the New Frontier

Accessible via the Red Line ("T" Red Line JFK/UMass stop, and shuttle bus) is the striking **John F. Kennedy Library** (9am–5pm daily; tel: 866-535 1960), designed by I.M. Pei and occupying a stunning location on Columbia Point. The Library contains the president's papers; public exhibits cover his life and the history of the US during his era. Personal items on display include JFK's desk and the coconut shell on which he carved a cry for help after his PT boat was sunk during World War II. A 30-minute film is part of the tour. The *Ventura*, the president's sailboat, sits behind the library.

Two miles (3 km) north of Columbia Point,

in South Boston's Thomas Park ("T" Red Line, Broadway stop) is **Dorchester Heights National Historical Site** (irregular hours), marking the spot where Washington's army placed cannon to force the British from Boston in 1776. A 215-ft (65-meter) white marble monument commemorates the victory.

## Brookline

Nestled by Boston's outlying neighborhoods to the north and south, **Brookline** by the 19th century was Boston's wealthiest suburban enclave. The heart of Brookline is Coolidge Corner, a stop on the "T" Green Line. (Note: If you're boarding the Green Line downtown or at Back Bay stops before Copley Square, make sure you're getting on the right train. The line splits into several different routes past Copley, before emerging from the tunnels and operating as a surface-level trolley service.)

A 10-minute walk northwest on Harvard Street leads to Beals Street; turn right to reach Number 83, the **John F. Kennedy National Historic Site** (May–Nov Wed–Sun 10am–4:30pm; tours to 3pm; tel: 617-566 7937), the 1917 birthplace of the president. His parents lived in this modest, two-story house from 1914 to 1921. Under the supervision of the late Rose Kennedy, the president's mother, the house was restored to its 1917 appearance.

A bit over a mile (1.6 km) south of Cleveland Circle, the Green Line terminus, is the **Olmsted National Historic Site** (43 Warren Street; grounds open Fri–Sun 10am–4:30pm; call for tour schedules; tel: 617-566 1689), where Frederick Law Olmsted had his office and home during and after the construction of the Emerald Necklace. Drawings, plans and papers are on display.

Another 1½ miles (2 km) beyond is the **Larz Anderson Museum** (Larz Anderson Park, 15 Newton Street; Tues–Sun 10am–5pm; tel: 617-522 6547). The Museum houses a superb collection of early automobiles and related exhibits in the carriage house of the former estate of diplomat Anderson. Across the road is The Country Club (scene of the 1999 Ryder Cup golf tour-

nament), founded in 1881 and the forerunner of hundreds of such establishments throughout the nation.

## Watertown

North of Brookline and the Boston neighborhood of Brighton, the suburb of **Watertown** lies on the other side of the Charles River. Just west of Watertown Square (bus from Harvard Square) is the **Armenian Library and Museum of America** (65 Main Street; tel: 617-926 2562; call for hours), containing a diverse collection of Armenian textiles, ceramics, coins and religious art.

If you're driving, continue on Route 20 for 2 miles (3 km), then turn left on Gore Street to reach **Gore Place** (52 Gore Street, Waltham: guided tours Apr–Nov, Thur–Mon; tel: 781-894 2798), a treasure trove of early 19th-century European and American decorative arts. This 22-room brick mansion was designed by Rebecca Payne Gore – one of the first women to design a great home – and built in 1805 by her husband, Christopher Gore. Mrs Gore enjoyed her comforts, and the home has some of America's first flush toilets and showers. A later innovation is the flying staircase that spirals three full flights upward. The grounds, which run down to the river, cover 40 acres (16 hectares). ❑

**LEFT:** hanging out at the Arnold Arboretum.
**RIGHT:** John F. Kennedy's birthplace, Brookline.

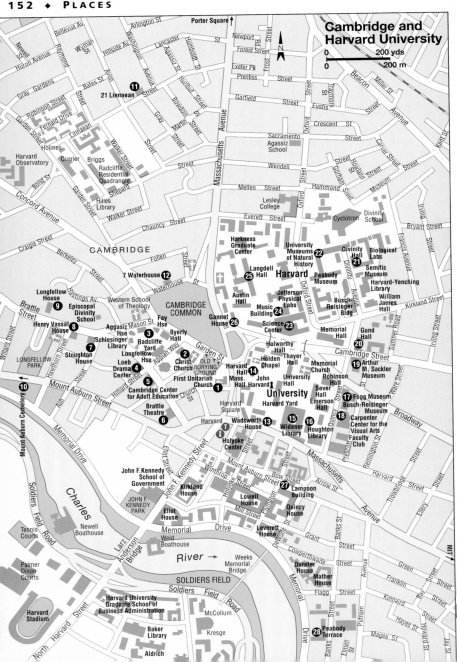

# Cambridge and Harvard University

# CAMBRIDGE

**Being as old as Boston, the former New Towne has its share of history and cemeteries. But these days it's a one-industry town – and the industry is education**

Cambridge, separated from Boston by the Charles River and linked to it by half a dozen bridges, was founded in the same year as Boston. Originally called New Towne, it was the Bay Colony's first capital. It is still a city in its own right: its population of more than 100,000 makes it one of the largest in Massachusetts. Each fall this number is swollen by about 25 percent by students attending Harvard University or Massachusetts Institute of Technology (MIT), both of which also attract many tourists to the city.

**Harvard Square**, the focal point of Cambridge for the visitor, can be reached readily from Boston on the Red line of the "T". The square and its immediate surroundings crowd with restaurants, cafés, and stores, including a notable concentration of bookshops. Newspapers from around the world are available at the large Out of Town News kiosk in the middle of the square.

A tall, abstract, granite sculpture entitled *Omphalos* stands next to the kiosk. If the sculpture had been commissioned by Harvard rather than by the Metropolitan Transport Authority, one would have cried hubris, knowing that it was the intent of the sculptor's patron to indicate that Cambridge and not Delphi was the navel of the world. In the square pierced and tattooed skateboarders mingle with undergraduates and tourists, and music fills the air as street musicians play at every corner. (There are more than four because the square is amorphous.)

## Colonial memories

Cambridge has a long and proud colonial history, quite apart from its university associations. Head north from the square on Massachusetts

Map on page 152

**BELOW:** outdoor chess in in Harvard Square.

*Memorials on
Cambridge Common
include a bronze
relief showing
George Washington
on horseback under
an elm tree, assuming
command. On the
reverse side is the
text of Washington's
orders given here on
July 4, 1775, the
Congressional docu-
ment that officially
melded the colonial
militias into a unified
Continental Army.*

**BELOW:**
Radcliffe Yard.

Avenue, leaving Harvard to the right, and immediately pass on the left the **First Unitarian Church ❶**. Adjacent is the Old Burying Ground, known as "God's Acre," in which Harvard's first eight presidents are interred. Several veterans of the Revolution, including two black soldiers, also lie here.

Bear left onto Garden Street where, on the left, is **Christ Church ❷** *(see panel below)*. Immediately across the road from Christ Church is a traffic island with a granite lectern topped by a bronze plaque honoring William Dawes, sent at the same time as Paul Revere to warn outlying villagers of the coming of the British. Footprints of his galloping horse are simulated in brass on the pavement.

To the north is **Cambridge Common**, a treasure trove of markers, memorials and monuments and a place inexorably associated with George Washington. It was here on July 4, 1775, that he took command of the Continental Army. Make for the flagpole and the cluster of three cannons, abandoned when the British left Boston on March 17, 1776 and placed about cobblestones on the west side of the Common.

## Education for women

Cross Garden Street and enter the old **Radcliffe Yard ❸**, where the renowned women's college began life in 1879. Until recent years, women who attended Harvard were required to apply to Radcliffe, but in 1999 Radcliffe College as such was fully integrated with Harvard, with the Radcliffe name retained by an Institute of Advanced Study within the university. To the right and left are Byerly Hall and Fay House. The latter, a Federal-style building from 1806, is the oldest structure in the Yard and once housed the entire college apart from student rooms.

Across the Yard is striking **Agassiz House** with its Ionic portico. Named after Radcliffe founder Elizabeth Cary Agassiz, it contains a 350-seat theater where Eugene O'Neill's first play opened and failed and where Jack Lemmon got his start. On either side are the Radcliffe Gymnasium and the Schlesinger

### Christ Church

**C**hrist Church is Cambridge's oldest house of worship (1761). Its simple design fulfilled the congregants' request to Peter Harrison, America's first noted architect (he also designed Boston's King's Chapel), for "no steeple, only a tower with a belfry." When most of the Tory congregation fled in 1774, the church was used as a barracks and the organ pipes were melted down for bullets. A bullet hole in the vestibule is said to be from the rifle of a Redcoat as he marched toward Lexington in the early hours of April 18, 1775. The church was reopened on New Year's Eve, 1775, when George and Martha Washington attended worship.

Library. The Murray Research Center, which studies the impact of social changes on lives, especially those of women, now occupies the first floor of the gymnasium. Upstairs is the Radcliffe Dance Center.

The **Schlesinger Library** has an outstanding collection of literature on the history of women in America and is the country's top research center devoted to women's studies. The library, open to the public, includes a Culinary Collection with more than 2,300 cookbooks. On the other side of the Yard is **Longfellow House**, a long red-brick neo-Georgian affair with paired entrances framed by pilasters. It houses the Graduate School of Education.

## Tory Row

Exit from Radcliffe Yard onto Brattle Street, once known as Tory Row because in the 18th century most of its houses were owned by loyalists. It was also called Church Row, because its residents both built and worshipped at Christ's Church.

A left turn and a 300-yard stroll through the hustle and bustle of commerce to Brattle Square might cast some doubt that this is the most prestigious street in Cambridge, famous for both history and architecture, but a right turn and a walk of about three-quarters of a mile (1.2 km) fully justifies these claims. Here, all the hubbub is gone and the leafy, tranquil street is lined by splendid large clapboard houses fronted by elegant porticoes, most from the 19th century but some dating to the 18th, each standing in its own spacious grounds. Many bear blue plaques commemorating the greats who have lived in them.

Stroll first to Brattle Square. En route, on the right stands Harvard's handsome, modern **Loeb Drama Center** ❹. Nearby, an outdoor café fronts No. 56, a simple two-story, hip-roofed, Federal-style building,

home to Longfellow's "village blacksmith." But don't search for the chestnut tree under which Longfellow met Dexter Pratt: it suffered the fate of Washington's elm and was chopped down in 1870 when Brattle Street was widened.

Farther along, at No. 42, stands the first of the famous mansions that line the length of the street. Aside from the projecting entrance this three-story gambrel-roofed clapboard house is true to its 1727 origins. It was built by the future Major General William Brattle, doctor, lawyer and minister, commander of all the militia of the province and one of the wealthiest men in Cambridge. He fled to England in 1774. The mansion is now the **Cambridge Center for Adult Education** ❺.

Next door is the **Brattle Theatre** ❻. Paul Robeson and T.S. Eliot trod the theater's boards, as did Jessica Tandy and Hume Cronyn, Hermione Gingold and Zero Mostel. Since 1953 it has been a movie revival house.

Return along Brattle Street past Radcliffe Yard. **Stoughton House** ❼,

Map on page 152

*Loeb Drama Center.*

**BELOW:** the parlor in the Longfellow House.

the dark building on the left at No. 90, was designed by H.H. Richardson of Boston's Trinity Church fame, and is renowned as one of the first and best examples of domestic American shingle style.

Next door at No. 94 stands the **Henry Vassal House** ❽, originally built in the 17th century; its eponymous owner gambled away his fortune. It was medical headquarters for the first American Army during the Revolution.

Across the road is the red puddingstone Episcopal Divinity School, whose faculty house (No. 101) with its curved central bay has the grace of an English Regency villa. And so to the **Longfellow House** ❾ at No. 105 (guided tours May–Oct, Wed–Sun; tel: 876 4491), a yellow clapboard building that is the most historic house on Tory Row. The Georgian mansion, started in 1759, originally stood amid 116 acres (47 hectares); it was one of seven Tory estates occupying the area between Brattle Square and Elmwood Avenue whose lands stretched down to the river. The house was abandoned by its owner, John Vassal Jr, in 1774, when

patriots made life difficult for loyalists in Cambridge, and it was George Washington's headquarters for nine months during the siege of Boston.

Longfellow first arrived here as a lodger in 1837. After receiving the house as a wedding gift from his father-in-law, he remained until 1882. Tragically, his young wife Fanny was fatally burned here in 1861. The gardens, old carriage house and the house are kept virtually as they were in Longfellow's time, with myriad memorabilia including a chair made from the "spreading chestnut tree."

Across the street is Longfellow Park, through which the poet would walk on his way to bathe in the river. The Mormon Center occupies the northeast corner of the park; the Friends Meeting House stands on the west side. Continue on Brattle Street, passing the large white-brick Holy Trinity Armenian Church with its strong eastern influence, and many distinguished homes. These include the houses (Nos. 113, 115) that Longfellow built for his two daughters, and the Hooper-Lee-Nichols House (No. 159), built in

*Henry Wadsworth Longfellow (1807–82) devoted his life to writing after he retired in 1854 from teaching at Harvard. His myth-creating poems include "The Village Blacksmith," "The Wreck of the Hesperus" and " The Song of Hiawatha." His best-known later work, "Tales of a Wayside Inn," was published in 1863.*

**BELOW:**
the Longfellow House on Brattle Street.

the 1680s and now owned by the Cambridge Historical Society (open to the public on occasion).

Then, across Kennedy Road (named after a Cambridge cookie manufacturer and not the President), there is No. 163, former home of Edwin Land, inventor of the Polaroid camera, and No. 165, built in 1870 by John Bartlett, the Cambridge bookseller responsible for *Bartlett's Familiar Quotations*.

Turn left onto short Elmwood Avenue and proceed to the end, to No. 33, a splendid three-story Georgian affair from 1767. It was used as a hospital for Americans during the Revolutionary War and has since been occupied by an illustrious line of owners. Today, it is owned by Harvard and occupied by its president.

## Mount Auburn Cemetery

Continue west along Mount Auburn Street for about 600 yards to the main entrance to **Mount Auburn Cemetery** ⑩. Consecrated in 1831, this is America's oldest and most beautiful garden cemetery, its grounds planted with a glorious collection of trees and shrubs. Among more than 70,000 people interred here are Charles Bulfinch, Oliver Wendell Holmes, Henry W. Longfellow and Mary Baker Eddy (whose tomb is rumored to contain a telephone with an unlisted number). In recent years novelist Bernard Malamud, inventor Edwin Land and engineer R. Buckminster Fuller have all been laid to rest here. Fuller's grave displays an image of his geodesic dome and the cryptic epitaph, "Call me trimtab" and lies near his relative, American 19th-century transcendentalist Margaret Fuller.

Although most tombs in this non-sectarian cemetery are modest, others are grand and the cemetery has been a showpiece of American funerary art for the past 150 years. A climb to the top of the George

Washington Tower located at the cemetery's center affords wonderful views of the landscape.

Return to Harvard Square either by walking or taking a bus along Mount Auburn Street.

Walking back toward Harvard Square on Brattle Street, take Craigie Street to Concord Avenue, turn left, then turn right on Bond Street to reach the old Radcliffe Residential Quadrangle, a pleasant affair of neo-Georgian buildings. The handsome, modern **Hilles Library**, in the southwest corner of the quadrangle, is much more than a library: it includes a movie theater and art gallery and is the site of the quadrennial Music-Listening Orgy during which hundreds of classical tapes are played from beginning to end without interruption.

Exit from the north of the quadrangle onto Linnaean Street. Turn right and, after 600 yards, you will reach **No. 21** ⑪, a simple white two-story structure that dates back to the second half of the 17th century; it is the oldest entire dwelling place in Cambridge.

Map on page 152

TIP

The Friends of the Mount Auburn Cemetery offers special walks and talks: 547-7105. A map of notable graves and memorials is available at the front gate of the cemetery, which is also one of New England's favorite spots for birdwatching, especially during the spring migration.

**BELOW:** memorial at Mount Auburn Cemetery.

**BELOW:**
students pay tribute
to the notoriously
inauthentic statue
of John Harvard.

Linnaean Street now intersects
with Massachusetts Avenue, which
in recent years has seen an increase
of exotic restaurants and boutiques,
many of which recall the atmosphere of Harvard Square in the
1960s and 1970s. From here it is a
stroll of three quarters of a mile
down the avenue to Harvard Square,
with Lesley College and Harvard
Law School on the left.

Walking down Massachusetts
Avenue, spare a glance on the north
side of the Cambridge Common for
the two-story, gray, clapboard house
at **No. 7 Waterhouse Street** ⑫. It
was here that Dr Benjamin Waterhouse lived and "cut the claws and
wings of smallpox" by introducing
into the US, in 1800, a vaccination
with "vaccine threads" that he had
received from Dr Edward Jenner.

### Harvard Yard

Begin an exploration of the heart of
Harvard by entering the gate to Har-
vard Yard that stands just south of
Harvard Square, on the right side of
Massachusetts Avenue. **Wadsworth
House** ⑬, the yellow clapboard

building to the right of this entrance,
was built in 1727 and was the home
of Harvard presidents until 1849. It
was George Washington's headquarters for a few nights when he
arrived in Cambridge. Today it
houses the Alumni Office and other
university offices.

The Yard is a delightful shady
oasis rather than the "unkempt
sheep-commons" that John Kirkland saw when he became president
of the college in 1810. Then it was
cluttered with a brewery and sundry
privies. Kirkland is responsible for
the trees, the footpaths and the tradition of care which still prevails.

In the center of the Yard is **University Hall**, an 1816 granite building
designed by Bulfinch. It now houses
university offices but originally had
dining rooms, classrooms, a chapel
and the president's office. Fortunately,
the architect anticipated the future,
and designed the rear of this building
to be almost as handsome as the front.
And it is this rear that is now the western side of the New Yard or Tercentenary Quadrangle.

The larger than life-sized bronze

### John Harvard

John Harvard, a butcher's son, was
born in London in 1607. Shortly
after he was married in 1637, he sold
the Queen's Head inn in Southwark
bequeathed to him by his mother and set
sail for the New World. Although he was
never formally ordained as a minister,
he served for a time as assistant pastor in the First Church of Charlestown.
But, within a year of his arriving in New
England, he died of tuberculosis. In his
will he left half of his £1,600 of inherited wealth, together with his library of
classical and theological literature, to a
school in New Towne, soon to be renamed Cambridge. The future of the
school was assured, and in 1639 it was
named Harvard College.

Map on page 152

**statue of John Harvard** which sits below the American flag in front of University Hall is often referred to as "the Statue of Three Lies." The statue is not of John Harvard but an idealized representation, modeled by an undergraduate in 1884, the year that the figure was sculpted by Daniel Chester French. The inscription on the base refers to John Harvard as the founder of Harvard College. He was not: he was the first major benefactor. The inscription also says that the College was founded in 1638, the year of the John Harvard bequest. It was not: the correct date of its founding is 1636.

To the west of University Hall, and facing each other, are Massachusetts and Harvard halls. The former, erected in 1720, is the oldest Harvard building still standing, and the College Clock, part of the original structure on the western gable, has been painted to resemble its 18th-century appearance. During the Revolutionary War, Continental Army soldiers were billeted here.

The north side of the Old Yard is occupied by four freshmen dormitories. To the west are the twin dormitories of Hollis and Stoughton. The former, Harvard's fourth oldest building (1763), was home, at different times, to President John Quincy Adams, Ralph Waldo Emerson, Henry Thoreau and Charles Bulfinch. During the war 600 Colonial troops were quartered here. The wooden pump outside Hollis is a 1936 replica of the Old College pump at which students would perform their ablutions.

**Harvard Hall** ⑭ (1766) is the third college building to stand on this site. Its predecessor was razed by a 1764 fire which was called "the greatest disaster in the history of the College," destroying as it did the largest library in the colonies, including John Harvard's books. One of the latter was saved because, on the night of the fire, an undergraduate had removed it from the library. Next day, realizing the treasure he possessed, he took the book to President Holyoke who thanked him graciously, accepted the volume and expelled the student for removing it without permission.

*Continental Army troops occupied Harvard Hall in 1775–76, removing 1,000 pounds (450 kg) of lead from the roof to make bullets. The hall's fine Georgian architecture was compromised in 1842 and 1872 by new extensions.*

**BELOW:**
Harvard in winter.

*The Houghton Library: noted for its incunabula.*

Standing between and slightly back from Hollis and Stoughton is **Holden Chapel** (1742), Harvard's third oldest building. The chapel, built in glorious high Georgian style, with its pediments decorated with the elaborate crest of the Holdens, was called "a solitary English daisy in a field of Yankee dandelions." Even though Harvard was founded as a ministerial school, Holden was its first chapel – more than a century after the college was founded. Later, it was the home of the Medical School; it now houses offices of choral groups.

At the north end of the Yard is the granite **Holworthy Hall** (1812). To the east is **Thayer Hall**, a stripling which first housed students in 1870.

Grander by far than the Old Yard is the Tercentenary Quadrangle or **New Yard**, which, on the first Monday of each June, is the scene of Commencement. This Yard is dominated on the south by the Widener Library's massive Corinthian colonnade standing atop a monumental flight of stairs and on the north by the soaring, delicate, white spire of

Memorial Church, which honors the Harvard dead in both world wars. The rear of University Hall is on the west side, and facing this is H.H. Richardson's **Sever Hall**, its entrance flanked by turreted towers and the entire building rich in decorative brickwork. Built in 1880, it has been called "a turning point in the course of American architecture."

**Widener Library** ⓯ is the third largest library in the US and the world's largest university library *(see panel below)*. Three interesting Cambridge dioramas (1677, 1755 and 1936) can be seen in the building, whose Widener Memorial Room, a glorious affair of wood paneling and stained-glass windows, contains Harry Widener's original private library, which includes a copy of the Gutenberg Bible and a first folio of Shakespeare. Some claim that John Singer Sargent's murals in the anteroom to the Memorial Room "are the worst works of public art ever done by a major American painter."

The adjacent **Houghton Library** ⓰ has a brilliant collection of incunabula and the libraries of,

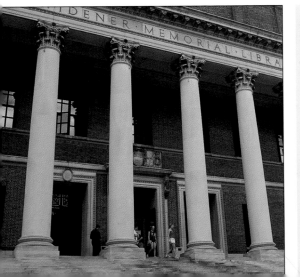

### The Widener Library

The library contains more than 3 million volumes stacked on 50 miles (80 km) of shelves. It is the administrative center of the university network of nearly 100 libraries which house 11 million books. The library is a memorial to Harry Elkins Widener, a young bibliophile who drowned in the sinking of the *Titanic*. As he had already indicated that he would donate his library to Harvard, his mother gave the university his books and the money to build space for millions more. Mrs Widener believed that if Harry had been able to swim he would have survived the sinking, and so, as part of her bequest, she stipulated that all Harvard students pass a swimming test before graduation.

Map
on page
152

among others, Cotton Mather and John Masefield. The John Harvard collection has the one book that survived the 1764 fire and "sisters" of many other works destroyed.

The rear of Sever Hall, just as handsome as the front, is flanked on the south by **Emerson Hall** and on the north by **Robinson Hall**. These three buildings, sometimes called Sever Quadrangle, form a unifying structure pulled together by the common use of brick and simple rectangular shapes. The first school of architecture and the first school of city planning in the nation were originally located in Robinson Hall, which has the names of celebrated architects, sculptors and philosophers embossed below the upper windows.

## An artistic hodgepodge

On exiting onto Quincy Street from Sever Quadrangle, you are directly opposite the **Fogg Art Museum ⑰** with the Arthur M. Sackler Museum to the north on Broadway and the striking **Carpenter Center for the Visual Arts ⑱** on the Fogg's right (museums open Mon–Sat 10am–5pm, Sun 1pm–5pm; tel: 495-9400).

The Fogg and the Sackler art museums contain collections any provincial city in the world would love to own. Their purpose is not to entertain the casual visitor but rather to educate students; however, they are open to the general public. Collectively, these three museums have nearly 150,000 objects; the great majority are bequests; others are on long-term loan, although occasional items have been purchased.

Outstanding in the Fogg are the Ingrès canvases, the best collection outside France; a splendid assembly of pre-Raphaelite works and French impressionists; 27 Rodins; a Fra Angelico crucifixion; 54 Blake watercolors; and a print room with 300 Durers and 200 Rembrandts. The Fogg also has an excellent col-

lection of Western sculpture featuring Romanesque works from the late 11th and 12th centuries and a dazzling display of silver.

The **Busch-Reisinger collection**, displayed in Werner Otto Hall, a large extension of the Fogg, is devoted to the art of Germany, with some works from other North European countries. Outstanding is the 20th-century Expressionism, with canvases by Klee and Kandinsky and Max Beckman's *Self Portrait in Tuxedo*. Here, too, are a wonderful Pear Tree by Gustav Klimt and the largest collection outside Germany of Bauhaus material, including the archives of Gropius and Feininger. Among older paintings the collection is especially strong in 15th- and 16th-century items from the German, Dutch and Flemish schools. Romanesque and Gothic ecclesiastical sculpture, 18th-century rococo porcelain, jewelry, textiles, furniture and metalcraft are also on display.

The Carpenter Center is the only Le Corbusier building in North America, and just one of a variety of modern buildings on the Harvard

*"William F. Buckley Jr. once remarked that he would rather be governed by the first 100 names in the Boston telephone book than by the faculty of Harvard University."*
*–Richard Nixon*
The Real War *(1980)*

**BELOW:**
the Fogg Museum.

**BELOW:** yesterday's body beautiful, from the Sackler Museum.

campus. When James Stirling, the English architect and designer of the Sackler Museum, was severely criticized for his design, he was reported to have exclaimed: "Doesn't fit in! I've simply created another animal for the Harvard architectural zoo!" And, indeed, the Carpenter is incongruous among the conventional buildings to its north and south and facing it from across the road – the Fogg Museum, the Faculty Club and the President's House respectively. (The President no longer lives in the house that bears his name: it is now used by the governing body.)

The most striking features of the Carpenter Center, which proper Bostonians have compared to two rhinos wrestling, is the sweeping ramp that leads from the street to the heart of the building on the upper level; the Corbusier trademarks of tall pillars, upon which the building appears to float; and concrete sun breakers that admit natural light while blocking out the sun's direct rays. Ascend the ramp and look down into the studios where artists are at work, or visit one of the many temporary exhibitions the Carpenter hosts. In the basement of the building is the **Harvard Film Archive** (tel: 495-4700), dedicated to screenings of both new and classic films.

Head north across Broadway to be immediately faced by Stirling's zebra, the **Arthur M. Sackler Museum ⓭**, a somewhat geometrical building with orange and gray striations. Its collection is devoted to works of Ancient, Oriental and Islamic art. Here is what many agree is the most magnificent collection in the world of Chinese jades. Also on show are Japanese prints and woodblocks, Persian miniatures and Greek and Roman statues and vases.

Farther north, across Cambridge Street, is the slender-pillared **Gund Hall ⓴**, home of the Graduate School of Design. The vast studio area, which is four levels high and devoid of interior walls, is a stunning highlight of this 1972 design by John Andrews. Gund is home to the Frances Loeb Library, specializing in books about architecture and urban design.

## Memorial Hall

Across from Gund is **Memorial Hall**, a huge Ruskinian Gothic pile which, like nearly all great Harvard buildings, has its admirers and detractors. Among the latter is G.E. Kidder Smith, the architectural historian: "Though not lovely [it] is loved, a mammoth ugly duckling, an almost fantastic statement of the taste of its time." Memorial Hall was built in the last quarter of the 19th century to honor Harvard men who fell in the Civil War. Its steep polychromatic roofs were at one time topped by a soaring clock-tower whose bells called and dismissed classes. The tower was destroyed in 1956 in a spectacular conflagration.

Although from the outside Memorial Hall looks like a cathedral and

although its interior is tripartite, one has only to enter to realize that this is a secular building. The vast, oblong nave was used for commencement exercises and as an undergraduate dining hall. (It has been restored to serve that purpose.) The transept, in ecclesiastical terms, is the memorial part of the hall, and its 17 stained-glass windows are a veritable museum of American stained glass: note especially the "Battle Window" by John la Farge. The apse, again in ecclesiastical terms, is Sanders Theater, which, with seating for 1,200, is still the largest auditorium in the university. It has superb acoustics and sightlines.

Continue northward, crossing Kirkland Street, and enter Divinity Avenue. At the corner stands a building that might look more at home in Bavaria than New England: the **Busch-Reisinger building**, which formerly housed the university's collection of German art. On the other side of Divinity Avenue stands the 15-story **William James Hall**, which houses the university's behavioral sciences department. It was designed by Minoru Yamasaki, whose work included the twin towers of New York's former World Trade Center.

Homogeneity is the keynote to the other buildings on 300-yard-long Divinity Avenue, even though they were built over a span of 150 years and serve a wide variety of purposes. To the right are the Harvard-Yenching Library and the Semitic Museum. The **Semitic Museum** lacks the mass appeal of its neighbors; its main attraction is a collection, changed from time to time, of old photographs of the Middle East.

**Divinity Hall** ㉑ is the last building on the east of Divinity Avenue, and is the oldest Harvard building (1816) devoted to its original purpose: a dormitory for divinity students. It was built because President Kirkland believed that divinity students should be isolated from the rest of the university in case they adopted "more of the spirit of the University than of their profession."

At the end of Divinity Avenue are the vast **Biological Laboratories**. Enter the courtyard of the last and observe Bessie and Victoria, two monster rhinos who guard the main entrance. The red and green doors are covered with intricate grillework representing the flora and fauna of sea, air and earth.

On the left of Divinity Avenue are the Sherman Fairchild Biochemical Laboratories and the University Museums. Closing the avenue at its northern end is the **Farlow Herbarium** *(see margin note)*, which has the world's largest orchid collection.

## Museums of Natural History

With their primary entrance on Oxford Street, the **University Museums of Natural History** ㉒ (admission times vary; tel: 495-3045) are comprised of the Peabody Museum of Archeology and Ethnology, the Museum of Comparative Zoology, the Geological and Mineralogical

*Harvard's Farlow Herbarium, founded by William G. Farlow who held the first chair of cryptogamic botany in the US in 1879, contains more than 1.3 million specimens of lichens, fungi, algae and bryophytes. It also has a large library of associated books and manuscripts.*

**BELOW:** today's bodies beautiful – Harvard football players.

**BELOW:** head to head at the Museums of Natural History.

Museum and the Botanical Museum.

Giant totem poles, Navaho blankets, Hopi ceramics and African masks are among the items on display at the **Peabody Museum of Archeology and Ethnology**, the oldest such museum in the Americas and the most important of the four museums. Outstanding is the Hall of the North American Indian, which focuses on the interaction between Native Americans and newcomers. Other, less exciting, galleries cover the Indians of Central and South America, especially the Maya. The Tozzer Library is said to contain America's best anthropological collection.

The natural history museums' top attraction is the Ware Collection of Glass Flowers in the **Botanical Museum**. These 847 remarkably accurate models are a unique collection made near Dresden, Germany, by the Blaschkas, father and son, between 1871 and 1936.

The **Museum of Comparative Zoology** contains such treasures as Kronosaurus, a 42-ft (13-meter) long fossil sea-serpent from Australia; the 25,000-year-old Harvard mastodon, a 65-million-year-old dinosaur egg, extinct birds such as the great auk and the passenger pigeon and hundreds of stuffed birds and animals.

Rounding off this quartet of museums is the **Geological and Mineralogical Museum**, which exhibits a large collection of gems, minerals, ores and over 500 meteorites.

Farther down Oxford Street, toward Memorial Hall, is the airy, light and white, glass and concrete **Science Center** ㉓, the largest of all Harvard buildings and winner of an American Institute of Architecture award for its architect, Josef Louis Sert, once dean of the university's Graduate School of Design. A mini-museum in the Science Center houses a permanent exhibition of fascinating early scientific instruments dating back to around 1550. The collection illustrates the history of instrumentation in a broad range of subjects, from astronomy to navigation, and includes telescopes and early computing devices.

Walk down Oxford Street on the eastern flank of the Science Center and turn left to see three entirely disparate buildings. To the west is the discrete, almost genteel, **Music Building** ㉔. Inscribed above its entrance are the words: "To Charm, To Strengthen and To Teach, These are the Three Great Chords of Might." To the east is the all-glass Gordon McKay Building of Engineering and Applied Physics and the Jefferson Physical Laboratory, a large red-brick Victorian monster. Here, in the 1920s, a laboratory was made available to Edwin Land, a bright young undergraduate who subsequently made his fortune by inventing the Polaroid camera.

## The Law School

Walk westward and immediately enter an irregular yard, part of which, deplorably, is a parking lot.

It is flanked by a variety of buildings. Prominent is the white limestone **Langdell Hall** ㉕, which is the heart of the Law School and delineates the west side of Law School Yard. Because of the great length of Langdell and the lack of depth of the yard, it is impossible to appreciate fully the glory of the grand ivy-covered portico of this building with its Ionic columns and pilasters. It houses part of the largest (1.4 million volumes) law library of any university in the world. The Law School, established in 1817 with six students, is now attended by 1,800 students: it is America's oldest law school.

The back of Langdell Hall, almost as handsome as the front, forms the east side of a small, leafy quadrangle, around which, and spreading out from, are the 17 other buildings that constitute the Law School. Much appreciated in winter are the tunnels that connect some of these to Langdell Hall.

The Law School's polychromatic **Austin Hall** is somewhat evocative of Sever Hall and bears the characteristic Richardson imprint. The portico of this Romanesque building, completed in 1881, has three glorious round arches supported by groups of intricate colonettes and a conical-capped asymmetrical turret.

To the west, and unsuccessfully attempting to close this pseudo-yard from Massachusetts Avenue, is the somewhat incongruous **Gannet House** ㉖ a small white Greek-Revival building from 1838, home of the renowned *Harvard Law Review*.

Facing Austin Hall is the back of Littauer Center, which is now occupied by the university's government and economic departments.

The north side of the Law School Yard is enclosed by the modern buildings of the **Harkness Graduate Center**, opened in 1949 and designed by Architects Collaborative under the leadership of Walter Gropius *(see panel, below left)*.

## Closer to the Charles

Harvard's domain also extends south of the Square. At the rear of a wide triangular area on Mount Auburn Street, the whimsical build-

> Map on page 152

*Law School students, when in Harvard Square, will gleefully point out to you the joke window above the Curious George bookstore advertising the law firm of Dewey, Cheetam and Howe (try saying it out loud).*

**BELOW:** Harvard Law School graduate wave inflatable sharks as a tribute to their chosen profession's reputation.

## Harkness Graduate Center

All the buildings are dormitories except the Harkness Commons; it contains dining areas, public rooms and some unusual works of art. The Commons faces a sunken quadrangle, frozen in winter for ice-skating. The central work of art and the focal point of the complex is the 27-ft (8.2-meter) high stainless steel *World Tree* by the sculptor Richard Lippold. Nicknamed "Jungle Gym," "Clothes Rack" and "Plumbing," it represents a primitive religious symbol common among such people as the Australian aborigines who believed that their sacred *World Tree* is the hub of the universe. To welcome the spring, law students have been known to indulge in strange fertility rites around this tree.

*Harvard has two celebrated student publications. The "Harvard Crimson" is the undergraduate newspaper, located at 14 Plympton Street, and the "Harvard Lampoon" is a humor magazine, housed in castle-like offices on Mount Auburn Street built on land donated by William Randolph Hearst, once its business manager.*

**BELOW:**
a class at Harvard Business School.

ing with a gaudy door and topped by an ibis is the headquarters of the ***Lampoon*** **㉗**, Harvard's famous humor magazine. To the left of this once stretched Harvard's Gold Coast, so-called because of the opulent lifestyle of the students who lived in these buildings, which were, at the start of the 20th century, luxurious private apartments.

Also on Mount Auburn Street, next to Lowell House, note a red-brick building with a six-pillared entry. This is the Fly Club, one of eight once snooty Harvard "final clubs," which have shed much of their exclusivity in recent years. Theodore and Franklin Roosevelt were both members here, presumably because even they couldn't pass muster at the lordliest Harvard club of all, the Porcellian.

Walk south on John F. Kennedy Street for 600 yards to the river. The first half of this street is occupied by stores and restaurants while the right side of the lower half is occupied by the **John F. Kennedy School of Government**, which, like most of Harvard, just grows and grows. A small attractive public park lies between this school and the river.

On the left side of John F. Kennedy Street are **Kirkland** and then **Eliot**, two of Harvard's seven original neo-Georgian residential houses, distinguished by their graceful cupolas, enclosed courtyards and mellow red-brick walls. The houses, together with newer, more modern fellows, stretch to the left along the river, ending in the contemporary **Peabody Terrace** **㉘**, a 21-floor, three-towered complex for married students; the building came from the drawing board of Josef Luis Sert.

Across the Larz Anderson Bridge sprawls, on the left, the **Business School** campus and, on the right, Harvard's vast Elysian playing fields, which are both in Brighton, a suburb of Boston. (The boathouse on the left of the bridge is used by women's crews while that on the right is used by Harvard men.) The Business School is a sizeable village of relatively modest neo-Georgian buildings which display a consistent rhythm of green doors, white window frames and red-brick walls. Worth seeking out is the **Class of 1953 Chapel** designed by Moshe Safdie. From the exterior it may look a bit like a greenish oil tank; however, once past the tall weighty doors, one finds an oasis for quiet contemplation complete with a small Zen garden stocked with Japanese goldfish.

Back in Harvard Square, exit to the southeast on Massachusetts Avenue. On several blocks leading to Sullivan Square, and continuing beyond, there are more stores and restaurants similar to those found around Harvard Square.

About a quarter-mile farther, immediately before Central Square, stands the imposing Romanesque **Cambridge City Hall** with its campanile. The large rusticated building with cupolated tower facing the

Town Hall is an office building. In and around Central Square, are several inexpensive ethnic (especially Indian) restaurants.

## The Massachusetts Institute of Technology

Half a mile beyond Central Square, you reach the first MIT buildings. A thoroughly unprepossessing structure on the left houses the **MIT Museum**  (265 Mass Ave; Tues–Fri 10am–5pm, Sat–Sun 12pm–5pm; tel: 253-4444) founded in 1971 and containing treasures that have made MIT a leader in computer, electronic and nuclear technologies.

Two other MIT museums are open to the public. In the **Hart Nautical Museum** (55 Mass Ave; daily except Sat 9am–8pm; weekends noon–5pm; tel: 253-4444) are model craft ranging from Donald McKay's great Yankee clipper *Flying Cloud* to modern guided missile warships by way of America's Cup defenders. Temporary exhibits of outstanding contemporary art are featured in the **List Visual Arts Center** in the Wiesner Building (20 Ames St; Tues–Thur 12pm–6pm, Fri noon–8pm; weekends 12pm–6pm; tel: 253-4444) at the eastern end of the campus.

Continue from the MIT Museum along Massachusetts Avenue and cross the railroad to reach the main campus. The west campus, on the right, is devoted to the students' social life; the larger east campus, to the left, is the workplace of MIT.

**Kresge Auditorium** and the Chapel are two outstanding buildings designed by a Finnish architect, Eero Saarinen. The former, completed in 1953, is an enormous tent-like structure rising out of a circular brick terrace; its roof appears to be supported at only three points by delicate metal rods, and it is enclosed by thin-mullioned curtains of glass. It is very much an outward-looking building. The oak-paneled

**Maps: on page 152, 167**

*Cambridge City Hall.*

**BELOW:** the Stata Center for Computer Information and Intelligence Sciences at MIT.

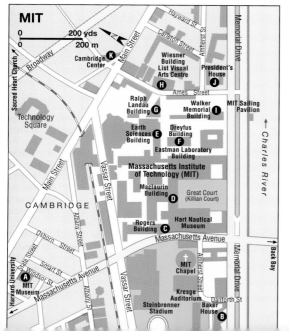

*A large Henry Moore sculpture adorns Great Court. Until the 1950s MIT did not acquire works of art, but it now has an active Council for the Arts and major pieces of sculpture by, among others, Picasso, Nevelson, Lipschitz and Calder dot the campus.*

**BELOW:** the Maclaurin Building at MIT.

auditorium seats 1,238 and a small theater accommodates 200.

The much smaller non-denominational chapel, a windowless, brick cylinder set in a moat and adorned with a sculptural bell tower, is inward-looking. Light reflected from the moat illuminates the interior, where a delicate bronze-toned screen hangs behind the white marble altar block. Slightly farther west is **Baker House B**, an undulating dormitory designed by the Finnish architect Alvar Aalto so that all its rooms have a view of the river.

Back on Massachusetts Avenue is the imposing domed neoclassical facade of the **Rogers Building C**, completed in 1937 and named after William Barton Rogers, who founded MIT in 1861. Its steep stairway and four pairs of Ionic columns provide the main entrance to the teaching buildings of the School of Architecture and Planning and leads to an extensive system of tunnels claimed to be the third largest in the world. These link many of the east campus buildings.

Rather than entering here, con-

tinue on Massachusetts Avenue for a further couple of hundred yards to the Charles River. Turn left onto Memorial Drive and immediately on the left is the aptly named Great Court (also called Killian Court) in front of the monumental **Maclaurin Building D** with its Pantheon-like dome and broad Ionic portico. (Richard C. Maclaurin, a Scot, was the president of MIT who moved the institute from Boston to Cambridge.) Inscribed on the buildings enclosing the court are the names of great scientists, including Darwin and da Vinci, Faraday and Franklin and two MIT benefactors, DuPont and Lowell.

Farther eastward is McDermott Court, dominated by the **Earth Sciences Building E**, the tallest structure on campus and readily recognized by the large white sphere on its roof. In front of it stands Alexander Calder's *Big Sail*, a giant freeform metal sculpture. The Earth Sciences Building is just one of four on campus designed by I.M. Pei, a Harvard graduate who also studied at MIT. The others are the **Dreyfus Building F** and the **Ralph Landau Building G**, which flank Earth Sciences, and, somewhat farther east, the **Wiesner Building H**.

Farther along Memorial Drive it is back to neoclassicism with the **Walker Memorial Building I**, which is used for a variety of purposes. Facing this is the MIT Sailing Pavilion. And then, still on Memorial Drive, is the austere, limestone, ivy-covered **President's House J**.

Main Street and Kendall Square, to the east of Wiesner, are today tree-bordered areas lined by handsome, soaring buildings, most of which are of red brick. A few years ago they were a desolation. Visit the landscaped garden atop the parking lot in the heart of the **Cambridge Center K**, a modern hotel, laboratory and office complex. Farther west, across the rail tracks, is more of the same in

**Technology Square**, an urban redevelopment project in which MIT joined with the city to clear away old factories and tenements.

The name Polaroid on some of these buildings reflects the birth of the instant camera in Cambridge. Polaroid's rival, Eastman Kodak, is well represented on the MIT campus with the Eastman Laboratory Building and Eastman Court. George Eastman left much of his not inconsiderable estate to MIT.

## East Cambridge

Proceed north from Technology Square for about a half-mile on Fulkerson Street. Turn right onto Otis Street where, on the right, stands the **Sacred Heart Church**, a Victorian Gothic edifice in blue trimmed with granite and built between 1874 and 1883 to serve East Cambridge's ever-increasing number of Irish immigrants.

A large, terra cotta and brick building 300 yards farther along Otis Street now houses the elderly and stands on the site of Fort Putnam. It was from here, the highest point of East Cambridge, that in March 1776 the Patriots bombarded the British during the final days of the siege of Boston.

Continue along Otis Street, lined with trim, wooden Greek Revival houses representative of the decorous vernacular architecture of 1820–70, until the corner of Third Street. Here stands the simple, Federal-style **Holy Cross Polish Church** sans cupola. Originally built for a Unitarian congregation in 1827, this is the oldest church in East Cambridge. It testifies to the many Polish who, together with Portuguese, Italian and Lithuanians, arrived in East Cambridge following the Civil War. They joined, in the city's factories, the Irish and Germans who had begun to arrive half a century earlier. The handsome

19th-century red-brick apartments on the same side of Third Street led to the sobriquet Quality Street.

The red-brick building across the road with Georgian cupola and modest Italianate campanile is **Bulfinch Place** , a courthouse brilliantly rehabilitated by Graham Gund into offices and the Cambridge Center for the Performing Arts. The original structure, built to Bulfinch's plans in 1812, was poorly constructed and in 1848 was redesigned as a courthouse by Ammi Young.

North of Bulfinch Court is the monumental red-brick 19th-century **Middlesex Country Registry** with four brick porticoes. On the Second Street side are some superb wrought-iron lantern-holders.

In the early part of the 20th century Cambridge was the third most important manufacturing city in New England, but industry has been replaced by commerce. Walk a few blocks down First Street to reach the **Cambridgeside Galleria**, an upscale shopping mall. It stands alongside a circular basin in the center of which is a soaring fountain whose

*The proud eagle that stands in Bulfinch Place's central courtyard formerly crowned the main Boston Post Office. A stele at the northeast corner of this block marks where 800 British Redcoats landed on April 19, 1775, to begin their march on Lexington and Concord.*

**BELOW:** graduating at MIT.

Maps: pages 167, 170

Map below

*Studying the Sun at the Museum of Science.*

waters join the 200-yard long **Lechmere Canal**, which enters the Charles River. River-boat excursions leave from the basin. East Cambridge (Lechmere stop) can be reached on the Green line of the "T".

## Museum of Science

Perched on the Charles River Dam (Monsignor O'Brien Highway, just across the Lechmere Canal from the Galleria Mall) is the **Museum of Science** (Sat–Thur 9am–5pm, Fri 9am–9pm; July–Labor Day Sat–Thur 9am–9pm; tel: 723-2500). The museum began life in 1830 as the Boston Society of Natural History, and moved here in 1951.

Before entering, observe the garden bordered by rock samples, some quite beautiful, from throughout the world. These include pieces from the Giant's Causeway in Northern Ireland, the Rock of Gibraltar and Mont Blanc. The museum, a hands-on affair, contains hundreds of exhibits in six major fields: astronomy, computing, energy, anthropology, industry and nature. Visitors can determine their weight on the moon, listen to a transparent talking woman, see bolts of lightning created indoors, and watch chickens hatching. Computing exhibits include the Virtual Fish Tank, a computer-simulated model, and the Best Software for Kids Gallery. The 20-ft-high (6-meter) model of a Tyrannosaurus Rex is a big draw.

The adjacent **Hayden Planetarium's** projector and multi-image system offer excellent programs on astronomy, plus laser light shows.

Those prone to motion sickness should skip the museum's **Mugar Omni Theater**, where wrap-around state-of-the-art movies are projected onto a 76-ft (23-meter) high domed screen, with sound blasting from 84 speakers; but for the strong of stomach it's well worth a visit. There are late shows at weekends. ❑

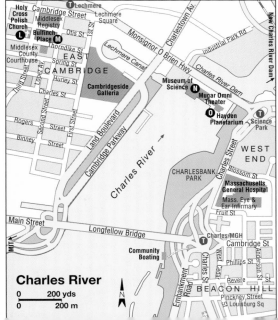

**Charles River**

0 — 200 yds
0 — 200 m

# The Education Industry

Boston has been firmly linked to learning ever since William Blackstone, the first white settler, lugged 200 books with him to the cabin where he lived alone on what is now Boston Common. Today there are 60 college and universities in Boston and its surrounding communities, adding some 250,000 students to the region's population. Some notable educational institutions:

● **Harvard University** is the oldest and richest university in the US. It has nearly 40 Nobel laureates on its faculty, 18,000 students and 23,000 faculty and staff.

● **Massachusetts Institute of Technology**, has 10,000 students, more than half of whom are enrolled in graduate programs.

● **Boston University** has more than 30,000 full- and part-time students, and more international students than any other US university or college. Alexander Graham Bell taught here while he was developing the telephone. BU has 17 schools, including communications, medicine, law, theology and dentistry.

● **Boston College**, one of 28 Jesuit colleges in the US, is the nation's largest Catholic university with an enrollment of nearly 15,000. A university in all but name, it has 11 schools, colleges and institutes, and a satellite law school campus in Newton.

● **Northeastern University**, with 26,000 students, has nine undergraduate and 10 graduate and professional schools. The best known are in law and criminal justice.

● **Emerson College** is the only private four-year college in the US devoted exclusively to the study of communication and the performing arts at the undergraduate and graduate level. Alumni include Jay Leno, Henry Winkler, Spalding Gray, and Dennis Leary.

● **Suffolk University**, also downtown, was founded to serve students otherwise denied access to college because of income, religion or class; its fees are about half those of competing schools.

● **Tufts University**, about 5 miles (8 km) north of Boston in Medford, has an enrollment of about 5,000 undergraduate students. P.T. Barnum of Barnum & Bailey's Circus was one of its founders.

● **Wellesley College**, about 13 miles (21 km) west of Boston, has remained women-only, with 2,300 students. Its pastoral 500-acre (200-hectare) campus is one of the finest in America, with its own lake, a nine-hole golf course and 24 tennis courts.

● **Babson College**, also in Wellesley, has one of the top MBA programs in North America and Europe; 2,000 of its students are in the graduate school, and most of the 1,500 undergraduates plan careers in business.

● **Brandeis University**, in the western suburb of Waltham, is known for its Gordon Public Policy Center, and its Judaic studies program is the largest outside Israel.

● **Simmons College**, in Fenway, has four graduate schools, including the world's only graduate business school for women.

● **New England Conservatory**, with just over 800 graduate and undergraduate students, stages 600 free concerts a year.

● **Berklee College of Music** has become the world's largest independent music college, and has a focus on contemporary music.

● **University of Massachusetts**, across town on Dorchester Bay, has about 12,000 students, all commuters and many working full-time to subsidize their educations. ❏

**RIGHT:** in the science lab at Boston College.

# RESTAURANTS & BARS

## Restaurants

### American

#### Bambara
25 Edwin H. Land Boulevard; Tel: 617-868 4444. Open: B Mon-Fri, L & D daily. $$–$$$
Located in the boutique Hotel Marlowe near the Charles River and attracting a clientele from the high-tech businesses surrounding MIT, this sleek brasserie offers a bar menu, inventive cocktails (a basil margarita?), and "modern American comfort food," including roasted pork loin, braised lamb shank, and chocolate bread pudding. The outdoor patio can get noisy at rush hour.

#### Flora
190 Massachusetts Avenue, Arlington; Tel: 781-641 1664. Open: D nightly except Mon. $$$$
www.florarestaurant.com
Just over the line in Arlington, this chic spot has taken up residence in a rehabbed 1920s bank. Entrées include maple-brined pork loin with mango ginger sauce or baked salmon roulade with deviled crab and a wild rice pancake. The wine and beer list – including Belgian Trappist beers – is carefully synched with the menu.

#### Harvest
44 Brattle St. Tel: 868-2255. Open: L & D daily, Sun brunch. $$$–$$$$
www.the-harvest.com
A Harvard Square institution, specializing in American cuisine, with a good assortment of grilled fish and meats, an open kitchen, and a sleek bar. The three-course Sunday brunch ($33) includes treats such as salmon carpaccio, and a Maine lobster and bacon frittata; and the delightful shaded garden terrace stays open well into the fall (there are outdoor heaters).

#### Mr. & Mrs. Bartley's Burger Cottage
1246 Massachusetts Ave. Tel: 465-6559. Open: L, D Mon–Sat. $
www.mrbartleys.com
The premier place for burgers in Harvard Square since 1961. Traditionalists will order a side of onion rings, and a frappé or lime rickey to wash it all down.

#### 1369 Coffee House
1369 Cambridge St. Tel: 576-1369 (also 757 Massachusetts Avenue. Tel: 576-4600). Open: light breakfast, L & D daily. $
Described as the anti-Starbucks, the light fare – soups, salads, sandwiches, and baked goods – is quite good, and the laid-back atmosphere reminiscent of Cambridge in the 1960s.

### BBQ

#### Brother Jimmy's BBQ
96 Winthrop St. Tel: 547-7427. Open: L daily except Mon & Tues in winter, D daily. $$–$$$
www.brotherjimmys.com
"Put some South in Yo' Mouth" at this New York-based chain which specializes in Blues, St. Louis-style ribs and a large menu of Southern-style treats. Sunday night the joint is packed with students who come for the all-you-can-eat ribs and all-you-can-drink drafts ($22.95, with a two-hour maximum stay permitted).

### Asian

#### All Asia
334 Massachusetts Ave. Tel: 497-1544. Open: D nightly. $
A continental gastronomic tour, including soups from Thailand, fish from Indonesia, satés from Malaysia, and more-familiar standard Chinese dishes, all served in somewhat unprepossessing surroundings.

#### Elephant Walk
2067 Massachusetts Ave. Tel: 492-6900 (also 900 Beacon St. Tel: 247-1500). Open: L Mon–Fri, D nightly. $$–$$$
www.elephantwalk.com
The owners grew up in Cambodia when it was a French Protectorate, and since 1991 have been serving classic French cuisine as well as traditional street dishes and royal Khmer specialties. Three- and four-course tasting menus are offered Sun–Thur ($19.95 and $29.95), and there are a large number of vegetarian choices as well as a celiac (gluten-free) menu.

#### Mary Chung
464 Massachusetts Ave. Tel: 864-1991. Open: L & D daily. $
Those who like their Chinese food hot are happy to cool their heels waiting for a table at this extremely plain and very popular Central Square eatery. Dim sum weekend brunch.

### Ethiopian

#### Asmara
739 Massachusetts Ave. Tel: 864-7447. Open: L & D daily. $$
A variety of traditional spicy dishes are the specialty at this friendly and informal family-owned spot in Central Square.

### Indian

#### Bombay Club
57 JFK St. Tel: 661-8100. $$
www.bombayclub.com
Mildly spicy cuisine in an elegantly-decorated, second floor dining room overlooking Harvard Square. Spices are all freshly ground, yogurts

and cheeses are made from scratch, and the 10-course weekday luncheon and weekend brunch buffets are among the best values in town. For a special occasion, the Maharaja Dinner, served Tues–Thur ($60) concludes with a demonstration of Mehendi (henna body painting), and audience participation is welcome.

### Italian

**Pinocchio's**
74 Winthrop St. Tel: 876-4897. Open: L & D daily. $
The most popular spot in town for a slice or a whole pizza, although folks also queue up for the cheeseburger subs. Seating is limited.

### Korean

**Koreana**
154 Prospect St. Tel: 576-8661. Open: L & D daily. $–$$
www.koreanaboston.com
Grills are built right into the tables at this Korean-style barbecue. Customers can cook up dishes like Galbi (prime beef ribs with traditional sauces) or leave the cooking in the capable hands of the chefs. There's an excellent sushi bar.

### Mexican

**Picante Mexican Grill**
735 Massachusetts Ave. Tel: 576-6394 (also, 217 Elm St., Somerville. Tel: 628-6394). Open: L, D and weekend brunch. $
www.picantemex.com
Very informal atmosphere and very good Cal-Mex dishes, all prepared without lard. The homemade soups are particularly satisfying, and weekend brunch is an enduringly popular affair.

### Portuguese

**Atasca**
279 Broadway, Tel: 354-4355; 50 Hampshire St., Tel: 621-6991. Open: L & D daily. $$
www.atasca.com
Portugal meets Brazil at this old-world restaurant designed to satisfy new-world tastes. Many of the dishes are available in either small or large plates, and include treats such as sautéed squid with garlic, spicy poached mussels; and baked dry salt cod with caramelized onions, roast peppers and home fries.

### Seafood

**East Coast Grill & Raw Bar**
1271 Cambridge St. Tel: 491-6568. Open D, Sun. brunch. $–$$$
www.eastcoastgrill.com
Here's an ideal find – a restaurant whose menu includes both a raw bar platter and oak-smoked pit BBQ. To pile on the perfection, Sunday brunch includes a "Make Your Own Bloody Mary Bar". This seafood restaurant, which still honors its BBQ roots, excels at both. Park in the Nissan lot across the street ($5).

### Bars

Moroccan snacks, great drinks and cozy divans make the **Enormous Room** (567 Massachusetts Ave., Tel: 491-5550), upstairs from Central Kitchen, one of the happening places in Central Square.
Cambridge's beautiful people enjoy the ambiance of the swank **West Side Lounge** (1680 Massachusetts Ave. Tel: 441-5566).
Stop in at **Charlie's** (10 Eliot St.; Tel: 492-9646), upstairs from Charlie's Kitchen, for a late-night brew and to catch a glimpse of the pre-yuppified Harvard Square.
For a bit of off-the-beaten path nightlife, head over to Davis Square in nearby Somerville, home to Tufts University and two great venues for live music: **Johnny D's Uptown Restaurant & Music Club** (17 Holland Street, Tel: 776-2004), featuring everything from Zydeco to pop nightly; and **Orleans** (65 Holland Street, Tel: 591-2100), where the accent is mainly on jazz.

### PRICE CATEGORIES

Prices for three-course dinner per person with a half-bottle of house wine, tax and tip:
**$** = under $25
**$$** = $25–$40
**$$$** = $40–$50
**$$$$** = more than $50

**RIGHT:** satisfied customer at a Cambridge sushi bar.

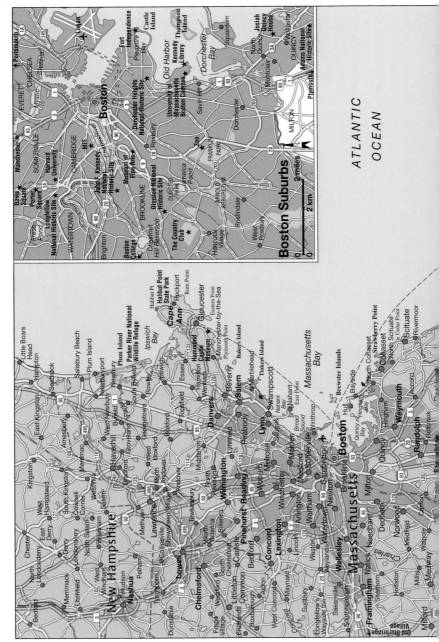

Boston Suburbs

ATLANTIC OCEAN

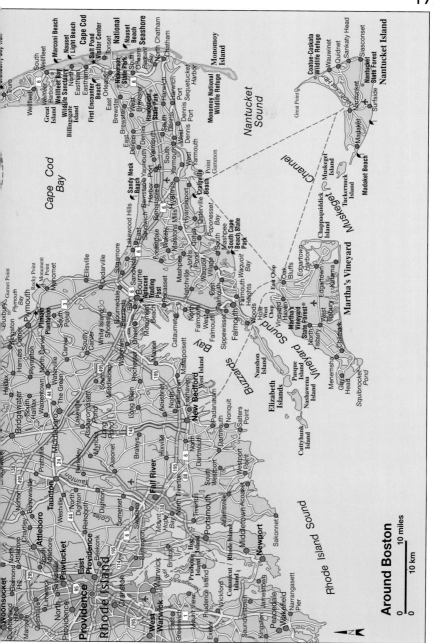

**Around Boston**

0 — 10 miles
0 — 10 km

# EXCURSIONS WEST

Within easy reach of Boston are the Revolutionary
sites of Lexington and Concord, the literary
shrine of Walden Pond, and the historical
reconstruction of Old Sturbridge Village

For most visitors, an excursion into Boston's western outskirts invariably means a pilgrimage along the famed "Battle Road" followed by combatants on those fateful days of April, 1775, when simmering American resentments flared into all-out war wih Britain. But there's more out this way, including mementoes of Concord's literary immortals, the real "Wayside Inn" of Longfellow's tales, and one of America's finest living history museums, Old Sturbridge Village.

## Lexington

To reach **Lexington ❶**, site of the first battle of the Revolution, leave Boston on Route 2 (Boston University Bridge to Cambridge's Memorial Drive, then west) and, after 10 miles (16 km), turn right onto Route 4–225. On the left as you enter Lexington is a contemporary building which houses the **National Heritage Museum** (33 Marrett Road; Mon–Sat 10am–5pm, Sun noon–5pm; tel: 781-861-6559) featuring changing exhibits of Americana. Soon after, still on the left, is the russet-colored 1635 **Munroe Tavern** (1332 Massachusetts Avenue; Patriots' Day weekend; late May–late Oct Mon–Sat 11.30am–4.30pm, Sun 1–4.30pm; tel: 781-862-1703), which served as headquarters for the

Redcoats and as a hospital on their retreat from Concord. The **Battle Green ❷**, a triangular park in the heart of Lexington, is a mile farther on. Here, early on the morning of April 19, 1775, the colonials' Captain Parker told his men: "Stand your ground, don't fire unless fired upon, but if they mean to have a war, let it begin here!"

Atop a heap of boulders, taken from a wall behind which the Americans shot at the British, is the **Minuteman Statue** (the "minutemen"

Map
on page
181

**PRECEDING PAGES:**
old coastguard
station, Eastham
**LEFT:**
getting hitched on
Lexington Green.
**BELOW:**
defending tradition
on Patriots' Day.

were so called because they were members of a militia supposed to be ready at a minute's notice). To the right (east) is the 1690 **Buckman Tavern** (1 Bedford Street; mid-Mar–Nov Mon–Sat 10am–5pm, Sun 1–5pm; tel: 781-862-5598), where 77 minutemen gathered to await the British. Following the battle, wounded minutemen were carried here for medical attention. It has been restored to its original appearance. Guided tours highlight a bullet hole in the door, muskets, cooking equipment and furniture.

A quarter-mile north of the Green is the mocha-colored 1698 **Hancock-Clarke House** (35 Hancock Street; Patriots' Day weekend; late May–late Oct Mon–Sat 11.30am–4.30pm, Sun 1–4.30pm; tel: 781-861-0928) where, on April 18, wanted men John Hancock and Samuel Adams were roused from their sleep by Paul Revere and warned of the coming of the British.

*Memorial Day in Concord.*

**BELOW:** Minuteman statue, Lexington.

## Battle Road

Leave Lexington on Route 2A – the Battle Road – from the northwest corner of Battle Green to reach Minuteman National Historical Park. Stop at the **Battle Road Visitor Center ❸** (daily in season 9am–4pm; tel: 781-674-1920). This the best place to begin a Lexington-Concord exploration; a film shows the events that led to the initial battle, and there's an animated map of British and American troop movements.

Visit also the partly uncovered **Ebenezer Fiske farmhouse**, where, after refreshing himself with a drink from a well, a minuteman found himself facing a Redcoat. "You are a dead man," announced the minuteman. "And so are you," was the reply. Both leveled their muskets; both fired; both were killed.

## Concord

**Concord ❹** is 8 miles (13 km) away, after several further informa-

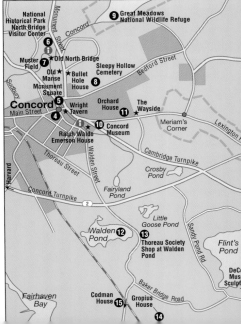

tive stops along the Battle Road. This handsome small town, now an upscale suburb, is doubly important. Here is where the second engagement of the Revolution took place and here, during the first half of the 19th century, lived a handful of renowned literati *(see page 39)*.

**Monument Square** ❺, at the center of town, is where, on April 19, 1775, a British sergeant burning a cache of captured supplies inadvertently set fire to a building. The Americans massing on the opposite side of the river saw the smoke and, assuming that the British were burning the town, decided to march to its defense "or die in the attempt." Their advance was blocked by a British detachment guarding the bridge. Several roads radiate from Monument Square: all should be explored.

Begin by driving north on Monument Street for a little over 1 mile and then turning left to reach imme-

diately the **National Historical Park North Bridge Visitor Center** ❻ (daily). Here, dioramas and a somewhat basic 12-minute audio-visual presentation explain the confluence of events that led to the battle. Visitors are invited to don colonial costume in one of the rooms. The gardens overlooking the Concord River with their view of **Old North Bridge** are quite beautiful.

Stroll the half-mile downhill past the **Muster Field** ❼ (to the right), along roughly the route of the militia until you reach sculptor Daniel Chester French's heroic statue of the Minuteman, rifle in one hand and the other clutching a plowshare. On the plinth are Ralph Waldo Emerson's immortal words chronicling "the shot heard round the world." And so to "the rude bridge that spanned the flood." Today's bridge was built in 1956.

The bloody skirmish seems distant ideed from today's idyllic surround-

Map below

*Old Manse, where Ralph Walso Emerson lived briefly.*

ings, perhaps best enjoyed by paddling a canoe along the winding river and under the bridge. (Canoes can be rented at South Bridge on Main Street: the river at this point is the Sudbury rather than the Concord.)

The simple, clapboard **Old Manse** (mid-Apr–Oct Mon–Sat 10am–5pm; Sun & holidays noon–5pm; tel: 978-369-3909), 200 yards south of North Bridge, was built in 1770 and was first occupied by the Rev. William Emerson, who watched the battle for the bridge from here. His grandson, Ralph Waldo Emerson, lived here for two short periods. Then, after their marriage, the Hawthornes moved in and remained for three years.

During this period Nathaniel wrote *Mosses from an Old Manse*, a collection of stories that secured a literary place for both house and writer. Meanwhile, Sophia was painting and scratching the study and dining room windows with her wedding ring. The longest and most charming of her inscriptions states: "Una Hawthorne stood on this window-sill January 22, 1845, while the

**BELOW:**
Old North Bridge.

trees were all glass chandeliers – a goodly show which she liked much though only 10 months old."

## Literary giants

Back in Monument Square, drive northeast on Bedford Street (Route 62) for 200 yards to **Sleepy Hollow Cemetery** ❽. Author's Ridge, in the northeast corner, is the final resting place of Hawthorne, the Alcotts, Emerson and Thoreau.

To escape all the history and just commune with nature, continue on Bedford Street for another mile and watch for a small sign noting the entrance to the **Great Meadows National Wildlife Refuge** ❾. Here serious birdwatchers mix with those only out for a bucolic stroll.

Backtrack from the Monument Square for less than a mile on the Lexington Road to the junction with the Cambridge Turnpike. Here stands the **home of Ralph Waldo Emerson** and the **Concord Museum** ❿ (200 Lexington Road; Jan–Mar Mon–Sat 11am–4pm, Sun 1pm–4pm; Apr–Dec Mon–Sat 9am–5pm, Sun noon–5pm; tel: 978-369-9609). In the former, Emerson wrote many of his celebrated essays and poems, while in the latter, a brick building, is Emerson's study, which, apart from one round table, was transferred in its entirety from the wooden Emerson home because of fear of fire. The excellent museum consists of a series of beautifully reconstructed rooms from the 18th and 19th centuries. Its Thoreau Gallery has the largest collection of artifacts associated with the author, including furnishings from his Walden Pond abode.

One mile farther along, at 399 Lexington Road, stands the shaded brown clapboard **Orchard House** ⓫ (Apr–Oct Mon–Sat 10am–4.30pm, Sun 1–4.30pm; Nov–Mar Mon–Fri 11am–3pm, Sat 10am– 4.30pm, Sun 1.30–4.30pm; tel: 978-369-4118),

where the Alcott family lived from 1858 to 1877. Here Louisa May Alcott wrote *Little Women* and *Little Men* and her father, Bronson, founded his school of philosophy. Family memorabilia is on display.

Just beyond, at No. 455, is **The Wayside** (not to be confused with Longfellow's Inn; *see page 185*), the home of the Concord Muster Man on the day of the battle (Mar–Dec Mon–Sat 10am–5pm; Sun 2–5pm; tel: 978-369-6993). The Alcotts resided here before moving to Orchard House. Hawthorne, who bought the house in 1851, lived and attempted to write here, eventually turning in desperation to travel writing and saying he would be happy if the house just burned down. It was later occupied by Margaret Sidney (real name Harriet Lothrop), author of the *Five Little Pepper* books.

## Walden Pond

Continue to **Walden Pond ⑫**, reached by returning toward Concord and then traveling south on Walden Street, which crosses Route 2, for 1½ miles (2.5 km). The pond

is relatively small and can be circled on foot in about an hour. The best time to visit is in the fall. During summer, when the pond is a popular swimming spot, Thoreau would have been unable to separate himself from "the mass of men [who] lead quiet lives of desperation" – or who just want to cool off on a hot day. A cairn of stones stands alongside the site where Thoreau lived between 1845 and 1847.

Thoreau enthusiasts will also wish to visit the **Thoreau Society Shop at Walden Pond ⑬** (915 Walden Street; May–Labor Day 10am–7.30pm; after Labor Day–Dec 1 10am–6pm; Dec 2–24 and mid-Jan–May 11am–4pm; tel: 978-287-5477), which houses much memorabilia. Nearby is a replica of his Walden Pond cabin.

(Concord can quickly "be done" in a couple of hours, but to explore any house usually necessitates joining a guided tour. This often requires a short wait. Most tours take about 40 minutes.)

Continue south from Walden Pond and, after a half-mile, turn left. Immediately to the right is the

*Walden Pond.*

**BELOW:** in memory of Henry David Thoreau.

*One of Lincoln's often-overlooked architectural gems is its charming, Richardson Romanesque town library, located on Trapelo Road not far from the DeCordova Museum.*

**BELOW:** in the Indian Museum at Fruitlands Museums.

**Gropius House** , which expresses the Bauhaus principles of function and simplicity (68 Baker Bridge Road, Lincoln. Jun–Oct 15 Wed–Sun 11am–4pm; rest of year Sat and Sun 11am–4pm; tel: 781-259-8098). This was the first building that the great German architect designed when he arrived in the US in 1937.

## A choice of museums

Another mile leads to the attractive **DeCordova Museum and Sculpture Park** (Sandy Pond Road, Lincoln; Tues–Sun 11am–5pm; tel: 781-259-8355), showcasing temporary exhibitions of modern art. The 30 acres (12 hectares) of grounds, high above **Sandy Point Pond**, are a splendid setting for sculpture. In summer, outdoor concerts are held in the amphitheater.

Also in Lincoln is a gem of a three-story blue clapboard house with an Ionic portico. The **Codman House** , its grounds landscaped like an English country estate, is a treasure trove of 18th- and 19th-century furniture and decorative arts.

To reach **Harvard Village** and the

**Fruitlands Museums**, return to Concord and drive west on Route 2. After 13 miles (21 km), turn south on Route 110 and immediately right onto Old Shirley Road. This crosses Depot Road to become Prospect Hill, where the entrance to Fruitlands is located 2 miles (3 km) after leaving Route 2. Fruitlands, with magnificent views across the Nashua River Valley, is a handsomely landscaped property featuring four excellent museums (102 Prospect Hill Road; mid-May–mid-Oct Mon–Fri 11am–4pm, Sat and Sun 11am–5 pm; tel: 978-456-3924). The Tea Room is a lovely spot for lunch or Sunday breakfast buffet.

An 18th-century farmhouse where, for some months, Bronson Alcott and his family, an English friend, Charles Lane, and others attempted an experiment in communal living is now a **Transcendentalist Museum**. The **Shaker House**, built in the 1790s, was an office for the Harvard Shakers Society, which flourished until 1918. Shaker handicrafts are displayed, and a variety of exhibits offer

insight into the Shaker way of life, which involved celibacy, communal ownership of property and worship joyfully expressed in dance.

The other two museums are the **American Indian** and the **Picture Gallery**. The former houses a selection of North American (not New England) Indian relics, historic Indian arts and dioramas. The west gallery of the latter displays delightful "primitive" portraits by early 19th-century itinerant artists, while the east gallery showcases the works of landscape painters associated with the Hudson River School.

## Longfellow's Wayside Inn

Head south for 6 miles (10 km) past Walden Pond on Route 126, then turn right onto Route 20 and continue for 5 miles (8 km) to Sudbury and **Longfellow's Wayside Inn**, which claims to be the country's oldest operating inn. Known as John How's Black Horse when built in 1661, the tavern became inexorably linked with Henry Wadsworth Longfellow when *Tales of a Wayside Inn* appeared in 1863.

The inn still offers "Food, Drink and Lodging for Man, Woman and Beast," and can be explored by those not staying for a meal or a night. It was restored by Henry Ford in the 1920s. In its grounds stand the Red Schoolhouse supposedly attended by Mary and her little lamb of nursery rhyme fame, and a working reproduction of an 18th-century gristmill.

## Old Sturbridge Village

Although well beyond Boston's western suburbs, **Old Sturbridge Village** (Apr–Oct daily 9.30am–5pm; Nov–Jan 1 daily 9.30am–4pm; Jan 2–Mar Wed–Sun 9.30am–4pm; tel: 508-347-3362) shouldn't be missed by anyone with an interest in history and an extra day to spend in Massachusetts. From Boston, the best approach is via the Massachusetts Turnpike; get off at Exit 9 for Sturbridge (same exit as for I-84 south). The Village can also be reached by bus from Boston.

More than 40 original buildings, dating from 1730 to 1840, have been collected from throughout New England and placed here to create a *circa* 1830 village and a 70-acre (28-hectare) farm. Many stand around a central green, and a lake is spanned by a covered bridge. A blacksmith, potter, cobbler, and other tradespeople work in period attire; there's a working general store, and a restaurant serving old-time New England cuisine. A pair of oxen harnessed to a plow are used to turn the sod, and the same strains of crops common to the region in the early 19th century are grown. Houses are authentically furnished, and a variety of religious and civic events punctuate the daily and seasonal rhythm of village life and farm work.

Two small but superb museums, one devoted to clocks and the other to glass, round off an enjoyable family destination. ❏

Maps: pages 176, 181

*Traditional dress, Old Sturbridge Village.*

### Restaurants

#### Concord

**Colonial Inn**
48 Monument Square, Concord, Tel: 800-370-9200 or 978-371-1533. Open: B, L, & D daily. $$$
www.concordscolonialinn.com
Classic fare at this 1716 inn include chicken pot pie, baked stuffed lobster, fresh grilled fish, and Yankee pot roast. High tea ($21.95) is served Fri–Sun.

**Publick House**
On the Common, Route 131; Tel: 508-347-3313 or 800-782-5425. Open: B, L & D daily. $$–$$$
www.publickhouse.com
This 1771 inn's timeless menu includes prime rib with Yorkshire pudding, lobster pie, and full turkey dinner. A tavern serves a lighter menu.

#### Lexington

**Peking Garden**
27 Waltham St./ Lexington, Tel: 781-862-1051-371-1533. Open: L, & D daily. $
Well-prepared Chinese dishes served in a spacious room. The luncheon and dinner buffets are well-stocked and offer a broad assortment.

● ● ● ● ● ● ● ● ● ● ● ● ● ● ● ● ● ●
*Prices for three-course meal for one, with half-bottle of house wine, tax and tip.*
**$** *under $25.* **$$** *$25–40.*
**$$$** *$40–50.* **$$$$** *$50-plus.*

# THE NORTH SHORE

**The delightful, wild coast of Cape Ann is a major attraction. Characterful seaports such as Gloucester and Marblehead cast a potent spell. So do Salem's witches**

**BELOW:** picnicking at Chandler Hovey Park, Marblehead.

The North Shore, far more rocky and rugged than the South Shore and Cape Cod, is famed not only for its natural scenery but for the splendid architecture and quaint streets of 18th- and 19th-century seaports such as Salem, Marblehead, Gloucester and Newburyport. Leave Boston via the Callahan or Ted Williams tunnel (Route 1A), or by heading over the Bunker Hill and Tobin bridges (Route 1). The former route, which hugs the shoreline more closely, will take you through the old shoe manu-facturing city of Lynn and then into the handsome suburban precincts of Swampscott. As you enter Swamp-scott, veer left off Route 1A onto Atlantic Avenue, which passes some of the town's grand turn-of-the-20th-century homes on its way to the colonial port of Marblehead.

## Yachties' haven

At Marblehead, Turn right onto Ocean Avenue and drive across the causeway at the base of Marblehead Harbor to arrive at exclusive **Marblehead Neck ❶**. Harbor Avenue makes a 3-mile (5-km) loop around the Neck, passing some splendid homes and, on the harbor side, the Eastern Yacht Club, the East Coast's most prestigious yacht club – although that statement will certainly be challenged by members of the neighboring Corinthian Yacht Club. Chandler Hovey Park, in the lee of the lighthouse at the tip of the Neck, is a glorious windswept point from which to watch dozens of white sails scudding in and out of the deep, pro-tected harbor.

Return across the Ocean Avenue causeway, then turn right onto Atlantic Avenue and immediately arrive in **Marblehead ❷** proper, a twisting labyrinth of busy, narrow one-way streets lined with old clap-board houses.

The **Jeremiah Lee Mansion** (161 Washington Street; tel: 781-631-1768; open June–mid-Oct Mon–Sat; Sun pm), built in 1768, is an excellent example of Georgian architecture. Its exterior is of wood cut to imitate stone, while its interior has a grand entrance hall, elegant furnishings and original paneling. Also worth a visit is the **King Hooper Mansion**, an early 18th-century building with slave quarters, ballroom and garden.

Washington Square in the heart of the town is its highest point and provides pleasant views. The square is surrounded by private mansions that once belonged to sea captains and merchants; it is fronted by **Abbot Hall** (Washington Street; open daily; tel: 781-631-0000), the town hall, which has earned a niche in history by being home to Archibald Willard's renowned painting *The Spirit of '76*.

Leave the town by Lafayette Street; this immediately becomes Route 114, which, in turn, soon joins Route 1A and, after another 3 miles (5 km), enters Salem.

## Bewitched Salem

Follow Route 114 west and north from Marblehead to **Salem ❸**, also accessible via the MBTA Rockport commuter rail line from Boston. Some 200 years ago Salem – the word is derived from the Hebrew *shalom* ("peace") – was so great a seaport that many in foreign parts believed that New York was a town in a land called Salem. Today, it is a shadow, albeit a delightful one, of its former self, rich in museums and historic sites.

All places mentioned here can be visited by following the red line painted on the sidewalk. Alternatively, board a trackless trolley for a narrated tour of all the historic sites, alighting at will and rejoining a later car. Best to start your visit at the **National Park Visitors Center ❹**

**Maps:**
**Area 190**
**City 187**

*Low-flying witches.*

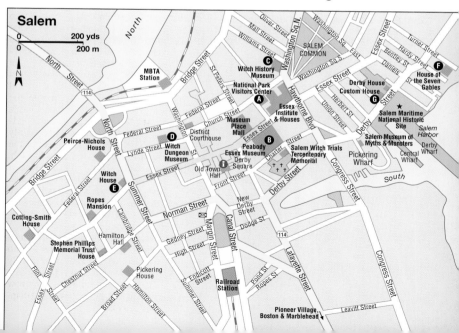

**Salem**

0   200 yds
0   200 m

# Salem's Witches

I n the mid-1600s, when the fever for witch-killing blew across the North Atlantic from Europe, the colonies of Rhode Island, Connecticut and Massachusetts joined the pack with decrees of death. Connecticut quickly seized and executed nine victims. Bostonians hanged Margaret Jones of Charlestown on a bright June day in 1648, and for an encore on Boston Common they hanged the beautiful and cultured Anne Hibbins, widow of the colony's former representative to England.

Against that lunatic background, the fanatical Rev. Cotton Mather sensed a great opportunity for self-promotion and professional success. He was already the colony's most highly acclaimed clergyman. He was learned, brilliant, ambitious, but he yearned for more. He longed to succeed his father, the Rev. Increase Mather, as the president of Harvard. He decided it would boost his reputation and enhance his career if he could identify assorted witches and promote their executions. So he went to work and soon focused on a witch-suspect named Goodwife Glover, the mother of a North End laundress. With Mather's help, poor Mrs Glover quickly wound up in the noose of a Boston Common gallows rope.

In that same year, the fever struck Salem. The initial case involved a hot-tempered, trouble-making minister named Samuel Parris. He upset the serenity of his neighbors by arriving in town with two black slaves from the West Indies, a man named John and his wife, Tituba. Within two years, Tituba was teaching voodoo to a pair of young girls, Ann Putnam and Mercy Lewis. When they had learned all they needed to know from Tituba, they turned against the black woman with hysterical charges of witchcraft. And Tituba wound up in jail.

At this point, Salem's witchcraft surge really took off. Tituba pointed the witch-finger against two other Salem women, Sarah Osburn and Sarah Good. They in turn dragged in Rebecca Nurse and Martha Corey. And the madness kept spreading like infection, with every suspect accusing somebody else, until scores of victims awaited death. Between June and September in 1648, the Salemites executed 14 women as witches and six men as warlocks. And, to leave nothing to chance they also convicted and hanged two dogs.

Throughout the year, Cotton Mather was a frequent visitor to the town. He never missed an execution. He was a roaring orator at all hangings. He was quick to gallop his horse to the front of a crowd of onlookers and to leap from his saddle to the gallows platform. There he would rant and rave, preach and pray, devoting most of his performance to berating and denouncing the victim who was waiting to die, and thereafter adding a modest personal statement calculated to move his steps toward the presidency of Harvard.

Such was the situation in 1693 when William Phips, who had been busy fighting the Indians and the French in the northern woods, returned to his duties as the colony's governor. Phips took one disgusted look at the witchery set-up and issued a proclamation freeing all suspects still incarcerated. Mercifully, the madness braked to an abrupt halt. ❑

**LEFT:** Salem's Witch History Museum.

(2 Liberty Street; tel: 978-740 1650), just off The Mall (Essex Street), which screens a prize-winning film about Essex County, and has an excellent shop.

Salem's historic houses cover the evolution of architecture and furnishings in the region from the 17th to the 19th centuries. In a row on Church Street are the Derby-Beebe summerhouse (1799), the John Ward house (1684) and the Andrew-Safford house (1819).

Diagonally across Essex Street from the Peabody Essex Library is the world-class **Peabody Essex Museum ❸** (East India Square; tel: 978-745-9500; daily 10am–5pm), whose collections date from 1799, when 22 Salem men who had sailed beyond Cape Horn and the Cape of Good Hope founded the East India Marine Society, whose mission included forming a "museum of natural and artificial curiosities" to be collected by members on their voyages. Ships' models, figure-heads, nautical instruments, charts and maps abound in the Museum's Maritime Department, while the Asian Export Department glitters with porcelain, gold, silver, furniture and textiles created by Chinese, Japanese and Indian artisans in the 19th century. Artifacts from the South Pacific and the Far East abound in the Ethnology Department. A Natural History Department rounds off the collection. The Yin Yu Tang House is the only complete Qing Dynasty house outside China.

West of these museums, elegant homes, many built for sea captains, line Chestnut, Essex and Federal streets. The first of these streets is a National Historic Landmark and has often been cited as one of the most beautiful streets in America.

North next to Salem Common is the **Witch History Museum ❸** (Washington Square; Apr–Nov daily 10am–5pm; tel: 978-744-1692). It and the **Witch Dungeon Museum ❶** (16 Lynde Street; Apr–Nov daily 10am–5pm; tel: 978-741-3570), both in former churches, present their versions of the witch trials that made Salem notorious in 1692–93 *(see opposite page)*. Learn more about this mass delusion in the **Witch House ❸** (310 Essex Street; May–early Nov 10am–5pm with last tour at 4.30pm; tel: 978-744-8815), where Judge Corwin questioned more than 200 suspected witches.

At the other end of town the nine-acre **Salem Maritime National Historic Site**, under the auspices of the National Park Service (193 Derby Street; daily 9am–5pm; tel: 978-740-1660), preserves and interprets the maritime history of New England. The nearby **House of the Seven Gables Historic Site ❻** (54 Turner Street; daily 10am–5pm; until 7pm July 2–Oct; tel: 978-744-0991), was the setting for Hawthorne's novel of that name. Several other houses at the site include his birthplace.

Across the street are the 1761 **Derby House** (Derby, a ship-owner, was probably the nation's first

Map on page 187

*Arthur Miller based his 1953 play "The Crucible" on the Salem trials, though its real target was the recent witch hunts then being carried out by Congress against supposed Communists.*

**BELOW:** Ropes Mansion, Salem.

*More "witches" were exterminated in Salem than anywhere else in New England.*

millionaire) and the 1819 **Custom House G** with an office once used by Nathaniel Hawthorne. To the southeast is the desolate 2,000-ft (600-meter) long Derby Wharf, one of 40 wharves once crowded with merchantmen. Adjacent **Pickering Wharf**, with its many restaurants and stores, including several antiques shops, will delight those who enjoy Boston's Quincy Market. But caveat emptor: 200 years ago the English were making and exporting to Salem copies of Chinese export-ware.

A trackless trolley takes visitors to the **Pioneer Village** (late Apr–late Nov Mon–Sat 10am–5pm; Sun noon–5pm; tel: 978-744-0991), 4 miles (6 km) south of Salem, where interpreters in period costume introduce visitors to Salem of the 1620s when it was the first capital of Massachusetts. The buildings range from rough dugouts and wigwams to thatched cottages. Crafts demonstrated include making tallow candles and spinning wool.

## Seafront mansions

From Salem, travel north on Route 1A to Beverly; then turn east on Route 127 to drive through Beverly Farms,

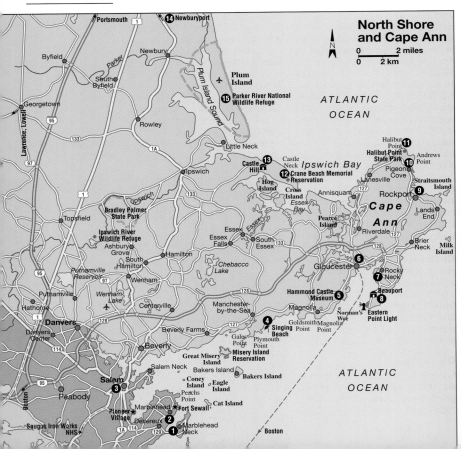

Pride's Crossing and Manchester-by-the-Sea, all Brahmin summer retreats. **Singing Beach ❹** in Manchester, 31 miles (50 km) from Boston, is especially attractive. It derives its name from the crackling sound made when walking on the sands. (There is parking only at the railway station, a half-mile from the beach.)

Six miles (10km) past Manchester, turn right off 127 toward Magnolia and follow Hesperus Avenue to the **Hammond Castle Museum ❺** (daily 10am–4pm in summer, Sat–Sun only Sept–May; tel: 978-283-2080). This massive building was constructed in the mid-1920s with bits and pieces of European châteaux. The eponymous owner was an inventor; the castle was his home, his laboratory and a gallery for his art collection. The castle, which has secret passageways and a 100-ft (30-meter) long hall for the 8,200-pipe organ (advance arrangements can be made for a mini-organ concert), stands on a bluff overlooking the sea and Norman's Woe, a surf-pounded rock that is the setting for Longfellow's poem *The Wreck of the Hesperus*.

Hesperus Avenue now rejoins Route 127 and, after 3 miles (5 km), arrives at the drawbridge in Gloucester which spans the Annisquam Canal. On the other side of the bridge, those who have perished at sea are honored by the famed **Gloucester fisherman statue**, depicting a helmsman firmly gripping a wheel as he scans the horizon. Those familiar with the book and film *The Perfect Storm*, about an ill-fated Gloucester crew, know that the poignancy of this memorial is not merely a matter of ancient history.

## Gloucester

**Gloucester ❻**, the nation's oldest seaport, was founded in 1623 by a group of Englishmen who had come "to praise God and to catch fish."

How well they succeeded can be observed in the harbor, where local and foreign boats still unload their catch. Many fishermen in this, one of the world's leading fishing ports, are of Portuguese or Italian descent. Whale-watching cruises also leave from the harbor.

In town, visit the **Sargent House Museum**, the handsome Georgian home of Judith Sargent and John Murray at 49 Middle Street (Memorial Day–Columbus Day, Fri–Mon noon–4pm); its rooms are arranged as they might have looked in 1790. The country's first Universalist Church, a movement that Murray founded, is across the street. Displayed in a large Federal-style house at 27 Pleasant Street, the headquarters of the **Cape Ann Historical Association**, are fine seascapes by the renowned American marine painter Fitz Hugh Lane and an interesting collection of furniture, silver and porcelain and a maritime room. Farther inland, on Main Street, is the **Portuguese Church of Our Lady of Good Voyage**, recognizable by its two blue cupolas.

Maps:
Area 190
City 187

*A recent literary landmark in Gloucester is the Crow's Nest, the bar featured in Sebastian Junger's 1997 bestseller "The Perfect Storm," later made into a movie starring George Clooney.*

**BELOW:**
"They that go down to the sea in ships…" reads the inscription on the fisherman's statue in Gloucester.

*Rockport's
Motif No. 1.*

From the church, drive around the harbor to East Main Street, which leads to **Rocky Neck ❼**, an artists' colony containing lively restaurants. Rudyard Kipling worked on *Captains Courageous*, about Gloucester fishermen, while staying here.

On leaving Rocky Neck, turn right onto Eastern Point Road. After about 3 miles (5 km), take the right fork, even though it's marked "Private." This is the exclusive enclave of Eastern Point, which has a score of magnificent homes. Notable, and open to the public, is **Beauport ❽** (June–mid-Sept Mon–Fri 10am–last tour at 4pm; mid-Sept–mid-Oct daily 10 am–last tour at 4pm; tel: 978-283-0800), built and furnished between 1907 and 1934 by Henry Davis Sleeper, a collector of American art and antiquities. Tours take in more than half of the 40 rooms, each designed and decorated to cover a different period of American life.

### Farther along Cape Ann

Return to the entrance to Eastern Point, turn right onto Farrington Avenue and then left onto Atlantic Road. You are now on a counter-clockwise loop of Cape Ann, following by land, if not by sea, the exploration made in 1604 by Champlain, the French explorer, and then in 1614 by John Smith, who mapped the area and named it in honor of his queen. Cape Ann combines outstanding scenery, along its sometimes rocky, sometimes sandy shores, with a splendid selection of boutiques, galleries and restaurants.

The route passes **Good Harbor, Long** and **Pebble beaches** before reaching, after about 7 miles (11 km), **Rockport ❾**. A tranquil fishing village prior to the 1920s, Rockport was discovered by artists and subsequently became a day-trippers' paradise. Most of the town's two dozen galleries, which display works of both local and international artists, are on Main Street, but the lure which attracts most tourists is **Bearskin Neck**. This narrow peninsula, jutting out beyond the harbor, is densely packed with tiny dwellings and old fishing sheds, now converted into galleries, antique stores and restaurants.

A photographers' favorite is a red lobster shack called **Motif No.1** because of the infinite number of times it has been photographed and painted. Beyond, enjoy magnificent views of the Atlantic from the breakwater at the end of the Neck.

Leave Rockport for **Pigeon Cove ❿**, a couple of miles along Route 127, and turn left to visit the **Paper House**; its walls and furnishings are made of Boston newspapers whose pages were compressed together – 215 sheets for the walls – and then lacquered. One desk is made exclusively of *Christian Science Monitors*, another of accounts of Lindbergh's transatlantic flight. This is one of those attractions whose fame lies in the fact that it exists at all, rather than in any intrinsic value.

Return to Route 127 and continue

for another couple of miles to **Halibut Point State Park ⑪**. A half-mile walk from the parking lot through blueberry bushes leads to the outermost tip of Cape Ann, where huge tilted sheets of granite and fascinating tidal ponds have their devotees. A former quarry near the parking lot is a reminder that Rockport and its surroundings provided the granite for many buildings in Boston and beyond.

Continue on the loop through **Annisquam**, an exclusive summer community freshened by the tang of the ocean. Rather than returning directly to Gloucester, turn west onto Route 128 and take Exit 14 to reach Route 133 and head north.

The appearance of Woodman's, a rustic restaurant in **Essex**, belies its contribution to mankind. This is where, on a hot July day in 1916, Lawrence Woodman tossed some cornmeal-coated clams into a pan of boiling oil and created the heavenly dish of fried clams. Essex's other main draws are its many antiques shops and the **Essex Shipbuilding Museum**, at 28 Main Street (May–Oct Wed–Sun 10am–5pm; Nov–Apr Sat–Sun noon–4pm: tel: 978-768-7541), displaying drawings, tools, photographs, and rigged ship models in an 1834 schoolhouse.

Turn right onto Spring Street to **Cogswell's Grant** (June 1–mid-Oct Wed–Sun 11am–4pm; tel: 978-768-3632), the *circa* 1730 summer home of Bertram K. and Nina Little, mid-20th-century preeminent collectors of American decorative arts. Their riverfront farmhouse is crammed with their eclecic collection.

Just before reaching Ipswich, turn right onto Argilla Road, bordered by country estates. After about 3 miles (5 km), it leads to the **Crane Beach Memorial Reservation ⑫**, covering over 1,400 acres (570 hectares) and with more than 5 miles (8 km) of magnificent white sands and

dunes. However, nothing is perfect and the greenhead fly season from mid-July to mid-August can be hell. (The pests bite ferociously, but are successfully warded off by applying a product called Skin-So-Soft, sold locally, to exposed areas. Ticks carrying lime disease are more than a mild nuisance, however – this is one of their prime haunts, so wear long trousers and use repellent.) The Pine Hollow Interpretive Trail is an enjoyable stroll over dunes into pine hollows and onto a boardwalk in a red maple swamp.

Overlooking the beach is **Castle Hill ⑬** (June–early Oct Wed–Thur 10am–4pm; tel: 978-356-4351), a 59-room mansion where glorious concerts are held on summer weekends. It's named for its builder, plumbing-fixture magnate Richard Crane, whose name travelers will doubtless encounter everywhere.

Return on Argilla Road to South Main Street, which borders the Ipswich village green. On the left, at 53 South Main Street, is the dark-brown **John Whipple House**, with its lovely 17th-century garden.

Map on page 190

*The lighthouse at Annisquam.*

**BELOW:** lining up for clams at Woodman's.

Map on page 190

**TIP**

After Labor Day, visitors are permitted to pick beach plums and cranberries in Parker River National Wildlife Refuge. A limited number of cars are allowed on the reserve, so get there early in summer to avoid disappointment.

**BELOW:** the Theater in the Open at Maudsley State Park, Newburyport.

Across the road at No. 40, the white Federal-period **John Heard House**, built with profits from the China trade, is filled with Chinese and early American artifacts; it has a collection of antique carriages on its grounds. Both houses are owned by the **Ipswich Historical Society** (tel: 978-356 2811) and are just two of 40 restored 17th- and 18th-century houses in the town.

## Newburyport

Continue north from Ipswich on Route 1A. After 12 miles (20 km), 1A becomes **Newburyport's** ⑭ elegant High Street, lined by magnificent clapboard Federal-period houses. At No. 98, the **Cushing House** (May–Nov Tues–Fri 10am–4pm, Sat noon-4pm; tel: 978-462-2681), headquarters of the Old Newbury Historical Society, has 21 splendidly furnished rooms, varied artifacts and a garden with many plants more than a century old.

Turn right off High Street to reach the Merrimack River and the waterfront. The story of the town's 18th- and 19th-century glory days of sea-borne commerce is recounted in the **Custom House Maritime Museum** (25 Water Street; Apr–Dec Tues–Sat 9am–5pm, Sun noon–4pm; tel: 978-462-8681).

Between the waterfront and High Street is the reconstructed **Market Square** and **Inn Street Mall**, a pleasing ensemble of early 19th-century three-story brick and granite buildings that owe their architectural cohesiveness to the all-at-once rebuilding of downtown after a disastrous 1811 fire. Both areas, along with busy State Street, are filled with shops, galleries, restaurants, and taverns. Two churches in town are worth visiting. **Old South**, the older (1785), has a whispering gallery and a bell cast by Paul Revere; the newer (1801) **Unitarian** is renowned for its delicate wooden spire.

From Newburyport, a 3-mile (5-km) drive across a causeway leads to Plum Island, a 4,700-acre (1,900-hectare) reservation, **Parker River National Wildlife Refuge** ⑮, with a 6-mile (10-km) stretch of superb sands that is nirvana for both bird watchers and beach bums. Turtles and toads, raccoons and rabbits, pheasant and deer thrive here.

For a quick return to Boston, take either Route 1 or – faster yet – Interstate 95 south, switching to Route 1 at Peabody. If you're interested in industrial history, watch for signs indicating the **Saugus Iron Works National Historic Site**, the country's first iron works (1646), just east of Route 1 about 10 miles (16 km) north of Boston (244 Central Street, Saugus; Apr–Oct daily 9am–5pm; Nov–Mar daily 9am–4pm; tel: 781-233-0050). Rangers lead visitors through the impeccably reconstructed plant and explain how iron was made in the mid-1600s. The Iron Works House, the only surviving part of the original complex, is a good example of 17th-century American Elizabethan architecture. ❑

# RESTAURANTS

## Marblehead

### The Landing

81 Front St., Tel: 781-639-1266. Open: L & D daily, Sun brunch. $$–$$$

www.thelandingrestaurant.com

Fresh seafood, prime beef, and poultry specialties share the menu at this pleasant spot overlooking the harbor. A pub menu is also available.

### Pellino's

261 Washington St., Tel: 781-631-3344. Open: D nightly. $$$

www.pellinos.com

The Italian-born chef/owner specializes in regional Italian cuisine, with an emphasis on the north. The atmosphere is cozy and romantic, the antipastos imaginative, and entrées such as lobster ravioli with baby shrimp and garlic-crusted rack of lamb superb. There's also an award-winning wine list, and the house special dessert, warm chocolate volcano cake, is terrific.

## Salem

### Finz Seafood Grille

Pickering Wharf, 76 Wharf St., Salem, Tel: 978-744-8485. Open: L & D. $$–$$$

www.hipfinz.com

With huge windows overlooking the harbor, this upscale spot draws a loyal local crowd who favor the great raw bar, seafood pot pie, lively bar, and weekend jazz.

### Grape Vine

26 Congress St., tel: 978-745-9335. Open: D nightly. $$$$

Seasonal New American fare is the specialty at this cozy, romantic bistro. Tasty items include homemade chowder and ravioli, seared duck breast, spring rolls, and risotto. Dine al fresco in the garden from May to Sept.

### Red's Sandwich Shop

15 Central St., tel: 978-745-3527. $

A terrific spot for hearty breakfasts and lunches.

## Gloucester

### Gloucester House Restaurant

7 Seas Wharf, Tel: 978-283-1812. Open: L & D daily. $$

www.lobster-express.com

Since 1958 the Linguata family has been serving seafood on premises overlooking a historic working wharf. The more casual Seven Seas Café serves lobster and seafood "in the rough"; and breakfast and lunch is served at the Morning Glory Coffee Shop, open 6am–12:30pm summer.

### White Rainbow

65 Main St., Tel: 978-281-0017. Open: D nightly; Jan, Tues–Sun. $$–$$$

www.whiterainbowrestaurant.com

Housed in an 1830s Federal-style brick building, this local favorite has a changing Continental menu and elegant

ambiance. There's an extensive light fare, mezes and tapas menu, and a long list of fine wines, martinis, and house specialty drinks.

## Rockport

*Note: Rockport is a "dry" town, but you can bring your own wine to most restaurants.*

### Brackett's Oceanview Restaurant

25 Main St., Tel: 978-546-2797. Open: L & D nightly; closed Nov–mid-Apr. $$

www.bracketts.com

Seafood, burgers, and homemade desserts in a pleasant spot overlooking the harbor.

### Portside Chowder House

7 Tuna Wharf, Tel: 978-546-7045. Open: L & D daily in summer; L daily winter and fall; L&D on spring weekends. $

A fine spot for a hearty bowl of chowder, a sandwich or salad, and a terrific water view.

## Essex

### Woodman's of Essex

Route 133, 121 Main St., Essex, Tel: 800-649-1773. Open: L & D daily. $–$$

www.woodmans.com

The first clam was fried here more than 85 years ago, and today the expanded seafood shack serves up lobster in the rough, steamers, fresh fish, and fabulous fried clams. No credit cards.

## Newburyport

### The Grog

13 Middle St., Tel: 978-465-8008. Open: L & D daily. $–$$

www.thegrog.com

The city's premier rendezvous for burgers, seafood, chowder, and beer in a laid-back atmosphere.

### Joseph's Winter Street Cafe

24 Winter St., Tel: 978-462-1188. Open: L Fri, D nightly. $$$–$$$$

www.josephswinterstcafe.com

The elegant European-style bistro has an open dining room with the feel of a supper club and acoustics that do justice to the nightly jazz. The quieter Terrace Room is more intimate. A three-course Sunset Supper is served Sun–Thur for $14.

### Szechuan Taste & Thai Café

19 Pleasant St., Tel: 978-463-0686. Open: L & D daily. $$

www.szechuantaste.com

A superb selection of Chinese, Japanese and Thai delicacies, and a deft touch with seafood, in a handsomely decorated spot just off State St. There's a sushi bar.

---

### PRICE CATEGORIES

Prices for three-course dinner per person with a half-bottle of house wine, tax and tip:

$ = under $25
$$ = $25–$40
$$$ = $40–$50
$$$$ = more than $50

# The Industrial Heritage

New England's first fortunes were made on the seas, but by the early 19th century Boston money was financing America's first great wave of industrial expansion. Manufacturing was not entirely new to the region: America's first iron works had been established in Saugus in the 1600s and shipbuilding had long been vital to the coastal economy. But the Industrial Revolution in New England truly dates to Samuel Slater's establishment of America's first mechanized textile mill in Pawtucket, Rhode Island in 1793.

Two decades later, Boston's Francis Cabot Lowell returned from England having memorized the details of the power loom – a device so jealously guarded by the British that the export of its plans was forbidden by law. Lowell set up his first looms at a small plant in Waltham, near Boston, and with partner Nathan Appleton soon plotted a much larger operation at a site on the Merrimack River that would bear his name.

## Lowell

The mills of **Lowell** began operating in the 1820s and grew to become part of a chain of leviathan textile enterprises, all powered

by the waters of the Merrimack, in New Hampshire and Massachusetts. Having reached their peak of production a century ago – and having long been eclipsed by mills in the southern US and abroad – Lowell's hulking brick canalside factories have been painstakingly preserved as **Lowell National Historical Park** (Visitor Center, 246 Market Street; open daily, hours vary with season; tel: 978-970-5000).

Begin a tour of the park at the visitor center, which offers detailed exhibits and a slide show explaining the context of the Lowell mills in the story of American industrialization. A separate exhibit, "Mill Girls and Immigrants," tells how the spinning machines of "Spindle City" were first attended by girls from nearby farms who, thanks to the owners' paternalism, boarded in model dormitories and attended the city's handsome St Anne's Church each Sunday. Soon, though, the mills' capacity expanded beyond the ability of the "mill girls" to fill labor requirements, and the operators began to recruit successive waves of immigrants, beginning with the Irish, and then the French Canadians whose descendants still form a substantial part of Lowell's population. (The city boasts a kaleidoscopic ethnic diversity: Afro-Americans, Portuguese, Poles, Greeks, eastern European Jews, Armenians, Hispanics, and southeast Asians – Lowell has been called the "Cambodian capital of America.")

National Park rangers give a variety of tours through the mill buildings and along Lowell's streets and canals. The best tour involves genuine trolley rides, traveling on a barge through canals and locks and some walking. At the park's Boott Cotton Mill, vintage power looms still operate; when they crank up in unison, the racket is so intense that visitors are given earplugs – a luxury the millworkers did not enjoy. For further understanding of the Lowell story, the National Park experience can be augmented with a visit to **Lowell Heritage State Park** (500 Pawtucket Boulevard; hours similar to National Park; tel: 978-369-6312); and the **American Textile History Museum** (491 Dutton Street; Tues–Fri 9am–4pm; Sat–Sun 10am–5pm; tel: 978-441-0400), where exhibits explain the history of woolen textile manufacturing, stressing the transition from hand to machine production. Carding, spinning and weaving are demonstrated.

Non-mill-related Lowell sites close to the National Park Visitor Center include the **Whistler House Museum of Art** (243 Worthen Street; May–Oct 11am–4pm Wed–Sat, Sun 11am–4pm; closed Jan–Feb and Sun Nov–Apr; tel: 978-452-7641), located in the birthplace of painter James Abbott McNeill Whistler and exhibiting late 19th- and early 20th-century work by Whistler and his contemporaries. Lowell native Jack Kerouac, the central figure of the "Beat Generation" of American authors, is commemorated in Eastern Park Plaza with a series of quotes from his work emblazoned on large steel plaques. The **New England Quilt Museum** (18 Shattuck Street; Tues–Sat 10am–4pm; Sun noon–4pm May–Nov; tel: 978-452-4207) has antique and contemporary quilts.

From Boston, reach Lowell by taking I-93 north to I-495 south. Or, take an MBTA commuter train from North Station.

## Lawrence

Downstream from Lowell along the Merrimack River is another one-time textile capital, **Lawrence** (from Boston, I-93 north to I-495 north). Lawrence, whose principal output was woolen cloth, was known as "Queen of the Mill Towns," and much of its old, riverside factory infrastructure remains, capped by an immense clock tower that once ruled the lives of thousands. The mills at Lawrence have not been as well preserved as those upriver at Lowell; the old brick buildings present a melancholy aspect, especially when seen from the Merrimack at sunset.

It was in Lawrence that 23,000 mill workers went on strike for two months in 1912. The shutdown was called the "Bread and Roses" strike, after a line in a poem by James Oppenheim describing women workers' aspirations – "We want bread, and roses too" – and in fact the strike was largely orchestrated by women. Begun in response to mill owners' cutting pay after a new state law shortened the work week, the action was successful in attaining wage increases,

although the owners soon speeded production and, during a recession a few years later, again slashed pay. Nevertheless, the strike helped galvanize the American labor movement. The story is recounted at **Lawrence Heritage State Park** (1 Jackson Street; daily 9am–4pm; tel: 978-794-1655), located in a mill boarding house.

## Watches on the Charles

Closer to Boston, in the small city of **Waltham** (MBTA buses from Boston), the **Charles River Museum of Industry** (154 Moody Street; Thur–Sat 10am–5pm; tel: 781-893-5410) occupies part of the Boston Manufacturing Company textile mill, predecessor of the Lowell mills and New England's first integrated textile factory – raw material went in one end and the finished product came out the other. But Waltham eventually became far more famous as the "Watch City," with the Waltham Watch Company turning out 40 million timepieces over 100 years, in an astonishing array ranging from dollar watches to elaborate models fit for the vest pockets of tycoons. The museum exhibits Waltham watches, and also precision metalworking instruments, bicycles and automobiles – aficionados will love the Stanley Steamer – manufactured locally. ❏

**LEFT:** mill buildings, Lowell National Historic Park.
**RIGHT:** there is a long tradition of quilt-making.

# SOUTH SHORE AND CAPE COD

There's yet more history to be found at Quincy and Plymouth. Beyond lie the long sandy beaches and well-preserved communities of Cape Cod

**BELOW:**
John Quincy Adams's Library in the Adams National Historic Site.

Cape Cod's glorious beaches are the prime destination for most visitors traveling south from Boston. But rather than making a beeline for the Cape via busy, bland Route 3, try clinging more closely to the shoreline, and take in a wealth of history and scenic splendor that begins just beyond the metropolis.

Leave Boston via Route 3 (the Southeast Expressway). Take Exit 12 and join Quincy Shore Drive which crosses the Neponset River by a drawbridge, and, 9 miles (14 km) after

leaving Boston, arrive at **Quincy ❶**, "city of presidents." Both John Adams and his son, John Quincy Adams, were born here. (Quincy can also be reached on the Red line of the "T".)

## Quincy's heritage

The city boasts half a dozen buildings associated with the names Quincy and Adams. The 1770 Georgian **Josiah Quincy House** (20 Muirhead Street), is furnished with Quincy family heirlooms. A half-mile farther south is the **Quincy Homestead** (34 Butler Road), a handsome country mansion dating to the early 19th century. But it is the Adams legacy that shines brightest.

Right in downtown Quincy, at 1250 Hancock Street, is the visitors center for the **Adams National Historic Site** (house tours daily 9am–5pm mid-Apr–mid-Nov; visitor center only Tues–Fri 10am–4pm rest of year; tel: 617-770-1175). This is the place to go for a thorough orientation to the remarkable story of the Adams family, which produced both the second (John Adams) and sixth (John Quincy Adams) presidents of the United States, as well as an illustrious line of descendants including historian Henry Adams. Shuttle tours leave the center for several Adams sites, for which they are the only means of admission. These include the **Old House**, purchased by John Adams in 1787 and displaying four generations of family furnishings and memorabilia, and the adjacent baronial **Stone Library** containing John Quincy Adams's Library of 14,000 books; and, some distance away, the modest saltbox houses in which the presidents were born. (Simple though these dwellings may be, Abigail, wife of John, wrote that she preferred the charms of "my little cottage" to the grandeur of the London court.)

The **United Parish First Church**, 1306 Hancock Street, is known as the Church of the Presidents and contains the remains of the two presidents and their wives.

Continue south on Route 3A to the **Hingham Rotary**, passing along the way the now defunct **Bethlehem Shipyards**. Here the *Thomas W. Lawson*, the only seven-masted schooner ever built, was launched, as was the first atomic-powered surface ship. Exit on Summer Street, then turn left at Martin's Lane for a 1-mile drive to **World's End**, an idyllic 248-acre (100-hectare) oasis designed by Frederick Law Olmsted. Stroll on paths lined with oak, hickory and cedar trees and through rolling fields that are home to pheasant, quail, foxes and rabbits. Herons and egrets populate the rugged 5-mile (8-km) shoreline, and all the while the impressive Boston skyline can be seen in the distance.

Return to Summer Street, turn left and follow the road to Washington Boulevard. This leads to **Nantasket Beach**, the best beach close to Boston (16 miles/24 km). An **antique carousel**, operating in summer, is the only reminder of a vanished amusement park. Farther out on the peninsula is the town of **Hull**, which offers views of the Atlantic and the harbor islands. **Boston Light**, about 1½ miles (2.5 km) offshore on **Little Brewster Island**, is the successor to the nation's first lighthouse (see page 111).

## Hingham

Backtrack from Hull via Washington Boulevard and Summer Street to the polished town of **Hingham**, where the numbers on the handsome, usually white, clapboard houses on **Main Street** are not to assist mail deliveries but to announce with pride when the houses were built – more often than not, in the 19th century and, occasionally, in the 18th. The town has several inspiring churches, including the 1681 **Old Ship Church** on Main Street, the oldest building in the nation in continuous ecclesiastical service. The interior of its roof echoes an inverted ship's hull.

Continue south on Route 3A through **Cohasset**, where Jerusalem Road winds past mansions old and new overlooking a rocky coast. Fourteen miles (22 km) farther south is **Marshfield**, where the **Daniel Webster Law Office** is located in the grounds of the 18th-century Winslow House; the great

*The Hull Lifesaving Museum at 1117 Nantasket Avenue (open Jun–Sept Wed–Sun, Oct–May Fri–Sun) gives a good idea of the heroic measures needed when warnings from the Boston Light could not avert disaster.*

**BELOW:** a ship's figurehead near Hingham Harbor.

Map on page 202

*Statue of Massasoit at Plymouth.*

**BELOW:** *Mayflower II at Plymouth.*

orator spent the last 20 years of his life here and is buried in the town's **Winslow Cemetery**, on Winslow Cemetery Road.

Immediately to the south is **Duxbury**, with its gracious colonial homes and a 9-mile (14-km) long barrier beach offering superb bird watching. The energetic might wish to ascend the 116-ft (40-meter) high Myles Standish Monument for vistas reaching from Boston to Cape Cod. Standish and other Pilgrims lie in the picturesque **Old Burying Ground** on Chestnut Street.

## Plymouth

Continue on Route 3A to **Plymouth ❷**, 40 miles (64 km) south of Boston. This is the celebrated 1620 landing site of the Pilgrims – as the story has it, on **Plymouth Rock** – and the first permanent American settlement north of Virginia.

Plymouth is rich in Pilgrim connections; a trolley runs between the different sites. A stone's throw from the grandiose neoclassical monument over the Rock is the *Mayflower II* ❹ (Apr–Nov daily 9am–5pm; July–Aug until 7pm; tel. 508-746-1622). This replica was built in England and sailed to Plymouth in 1957. The 104-ft (32-meter) long vessel, staffed with period-costumed interpreters who act the parts of the passengers and crew, vividly conveys the hardships of the 66-day 1620 voyage endured by 120 souls. (Note: if you're visiting both the *Mayflower II* and Plimoth Plantation, a combination ticket is available.)

Across the road from the Rock is **Coles Hill**, where, during their first winter, the Pilgrims secretly buried their dead at night to hide the truth about their fast-dwindling numbers from the Indians. Nearby is the site of the original settlement. At 16 Carver Street is the **Plymouth National Wax Museum** ❸ (Mar–Nov daily 9am–5pm; July, Aug

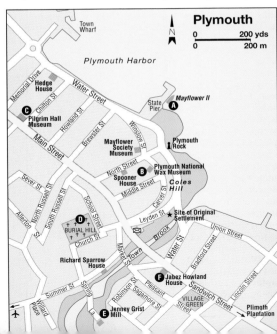

9am–9pm; June, Sept, Oct 9am–7pm; tel: 508-746-6468) with dioramas illustrating the Pilgrims' story from the emigration of the dissenting religious Separatists from England to Holland in 1607 to the first Thanksgiving celebration in 1621. An imposing **statue of Massasoit**, the Indian chief who helped the Pilgrims survive their first spring, stands in front of the Museum.

**Pilgrim Hall Museum** ● (75 Court Street; daily 9.30am–4.30pm, closed in Jan; tel: 508-746-1620), a Greek Revival building designed by Alexander Parris and the oldest public museum in the nation (the Peabody-Essex in Salem *(see page 189)* is older but began as a private institution) has the country's largest collection of Pilgrim memorabilia, including John Alden's halberd, Myles Standish's Bible and the cradle of Peregrine White, who was born aboard the *Mayflower*.

Farther east, beyond Main Street, is **Burial Hill** ●, with gravestones dating back to the colony's founding. The most famous epitaph reads: "Under this stone rests the ashes of Will^m Bradford, a zealous Puritan and sincere Christian, Governor of Plymouth Colony from April 1621–57 [the year he died, aged 69] except 5 years which he declined." The hill was the site of the Pilgrims' first meeting house, fort and watchtower. South of Burial Hill is the replica **Jenney Grist Mill** ●, where corn is still ground as in the days of the Pilgrims. The **Jabez Howland House** ● at 33 Sandwich Street (Memorial Day–Columbus Day daily; tours 10am–4.30pm; tel: 508-746-9590) is the only surviving house in Plymouth in which a *Mayflower* Pilgrim actually lived.

## Plimoth Plantation

The year is always 1627 at **Plimoth Plantation** (late Mar–late Nov daily 9am–5pm; tel: 746-1622), 3 miles (5 km) south of the Rock, where interpreters dressed in Pilgrim costumes and speaking in old English dialects assume the roles of specific historical residents of the colony. Query Mistress Alden about Captain Standish and she may well respond: "Oh, he lives next door and there are some, sir, who feel he is not the easiest man with whom to deal." Question the same Mistress Alden or Captain Standish about Paul Revere or George Washington and they will look at you with incomprehension. The interpreters do not simply stand around waiting for questions but go about their 1627 work and interact with one another. Even the livestock is painstakingly backbred to approximate 17th-century barnyard beasts.

Another part of the site is a **Wampanoag village**, reconstructing Indian life in Massachusetts in the 1620s. The visitors' center has audio-visual presentations and excellent changing exhibitions.

## Cape Cod

Leave Plymouth on Route 3, and head south 17 miles (27 km) to

Maps:
Area 202
City 200

*Acting the part at Plimoth Plantation.*

**BELOW:**
Plimouth Plantation.

*The Cape Cod Rail Trail.*

reach the **Sagamore Bridge**, which soars across the **Cape Cod Canal**. Beyond lies a land of marshes and meadows, pines and cranberry bogs and, above all, beaches.

For Henry David Thoreau, Cape Cod was "the bared and bended arm of Massachusetts." The **Upper Cape**, comprising the towns of Sandwich, Barnstable, Falmouth and Woods Hole, constitutes the upper arm beyond the canal; the **Mid-Cape**, which stretches from Hyannis to Orleans and which includes the towns of Chatham, Harwich, Brewster, Dennis, Yar-

mouth and Barnstable, takes in the elbow; and the **Lower Cape** – that part generally likened to the forearm, stretching northward to end with the "sandy fist" of Provincetown – includes the towns of Eastham, Wellfleet and Truro.

The Sagamore Bridge opens onto Route 6 (the Mid-Cape Highway), which runs first east and then north and ends, after 60 miles (100 km), at Provincetown. This is the quickest route to take, but much more intriguing is Route 6A (the old King's Highway). It parallels, more or less, Route 6 and passes through

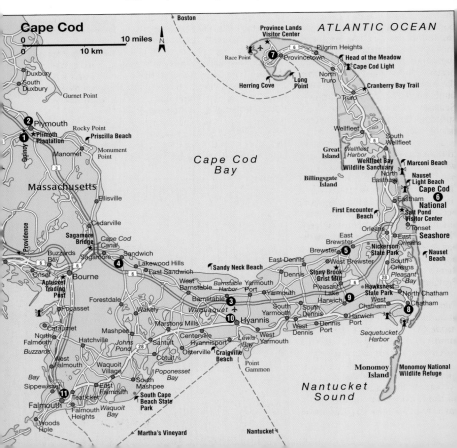

many of the Cape's prettiest villages, most with weathered cedar-shingle saltbox houses and a white-steepled church.

The Cape has about 300 miles (500 km) of sandy beaches, some backed by dunes rising 100 ft (30 meters) or more. Thunderous surf pounds the Atlantic side of the Upper Cape, while gentler waters prevail in **Cape Cod Bay**. Slightly rougher are **Buzzards Bay**, to the southwest of the Upper Cape, and **Nantucket Sound**, to the south of the Mid-Cape.

## Leisure activities

Because the Cape is so narrow, it is possible to spend the morning in roaring surf and, half an hour later, loll in placid, shallow waters. (Parking permits are required at some beaches, but are easily obtained; for the expansive beaches and dunelands of the Cape Cod National Seashore, the best bet for those spending more than a couple of days is to buy a season permit).

The Cape's 365 ponds are home to brown, rainbow and brook trout, white and yellow perch, and black bass. A non-resident Massachusetts license is required for fresh-water fishing, but not for surfcasting from ocean beaches, where striped bass and bluefish are the favorite quarry. "Party boats," which go out onto the bay for trips of several hours, are a popular fishing option; a number of them sail from MacMillan Wharf in Provincetown.

Nearly 40 golf courses dot the Cape. The greatest concentration is in the largest two towns of **Barnstable ❸** (seven courses) and **Falmouth** (five courses). Only about a dozen courses are strictly private.

Each community has set aside special areas for bicycling, but cyclists really come into their own on the **Cape Cod Rail Trail**, a paved recreational trail that runs on an abandoned railroad bed for 26 miles (42 km) from Route 134 in Dennis to Wellfleet. Its route passes quintessential Cape scenery and several cultural and historical sites. The **Salt Pond Visitor Center** of the **Cape Cod National Seashore** is right off the trail in Eastham.

**Sandwich ❹**, the town that glass built and the first community reached after crossing the canal, is a good place to be if the weather is bad. It's a lovely little village that has more museums than anywhere else on the Cape. Colorful utility and decorative glassware once made here is showcased in the **Sandwich Glass Museum** (129 Main Street; Feb–Mar Wed–Sun 9.30am–4pm; Apr–Dec daily 9.30am–5pm; tel: 508-888-0251).

Several interesting historic sites border Shawme Pond. These include the **Hoxie House**, which, with its 17th-century furnishings, is believed to be the oldest (1637) house on the Cape. The **Thornton Burgess Museum** (Apr–Oct Mon–Sat 10am–4pm; Sun 1–4pm; tel: 508-888-4668), in an 18th-century

Map on page 202

**TIP**

Distances between communities are short, and you can travel the entire Cape, with frequent stops, in a day. But it's better to take your time. Most visitors make one township their base, though some prefer to mosey from town to town. Each has its own distinctive character, but they have one thing in common: all are close to superb beaches.

**BELOW:** Shawme Pond, Sandwich.

*Carousels such as this one at Heritage Plantation are a New England favorite.*

house, memorializes the beloved children's author (*Peter Cottontail* and other animal favorites) who lived here. At **Dexter's Grist Mill**, in use since the 1650s, you can see cornmeal being stone-ground and buy the delicious finished product.

Best of all is the **Heritage Plantation** (130 Grove Street; May–Oct Mon–Sat 9am–6pm, Wed until 8pm; Nov–Apr Wed–Sat 10am–4pm; tel: 508-888-3300), located on 76 acres (31 hectares) of gardens rich in rhododendrons and day-lilies. It houses an eclectic collection of Americana in several buildings. A replica of the round Shaker Barn at western Massachusetts' Hancock Shaker Village contains a magnificent collection of antique cars dating from 1899 to 1937 (Gary Cooper's 1930 Duesenberg is the star). Another replica, this time of the "Publick House," a recreation hall for the Continental Army (1783), is filled with antique firearms, flags, Indian artifacts and 2,000 miniature soldiers. The Art Museum has a fine collection of folk art, including Cape-crafted antique

decoys and more than 100 Currier and Ives prints. And there's a working 1912 carousel for the kids.

Twenty-eight miles (45 km) farther along Route 6A, near the elbow of the Cape, is **Brewster ❺**, another rainy-day favorite. The **Stony Brook Grist Mill** still grinds corn as it did in 1663. During April and May, schools of alewives (herring) returning from the Atlantic struggle in the mill-stream to leap up ladders that will lead them to the tranquil mill ponds where they spawn.

Brewster's **New England Fire and History Museum** (Memorial Day–Labor Day, Mon–Fri 10am–4pm; Sept–Oct Sat, Sun noon–4pm; tel: 508-896-5711) has one of the world's largest collections of antique fire equipment and memorabilia. There are also period buildings, including an apothecary, on the site.

## The Lower Cape

In 1961, in order to preserve the beauty of the Cape and to highlight a number of natural and historic sights, the ocean shorelines of six towns – Chatham, Orleans, Eastham, Wellfleet, Truro and Provincetown – were dedicated as the **Cape Cod National Seashore ❻** (CCNS) under the aegis of the National Park Service. Visitor centers, offering displays, films, and natural history interpretative programs, are located just off Route 6 at Eastham (**Salt Pond**) and at Provincetown (**Province Lands**). The view of dunes and ocean from the upper deck of the latter is spectacular.

The **Marconi Area** (South Wellfleet), where Guglielmo Marconi sent the first radio signal across the Atlantic (1903) is part of the CCNS. At **Race Point** in Provincetown, visit the **Life Saving Museum**, which displays the crude equipment used to rescue mariners from the hundreds of vessels once wrecked along this stretch of coast.

What attracts most people to the CCNS, however, are its magnificent beaches, sprawling, desert-like dunes, and heather-covered highlands, resembling, in Thoreau's words, a "Turkey carpet" in autumn. The best oceanside beaches are **Nauset (Orleans), Nauset Light (Eastham), Marconi (South Wellfleet), Head of the Meadow (Truro), Provincetown** and, above all, **Longnook (Truro)**. Arrive early to find parking at any of these spots – and bring a tolerance for bracing water temperatures.

Provincetown's popular beaches are **Herring Cove**, about a mile from town and whose southeast section is predominantly gay, and **Race Point**, a few miles north of town. It was at Race Point that Thoreau, after strolling, wrote: "Here a man may stand, and put all America behind him." Then there is **Long Point**, gained by walking across a mile-long causeway beginning at the west end of Commercial Street, near the Provincetown Inn. Near the start of the causeway a commemorative stone notes that it was "somewhere near here" that the Pilgrims first landed (no, it wasn't at Plymouth, as you'll see below).

## Provincetown

**Provincetown ❼**, at the very tip of the Cape, is a three-ring, often raucous circus. (If you wish to get there directly and avoid the town's notorious traffic, a high-speed passenger-only ferry operates from Boston's Long Wharf to Provincetown from May–Oct, tel: 617-227-4321; there's also air service from Boston). Thick with crafts shops, art galleries, stores (both elegant and tawdry), and restaurants, "P-town" combines a long-standing community of Portuguese fishing folk, a large gay population, and, during the summer, hordes of tourists. And yet serious artists maintain a tradition that

started in 1899 with the founding of the Cape Cod School of Art.

**Commercial Street** parallels the harbor and is the center of activity. Parallel and just inland is **Bradford Street**. Near Bradford Street on High Poll Hill Road is the **Pilgrim Monument** (Apr–Nov 9am–4.15pm daily; July and Aug until 6.15pm; tel: 508-487-1310), which commemorates the Pilgrims' stop in Provincetown in 1620 for six weeks before they moved on to Plymouth because of its more protected harbor and better water supplies. The monument, a slim and stately affair adapted from the Torre del Mangia in Siena and built in the early 1900s, is the tallest granite structure in the country. It towers 352 ft (107 meters) above the town and can be ascended (no elevators, but a tolerable climb via gentle ramps) for a grand view of the Lower Cape.

The **Provincetown Museum** at the base of the monument is strong on local history and commemorates the arctic explorations of townsman Donald MacMillan. Works of local artists are on show in the **Province-**

Map on page 202

*Pilgrim Monument, Provincetown.*

**BELOW:** tourist cabins at Provincetown.

Map on page 202

*Painting by Michael McGuire at the Provincetown Art Association.*

**BELOW:**
Hyannis Harbor.

**town Art Association & Museum** (460 Commercial Street; tel: 508-487-1750).

Leaving Provincetown, backtrack for 28 miles (45 km) on Route 6 to the traffic circle at **Orleans** and take Route 28 for 9 miles (14 km) south to **Chatham ⑧**, at the Cape's elbow. Though not without shops, galleries, inns, and restaurants, Chatham is everything Provincetown isn't – quiet, sedate, and more like an old-money Maine resort. (For excitement, head for the observation deck above the Fish Pier to watch the fishing boats return in early afternoon.)

The 1752 **Old Atwood House Museum** (347 Stage Harbor Road; June–Sept, Tues–Fri 1pm–4pm; tel: 508-945-2493) offers local history and seafaring exhibits and a remarkable series of paintings of local residents by Alice Stallknecht Wight.

From Chatham, continue west on State 28 along the Cape's South Shore, passing **Harwich ⑨**, where cranberries were first commercially cultivated. Old Harwich, incorporated in 1694, has resisted the overdevelopment that has plagued other towns, and its Winchmere harbor is one of the prettiest on the Cape.

After an overbuilt commercial stretch, you reach **Hyannis ❿** after 17 miles (27 km). It and neighboring Hyannisport are the commercial center and transportation hub of the Mid-Cape, with scheduled airline services to Boston, Martha's Vineyard and Nantucket and ferries to the two islands. A vintage train provides a one-hour sightseeing ride to Sandwich or to Buzzards Bay.

Oddly, the magnet at **Hyannisport** is the private Kennedy Compound, which isn't visible from the road (harbor cruise boats do advertise a glimpse). Visit, instead, the **Kennedy Memorial**, located on Lewis Bay (a pleasant walk); the **John F. Kennedy Museum**, on Main Street (508-790-3077), is primarily a photo gallery.

### History and oceanography

A further 17 miles (27 km) on Route 28 leads to elegant **Falmouth ⑪**, whose delightful green is surrounded by 18th- and 19th-century houses shaded by graceful elms. The **Julia Wood House** and the **Conant House Museum** (tel: 508-548-4857) are maintained by the Falmouth Historical Society: the former, dating from 1790, has a genuine widow's walk, while the latter features exhibits of whaling times. Eight miles (13 km) beyond Falmouth, at the southernmost tip of the Cape, is **Woods Hole**, famous for its **Oceanographic Institute** (tel: 508-457-2034). From here, ferries leave for Martha's Vineyard.

Leave Woods Hole on Route 28 and travel north 17 miles (27 km) to Bourne at the canal. Either cross the canal by the Bourne Bridge and then drive east for 3 miles (5 km) on Route 6 to join Route 3, or take Route 6 along the south side of the canal, which you'll then cross via the Sagamore Bridge. ❏

# RESTAURANTS

*Many of the restaurants below have limited hours and/or are closed off-season (generally October–May). Be sure to call ahead at those times.*

## Brewster

### Chillingsworth
2449 Main St., Route 6A, Tel: 508-896-3640. Open: L & D Tues–Sun. $$$$
www.chillingsworth.com.
Often cited as the finest dining spot on the Cape, the restaurant/inn (three guest rooms) is in a 300-year-old estate on six landscaped acres, and specializes in French and "sublimated" New England cuisine. Diners can choose from an à la carte, or 7-course table d'hôte, menu, and might opt for an appetizer of oysters in puff pastry, and an entrée of rare seared tuna tornadoes with fois gras.

## Cohasset

### Atlantica
Cohasset Harbor Inn 44 Border St., Tel: 781-383-0900. Open: D nightly, Sun brunch Oct–mid-June. $$–$$$
www.cohassetharborinn.com
With a fabulous harbor view, an outstanding raw bar, and a varied menu including maple hardwood grilled meats and fish with an assortment of sauces, this is a fine place on a clear summer's eve. An all-you-can eat Sunday brunch ($14.95) includes smoked salmon, a carving station, and choice of omelettes.

## Hingham

### Tosca
14 North St., Hingham, Tel: 781-740-0080. Open: D nightly Memorial Day–Columbus Day, Tues–Sun rest of year. $$$
www.eatwellinc.com
Italian-inspired cuisine with an American influence is served in a renovated 1910 Granary Marketplace building. The setting, with exposed brick, mahogany tiles and an open kitchen, is decidedly theatrical; the menu runs to specialties such as wood oven baked lasagna and pork osso buco.

## Falmouth

### Coonamessett Inn
311 Gifford St., Tel: 508-548-2300. Open: L&D year-round. $$$–$$$$
www.capecodrestaurants.org
Located in a 200-year-old inn on 6 manicured acres, this Cape perennial serves regional specialties such as grilled duck breast with southern peach sauce, and herb-crusted cod. Sunday all-you-can-eat brunch ($20) is a standout. A full menu or pub fare is served in the lounge, where there's music Fri–Sat nights.

## Hyannis

### Baxter's Fish 'n' Chips
Pleasant St., Tel: 508-775-4490. Open: L & D summer, daily; weekends May & Sept. $
All the right summertime ingredients: fried clams and other fresh seafood, homemade tartar sauce, a superb raw bar, and al fresco seating.

### The Paddock
20 Scudder Ave., Tel: 508-775-7677. Open: L Mon–Sat, D Mon–Sat, from noon on Sun. Open Apr–mid-Nov. $$$
www.paddockcapecod.com
Linens, candlelight and fresh flowers set the mood in this dining room which has been serving contemporary American cuisine for almost 35 years. Look for polenta crab cakes, a large selection of fresh fish, and prime beef.

## Provincetown

### Napi's
7 Freeman St., Tel: 800-571-6274. Open: L Oct–Apr, daily; D nightly. $$–$$$
www.napis-restaurant.com
Built from an hodge-podge of salvaged materials, furnished with antiques, and decorated with works of local artists, this offbeat establishment's offerings are every bit as eclectic – linguine and clams, bouillabaisse, Brazilian shrimp, and Thai chicken and shrimp.

## Plymouth

### Isaac's on the Waterfront
114 Water St., Plymouth; Tel: 508-830-0001. Open L&D Mon–Sat; D served all day Sun. $$$
With a magnificent view of Plymouth Harbor, and a deft touch with dishes such as shrimp in garlic butter and Lobster Fantasy, Isaac's has become one of Plymouth's most popular dining spots for both couples and families. Beef and poultry are also on the menu. Valet parking weekends.

## Sandwich

### Dan'l Webster Inn & Spa
149 Main St., Tel: 508-888-3622 or 800-444-3566. Open: B, L, D daily. $$$
www.dnlwebsterinn.com
The four dining rooms in this 300+-year-old inn are elegant and candle-lit, but don't expect just the usual standard Yankee fare: the menu includes sophisticated dishes such as hazelnut encrusted rack of pork, veal Oscar, and artichoke and mascarpone ravioli.

---

**PRICE CATEGORIES**

Prices for three-course dinner per person with a half-bottle of house wine, tax and tip:
**$** = under $25
**$$** = $25–$40
**$$$** = $40–$50
**$$$$** = more than $50

# **T**RANSPORTATION

# GETTING THERE AND GETTING AROUND

*Note: Unless indicated otherwise, Boston telephone numbers have a 617 area code.*

## GETTING THERE

### By Air

Logan International Airport handles more than 1,200 flights daily, with 52 carriers, including 14 international airlines, serving the airport. It is the northern terminal of the world's busiest airline market: the New York–Boston run. Delta and the US Air shuttles run hourly throughout the day between Logan and New York's LaGuardia Airport. Delta also services Kennedy Airport in New York less frequently.

Logan has five terminals (A–E). Note that domestic and international flights of the same airline do not necessarily use the same terminal. There is a free shuttle bus service between the terminals.

**Currency** may be exchanged at BankBoston at terminal E. **Rental lockers** are available at all terminals, except terminal D. It costs $3 to rent a cart. Hotel reservation information is available at the information booths in each terminal. **Hotels** near the airport include Holiday Inn

Boston-Logan Airport (tel: 569-5250) and Hilton Boston Logan Airport (tel: 568-6700).

Logan, just 3 miles (5 km) from downtown Boston, is closer to town than any other major airport in the nation: this refers to distance and not to time. Traffic can back up at the tunnels that go under the harbor to connect the airport and city. For up-to-date information on airport **traffic conditions**, call Massport's Ground Transportation Hotline (tel: 1-800-235-6426; www.massport.com),

operators are available Mon–Fri 8am–7pm, but be prepared to wait; recorded information is available at the same number outside these hours.

### *Getting into Town*

The **MBTA Blue Line** from Airport Station is the fastest and cheapest way to downtown (the $1 ride takes about 10 minutes) and to many other places. Free shuttle buses run between airport terminals and the subway station.

**Cabs** are located outside each

## AIRLINE TELEPHONE NUMBERS

Call Logan's public information office on: 800-235 6426 or 561-1800 (www.massport.com) for your airline's current terminal, as airlines often move about.
● Some useful telephone numbers include:
**Aer Lingus**, tel: 1-800-474-7424.
**Air Canada**, tel: 888-247-2262.
**Air France**, tel: 1-800-237-2747.
**American**, tel: 1-800-433-7300.
**British Airways**, tel: 1-800-247-9297.
**Cape Air**, tel: 1-800-352-0714.
**Continental**, tel: 1-800-525-0280.

**Delta**, tel: 1-800-221-1212.
**Delta Express**, tel: 1-800-325-5205.
**Frontier**, tel: 800-432-1359.
**Iceland Air**, tel: 800-223-5500.
**KLM**, tel: 1-800-374-7747.
**Korean Air**, tel: 1-800—438-5000.
**Lufthansa**, tel: 1-800-645-3880.
**Northwest (International)**, tel: 1-800-225-2525.
**Southwest**, tel: 800-445-9267.
**United Airlines**, tel: 1-800-241-6522.
**US Air**, tel: 1-800-428-4322.
**Virgin Atlantic Airways**, tel: 1-800-862-8621.
● Other useful airport number: **Traveler's Aid** tel: 542-7286.

terminal. Fares to downtown should average about $25–$30, including tip, providing there are no major traffic jams. Airways Transportation **buses** leave all terminals every half-hour for downtown and Back Bay hotels, and several major bus companies, including Bonanza, Concord Trailways, Peter Pan and Vermont Transit, serve many outlying suburbs and distant destinations.

A delightful way to approach the city and especially useful for those staying in downtown hotels (Boston Harbor, Boston Marriot Long Wharf, Langham Hotel, Marriott Residence Inn, Boston Harbor on Tudor Wharf, Millennium Bostonian) is by **water taxi**. Harbor Express (tel: 222-6999; www.harborexpress.com ) docks at Long Wharf before continuing on to the South Shore. The shuttle operates year-round. Call or check their website for times. City Water Taxi (tel: 422-0392; open Apr–Nov; www.citywatertaxi .com) offers service from the airport to many of the hotels, as well as to the World Trade Center, North Station, and to Pier 4 in Charlestown, just a few minutes walk from the USS *Constitution*. Rowes Wharf Taxi (tel: 406-8584; www.roweswharfwatertaxi.com) operates year-round, from 7am to 7pm on demand, and also charges $10; round trip $17. The voyage to Boston Harbor locations takes just about 10 minutes. Tickets are sold on board.

A free shuttle bus (Route #66) operates between the airport ferry dock and all of the airline terminals.

## By Rail

Boston is the northern terminus of **Amtrak**'s Northeast Corridor. Passenger trains arrive at South Station (Atlantic Avenue and Summer Street, tel: 482-3660/1-800-872-7245; for the hearing-impaired, tel:1-800-523-6590; www.amtrak.com) from New York, Washington, DC, and Philadelphia, with connections from all points in the nationwide Amtrak system. They also stop at Back Bay Station (145 Dartmouth Street, tel: 345-7958).

Trains travel between New York and Boston daily; the average travel time is 5 hours, but the Acela high speed train makes the journey in 3¾ hours. South Station is also the eastern terminus for Amtrak's Lake Shore Limited, which travels daily between Chicago and Boston by way of Cleveland, Buffalo, Rochester and Albany. One train daily makes the journey in 20 hours.

## By Bus

Several intercity bus companies serve Boston. The two largest, **Greyhound** (tel: 526-1800/1-800-231-2222; www.greyhound .com) and **Peter Pan/Trailways/ Bonanza** (tel:1-800-343-9999; www.peterpanbus.com), have frequent daily services from New York City and Albany, NY, as well as services from points within New England. Greyhound serves the entire United States and parts of Canada; it offers unlimited advance purchase fares for 7, 14 or 30-day periods.

Nearby destinations are served by smaller bus companies such as American Eagle, C & J Trailways, Concord Trailways, and Plymouth & Brockton. All converge at South Station Transportation Center, 700 Atlantic Avenue.

Both Greyhound and Peter Pan also have terminals at Riverside in Newton, on the "D" Branch of the Green Line.

## By Car

**From the west**:
Route I-90 (Mass. Pike) is the most clear route inbound, and feeds directly into the Ted Williams Tunnel to Logan Airport and points north. Three major exits before WIlliams Tunnel: Exits 18–20 (Cambridge/Allston) are best for Cambridge and Charles River locations;

Exit 22 (Prudential Center/Copley Square) is best for Back Bay, Fenway, Kenmore Square and Boston Common (via Boylston, Charles, Beacon, Park and Tremont Streets); Exit 24 (Expressway/Downtown) is best for Downtown and Liberty Tunnel (former Central Artery, now underground) access.
**From the south**:
Routes I-95, 24 and 3 all "feed" into Route I-93 inbound.
Two major exits are:
● Kneeland Street/Chinatown – best for Back Bay, Theater District and Boston Common Visitor Center (via Kneeland, Charles, Beacon, Park and Tremont Streets);
● Dock Square – best for Airport, North End, Waterfront and Faneuil Hall Marketplace.
**From the north**:
Routes 1 and I-93 enter Boston on elevated highway structures. Major exits:
● Storrow Drive – best for Back Bay, Beacon Hill, Cambridge and Boston Common Visitor Center (via Government Center exit and Cambridge Street, which becomes Tremont Street);
● High Street – for Downtown;
● Kneeland Street – best for Chinatown and Theater District.

## Car Rentals

Car rentals can be arranged at the ground level of all terminals. Firms represented include: **Alamo** (tel:1-800-327-9633); **Avis** (tel: 1-800-831-2847); Budget (tel: 497-1800, 1-800-527-0700); **Dollar** (tel: 634-0006, 1-800-800-4000); **Enterprise** (tel: 561-4488, 1-800-325-8007); **Hertz** (tel: 1-800-654-3131); **National** (tel: 1-800-227-7368); **Thrifty** (tel: 1-800-847-4389).

If you are driving from Logan to downtown Boston, you can use either the **Sumner Tunnel** or the **Ted Williams Tunnel**. Both have a $3 inbound fee, and no outbound fee. Opinions differ as to which is faster, but the Williams, which is newer, generally can save a few minutes – especially if you are heading for points west or south. When bad traffic delays occur at the tunnels, take Route 1A North to Route 16 to Route 1 South and cross the **Tobin Bridge** into Boston.

## GETTING AROUND

### Public Transportation

#### General

Boston, it's justly claimed, is a walker's city – a good thing, for it is certainly not a driver's city. The city planners, as Emerson noted, were the cows, and it has been suggested that the Puritan belief in predestination extended even to urban design. Streets appeared where Providence chose to lay them – along cow paths, Native American trails and colonial wagon tracks – and are linked by crooked little alleys.

City planners, however, did come into their own in the middle of the 19th century and as a result the Back Bay and, to a lesser extent, the South End have impeccable grid systems.

If you attempt to drive in the city, and feel frustrated and inadequate, be consoled that many Bostonians feel the same way. Being faced by cars coming the wrong way on a one-way street, being stuck in a traffic jam, getting lost and then being unable to find a parking space is about par for the course. It's said that indicating a turn is considered "giving information to the enemy."

#### Parking

Conveniently located public parking facilities are found throughout the city, including at Government Center; Post Office Square; the Public Garden; the Prudential Center; and on Clarendon Street near the John Hancock Tower. Private lots are scattered around.

A number of parking garages are situated close to Harvard Square in Cambridge. Try Charles Square Garage, 1 Bennett Street; Church Street Parking Lot, Church Street; Harvard Square Garage, JFK and Eliot streets; and Holyoke Center Garage, access via Dunster and Holyoke streets.

Better by far to use the subway (aka rapid transit or "T") and bus services provided by the MBTA (Massachusetts Bay Transportation Authority).

### Transport

#### Rapid Transit

Massachusetts Bay Transportation Authority (MBTA; www.mbta.com; for general information tel: 222-3200/1-800-392-6100; for the hearing impaired tel: 722-5146; weekdays 6:30am–11pm, weekends 9am–6pm. For customer service tel: 222-5215; for MBTA police emergency tel: 222-1212. For easy reference, see the subway map on page 257.

Ever since it was inaugurated in 1897, the subway (nowadays the rapid transit or, more usually, the "T") has been a source of amusement for Bostonians. One ditty, "The Man Who Never Returned," tells of poor Charlie who was "doomed to ride forever 'neath the streets of Boston" because he lacked the nickel fare necessary to alight.

However, despite severe overcrowding during rush hours the "T" is a fairly efficient, clean and user-friendly system.

The five rapid transit lines – Red, Green, Orange, Blue, and Silver – that radiate out from downtown Boston cling to the name "subway" even though all lines run above ground for part of their route, and the Silver Line is actually served by buses.

There are more than 75 rapid transit stations, usually named for a nearby square, street, or landmark. In addition, Green Line trains stop at many street corners along the surface portion of their routes. All five lines intersect in downtown Boston. Transfers between lines, at no extra charge, are possible at:

**Park Street** – Red and Green Lines (with underground walkway to the Orange Line at Downtown Crossing).

**Downtown Crossing** – Red and Orange Lines (with underground walkway to the Green Line at Park Street).

**Government Center** – Blue and Green Lines.

**State** – Blue and Orange Lines. Haymarket and North Station – Green and Orange Lines. (This connection is considerably more convenient at Haymarket than at North Station).

"Inbound" is always towards downtown Boston – Park Street, Downtown Crossing and Government Center. "Outbound" means away from downtown. Outside of central Boston, both the Red and Green Lines have branches. Check the sign on the front of the train. Green Line trains (also called streetcars or simply cars)

### TAXICABS

Taxi stands are common at popular tourist sites. Companies to call include: **Bay State Taxi Service**, tel: 566-5000.
**Boston Cab Association Inc**, tel: 262-2227.
**Checker Taxi Co.**, tel: 536-7500.
**Independent Taxi Operators Association**, tel: 426-8700.
**Red Cab**, tel: 734-5000.
**Town Taxi**, tel: 536-5000. Tolls for bridges and tunnels are paid by the passenger. The charge for each ⅙ mile is 30 cents. There is no extra fare for additional passengers. The driver may charge extra for trunks or unusual cargo (e.g. crocodiles). For trips over 12 miles (19 km) from downtown flat rates are charged – $2.30 per mile plus tolls. Tipping is not mandatory but it is a brave (or callous) soul who does not add 15 percent to the fare.

## DISABLED TRAVELERS

The MBTA (Massachusetts Bay Transit Authority) has a good website (www.mbta.com) with information about which means of transportation are accessible to disabled travelers. The City of Boston's Disabled Person's Commission can be reached on 635-3682.

carry letters to indicate different branches: B – Boston College; C – Cleveland Circle; D – Riverside; E – Heath Street or Arborway. A red line through the letter on a sign means that the train goes only part way on that branch.

Turnstiles in the underground stations of the "T" accept only **tokens**. These can be purchased at the collectors' booths. One token ($1.25 for adults, 35¢ for seniors with MBTA senior citizen card; 60¢ for ages 5–11.) permits adult travelers to ride as far as they wish without extra payment. When boarding the "T" at surface stations one token or the exact change is necessary. Getting there on the "T" can be cheaper than getting back.

Although most outbound fares (except to Quincy Adams and to Braintree), regardless of distance, are $1.25, an inbound journey from outlying stations is $2 or more.

The Rapid Transit operates 20 hours each day – from shortly after 5am until past 1am. On Sundays, service begins about 40 minutes later than on other days. Last trains leave downtown Boston at 12.45am. On Friday and Saturday, a Night Owl bus, which parallels the subway lines, runs until 2:30am.
● For information on the one, three, or seven day MBTA discount pass, see *Discounts* in the A-Z section *(page 236)*.

### By Bus
The majority of the MBTA's 160-plus bus routes operate feeder services linking subway stations

to neighborhoods not directly served by the rapid transit system. Some crosstown routes connect stations on different subway lines without going into downtown. Only a few MBTA buses actually enter downtown Boston, and most of these are express buses from outlying areas.

One service that visitors might wish to use is Route 1, which travels along Massachusetts Avenue (at the western end of the Back Bay) across the Charles River to MIT and onto Harvard Square. MBTA buses also serve Lexington (board the T-62 or T-76 at Alewife) and Marblehead (board the T-441 or T-442 at Haymarket).

The basic MBTA bus fare is 90¢, seniors 25¢. On a few relatively long routes, zone fares – charges per additional zone, up to $2 – are imposed. Express bus fares range from $2.20 to $3.45, depending on the length of the route. Exact change is required on buses, and dollar bills are not accepted. MBTA tokens are accepted, but change is not returned.

### Commuter Rail
The MBTA Commuter Rail extends from downtown Boston to as far as 60 miles (100 km) away and serves such tourist destinations as Concord, Lowell, Salem, Ipswich, Gloucester and Rockport. In addition, Amtrak's "Downeaster" serves Portland, Maine.

Trains to the north and northwest of Boston depart from **North Station**, while trains to points south and west of the city leave from **South Station**. All south side commuter trains, except the Fairmount Line, also stop at the **Back Bay Station**. For information, tel: 222-3200.

Commuter rail fares are zoned according to distance. A trip from Boston to Salem, for example, costs $3.45. Tickets are sold at the railway stations or can be purchased on the train, subject to a surcharge.

### Limousine Services
**Carey Limousine**, tel: 623-8700.
**Commonwealth Limousine**, tel: 1-800-558-5466/787-5575.
**Escort**, tel: 926-6900.
**Fifth Avenue**, tel: 1-800-343-2071/884-2600.
**LTI Wordwide Limousine Service**, tel: 523-0727.

### Commuter Boat
Several water taxis offer service between waterfront hotels and waterfront attractions and Boston Harbor wharves. Among them: **Harbor Express** (tel: 222-6999; www.harborexpress.com), which goes to Hull and Quincy; **City Water Taxi** (tel: 422-0392; open Apr–Nov; www.citywatertaxi.com), which also continues on to Pier 4 in Charlestown for visits to the USS *Constitution;* **Rowes Wharf Water Taxi** (tel: 406-8584; www.roweswharfwatertaxi.com); and **Boston Harbor Cruises** (tel: 781-749-8009; www.bostonharborcruises.com), which travels between Rowes Wharf and Hingham Mon–Fri year-round: the one-way fare is $6.

### Driving

### Getting out of Boston
**To the west**:
Route I-90 (Mass Pike) is the best route. From Downtown, enter the "Pike" at Kneeland Street; from the Back Bay take Arlington Street, Copley Square or Mass. Avenue at Newbury Street.
**To the south and the north**:
Route 93 (Southeast Expressway) serves the South Shore and Cape Cod (via Route 3) and Rhode Island and New York (via Route I-95). Route I-93 (North) serves the North Shore and the New England Coast (via Routes 1 and I-95), New Hampshire (via Route I-93) and Vermont (via Routes I-93 to I-89 at Concord, NH).

# ACCOMMODATIONS

## HOTELS, YOUTH HOSTELS, BED & BREAKFASTS

### Choosing a Hotel

The city of Boston is fairly well endowed with hotels, although one might be tempted to question this during spring and fall when conventions are in full swing. Hard facts are that the metropolitan area has more than 31,000 hotel rooms, of which almost half are in Boston and Cambridge. Bed and breakfast accommodations are becoming increasingly popular and can be of a high standard. And then, of course, there's the inevitable "Y" and youth hostels.

Some visitors might prefer the rarefied atmosphere of Cambridge, a 10- to 20-minute trip from Boston and easily reached by public transport. Another alternative is to stay in one of the many hotels in Greater or Metropolitan Boston and join the MBTA (Massachusetts Bay Transportation Authority) commuters for a 30–40-minute journey every morning and evening. These suburban hotels, most of which belong to major chains, tend to be less expensive than city center hotels. The lodging tax in the Boston area is 12.45 percent.

### Hostels & "Ys"

Youth hostels offer basic and clean accommodations for very little money. You may purchase a membership on site ($28/year) or pay an extra $3 per night for your stay.

**Boston International Youth Hostel**, 12 Hemenway Street, Fenway. Tel: 536-9455, fax: 424-6558, www.bostonhostel.org
Male, female and co-ed rooms with shared baths for members and non-members. Kitchen, laundry rooms, and continental breakfast. Guests under 18 must be accompanied by parent or legal guardian.

**Hostelling International Boston @ Fenway**, 575 Commonwealth Avenue. Tel: 536-9455, fax: 424-6558, www.bostonhostel.org
On the campus of Boston University, the facility, a dormitory during the academic year, is open May–Aug. Private rooms or small dormitories with three beds are available, and there's internet access and a laundry.

**YMCA of Greater Boston**, 316 Huntington Avenue, Fenway. Tel: 536-7800, fax: 267-4653, www.ymcaboston.org
Clean single and double rooms with color TV for men only. Also three- and four-person accommodations. Guests have full use of all athletic facilities. Maximum stay is 10 days.

**Berkeley Residence YWCA**, 40 Berkeley Street. Tel: 375-2524, fax: 375-2525, www.ywcaboston.org/berkeley
The 200-room facility close to Copley Square has gone co-ed, renting singles and doubles for up to 13 nights per stay.

### A Place of Your Own

If you are planning to stay in the area for an extended period, it may be more economical to choose a short- or long-term rental. Among the agencies that offer this service:

**A B&B Agency of Boston**
47 Commercial Wharf
Tel: 720-3540 or 800-248-9262
www.boston-bnbagency.com
**AAA Corporate Rentals, Ltd.**
120 Milk St.
Tel: 357-6900 or 800-487-5020
www.furnishedapt.com
**Back Bay Accommodations**
Marlborough St.
Tel: 866-449-5302
www.bnbboston.com
**Greenhouse Apartments**
150 Huntington Avenue
Tel: 267-6777 or 800-330-4020
www.greenhouseapt.com
**Phillips Club at Boston Commons**
(specializing in long-term rentals)
Three Avery St.
Tel: 423-8500
www.phillipsclub.com

## CENTRAL AREA

### BEACON HILL

#### Luxury

**XV Beacon**
15 Beacon Street
Tel: 670-1500
Fax: 670-2525
www.xvbeacon.com
61-room boutique hotel, combining classic opulence and high-tech toys. All 60 rooms in the 1903 beaux arts building have working gas fireplaces, queen 4-poster beds, CD players, and heated towel racks. Complimentary in-town car service is included, plus 24-hour room service.

#### Moderate

**Beacon Hill Hotel**
25 Charles Street
Tel: 723-7575
Fax: 723-7525
www.beaconhillhotel.com
Just steps from Boston Common, the privately owned hotel, in a converted 1830s townhouse, has 12 rooms and a suite, all with flat screen TVs and abundant amenities. There are great views of Charles Street and Beacon Hill. The hotel is also home to the popular Beacon Hill Bistro.
**Holiday Inn-Government Center**
5 Blossom Street
Tel: 742-7630. Fax: 742-7804
www.holidayinnselectboston.com
Situated at the foot of the "wrong" side of

Beacon Hill, but next to the Massachusetts General Hospital and with the river just a few yards away. All 303 rooms offers standard hotel amenities, and Foster's Bar & Grill is on site.
**John Jeffries House**
14 David G. Mugar Way
Tel: 617-367-1866. Fax: 617-742-0313
www.johnjeffrieshouse.com
Comfortable, 46-room inn with elegant common rooms and accommodations ranging from studios for singles to deluxe units for up to three persons. All have full baths, phones, and TVs, and most have kitchenettes. Elevator.
**Onyx Hotel**
155 Portland Street
Tel: 557-9955
Fax: 557-0005
www.onyxhotel.com
The 112 rooms in this boutique hotel are decorated in a sophisticated palette of black, taupe and red, and offer all of the latest high-tech amenities. The Ruby Room on the ground floor hops at cocktail hour. Pet-friendly.

### DOWNTOWN

#### Luxury

**Boston Omni Parker House Hotel**
60 School Street
Tel: 227-8600. Fax: 742-5729
www.omnihotels.com
The country's oldest

continuously operating hotel (since 1854), across from Boston Common, has 551 guest rooms and common areas have been given a multi-million-dollar overhaul, and amenities include several bars, a 24-hour gym, and dataport and ethernet connections.
**Nine Zero**
90 Tremont Street
Tel: 772-5800
Fax: 772-5810
www.ninezero.com
One of Boston's sleekest new hotels, offering high-tech, high-speed, high-touch amenities along with personalized service, custom-designed beds and down comforters. Spire restaurant serves fine contemporary American fare.
**Ritz-Carlton Boston Common**
2 Avery Street
Tel: 574-7100 or 800-241-3333. Fax: 574-7200
www.ritzcarlton.com
Between the Financial and Theater Districts and overlooking the Common, the hotel is a "contemporary luxury urban sanctuary". It offers all the amenities of its older sister across the Common, but the 193 rooms, including 43 suites, have modern furnishings.

#### Moderate

**Harborside Inn**
185 State Street
Tel: 723-7500 / 888-723-7565

Fax: 670-6015
www.harborsideinn.com
The 54 rooms on eight floors of a renovated warehouse (not near the water) have high ceilings, exposed brick walls, Oriental rugs, and hardwood floors. Quieter rooms are away from State Street.

### NORTH END

#### Luxury

**Millennium Bostonian Hotel**
Faneuil Hall Marketplace
26 North Street
Tel: 523-3600. Fax: 523-2454
www.millenniumhotels.com
In two adjoining renovated warehouses, the hotel has 201 rooms and suites, some with working fireplaces and small, private balconies. Some rooms are quite small, and those overlooking Quincy Market can be very noisy, but the location is incomparable. There's a gym, the Atrium Lounge featuring piano jazz, and the popular Seasons restaurant.

#### PRICE CATEGORIES

A very approximate guide to current room rates for a standard double per night is:
**Luxury** = over $300
**Expensive** = $200–300
**Moderate** = $100–200
**Inexpensive** = under $100

# WATERFRONT

**HOTELS**

### Luxury

**Boston Harbor Hotel**
70 Rowes Wharf
Tel: 439-7000
Fax: 330-9450
www.bhh.com
Board the airport water shuttle at Logan and, seven minutes later, step into the luxury of the city's foremost waterside hotel. Each of the 230 rooms has either a harbor or skyline view. Eighteen rooms are specially designed for the physically disabled. A museum-quality art collection decorates the public areas. Meritage (*see Restaurant listings*) offers superb dining.

**Boston Marriott Hotel Long Wharf**
296 State Street, Long Wharf
Tel: 227-0800
Fax: 227-8595
www.marriott.com
Situated at the waterfront immediately next to the Aquarium and within a minute's walk of Quincy Market. Many of the 400 rooms have panoramic views of the harbor; all are well-appointed with standard hotel amenities.

**Seaport Hotel**
1 Seaport Lane
Tel: 385-4000
Fax: 385-4001
www.seaporthotel.com
One of the city's newest waterfront hotels, close to the World Trade Center and South Station, has 427 state-of-the-art, non-smoking guest rooms with hand-crafted cherry furnishings, marble baths, and work desks. The luxurious health club includes a 50-ft heated pool and extensive exercise facilities. Aura Restaurant (*see restaurant listings*) specializes in seafood. Pets weighing up to 50 lbs. are welcome.

# CHARLESTOWN

**HOTELS**

### Moderate

**Residence Inn by Marriott Boston Harbor on Tudor Wharf**
34-44 Charles River Avenue
Tel: 242-9000
Fax: 242-9000
www.marriott.com/bostw
All 168 suites at this new waterfront hotel offer views of the harbor or downtown and have fully-equipped kitchens. There's a heated indoor pool, fitness room, and complimentary hot breakfast buffet. A private water taxi ($) transports guests to Logan Airport and other harbor destinations.

### Inexpensive

**The Constitution Inn**
150 Second Avenue
Charlestown Navy Yard
Tel: 241-8400/800-495-9622
Fax: 241-2856
www.constitutioninn.com
This former YMCA is just five blocks from the USS *Constitution* and has 147 plainly-furnished, non-smoking rooms with air conditioning and some kitchenettes. Rates include a pass to the state-of-the-art health club, which includes an indoor heated pool, sauna, and weight room. Special rate for military personnel. Parking, a block away, is $6. Children over the age of 12 are welcome.

# BACK BAY & FENWAY

### Luxury

**Boston Marriott Copley Place Hotel**
110 Huntington Avenue
Tel: 236-5800
Fax: 236-5885
www.marriott.com/marriott/bosco
Large, reliable hotel with 1,149 handsomely-appointed rooms, including 36 suitable for the disabled. The hotel is linked by indoor passages to the Copley Place shopping mall and to the Prudential Center.

**Boston Park Plaza Hotel & Towers**
64 Arlington Street
Tel: 426-2000
Fax: 426-5545
www.bostonparkplaza.com
Historic hotel near Boston Common has a spacious, chandeliered lobby, 950 guest rooms (some on the small side, others recently renovated), eight restaurants and lounges, and spa services; a popular spot for conventions.

**The Eliot Suite Hotel**
370 Commonwealth Avenue
Tel: 267-1607
Fax: 536-9114
www.eliothotel.com
European-style boutique hotel offers 95 elegantly-furnished rooms and suites (some with kitchenettes and sitting areas), and Clio, one of the city's finest restaurants (*see restaurant listings*).

**The Fairmont Copley Plaza**
138 St. James Avenue
Tel: 267-5300
Fax: 24706681
www.fairmont.com.
With 383 European-style rooms, many with period furnishings, the hotel overlooking Copley Square remains *la grande dame* of Boston hotels. Some rooms are on the small side

and rather plain; those overlooking the Square are much in demand. Be sure to have a drink at the Oak Bar.

**Four Seasons Hotel Boston**
200 Boylston Street
Tel: 338-4400
Fax: 351-2051
www.fourseasons.com
Elegance and sybaritic living are hallmarks of this 15-story, 274-room red-brick hotel overlooking the Public Garden. The service and cuisine, particularly in the restaurant Aujourd Hui (see restaurant listings), set standards city-wide.

**The Lenox**
61 Exeter Street
Tel: 536-5300
Fax: 266-790
www.lenoxhotel.com
Understated elegance and attention to detail define this 212-room hotel, privately owned since it opened in 1900. Rooms are decorated in French Provincial, Oriental, or Colonial decor, and the corner rooms are particularly spacious.

Azure Restaurant (see restaurant listings) has a fine reputation.

**The Ritz-Carlton**
15 Arlington Street
Tel: 536-5700 or 800-241-3333. Fax: 536-9340
www.ritzcarlton.com
Not quite as glitzy as the Four Seasons, but in its own way every bit as luxurious. Some of the 278 rooms overlook the Public Garden. Forty-one are suites (many with wood-burning fireplaces), including one for children, with specially scaled-down fixtures.

### Moderate

**463 Beacon Street Guest House**
Tel: 617-536-1302. Fax: 617-247-8876
www.463beacon.com
A great hotel alternative for stays of a week or longer, this turn-of-the-20th-century brownstone close to Massachusetts Avenue has 20 comfortable rooms with private baths, phones, TVs and air conditioning; many

have kitchenettes or full kitchens. Rooms available by the night.

**Best Western Boston-The Inn at Longwood**
342 Longwood Avenue
Tel: 731-4700
Fax: 731-4870
www.innatlongwood.com
161 nicely-furnished and fully-equipped rooms in the heart of Longwood Medical area and near Back Bay attractions.

**Boston Hotel Buckminster**
645 Beacon Street
Tel: 236-7050
Fax: 262-0068
www.bostonhotelbuckminster.com
This hotels, built in 1897, has 94 rooms, including 24 suites. All have private baths and one to three beds (the one-bed units fall into the budget price range) and offer either a view of Kenmore Square or the skyline. Continental breakfast included.

**Days Hotel Boston**
1234 Soldiers Field Road
Tel: 254-1234
Fax: 254-4300
www.dayshotelboston.com
Three miles from Fen-

way Park, this chain hotel has 117 rooms and suites, a fitness room, outdoor pool, and free parking.

**Howard Johnson Hotel Fenway**
1271 Boylston Street
Tel: 267-8300
www.hojo.com
Simple motel accommodations close to Fenway Park and Kenmore Square.

**The MidTown Hotel**
220 Huntington Avenue
Tel: 262-1000 / 800-343-1177
Fax: 262-8739
www.midtownhotel.com
Standard 159-room motel with outdoor pool; near Symphony Hall, Christian Science complex and Prudential Center. Free parking.

**Newbury Guest House**
261 Newbury Street
Tel: 437-7666 / 800-437-7668
www.newburyguesthouse.com
Three 1880s single-family Victorian homes were renovated in the 1990s to create this elegant, 32-room inn. Handicapped rooms and elevator. Quieter rooms are in the back.

# THE SOUTH END

### HOTELS

### Moderate

**Chandler Inn**
26 Chandler Street
Tel: 482-3450 or 800-842-3450. Fax: 542-3428
www.chandlerinn.com
Located between Copley Square and Park Square, all 56 rooms at this small, gay-friendly hotel have work desks, satellite TVs, and data

ports. Some are quite small, as are the baths, but the ambiance is good. If you want quiet, ask for a room away from the swinging ground-floor bar.

**Clarendon Square Inn**
198 West Brookline Street
Tel: 536-2229
www.clarendonsquare.com
This beautifully-appointed, gay-friendly circa 1860 Victorian B&B offers the amenities of a small luxury hotel and the warmth of

a small inn. Rooms have wood burning fireplaces, DSL, DVD players, and views of the Boston skyline. There's a rooftop hot tub.

### Inexpensive

**Nolan House B&B**
10 G Street
Tel: 269-1550 / 800-383-1550
www.nolanhouse.com
The three guest rooms in this circa 1860 nonsmoking Victorian home are air conditioned and

comfortably furnished. There's free parking, a full breakfast, and bus service right outside the door. Rooms have shared or private baths.

### PRICE CATEGORIES

A very approximate guide to current room rates for a standard double per night is:
**Luxury** = over $300
**Expensive** = $200–300
**Moderate** = $100–200
**Inexpensive** = under $100

# CAMBRIDGE

## HOTELS

### Luxury

**Charles Hotel**
1 Bennett Street
Tel. 864-1200. Fax: 864-5715
www.charleshotel.com
A touch of class on the edge of Harvard Square: All 299 rooms are well appointed and include high-tech amenities. The Regattabar is one of the best jazz venues in the region. A shopping mall is attached to the hotel, and the Square's shops and restaurants are at the doorstep.

**Hotel Marlowe**
25 Edwin H. Land Boulevard
Tel: 868-8000 or 800-825-7040. Fax: 868-8001
www.hotelmarlowe.com
A boutique hotel with 236 guest rooms and suites near the banks of the Charles River, combining high-tech amenities with family- and pet-friendly services. Fitness center.

**Hyatt Regency**
575 Memorial Drive
Tel: 492-1234. Fax: 491-6906
www.hyatt.com
The "pyramid on the Charles", with its striking glass atrium, is closer to MIT than to Harvard and just across the bridge from Boston University. Some of the 500 rooms offer great views of the river and Boston skyline. Fifteen rooms designed for the physically disabled.

**Royal Sonesta**
5 Cambridge Parkway
Tel: 806-4200. Fax: 806-4232
www.sonesta.com
400 rooms on the banks of the Charles offer great views of the Boston skyline. The hotel is close to the Science Museum and practically next door is the CambridgeSide Galleria, a popular shopping mall. Free shuttle service into Boston and Harvard Square.

### Moderate

**DoubleTree Guest Suites**
400 Soldiers Field Road, Boston
Tel: 783-0090. Fax: 783-0897
www.doubletreehotels.com
On the river, next to the Harvard Business School, this is a great hotel for families. All 310 suites have two rooms, each with a telephone and TV. The living rooms contain sofa-beds, and children under 18 stay free. Breakfast is included in the room rate. Harvard Square is just a 15-minute stroll away.

**The Harvard Square Hotel**
110 Mount Auburn Street
Tel: 864-5200. Fax: 492-4896
www.harvardsquarehotel.com
Totally renovated in 2003, the six-floor, 72-room hotel in the heart of Harvard Square offers all standard amenities. Parking is $25 per night.

**The Inn at Harvard**
1201 Massachusetts Avenue
Cambridge 02138
Tel: 491-2222/1-800-528-0444. Fax: 520-3711
www.innatharvard.com
Harvard graduate Graham Gund designed his four-story hotel, constructed in 1992, to blend in with the university. The 113 rooms, built around a four-story atrium, are pleasantly appointed and have data ports. Restaurant on the premises.

**Kendall Hotel**
350 Main Street
Tel: 577-1300. Fax: 577-1377
www.kendallhotel.com
Boutique hotel in a handsomely renovated, 1893 Victorian firehouse, with 65 antiques-filled rooms; those in the seven-story tower have jacuzzi baths with separate showers. Non-smoking. Underground parking.

**Marriott Cambridge**
2 Cambridge Center
Tel: 494-6600. Fax: 494-0036
www.marriott.com
A 25-story, 431-room hotel adjacent to a shopping complex. Subway stop at the hotel entrance.

**Mary Prentiss Inn**
6 Prentiss Street
Tel: 661-2929. Fax: 661-5989
www.maryprentissinn.com
This National Register of Historical Places neoclassical Greek Revival inn has 20 rooms with exposed beams, shutters and antiques. Some have wood-burning fireplaces and jacuzzis. Full breakfast and afternoon tea. Lush outdoor deck. Free parking.

**Sheraton Commander**
16 Garden Street
Tel: 547-4800/1-800-325-3535. Fax: 868-8322
www.sheratoncommander.com
An old-fashioned but well-kept 176-room hotel near Harvard Square. Some rooms have Boston rockers, four-poster beds, and kitchenettes.

**University Park Hotel**
20 Sydney Street (close to the mit campus)
Tel: 577-0200. Fax: 494-8366
www.univparkhotel.com
This 210-room hotel in a not very attractive area is owned by MIT and managed by Doubletree. All rooms have Sony playstations, dual phones and data ports, and are fitted with ergonomically- designed furniture and decorated with art from the MIT collection and the deCordova Museum. Rooftop garden.

### Inexpensive

**Howard Johnson Hotel Cambridge**
777 Memorial Drive
Tel: 492-7777. Fax: 492-6038
www.hojo.com
A modern, 204-room motel, popular with tour groups, situated on the Cambridge side of the Charles River about equidistant from Harvard College and MIT and across the river from Boston University. Many rooms offer splendid views of the Boston skyline.

### Budget

**A Friendly Inn at Harvard Square**
1673 Cambridge Street
Tel: 547-7851. Fax: 547-0202
www.afinow.com/afi
"The intelligent choice for those who want their brains stimulated and not their wallets" – a comfortable inn close to Harvard Square. All rooms have private baths, phones, air conditioning, TV, and DSL. Free Parking.

# SOUTH SHORE & CAPE COD

## HOTELS

### Cohasset

#### Moderate

**Cohasset Harbor Inn**
44 Border St., 02025
Tel: 781-383-06650. Fax:
781-383-2872
www.cohassetharborinn.com
Beautifully situated
overlooking the harbor,
this year-round inn
offers a variety of
accommodations includ-
ing standard rooms,
mini-suites, and spa-
cious suites overlooking
the water. Atlantica
Restaurant serves din-
ner Wed–Sun and Sun
brunch; the casual Olde
Salt Restaurant offers
al fresco dining.

**CAPE COD
Note: many lodgings on
the Cape are seasonal
and require a minimum
stay, especially on
weekends and holi-
days. Be sure to call
ahead for reservations.**

### Barnstable

#### Moderate

**Beechwood Inn**
2839 Main St., Route 6A,
02630
Tel: 508-362-6618/800-609-
6618. Fax: 508-362-0298
www.beechwoodinn.com
Two of the six guest

## PRICE CATEGORIES

A very approximate
guide to current room
rates for a standard
double per night is:
**Luxury** = over $300
**Expensive** = $200–300
**Moderate** = $100–200
**Inexpensive** = under $100

rooms in this three-
story, 1853 Queen
Anne home have fire-
places; all are furnished
with antiques. The par-
lor is pure Victorian,
and the porch swing is a
lovely spot to while
away a few hours.

### Brewster

#### Moderate–Expensive

**Captain Freeman Inn**
15 Breakwater Rd., 02631
Tel: 508-896-7481/800-843-
4664. Fax: 508-896-5618
www.captainfreemaninn.com
A luxurious 1860s ship-
builder's home with 14
antiques-filled spacious
rooms (some with
whirlpool tubs) and a
heated, outdoor pool.
Bicycles are available
for guests.

#### Inexpensive

**Old Sea Pines Inn**
2553 Main St., Route 6A,
02631
Tel: 508-896-6114. Fax: 508-
896-7387
www.oldseapinesinn.com
Rooms at this 1907,
non-smoking Shingle-
style mansion, once a
girls' boarding school,
range from small
with shared bath, to
spacious suites with
fireplaces. Two of the
24 rooms are suitable
for families. There's a
summer dinner theater
on the premises.

### Chatham

#### Luxury

**Chatham Bars Inn**
297 Shore Rd., 02633
Tel: 508-945-0096/800-527-
4884. Fax: 508-945-5491.
www.chathambarsinn.com
A 1914 private hunting

lodge-turned grand
hotel/resort on 22
acres has 205 rooms in
the inn and outlying cot-
tages, and a private
beach. There's a fine
dining room, entertain-
ment, and complimen-
tary supervised
children's activities
(ages 4–12) from mid-
June through Labor Day.

#### Moderate

**Chatham Tides
Waterfront Motel**
394 Pleasant St., 02659
Tel: 508-432-0379. Fax: 508-
432-4289
www.allcapecod.com/chathamtides
A variety of accommoda-
tions are available,
including a motel with
efficiency units, suites,
and townhouses with
private sundecks (for
rent by the week). The
motel is on Nantucket
Sound. Private beach.

### Falmouth

#### Moderate–Expensive

**Coonamessett Inn**
311 Gifford St., 02540
Tel: 508-548-2300. Fax: 508-
540-9831
www.capecodrestaurants.org
One and two-bedroom
suites at a 200-plus
year-old inn on six
manicured acres. The
rooms are unfussy, and
many overlook the
lovely pond and gar-
dens. Good restaurant.

#### Moderate

**Mariner Motel**
555 Main St., 02540
Tel: 508-548-8000/800-233-
2939. Fax: 508-457-9470
www.marinermotel.com
Non-smoking, family-
friendly motel a short
walk from the Vineyard

ferry has 30 pleasant
rooms. Outdoor pool.

#### Expensive

**Mostly Hall**
27 Main St., 02540
Tel: 508-548-3786/800-682-
0565. Fax: 508-457-5778
www.mostlyhall.com
1849 National Register
Italianate villa, built by a
seafarer to please a
homesick wife, has
large, handsome high-
ceilinged rooms and
knowledgeable hosts.

### Hyannis

#### Moderate

**Inn on Sea Street**
358 Sea St., 02601
Tel: 508-775-8030. Fax: 508-
771-0878
www.innonseastreet.com
A B&B with 10 rooms in
a cheerful inn made up
of two 19th-century
houses. It's only a short
stroll from downtown
and the beach.
**Sheraton Hyannis
Resort**
West End Circle 02601
Tel: 508-775-7775/800-598-
4559. Fax: 508-778-6039
www.sheraton.com
A full-service, two-story
hotel with 222 rooms
and suites, indoor and
outdoor pools and spa,
supervised children's
activities in the sum-
mer, and a restaurant.

### Martha's Vineyard

#### Expensive

**Charlotte Inn**
27 S. Summer St., 02539
Tel: 508-627-4751. Fax: 508-
627-4652
www.relais&chateaux.com
An exquisite country inn
with five buildings (from
18th century to new),

with 25 rooms romantically decorated. The elegant L'Étoile (dinner only) serves excellent French cuisine. Children over 14 welcome.

### Moderate–Expensive

**The Edgartown Inn**
56 N. Water St., 02539
Tel: 508-627-4794. Fax: 508-627-9420
www.edgartowninn.com
Built in 1798 for a whaling captain and an inn for over 150 years, this property has welcomed Daniel Webster and Nathaniel Hawthorne as guests. Accommodations, in the inn and two outbuildings, include private and shared baths. Non-smoking.

## Nantucket

### Expensive

**The Wauwinet Inn**
120 Wauwinet Rd. 02584;
Tel: 508-228-0145/800-426-8718. Fax: 508-228-6712
(Closed in winter)
www.wauwinet.com
Nantucket's most elegant inn is 9 miles (14 km) from the center of town and has 35 well furnished rooms and cottages, some in the dunes and many with water views. The restaurant, Toppers, is excellent, and the rate includes breakfast.

### Moderate–Expensive

**Jared Coffin House**
29 Broad Street, 02554
Tel: 800-249-2405 or 508-228-2400. Fax: 508-228-8549
In the heart of the historic district, the inn offers single bedrooms and two-room suites with radio and TV in the original building, a three-story 1845 mansion, as well as in

five other historic buildings. A room with a loft is well suited to families. Two restaurants, raw bar.

## Sandwich

### Moderate–Expensive

**Dan'l Webster Inn & Spa**
149 Main St., 02563
Tel: 508-888-3622/800-444-3566. Fax: 508-888-5156
www.danlwebsterinn.com
Daniel Webster really did stay here, but today the inn blends Colonial charm with contemporary amenities. Many of the rooms have canopy or four-poster beds; some have fireplaces and two-person showers, whirlpools, and private balconies. There's an excellent restaurant, and the non-smoking inn is open year-round.

### Inexpensive

**Earl of Sandwich Motel**
378 Route 6A, 02537
Tel: 508-888-1415/800-442-3275. Fax: 508-833-1039
www.earlofsandwich.com
Quiet, year-round motel with standard and upscale units; the lovely grounds include an outdoor pool. Continental breakfast included.

## West Dennis

### Moderate–Expensive

**Lighthouse Inn**
1 Lighthouse Rd., 02670
Tel: 508-398-2244. Fax: 508-398-5658.
www.lighthouseinn.com
Old-fashioned seaside resort lighthouse-turned-inn with 61 cottages and rooms. Supervised activities for children in July–Aug, and a private beach. Operated by the Stone family since 1938.

# WEST OF BOSTON

## HOTELS

### Concord

#### Moderate–Luxury
**Concord's Colonial Inn**
48 Monument Sq., 01742
Tel: 800-370-9200 or 978-371-1533.
www.concordscolonialinn.com
Fifteen of the 56 rooms are in the 1716 main building. The rest are in a newer wing and cottages. Fine food.

#### Expensive
**Northbridge Inn**
21 Monument Street, 01742.
Tel: 978-371-0014. Fax: 978-371-6460

www.northbridgeinn.com
This 1885 in-town lodging has six spacious, one- and two-bedroom suites with queen beds, tile baths, kitchens, TVs, phones, data ports. Lavish breakfast.

#### Moderate
**Hawthorne Inn B&B**
462 Lexington Road, 01742.
Tel: 978-369-5610. Fax: 978-287-4949
www.concordmass.com
This historic inn has seven antiques-filled and well furnished rooms with private baths, air-con, phones and data ports. Emerson Room has gas log fire. Children welcome.

## Lexington

### Inexpensive–Moderate
**Battle Green Inn & Suites**
1720 Massachusetts Avenue, 02421
Tel: 800 343-0235/781-862-6100. Fax: 781-861-9485.
www.battlegreeninn.com
Simple but comfortable lodgings in the heart of town. Accommodations range from single rooms to suites, and studio units are available for long-term stays. All rooms have cable TV and air-con, and microwaves and refrigerators are available on

request. Fitness room; seasonal indoor pool.

## Sudbury Center

### Moderate
**Longfellow's Wayside Inn**
72 Wayside Inn Rd.
Tel: 978-443-1776/800-339-1776. Fax: 978-443-8041
www.wayside.org
The country's oldest operating inn (1716), a two-story building first restored by Henry Ford and, after a fire, by the Ford Foundation, has 10 antiques-filled rooms and is close to Lexington and Concord. The restaurant serves traditional Yankee fare.

## HOTELS

### Gloucester

#### Moderate

**Bass Rocks Ocean Inn**
107 Atlantic Rd., 01930
Tel: 978-283-7600/800-528-1234
www.bestwestern.com/bassrocksoceaninn
All 48 rooms in this two-story, Georgian-style motel look straight out to sea. The main house is on the National Register of Historic Places. A breakfast buffet is served on the sun porch, and bikes are available for guests. Outdoor pool.

**Cape Ann Motor Inn**
33 Rockport Rd. Gloucester 01930. Tel: 978-281-29000
www.capeannmotorinn.com
This three-story property offers standard motel accommodations (some with kitchenettes), but all rooms have two double beds, are ocean front and have sliding doors onto balconies overlooking Long Beach. Rates include coffee and pastries. Open year round; pets accepted.

### Marblehead

#### Moderate

**Harbor Light Inn**
58 Washington St., 01945
Tel: 781-631-2186. Fax: 781-631-2216
www.harborlightinn.com
A formally decorated, 21-room inn with a 19th-century addition built around an 18th-century house. Decor ranges from traditional to contemporary. Many

rooms have fireplaces and some have whirlpool tubs.

**Marblehead Inn**
264 Pleasant St., 01945
Tel: 781-639-9999.
www.marbleheadinn.com
Nine suites with kitchenettes and Victorian-style furnishings.

### Newburyport

#### Inexpensive–Moderate

**Clark Currier Inn**
45 Green St., 01950
Tel: 978-465-8363
www.clarkcurrierinn.com
A dignified, three-story 1803 shipbuilder's home in the Federal mode. Many of the eight rooms (all with private bath) feature pumpkin-pine floors, pencil-post beds and other antique furnishings. The fireplaced parlor is comfortable and cozy. The inn is non-smoking.

#### Moderate

**Garrison Inn**
11 Brown Square, 01950
Tel: 978-499-8500. Fax: 978-499-8555
www.garrisoninn.com
A four-story, 1803 Federalist residence-turned-inn has 24 rooms and 6 suites with private baths and reproduction antiques; some rooms have fireplaces. All are equipped with phones and air conditioning. David's Tavern serves eclectic American fare nightly, and offers child care while you dine.

### Rockport

#### Inexpensive

**Sally Webster Inn**
34 Mount Pleasant St., 01966

Tel: 978-546-9251/877-546-9251
www.sallywebster.com
All seven antiques-filled rooms at this three-story, 1832 intown inn have private baths; several have wide-board pine floors and canopy beds. There is a cozy, fireplaced living room, and breakfast is served on the terrace in good weather.

#### Moderate

**Seaward Inn & Cottages**
44 Marmion Way, 01966
Tel: 978-546-3741/877-473-9273. Fax: 978-546-7661
www.seawardinn.com
A welcoming summer house turned B&B, perched on a beautifully-landscaped, five-acre seaside ledge. There are 38 rooms in the main inn, two nearby houses, and adjacent cottages. Natural, spring-fed outdoor pool, and complimentary full breakfast.

### Salem

#### Moderate

**Hawthorne Hotel**
18 Washington Square West, 01970
Tel: 978-744-4080/800-729-7829. Fax: 978-745-9842
www.hawthornehotel.com
The city's only full-service hotel is a renovated Federal-style lodging at the edge of the Green. All 89 rooms and 6 suites have 18th-century reproduction furnishings and modern amenities. Nathaniel's Restaurant serves a lively jazz brunch buffet and has live piano entertainment Thur–Sat

evening. The Tavern serves casual fare.

**The Salem Inn**
7 Summer St., 01970
Tel: 978-741-0680 or 800-446-2995. Fax: 978-744-8924
www.saleminnma.com
This downtown inn is actually a collection of three restored, historic buildings built between 1834 and 1874. Many of the 42 rooms have fireplaces (operable Nov–April), oversized whirlpool baths, and/or canopy beds. All rooms have TV and phones, and each of the inns has a fireplaced parlor. And what other town in America raises its rates during Halloween?

### Tyngsboro

#### Luxury

**Stonehedge Inn**
160 Pawtucket Blvd., Tel: 978-649-4400. Fax: 978-649-9256
www.stonehedge.com
Luxurious rooms, superb French cuisine and a first-class spa are hallmarks of this non-smoking, European-style luxury inn on 36 acres (15 hectares) near Lowell. Many of the 30 suites, decorated with French country furnishings, have fireplaces, jacuzzis, and balconies.

### PRICE CATEGORIES

A very approximate guide to current room rates for a standard double per night is:
**Luxury** = over $300
**Expensive** = $200–300
**Moderate** = $100–200
**Inexpensive** = under $100

# ACTIVITIES

# FESTIVALS, THE ARTS, NIGHTLIFE, SHOPPING, TOURS AND SPECTATOR SPORTS

## CALENDAR OF EVENTS

### Festivals and Holidays

Public holidays are marked with an ❶. For more details of events, phone the City of Boston Special Events Line; 635 3911; www.cityofboston.gov/arts.

### January

**Boston Wine Expo**, the nation's largest consumer wine event, showcasing more than 440 wineries from 13 countries, is held at the Seaport World Trade Center. Tel: 877-946-3976; www.wine-expos.com/boston.
**Martin Luther King Day** ❶, third Monday, ceremony at City Hall.
**Chinese New Year**, end of month or early February – celebrated in Chinatown with lion and dragon dances and firecrackers. Tel: 888-733-2678; www.bostonusa.com.

### February

**Washington's Birthday** ❶ ceremony held at Washington's statue in the Public Garden.
**New England Boat Show**, Bayside Expo. Tel: 474-6000.

### March

**Harpoon St. Patrick's Festival**, early March. Tel: 888-427-7666.
**New England Spring Flower Show**, a week-long event at Bayside Expo held the second week, is the oldest annual flower exhibition in the nation. Tel: 474-6000; www.masshort.org
**St. Patrick's Day Parade & Evacuation Day**, South Boston's 3.2 mile gala held on a Sunday near March 17, begins on Broadway and ends in Andrew Sq. Tel: 635-3911 or 268- 7955

### April

**Patriots' Day Re-enactments** ❶ over Patriot's Day Week-end: celebrations abound, especially in Concord and Lexington. Tel: 800-443-3332; www.battleroad.org
**Lantern service at Old North Church**, the Sun before Apr 19, commemorates Paul Revere's famous ride. Tel: 523-6676; www.oldnorth.com
**Boston Marathon**, the 26-mile world-renowned annual event, begins in Hopkinton and ends at Copley Square. Third Mon of month. Tel: 236-1652; www.bostonmarathon.org

### May

**Franklin Park Kite Festival**. Kite-flying, kite-making, music and refreshments for all the family.
**Boston Pops**, commencement of a two-month Tues–Sat (8.30pm) season at Symphony Hall begins mid-May. Tel: 266-1492; www.bso.org/pops

**Art Newbury Street**, mid-month festival when art in the galleries is joined by music on the streets: an art lover's nirvana.
**Lilac Sunday**, mid-May, the air at the Arnold Arboretum is redolent with the aroma from 400 varieties of varicolored lilacs in bloom. Tel: 524-1718; www.arboretum.harvard.edu
**Memorial Day** ❶ – May 31; celebrated Monday of last weekend in May.

### June

**Free Friday Evening Flicks at the Hatch Shell** on Memorial Drive. Tel: 727-8855 for program.
**Boston Pride**, first week, a lesbian and gay pride festival, commences with an Aids Walk around Charles River Basin and culminates in Saturday South End parade and Sunday carnival. Tel: 262-9405; www.bostonpride.org.
**Boston Harborfest**. Maritime and colonial festival at locations throughout the city the last week of the month, includes the popular Chowderfest. Tel: 635-4500 or 227-1528; www.bostonharborfest.com
**Bunker Hill Day**, mid-month, includes a costumed reenactment of the Battle of Bunker Hill and a parade in Charlestown. Tel: 242- 5642; www.nps.gov/bost
**Blessing of the Fleet**, on the last weekend, takes place at both

Gloucester and Provincetown: activities peak on Sunday.

## July

**Boston Pops**: free outdoor concerts at the Hatch Memorial Shell on the Esplanade. Tel: 266-1492; www.bso.org/pops

**Independence Day ①**. Fourth of July celebrations include: a reading of the Declaration of Independence from the balcony of Old State House; **Turnaround of the USS Constitution**, waterfront activities marked by the turnaround of "Old Ironsides" docked at the Charlestown Naval Yard; an evening **Pops Concert** at Hatch Shell on the Esplanade, culminating complete with the playing of the *1812 Overture* with cannons and fireworks (arrive early and bring a blanket or chairs).

**ArtBeat** hosts a week-long celebration of the arts with musicians, exhibits and performers in Davis Square, Somerville. Tel: 625-6000, ext. 2985; www.somervilleartscouncil.org/programs/artbeat.

**Boston Globe Jazz & Blues Festival**, the third week of the month, features well-known jazz and blues musicians at various venues. Tel: 929-3460; www.bostonglobe.com/promotions.

The **North End** lives up to its name of "Little Italy" with brass bands, religious processions and street food in several weekend festivals during the month.

**Feast of the Blessed Sacrament**, in New Bedford the last weekend of the month, is the country's largest Portuguese cultural event, with music, entertainment, and parades.

## August

The **North End** continues its religious processions and feasts.

**Chinatown Festival**. The first week of August, Chinatown celebrates with prancing lions and dragons, food, and martial arts displays. Tel: 635-3485.

**Gloucester Waterfront Festival**, in mid-August, includes a lobster bake, music, and exhibits. Tel: 978-283-1601; www.cape-ann.com/events.html

**Latin Nights** Thursdays from 6-10pm at Faneuil Hall Marketplace. Live bands and dance instructors. Tel: 523-1300.

## September

**Labor Day ①**-First Monday.

**Boston Tattoo Convention**, at the Boston Center for the Arts, 539 Tremont Street, hosts hundreds of tattoo artists, contests, vendors, and entertainment. Tel: 445-9090; www.bostontattoo convention.com.

**Art Newbury Street**: the Sunday after Labor Day the city's major concentration of galleries take to the street.

**Boston Film Festival** premiers new films and hosts discussions at Loews Copley Place, 100 Huntington Avenue, during first two weeks. Tel: 266-2533; www.bostonfilmfestival.org.

**New England Conservatory** hosts free concerts at Jordan Hall, 30 Gainsborough Street during the month. Tel: 536-2412.

**An Evening with Champions** raises money for the Jimmy Fund with skating champions, including Olympic medalists, at Harvard's Bright Hockey Center. Tel: 493-8172.

## October

**Columbus Day Parade**, on the Sunday closest to Oct. 12, is held in East Boston on even numbered years, and in downtown Boston on odd numbered years. Tel: 567-1811; www.cityof boston.gov/arts.

**Harvard Square Oktoberfest**. In mid-month the Square becomes a Bavarian township for a weekend, with oompah bands, dancers, ethnic food and a beer garden. Regional artists and merchants attend. Tel: 491-3434; www.harvardsquare.com/events/oktoberfest.

**Head of the Charles Regatta**, in the middle of the month, is the world's largest one-day crew race. Tel: 868-6200; www.hocr.org.

**Salem** comes alive (or plays dead) throughout the second part of the month with Halloween happenings. Tel: 978-744-3663; www.salemhauntedhappenings.com.

## November

**Veterans' Day Parade**, on the Sunday nearest Nov. 11, begins on Commonwealth Avenue at the corner of Hereford Street in Back Bay. Tel: 635-4455; www.cityofboston.gov/arts.

**Thanksgiving ①** Fourth Thursday

## December

**Christmas Tree Lightings**: the first weekend at the Prudential Center (tel: 800-746-7778), and Boston Common (tel: 635 4505).

**Boston Tea Party Re-enactment**, in the Old South Meeting House on the 16th, recounts Boston's patriots protest of King George III's taxations without representation. Tel: 482-6439; www.old southmeetinghouse.org.

**Louisburg Square**: Carol Singing on the 24th.

**Christmas Day ①**, the 25th.

**First Night:** on the 31st, citywide revels start in the afternoon and continue until the small hours. Tel: 542-1399; www.firstnight.org.

## THE ARTS

**BosTix** is Boston's only half-price, day-of-show ticket outlet and information source for theater, dance and music events. Half-price tickets go on sale at 11am on the day of performance and transactions are cash only. Two locations: Copley Square, open Mon–Sat 10am–6pm, Sun 11am–4pm; and Faneuil Hall, open Tues–Sat 10am–6pm. For information: tel: 482-2849; www.artsboston.org.

Many upcoming events are listed on: www.BostonUSA.com (tel: 888-SEE BOSTON), which also sells tickets on line.

## Theater

Boston theater runs the gamut from Broadway shows to amateur and professional college productions by way of repertory and experimental theater. It has long played the role of a try-out town for pre-Broadway productions.

### ACT Roxbury
2201 Washington St., tel: 541-4900. Sponsors a host of activities including art and history tours, a film festival, open studios, and an arts series.

### American Repertory Theatre
Loeb Drama Center, 64 Brattle Street, Cambridge, tel: 495-6228 The ever-controversial ART, Harvard's repertory troupe, presents neglected works of the past, as well as new American plays and modern interpretations of the classics.

### Boston Center for the Arts
539 Tremont Street, tel: 426-2787. Hosts experimental theater at several venues throughout the city.

### Charles Playhouse
74 Warrenton Street, tel: 426-6912. Home of the long-running and now-renowned Blue Man Group art troupe, and Shear Madness, a humorous audience-participation whodunnit.

### Colonial Theatre
106 Boylston Street, Theater District, tel: 426-9366 Boston's oldest theater, with a richly restored early 20th-century proscenium, features pre- and post-Broadway productions.

### Emerson Majestic Theater
219 Tremont Street, Theater District, tel: 824-8000 This jewel box of a theater, which belongs to Emerson College, has been lovingly restored. It presents accomplished productions of musicals by Emerson students and other non-commercial, non-profit groups including Boston Lyric Opera and Ballet Theatre of Boston.

### Huntington Theatre Company/Boston University Theatre.
264 Huntington Avenue, tel: 266-0800. The resident company mounts five professional productions, which include such varied fare as operettas by Gilbert & Sullivan and plays by Lillian Hellman, as well as more offbeat performances.

### Lyric Stage
140 Clarendon Street, tel: 437-7172. Boston's oldest residential professional theater company presents serious 20th-century plays including New England and American premieres.

### The Opera House
539 Washington Street, tel: 426-9366. The city's 1928 Opera House has been restored to its former glory and now hosts dazzling Broadway-quality performances such as The Lion King.

### Publick Theatre
Christian Herter Park, 1175 Soldiers Field Road, Brighton, tel: 782-5425. Boston's oldest resident theater company performs Shakespeare for all ages under the stars (summer only) on the banks of the Charles River.

### Shubert Theatre
265 Tremont Street, tel: 482-9393. This 1910 theater is frequently the setting for pre-Broadway try-outs and for touring Broadway companies.

### Wilbur Theatre
246 Tremont Street, tel: 423-4008. Opened in 1914, this intimate and elegantly restored theater has held several world premieres, including A Streetcar Named Desire and Our Town.

## Movie Theaters

The city and suburbs have a fair number of cinemas, many with multiple screens. The Boston Public Library, tel: 536-5400, and the Museum of Fine Arts, tel: 267-9300, regularly show classics. Some commercial cinemas in the city are:

### Allston Cinemas
214 Harvard Avenue, Allston, tel: 277-2140. Two screens.

### Brattle Theatre,
40 Brattle Street, Harvard Square, Cambridge, tel: 876-6837. Casablanca with Bogie and Bacall plays at least yearly. This former theater plays reruns of the classics and frequently mounts film festivals and author readings. One screen.

### Coolidge Corner Movie Theatre
290 Harvard Street, Brookline, tel: 734-2500. Boston's oldest art house shows independent and foreign films on its one screen.

### Harvard Square
10 Church Street, Cambridge, tel: 864-4580. Five screens for Harvard sophisticates.

### Kendall Square Cinema
1 Kendall Square, Cambridge, tel: 499-1996. Independent films on eight screens.

### Loews Boston Common
175 Tremont Street, tel: 423-5801. With 18 screens, you're sure to find a hit at this state-of-the-art, stadium-seating theater.

### Loews Copley Place
100 Huntington Avenue, tel: 266-1300. Showing independent films, family fare, and blockbusters on 13 screens.

### Somerville Theatre
55 Davis Square, tel: 625-4088 Second-run films at greatly reduced prices.

## Ballet

### Ballet Theatre of Boston
Old Cambridge Baptist Church, 1151 Massachusetts Avenue, tel: 354-7467. José Mateo and his troupe present the works of both masters and innovators, as well as new and classic works. The group's holiday Nutcracker is a popular alternative to more traditional presentations.

### Boston Ballet
19 Clarendon Street, tel: 695-6950. The city's premier dance company, with more than 50 full-time dancers, is one of the country's finest; the troupe presents both classical and modern works. The highlight of the year is their Christmas holiday presentation of Nutcracker.

### Dance Complex
536 Massachusetts Avenue,

Cambridge, tel: 547-9363
The community-run group presents creative works by local choreographers and dance classes for anyone who wishes to participate ($10 a class) .

**Impulse Dance Company**
Brookline Community Center for the Arts, 13 Green Street, tel: 469-8787. The Brookline-based troupe presents cutting-edge performances at "the studio" in Brookline and at venues throughout the area.

## Classical Music

As befits the "Athens of America," Boston is, considering its size, the most musical city in the nation. The city's prominence in education helps: playing, singing and dancing – for your pleasure and their own – are students from most of the 60 colleges and universities in Greater Boston.

**Boston Camerata**
145 Essex Street, Haverhill, tel: 866-427-2092. America's foremost early music ensemble, led by Joel Cohen since 1954, performs at various venues.

**Boston Cecilia**
1773 Beacon Street, tel: 232-4540. Professional musicians perform hits of the Baroque era using period instruments, as well as more contemporary music.

**Boston Landmarks Orchestra**
168 Brattle Street, Cambridge, tel: 520-2200. www.landmarks orchestra.org. Free classical music concerts at Boston's landmarks. Check the website for a complete schedule.

**Boston Philharmonic**
295 Huntington Avenue, tel: 236-0999. For more than 25 years Benjamin Zander has been conducting this orchestra, made up of professionals, amateurs, and students. A whole season might be devoted to a single composer. Performances are at Jordan Hall and Harvard University's Sanders Theatre.

**Boston Pops**
Symphony Hall, 301 Massachusetts Avenue, tel: 266-1200

The orchestra Arthur Fieldler made famous, with a host of guest performers, performs light favorites from May to mid-July; the Fourth of July concert on the Esplanade is an annual highlight.

**Boston Symphony Orchestra**
Symphony Hall, 301 Massachusetts Avenue, tel: 266-1200
One of America's "Big Five" orchestras, now led by James Levine of Metropolitan Opera fame, performs in acoustically sublime Symphony Hall Oct–Apr.

**Cambridge Society for Early Music**
Tel: 489-2062. Solo, chamber, choral and orchestral music from the Middle Ages through the early 19th century performed using historically-appropriate instruments at small halls and intimate venues throughout the area.

**Handel and Haydn Society**
300 Massachusetts Avenue, tel: 266-3605. America's oldest musical organization, which debuted in 1815, performs Baroque and classical works at Symphony Hall and Jordan Hall.

## Venues

**Cambridge Multicultural Arts Center**
41 Second Street, Cambridge, tel: 577-4100. The city's ornate arts center is the perfect setting for an on-going series of musical events, dance performances, and plays.

**Jorge Hernandez Cultural Center**
85 West Newton Street, tel: 927-0061. Home base for the Center for Latino Arts, which hosts a full roster of cultural events including Friday night salsa dances, performance art, jazz, and film.

**Hatch Shell**, The Esplanade, tel: 727-9547, ext. 450. Renowned for its free May–Sept concerts and dance performances in a memorable setting. Most famous are the Boston (Symphony) Pops concerts in July.

**Isabella Stewart Gardner Museum**
2 Palace Road, tel: 566-1401
Chamber music concerts in the

Tapestry Room at 1.30pm Sun from Sept to Apr.

**Longfellow House**
105 Brattle Street, tel: 876-4491
Summer Sunday music festival and poetry in the garden in July and early Aug beginning at 4pm.

**Museum of Fine Arts**
465 Huntington Avenue, tel: 267-9300. Hosts a year-long music program with a wide variety of performers. For schedule, check www.mfa.org

**New England Conservatory of Music**
290 Huntington Avenue, tel: 583-1100. Internationally acclaimed music conservatory that houses Jordan Hall, one of the country's finest concert halls. The NEC presents lectures, seminars and 600 free classical, jazz and improvisation music concerts each year.

**Sanders Theatre**
Memorial Hall, Cambridge & Quincy streets, Cambridge, tel: 496-2222. This 1,200-seat theater, renowned for its quirky Victorian architecture and fine acoustics and sightlines, has been hosting a variety of musical and literary events for more than a century.

**Symphony Hall**
301 Massachusetts Avenue, tel: 266-1492. Home of the Boston Symphony Orchestra, which presents concerts in the winter and moves to Tanglewood (in Lenox) for the summer, letting the Boston Pops take over. The hall is also used to stage a range of other classical performances, including a celebrity series.

**Wang Center for the Performing Arts**
270 Tremont Street, tel: 482-9393/800-447-7440. A big stage and huge auditorium showcases ballet, opera, concerts and Broadway plays.

## Opera

**Boston Lyric Opera**
45 Franklin Street, tel: 542-4912
Fully-staged productions from a varied repertoire using world-

class emerging singers and internationally-acclaimed directors and designers.

**Opera Boston**
25 Kingston Street, tel: 451-3388). New England's premier opera repertory company presents fully-staged performances at the Emerson Majestic Theatre in the Theater District.

## Church Music

**Emmanuel Church**
15 Newbury Street, tel: 536-3356. Sunday morning's 10am service, Sept—May, may include a cantata by J.S. Bach or a choral work by Handel. The church hosts a program of evening concerts.

**First Church in Cambridge Congregational**
11 Garden Street, Cambridge, tel: 547-2724. Sundays at 5:30pm, the church hosts a contemporary service based on jazz and gospel. At 7pm the first Friday of each month there's a Taize Worship Series of scripture, song, silence and light, based on the teachings of a French Community of Brothers.

**King's Chapel**
Corner School and Tremont streets, tel: 227-2155. Events include a Sunday 11am service with an 18-member choir; Tuesday's 12.15pm music recitals, which might include jazz, folk or classical music; Wednesday's 12.15pm prayer with an organ

prelude; and a 5pm Sunday concert series.

## Rock & Pop Concerts

**FleetBoston Pavilion**, 290 Northern Avenue, Wharf 8, South Boston, tel: 728-1600. www.fleetbostonpavilion.com. This enormous white marquee at the waterfront, which seats 5,000, is a glorious venue for rock, country, jazz and pop.

**Fleet Center**, 1 Fleet Center (Causeway Bay), tel: 624-1000, www.fleetcenter.com. Venue, seating 20,000, for rock and pop concerts, ice shows and circus.

**Orpheum Theatre**, 1 Hamilton Place, tel: 423-6398 or 423-6000. The historic 1852 Music Hall has been refurbished and now presents big names.

**The Wang Center for the Performing Arts**, 270 Tremont St., tel: 482-9393 or 800-447-7440. www.wangcenter.org. One of the nation's leading not-for-profit arts organizations, presents headliner performing artists.

## Jazz

**Berklee Performance Center**
136 Massachusetts Avenue, tel: 266-7455. Owned by the Berklee School of Music, this 1,200-seat auditorium is best known for its jazz concerts. Excellent musical events, keenly priced, are mounted by students and faculty.

## NIGHTLIFE

Boston's 250,000 students ensure the city of a busy nightlife. Bars and nightclubs, discos and comedy clubs abound in both Boston, especially in the Back Bay, and in Cambridge. Most remain open until 2am on weekdays and 1am on Saturdays, although Cambridge nightspots tend to close earlier than their Boston counterparts. Those under 21 cannot be served liquor, but many clubs admit customers 19 years and older on certain nights. It's best to call ahead and check an establishment's age policy.

### Nightclubs

The club scene is in a constant state of flux. Two areas where there is some degree of continuity are Landsdowne Street in the Fenway, which attracts a younger, edgier crowd, and Boylston Place ("the Alley") near the Theater District, which attracts older executive types. Some clubs are open only Wednesday or Thursday through Sunday.

**The Alley**
1 Boylston Place, tel: 351-7000. Three New Orleans-themed bars: The Big Easy (club with live band and DJs); the Sugar Shack (dancing to oldies and Top 40-music); and the Sweetwater Cafe (a "classic American" bar).

**Avalon**
15 Landsdowne Street, tel: 262-2424. Folks at the largest venue on the street (maximum capacity is 2,000) dance to both Euro and Top 40 music spun by big-name DJs, and, some nights, live performers. The place is packed Fri nights. Although Sun is officially a gay night, it's much attended by straights. No sneakers, jeans.

**BELOW:** making music at the Hatch Shell, home of the Boston Pops.

## Axis

13 Landsdowne Street, tel: 262-2437. Discs spin and hipsters hop to electro-pop, new wave and punk; Fri nights retro '80s new wave. One cover charge allows admission to Axis and Avalon. Mon, gay night, brings out the drag queens. Ages 18 and over welcome weekends; 19 and over weekdays.

## Buzz/Europa

51 Stuart Street, tel: 482-3939. The club, with two levels of dancing and shirtless bartenders, attracts well-heeled trendy Euros. Sat it becomes Buzz Boston and caters mainly to a gay crowd.

## DancePlex

262 Friend Street, tel: 720-1966. Retro feel as DJs play disco, techno, rave, and music of the last two decades. Sunday is gay night.

## Man Ray

21 Brookline Street, Cambridge, tel: 864-0400. Goths, gays and gawkers queue up for an on-going roster of events at this underground club. Thursday is gay night; Sat is disco/new wave night; Hell Night is the second Fri of the month.

## Pravda 116

116 Boylston Street, tel: 482-7799. A chic Russian-themed establishment with cocktail bar ("116" refers to the large selection of vodkas). DJs play Latin tunes for the mostly older crowd, which often dines here as well.

## Roxy

297 Tremont Street, tel: 338-7699. The city's grandest dance hall, a renovated hotel ballroom, is where the properly dressed gather – especially on weekends – to dance to live music.

## Sophia's

270 Boylston Street, tel: 351-7001. Salsa is the specialty at this four-story Latin restaurant and nightclub, which also presents live

bands as well as DJs. Has an outdoor deck. A tapas menu is available.

## Tequila Rain

145 Ipswich Street, tel: 437-0300. Nightly specials include Buff Fri for would-be male models, Girls Night Out, and wet T-shirt contests. The food is Tex-Mex and the music, accompanied by a wall of giant video screens, runs to top 40, hip hop and rock. Sneakers and sleeveless shirts are banned for men.

## Listening Rooms

### Club Passim

7 Palmer Place, Cambridge, tel: 492-7679. Enjoy folk and acoustic performers in the oldest folk club in the country, where Joan Baez had her first chance and musicians including Taj Mahal and Shawn Colvin launched their careers. A vegetarian restaurant and coffeehouse continues serving during show (nightly at 8pm). No alcohol.

### Common Ground

85 Harvard Avenue, Allston, tel: 783-2071. Funk, soul, rock, pop, ska, celtic and R&B mingle at this sports bar/Irish pub. The Irish pizza is topped with mashed potatoes, cheddar cheese, and bacon.

### Harper's Ferry

158 Brighton Avenue, Allston, tel: 254-9743. Wide-open bar where local musicians come to jam. There are pool tables behind the stage.

### The Living Room

101 Atlantic Avenue, tel: 723-5101. Nestle into a cozy couch, order a martini, gaze out at the harbor, and enjoy jazz and blues.

### Middle East

472 Massachusetts Avenue, Cambridge, tel: 864-3278. Ethnic cuisine and live music nightly in three rooms, each with a full service bar. Offers rock, jazz and blues, as well as folk and belly dancing.

## Regattabar

Charles Hotel, 1 Bennet Street, Cambridge, tel: 661-5000. An upmarket bar featuring top jazz names Tues and Wed at 8.30pm, and Thur–Sat 8 and 10pm. Essential to purchase tickets beforehand from Concentrix (tel: 876-7777).

## Ryle Jazz Club

212 Hampshire Street, Cambridge, tel: 876-9330. A great venue for new music and musicians. Downstairs it's jazz and smoke: upstairs it's lively dance music and special lesbian theme nights. Weekends it's salsa and swing dancing. Casual dress. Food served until midnight.

## Scullers Jazz Club

Doubletree Guest Suites Hotel, 400 Soldiers Field Road, Boston, tel: 562-4111. The long-time favorite, in a room with a panoramic view of the Charles River, attracts top-name groups Tues–Sat at 8 and 10pm. Advance reservations are suggested.

## Wally's Cafe

472 Massachusetts Avenue, South End, tel: 424-1408. This hole-in-the-wall bar, Boston's longest-running jazz joint, is much frequented by students from the nearby Berklee School of Music. No food (bring your own), no cover, no credit cards but lots of beer and fine music.

## Bars

### Black Rose

160 State Street, tel: 742-2286. A classic Irish pub, close to Faneuil Hall Marketplace, which teems with Boston business people primed to unwind. Live Irish music nightly and weekend afternoons.

### Boston Beer Works

61 Brookline Avenue, tel: 536-2337. A big, brash brew pub conveniently located across from Fenway Park

(there's a second location at 112 Canal Street).

**Bull & Finch**
Hampshire House, 84 Beacon Street, tel: 227-9605. Tourists come to gawk and guzzle at what is, in reality, nothing like what they see on TV in *Cheers*.

**Casablanca**
40 Brattle Street, Harvard Square, tel: 876-0999. "Here's looking at you, kid" – seated in a rickshaw-shaped wicker booth at a copper table, among other beautiful people. An institution.

**Cornwall's**
510 Commonwealth Avenue, tel: 262-3749. Bracing food and a truly international gamut of brews.

**Daisy Buchanan's**
240A Newbury Street, Back Bay, tel: 247-8516. Although there's no cover, proper dress is required at this long-established bar and restaurant with a great rock jukebox. Thirty-something crowd.

**John Harvard's Brew House**
33 Dunster Street, Cambridge tel: 868-3585. Microbrewery/ English-style pub. Decent bar fare, excellent house brews.

**Kitty O'Sheas**
131 State Street, tel: 725-0100. Popular Irish bar serving food and Thurs evening music to a mature crowd.

**The Plough and Stars**
912 Massachusetts Avenue, Cambridge, tel: 441-3455. A tiny but beloved Irish bar with a wide range of music, from bodhran to blue grass.

## Comedy Clubs

Few cities in the nation harbor as many comedy clubs as Boston. Some serve light snacks as well as drinks (bar and tables); all have a cover charge, and at some the show is continuous while at others there are discrete showtime hours, especially when big names perform. Most clubs have an admission fee, and

an "open mike" night when the audience may take to the stage.

**The Comedy Connection**
Quincy Market Building, Faneuil Hall, tel: 248-9700. Nightly local and national stand-up comedy.

**Comedy Studio**
Hong Kong Restaurant 1236 Massachusetts Avenue, Cambridge, tel: 661-6507. Dinner and a show, which might be a magic act, stand-up comedy, or a rather racy comedy-debate.

**ImprovBoston**
1253 Cambridge Street, Cambridge, tel: 576-1253. A creative troupe whips up humorous routines Wed–Sun.

**Improv Asylum**
216 Hanover Street, tel: 263-6887. Improvisation and sketch comedy Wed and Thurs at 8pm, and Fri and Sat at 8 and 10pm, with a special Sat Midnight Show.

**Nick's Comedy Stop**
100 Warrenton Street, tel: 482-0930. The city's longest-running comedy club hosts stars on their way up as well as many who have already arrived. Thurs–Sat.

## Gay Scene

Mostly in the South End. Many mainstream bars *(see above)* designate one night a week as Gay Night. For listings check *Bay Windows* (www.baywindows.com), a gay paper available throughout the city, including the Boston Public Library in Copley Square; Borders, 24 School Street; and Barnes & Noble, 395 Washington Street.

**Chaps**
100 Warrenton Street, tel: 695-9500. Wednesday evening is Latino Night, with go-go boys making the place rock. Boston's only tea dance, Sunday from 6–10pm, has become a tradition.

**Club Café**
209 Columbus Avenue, tel:

536-0972. One of the city's hottest spots for gays to dine and date. There's a full dinner menu, a lively bar, and video entertainment. Thur night it's packed, with lesbians in the front of the house, and gay men in the rear.

**Fritz**
Chandler Inn, 26 Chandler Street (South End), tel: 482-3450. Friendly gay neighborhood sports bar that serves brunch until 3pm weekends.

**Jacques Cabaret**
70 Broadway, tel: 426-8902 Boston's oldest gay bar is popular with the transgendered crowd. There are drag shows nightly at 10pm, and live music downstairs most Fri-Mon nights. Straights are also welcome.

**Paradise Cambridge**
180 Massachusetts Avenue, Cambridge, tel: 868-3000. Upstairs gay bar with strippers and go-go boys, and adult films after 10pm; downstairs dance club spins top 40 tunes. Youngish crowd.

**Ramrod/Machine**
1254 Boylston Street, tel: 266-2986. A long popular complex: Ramrod demands leather and Levis. The vast dance hall (Machine) plays the best in dance and techno and on Fri and Sat nights attracts a mixed crowd.

## Round-the-Clock

### Convenience Store

**Store 24**
1219 Commonwealth Avenue Allston, tel: 783-1034

### Locksmith

**USB Locksmith**
Tel: 208-1207. For when you're locked out of your car at 2am.

### Pharmacies

**CVS**
Porter Square Shopping Plaza, 35 White Street, Cam-

bridge, tel: 876-5519; and 587 Boylston Street, tel: 437-7916. Has a pharmacist on duty all night, and also carries a large supply of snack foods, cosmetics, stationary, postage stamps – whatever you might need at 4am.

## Restaurants

### News 24/7
150 Kneeland Street, tel: 426-NEWS. Food, drink, lottery tickets, five huge TVs, and a large selection of newspapers and magazines.

### South Street Diner
178 Kneeland Street, tel: 350-0028. Classic 1950s diner serving classic diner fare, including hot dogs, meatloaf, and apple pie.

## SHOPPING

Three major shopping areas attract strollers as well as serious shoppers. The Back Bay's **Newbury Street**, which stretches for eight blocks from the Public Garden to Massachusetts Avenue, is lined with boutiques, salons, and galleries. The Public Gar-

den end attracts the big spenders, while towards Massachusetts Avenue the atmosphere is more funky and shoppers are students, not international travelers.

Also in Back Bay, **Copley Place** and the **Shops at the Prudential Center** are glass-enclosed malls with high-end retailers and specialty shops. **Downtown Crossing**, an outdoor pedestrian mall, is anchored by Macy's. **Faneuil Hall Marketplace** has 150-plus shops and restaurants (see below).

In **Cambridge**, independently-owned shops line Massachusetts Avenue and the squares; the Harvard Square area, however, with numerous chain and independent stores, is the city's predominant shopping district.

Most stores open between 9–10am and close at 6–7pm. Some, especially at Faneuil Hall Marketplace, stay open later. Others, especially those in malls and tourist areas, are open on Sundays from noon until 5 or 6pm.

The state sales tax (5%) does not apply to clothing under $175.

## FANEUIL HALL MARKETPLACE

More than 150 shops and restaurants attract over 1 million visitors a month. Food stalls fill the Quincy Market Buildings, flanked by colorful pushcarts selling handmade crafts and souvenirs.

**Celtic Weavers** has a wide array of imported caps and capes, kilts and shawls and hand-knit fisherman sweaters, while **Dupre Kids** features funky junior sportswear. **Victoria's Secret** offers eye-catching underwear, as well as Italian shoes and boots.

**Whippoorwill** has crafts, **Henri's Glassworks** has hand-blown glass figures and hang-

ing decorations and the **Boston Pewter Company** has American pewter items. The **Discovery Channel Store** and an outlet of the **Museum of Fine Arts** are good for gifts. **Wacky Planet** specializes in items for left-handed people, and in **Cheers** everybody knows your name.

Across in the North Market, **Geoclassics** stocks museum-quality gems, minerals and fossils while the **Rockport Co.** and **Bill Rodgers Running Center** will shoe prospective prospectors. The **Boston City Store** in the basement of Faneuil Hall sells vintage street signs and Boston hard hats.

## Antiques

Newbury Street, Charles Street on Beacon Hill – with 40-plus shops —and Cambridge are prime locations.

### Autrefois Antiques
125 Newbury Street, tel: 424-8823. French and Italian furniture from the 18th to the 20th centuries. Functional antique lamps, chandeliers.

### Boston Antique Cooperative
119 Charles Street, tel: 227-9811. Estate goods from the 16th–20th centuries, with an emphasis on 18th-century Continental furniture, early textiles, American and English silver, armor, and arms.

### Brodney Gallery
145 Newbury Street, tel: 536-0500. Eclectic collection includes estate jewelry, sculptures, silver, pillboxes, furniture, paintings and bronzes.

### Cambridge Antiques Market
201 Monsignor O'Brien Highway, Cambridge (across from the Lechmere MBTA; tel: 868-9655. More than 150 dealers on five floors sell reasonably-priced furniture, lighting, glass, books, vintage clothing.

### City Lights
2226 Massachusetts Avenue, tel: 547-1490. For 1860–1950 working antique wall sconces and chandeliers.

### Devonia Antiques
43 Charles St., tel: 523-8313 Full sets of fine china, glassware and tableware as well as distinctive individual pieces of glassware and porcelain.

### Marcoz Antiques
177 Newbury Street, tel: 262-0780. Elegantly hand-crafted pieces include decorative arts, silver, jewelry; also, 18th–19th century French and English antiques.

## Art Galleries

More than a score of up-market galleries are centered on Newbury Street, from Clarendon to Fairfield, but others of note are sprinkled around the South End and Cambridge.

**Brickbottom Gallery**
1 Fitchburg Street, Somerville, tel: 776-3410. Many artists who display their works at Somerville's only non–profit contemporary gallery live and have their studios here, and open them to the public. Plus lectures, concerts, films, literary events.

**Copley Society of Boston**
158 Newbury Street, tel: 536-5049. The country's oldest nonprofit art association displays the works of its more than 600 members, as well as noted artists of the 19th and 20th centuries.

**Gallery NAGA**
Church of the Covenant, 67 Newbury Street, tel: 267-9060. Since 1977, a leading exhibitor of paintings by contemporary New England artists; also unique and limited-edition studio furniture, sculpture, photography, prints, and holography.

**International Poster Gallery**
205 Newbury Street, tel: 375-0076. More than 10,000 one-of-a-kind vintage posters from Europe and the US.

**Judi Rotenberg Gallery**
130 Newbury Street, tel: 437-1518. Displaying the works of contemporary New England artists for almost 30 years.

**List Visual Arts Center**
20 Ames Street, MIT, Cambridge, tel: 253-4680. Three galleries of modern art: contemporary, unconventional and works in progress, and sculpture.

**Out of the Blue Art Gallery**
106 Prospect Street, Cambridge, tel: 354-5287. The works of 40–50 community artists working in a variety of media displayed in an affordable setting.

**Pucker Safari Gallery**
171 Newbury Street, tel: 267-9473. Paintings, graphics, sculpture and ceramics from America, Europe, Israel, Asia

and Africa, including works by prominent artists including Chagall and Picasso.

**Washington Street Art Center**
321 Washington Street, tel: 623-5315. The 22-member artists' collective exhibits paintings, photography and fine crafts.

**Zeitgeist Gallery**
Inman Square, 1353 Massachusetts Avenue, Cambridge, tel: 876-6060. Artists working in a variety of media mount up to 20 exhibitions a year; nightly performances include art, poetry, music and theater.

## Bargains

**City Sports Basement**
11 Bromfield Street, tel: 423-2015. Sneakers, sportswear and outerwear at incredible prices, but the basement store is only open Mon–Fri, 11:30am–6pm.

**DSW Shoe Warehouse**
385 Washington Street, tel: 556-0052. Top-quality, well-known brands sold for up to 50 percent off retail.

**Filene's Basement**,
426 Washington Street, tel: 426-6645. The country's oldest bargain store opened in 1908. With its Automatic Markdown Plan, an $800 Brooks Brother suit may go on sale at $400; if unsold after 14 days it is reduced to $200; after 21 days to $100; after 28 days to $50. After that, proceeds go to charity.

**Keezer's**
140 River Street, Cambridge, tel: 547-2455. It's rumored that the members of the Boston Symphony Orchestra purchase their tuxedos here. Formal and informal wear, new and used, at phenomenally low prices.

**Second Time Around**
176 Newbury Street, tel: 247-5304; and 8 Eliot Street, Cambridge, tel: 491-7185. It's not unusual to find top-quality name brands at this

new, used, and consignment shop which marks down goods 20–50 percent over 90 days. Another store just up the street, at 252 Newbury St., also has menswear, as does the Cambridge store.

## Books

**Ars Libri**
500 Harrison Avenue, South End, tel: 357-5212. One of America's largest selection of rare and out-of-print art and art history books.

**Avenue Victor Hugo Bookshop**
339 Newbury Street, tel: 266-7746. Two jam-packed floors of all kinds of used books.

**Barnes & Noble**
660 Beacon Street, Kenmore Square, tel: 267-8484; and 395 Washington St., tel: 426-5184. Big chain with a huge selection of current titles.

**Borders Books & Music**
The other big chain. There are three Borders stores at Logan Airport: in Terminal E (International terminal), C, and A. There's also a large branch downtown, at 10–24 School St., tel: 557-7188.

**Brattle Book Shop**
9 West Street (downtown), tel: 542-0210. Established in 1825, the three-story antiquarian shop has more than 250,000 books, maps, prints, postcards and ephemera.

**Calamus Bookstore**
92B South Street, tel: 338-1931. Specializing in gay, lesbian, bisexual and transsexual subjects.

**Comicopia**
464 Commonwealth Avenue, Kenmore Square, tel: 266-4266. If you're looking for the *Adventures of Superman, #636*, you might just find it.

**Commonwealth Books**
526 Commonwealth Avenue, Kenmore Square, tel: 236-0182; and 134 Boylston St., tel: 338-6328. Specializing in affordable scholarly, used, out-of-print and antique

books, with an emphasis on arts, architecture, history, literature, philosophy, religion.

**Curious George**
1 John F. Kennedy Street at Harvard Square, tel: 498-0062. Classic and contemporary children's books, toys, stuffed animals, and lots of colorful art aimed at kids.

**Cuttyhunk**
540 Tremont Street, tel: 574-5000. Gay and lesbian literature, as well as information on the city's gay scene.

**Globe Corner Book Store**
28 Church Street, Cambridge, tel: 497-6277. One of North America's largest selections of guidebooks, maps, topographical maps, and software.

**Grolier Poetry Book Shop**
6 Plympton Street, Cambridge, tel: 547-4648. With more than 17,000 titles, the shop has specialized in poetry since 1927.

**Harvard Coop**
1400 Massachusetts Avenue, Harvard Square, tel: 661-1515. Prices are discounted for members – local students and faculty – but reasonable for all. There's an excellent selection of remaindered books at bargain prices.

**Israel Book Shop**
410 Harvard Street, Brookline, tel: 566-7113/800-323-7723. New England's oldest and largest supplier of Judaica sells books, art, music, gifts, and videos.

**New England Comics**
14A Eliot Street, Harvard Square, Cambridge, tel: 354-5352. New and back issue comic books, graphic novels, action figures, games, toys.

**Quantum Books**
4 Cambridge Center, Cambridge, tel: 494-5042. Discounted technical books, including computer, math, science, and psychiatry texts.

**Rand McNally Map & Travel Store**
84 State Street tel: 720-1125 Specializes in driving atlases,

domestic and international travel guides, and maps of every description.

**Schoenhof's Foreign Books**
76A Mt. Auburn Street, Harvard Square, Cambridge, tel: 354-5201. Books in more than 700 languages, including big selection of Joyceana; also literary T-shirts.

## Camping Supplies

**Hilton's Tent City**
272 Friend Street, tel: 800-362-8368. Anything and everything you might need for a trek into the bush is displayed on five jam-packed floors near the FleetCenter.

## Crafts

**Alianza Contemporary Crafts**
154 Newbury Street, tel: 262-2385. Exhibits an excellent selection of innovative ceramics, glassware and jewelry.

**Society of Art and Crafts**
101 Arch Street, tel: 345-0033. A wonderful showcase for American artists working with glass, wool, ceramics and about 200 other less conventional media.

## Department Stores

Most of the city's large department stores are in the Back Bay's Copley Place and Prudential Center malls, and at Downtown Crossing.

**Lord & Taylor**
760 Boylston Street, tel: 262-2000. Tasteful, conservative fashions. A favorite with Boston's Brahmins and suburban matrons in search of a wide range of clothing, shoes, and jewelry.

**Macy's East**
450 Washington Street, Downtown Crossing, tel: 357-3000. This New York spin-off, has a wide selection of merchandise of varying prices. It absorbed the business of the flagship Filene's department

store across the road, which ceased trading in 2006.

**Neiman-Marcus**
5 Copley Place, tel: 536-3660 Elegant high-end specialty store, a who's who of designer labels, and a purveyor of fine jewelry and furs.

**Saks Fifth Avenue**
800 Boylston Street, tel: 262-8500. Contemporary, upscale fashions and accessories for the entire family, as well as a full-service hair salon.

## Food

**Bread and Circus**
186 Alewife Brook Parkway, Cambridge, tel: 491-0040. The world's leading natural and organic foods supermarket has a megastore a few miles from Harvard Square.

**Cardullo's Gourmet Shop**
6 Brattle Street, Cambridge, tel: 491-8888. A long established purveyor of regional and global treats – everything from marzipan to maple syrup.

**DeLuca's Back Bay Market**
239 Newbury Street, tel: 262-5990; and 1 Charles Street, tel: 523-4343. Boston's first gourmet grocery (established in 1905) remains one of its best a century later, with a fine assortment of fresh fruit, homemade pastas, fresh baked goods.

**Formaggio Kitchen**
244 Huron Avenue, tel: 354-4750; and 268 Shawmut Ave., tel: 350-6996. An impressively vast assortment of 3,000 cheeses, artisanal oils, and delicacies from around the world. The cheeses are aged in a special "cave" at the Huron Avenue location.

**Mike's Pastry**
300 Hanover Street, tel: 742-3050. In a neighborhood famous for its Italian baked goods, Mike's remains one of the best.

TRANSPORTATION

ACCOMMODATIONS

ACTIVITIES

A – Z

**Savenor's**
160 Charles Street, tel: 723-6328. Boston's premier food shop carries those hard-to-find delicacies such as alligator tail and rattlesnake.

**Trader Joe's**
899 Boylston Street, tel: 262-6505. From sushi to salads, from exotic to basic, this national chain has it covered.

## Gifts

**Anthropologie**
799 Boylston Street, tel: 262-0545. Furniture, hip women's clothing, Burt's Bees skin products and a variety of eclectic goods are sold in this handsomely-appointed store.

**Bellazza Home and Garden**
129 Newbury Street, tel: 266-1183. High-quality, handmade and hand painted Italian bowls, vases, and tiles.

**The Flat of the Hill**
60 Charles Street, tel: 619-9977. Unique items, including painted furniture, picnic baskets, hand-painted signs.

**Shop at the Union**
Women's Education and Industrial Union, 356 Boylston Street, tel: 536-5651. A great place to buy cards, gifts, and children's clothing and support women's causes at the same time.

## Jewelry

**Cartier**
40 Newbury Street, tel: 262-3300. New England's only outpost for the high-end gems and jewelry purveyor.

**Dorfman Jewelers**
24 Newbury Street, tel: 536-2022. An elegant shop displaying a superb collection of first-class jewelry, watches, pearls, and diamonds.

**Shreve, Crump and Lowe**
330 Boylston Street, tel: 267-9100. North America's oldest jewelry store (established in 1796 at its first location, across the street from Paul

Revere's silversmith shop) is one of its finest.

**Tiffany & Company**
100 Huntington Avenue, Copley Place, tel: 353-0222. The little blue box made famous by Holly Golightly in the movie *Breakfast of Tiffany's* lives on in this elegant store.

## Men's Clothing & Shoes

**Alan Bilzerian**
34 Newbury Street, tel: 536-1001. An upscale boutique where the hip go for contemporary, European fashions.

**Brooks Brothers**
46 Newbury Street, tel: 267-2600; and 75 Court St., tel: 261-9990; and The Mall at Chestnut Hill, 199 Boylston St., tel: 964-3600. The bastion of conservative male clothing also offers duds for women and children, too.

**Emporio Armani**
210 Newbury Street, tel: 262-7300. Suits, khakis, blazers and sportswear for seekers of "fine fabrics and impeccable tailoring in a serene shopping environment".

**Ermenegildo Zegna**
39 Newbury Street, tel: 424-9300. An elegant, upscale boutique specializing in sportswear and luggage.

**Louis Boston**
234 Berkeley Street, tel: 262-6100 (closed Sun). Five-story emporium housed in the city's former Museum of Natural History. The upper stories sell designer clothing and accessories; gifts and home goods are on the first floor.

**Riccardi**
116 Newbury Street, tel.: 266-3158. For more than two decades Newbury Street's premier address for the latest European fashions and shoes.

**Thomas Pink the Shirtmaker**
100 Huntington Avenue, Copley Place, tel: 267-0447. Named for the London tailor who built his reputation in the 18th century, the store sells

custom-tailored shirts and accessories.

**Thom Browne**
331 Newbury Street, tel: 266-8722. Classic shoes including Kenneth Cole and Rockport, as well as funkier footwear.

## Women's Clothing & Shoes

**Betsey Johnson**
201 Newbury Street, tel: 236-7072. Cutting-edge clothing by the well-known designer.

**Chanel Boutique**
5 Newbury Street, Ritz-Carlton Hotel, tel: 859-0055. Clothing, fragrances, handbags, shoes and accessories from one of France's best-known designers.

**Jasmine Sola Boutique**
37A Brattle Street, Cambridge, tel: 354-6043; 344 Newbury Street, Back Bay, tel: 867-4636; Chestnut Hill Mall, 199 Boylston St., Chestnut Hill, tel: 332-8415. Business suits, casual wear, shoes, jewelry and accessories, all with a youthful, contemporary flair and an upscale price tag.

**Talbot's**
25 School Street, tel: 723-0660. Classic apparel and accessories that prove not all of Boston wants to look hip. Special department for sizes 12w–24w.

**Tall Girl**
211 Berkeley Street, tel: 424-7164. Fashions for taller women in sizes 5–20.

**Turtle**
619 Tremont Street, tel: 266-2610. Local designers and craftspeople create truly original women's clothing and jewelry.

## Music

**Cheapo Records**
645 Massachusetts Avenue, Central Sq., Cambridge, tel: 354-4455. Soul, R&B, and lots of country and rockabilly.

**HMV**
24 Winter Street, tel: 357-8444
1 Brattle Square, Cambridge, tel: 868-9696. The British rival to

Tower Records has a huge selection of music and videos.

**Mojo Music**

403 Massachusetts Avenue, tel: 547-9976. A small store with a big selection of used CDs and records, and memorabilia.

**Skippy White's**

538 Massachusetts Avenue, Central Square, Cambridge, tel: 491-3345. *The* place for soul, R&B, disco, and jazz, including a large selection of old 45s.

**Smash City**

304 Newbury Street, tel: 536-0216. Collector-quality CDs, tapes, and vinyl.

**Tower Records**

360 Newbury Street, tel: 247-5900. A grand renovated building at the corner of Newbury Street and Massachusetts Avenue offering a huge selection of music, books, magazines, and videos.

## Souvenirs

Several stores and kiosks at Faneuil Hall stock souvenirs of Boston, as do pushcarts at Downtown Crossing.

**Out of Left Field**

North Market Building, Faneuil Hall Marketplace, tel: 722-9401. The place to go for Red Sox gear.

## Toys

**Henry Bear's Park**

361 Huron Avenue, Cambridge, tel: 547-8424. Toys, games, and items for infants and pre-teens.

**Jack's Joke Shop**

226 Tremont Street, tel: 426-9640. The country's oldest joke shop, since 1922, is the place to find whoopie cushions, fake vomit, magic kits, and so on.

**Joie de Vivre**

1792 Massachusetts Avenue, Cambridge, tel: 864-8188. Games for sophisticated children and their parents – a kaleidoscopic collection.

**Stella Bella Toys**

1360 Cambridge Street, Cambridge, tel: 491-6290. Specializes in developmental toys, and scheduled activities include a

Saturday Sing-Along from 11am to noon, story tellers, infant massage, parent/child classes.

**Zoinks! A Wicked Cool Toy Store**

North market Building, Faneuil Hall Marketplace, tel: 227-6277. Packed to the rafters with stuff for kids of all ages.

## TOURS

### Guided Tours

### Bike Tours

**Boston Bike Tours**

Tel: 308-5902; www.bostonbiketours.com. Bicycles and helmets are provided for these three-four hour tours which leave from the Visitors Information Center on Boston Common Sat–Sun May–Oct at 11am. All ages welcome.

### Bus Tours

Bus companies run daily tours in summer. These cover not only Boston and its environs but venture farther afield.

**Boston History Collaborative**

650 Beacon Street, tel: 350-0358; www.bostondiscoveries.com. A three-and-a-half hour bus tour of Literary Boston begins at the Parker House Hotel, 60 School St., and visits historic sites in Cambridge, Lexington and Concord. It runs the second Saturday of each month.

**Brush Hill Tours**

14-16 South Charles Street, tel: 720-6342 or 800-343-1328; www.brushhilltours.com. Tours of Lexington, Concord, Greater Boston, Cambridge, Plimoth Plantation, Salem, Cape Cod, and Newport, Rhode Island departing from several downtown hotels.

**Sightseeing Boston Tours**

Tel: 781-899-1454. Air-conditioned coaches stop at 16 historic sites, including the Charlestown Navy Yard and Harvard University, and allow unlimited reboarding on later buses.

### TrolleyTours

**Beantown Trolley and Harbor Cruise**

14-16 S. Charles Street, tel: 617-720-6342; www.brushhilltours.com. Two-hour narrated tour aboard a San Francisco-style trackless trolley includes stops at the Museum of Fine Arts and the Seaport District. Visitors are picked up at their hotels, and can get off and on as they wish. Price includes harbor cruise May–Oct. Book 72 hours in advance.

**Discover Boston Multi-Lingual Trolley Tours**

519 East Second Street, tel: 742-1440; www.discoverbostontours.com. 100-minute historic tours of Boston and Cambridge available in six languages. Reboarding; all-day pass.

**Old Town Trolley**

380 Dorchester Avenue, tel: 269-8018; www.historictours.com. Cruises along Beacon Hill, Newbury Street, downtown, the waterfront, and Bunker Hill Pavilion, passing close to many Freedom Trail sites. The tour lasts 90 minutes, but passengers can alight and board a later trolley. The company also offers **Ghosts and Gravestones of Boston**, a two-hour tour which includes historic burial grounds.

### Boat Tours and Cruises

**Bay State Cruise Company**

200 Seaport Boulevard; tel: 748-1428. www.baystatecruises.com The *Provincetown III* catamaran speeds to Provincetown in 90 minutes. The *Provincetown II*, Boston's largest passenger cruise ship, makes the trip at a more stately pace. Music/dance cruises leave Fri– Sat evenings for those 21 and over.

**Boston Harbor Cruises**

1 Long Wharf, Tel: 227-4321 or 877-733-9425. www.bostonharborcruises.com. Three-hour whale watching, sightseeing, sunset and lighthouse cruises.

**Boston Duck Tours**

Leaves from Prudential Center and Science Park, Museum of Science, tel: 723-3825. www.

BostonDuckTours.com. Narrated historic tours of the city and the Charles River aboard World War II vintage amphibious vehicles.

**The Charles Riverboat Co.**
Lechmere Canal, CambridgeSide Galleria, 100 CambridgeSide Place, tel: 621-3001; www. charlesriverboat.com. One-hour narrated tours aboard the side-wheeler *Lexington*. Tours depart seven times daily (including sunset cruises at 5:30 and 7pm Jun–Aug; and weekends in Apr, May, and Sept). A cruise/lunch package includes a meal at the Cheesecake Factory Restaurant.

**Massachusetts Bay Lines**
Rowes Wharf, tel: 542-8000. www.massbaylines.com. Four-five hour sightseeing, music and whale-watching cruises; whales are guaranteed or guests receive a free ticket for another cruise.

**New England Aquarium**
Central Wharf, tel: 973-5200; www.neaq.org. Five-hour whale-watching cruises to Stellwagen Bank, feeding ground for whales, dolphins and seabirds, are accompanied by Aquarium naturalists and educators. Boats cast off from the aquarium's wharf summer weekdays at 9:30am and 1:30pm; and weekends at 10am and 2pm. If whales aren't sighted, guests receive a free ticket for another cruise.

**Odyssey Cruises**
Rowes Wharf, Boston Harbor Hotel, tel: 654-9700 or 888-741-0281. www.odysseycruises.com. Sightseeing, lunch, dinner/dancing, and midnight cruises.

## Walking Tours

Both Boston and Cambridge are ideal for walking. Many walking tours, both general and for the specialist, are available.

**Boston African-American Historical Park**
14 Beacon Street, 742-5415; www.nps.gov/boaf. Free 90-minute tours of the 1.6-mile Black Heritage Trail. Tours begin at the Robert Gould Shaw Monument on the Common and leave at

10am, noon, and 2pm Mon–Sat. Labor Day–Memorial Day, advance booking needed.

**Boston by Foot**
77 N. Washington Street, tel: 367-2345. www.bostonbyfoot.com. Ninety-minute walks include tours of: Beacon Hill, the Freedom Trail, Literary Landmarks, the North End, and the Victorian Back Bay. A 60-minute Boston by Little Feet tour is geared for ages 6–12 *(see page 235)*. Reservations not needed but tours begin at different locations, so call ahead.

**Boston History Collaborative**
650 Beacon Street, tel: 350-0358; www.bostondiscoveries.com. Non-profit body offering a free, self-guided walking map of historic waterfront attractions.

**The Boston National Historical Park**
15 State Street, tel: 242-5642; www.nps.gov/bost. Offers frequent free tours of the 2½-mile Freedom Trail from Patriot's Day weekend through November. A half dozen Freedom Trail sites are visited in the 90-minute tour.

**Boston Walks**
tel: 489-5020; www.walkboston.org. Irish, Italian and Jewish ethnic walking tours and bike rides in Boston, Brookline, Cambridge.

**Historic Neighborhoods Foundation**
286 Congress Street, tel: 426-1885; www.historic-neighborhoods.org. Offers a variety of Neighborhood Discovery Tours tours May–Nov. The Kennedy Roots Tour focuses on North End sites associated with the family of John F. Kennedy. Others include Chinatown, the Financial District, and a sunset stroll through Beacon Hill. Small children will adore the "Make Way for Ducklings" stroll *(see page 235)*.

**New England Ghost Tours**
P.O. Box 812128, Wellesley 02482; tel: 781-235-7149; www.newenglandghosttours.com. Boston's original ghost tour is a 90-minute walking tour of downtown's haunted locales.

**North End Italian Market**

**Tours/Michele Topor**
6 Charter Street, tel: 367-2185; www.micheletopor.com. Michele and her entourage visit the butcher, the baker, and the cheesemaker, and taste the best local food.

## SPORT

**BosTix** is Boston's only half-price, day-of-show ticket outlet and information source for sporting events. Half-price tickets go on sale at 11am on the day of performance for cash only. Two locations: Copley Square, open Mon-Sat 10am–6pm, Sun 11am–4pm; Faneuil Hall open Tues–Sat 10am–6pm. For information: www.artsboston.org.

### Spectator Sports

#### Baseball

**Boston Red Sox**
Fenway Park, Yawkey Way, tel: 267-8661. This cozy park, built in 1912, still has grass rather than artificial turf. The Kenmore Square (Green line of the "T", branches B, C, D) and Fenway stations (Green line, branch D) are close to the Park. Box office open Mon–Fri 9am–5pm. Tickets may be purchased on a 24-hour line at 482-4769.

#### Basketball

**Boston Celtics**
FleetCenter, 150 Causeway Street, tel: 624-1000 (recording). Accessible by the Green or Orange lines of the "T".

#### Football

**New England Patriots**
Sullivan Stadium, Foxboro, tel: 1-800-543-1776. Special "T" commuter trains to all Patriots home games from South Station, Back Bay Station, Hyde Park, Route 128 Station. By car take Route 3S (the Southeast Expressway) to Route 128N on to Route 95S. Take exit 9 and follow route 1S for about 3 miles (5 km) to the

stadium – a total distance of about 25 miles (40 km).

### Hockey
**Boston Bruins**
Fleet Center, 150 Causeway Street, tel: 624-1000 (recording).

## Annual Events

Each year Boston is host to three major sporting events:
**Boston Marathon**, tel: Boston Athletic Association at 236-1652; www.bostonmarathon.org. Held on third Monday (Patriots Day) in mid-April. The finish line is at Copley Square, but the Copley Station of the "T" is closed on Marathon day. To reach the final stretch, take the Orange Line to Back Bay Station or the Green Line to Auditorium or Kenmore; or the Green Line (C branch) to any stop on Beacon Street.
**Head of the Charles Regatta**, tel: 864-8415; www.hocr.org. Held on the second-to-last Saturday and Sunday of October, when thousands of oarspeople from all over the world race their shells on the Charles. Take the Red Line of the "T" to Harvard Square and walk south on J.F. Kennedy Street to the river. Or board the Green line (B branch) to Boston University campus and walk to the Boston University Bridge.
**United States Pro Tennis Championships**, tel: 731-4500. Held at the Longwood Cricket Club during the second week in July. The Green line (D branch) of the "T" stops next to the Club.

## Participant Sports

### Billiards
**Boston Billiard Club**
126 Brookline Avenue, tel: 536-7665. Features 42 oak tables against a maroon and green background. Full bar and snacks. Daily noon–2am.
**Flattop Johnny's**
1 Kendall Square, Cambridge, tel: 494-9565. Micro-brewed beer delivered to the accompani-

ment of ear-piercing alternative rock at the ultra-hip hall's 12 tables. Snacks. Mon–Fri noon–1am; Sat and Sun 3pm–1am.
**Jillian's and Lucky Strike**
145 Ipswich Street, tel: 437-0300. 55 tables and much, much more – arcade games, darts, ping-pong – on three floors. Bars. Billiards open Mon–Fri noon–1am; Sat and Sun noon–2am. Lucky Strike is the name of the bowling alley here.
**The Rack**
24 Clinton Street, tel: 725-1051. Upmarket hall with 22 tables and two full-service bars. Food served. Proper dress code. Open Mon–Fri 4pm–2am, Sat and Sun noon–2am.

### Canoeing
**Charles River Canoe and Kayak Center**
A kiosk is located at Artesani Park, off Soldiers Field Road, tel: 965-5110. Canoes, kayaks and rowing shells for hire. Instruction available. Apr–Oct Mon–Fri 10am–sunset, Sat–Sun 9am–sunset.
**South Bridge Boat House**
496 Main Street, Concord, tel: (978) 369-9438. Canoes and rowboats for exploring the Sudbury, Assabet and Concord rivers. Apr–Oct 9.30am–sunset.

### Cycling
Boston has plenty of dedicated trails that are good for cyclists and rollerbladers, including along the banks of the Charles or through Olmsted's Emerald Necklace. Bikes may be rented, in the warmer months, from:
**Ata Cycle**
1773 Massachusetts Avenue, Cambridge, tel: 354-0907
**Back Bay Bicycles**
366 Commonwealth Avenue, tel: 247-2336
**Community Bicycle Supply**
496 Tremont Street, tel: 542-8623

### Golf
**The Massachusetts Golf Association**

Tel: 774-430-9100/800-356-2201, represents more than 200 clubs in the state and will provide up-to-date information on which courses are open to the public.
● Two public 18-hole golf courses supervised by the Parks and Recreation Department are:
**Franklin Park**, 1 Circuit Drive, tel: 265-4084.
**George Wright Golf Course**, 420 West Street, Hyde Park, tel: 361-8313.
● Other 18-hole public courses close to the city:
**Newton Commonwealth Golf Course**
212, Kenrick Road, Newton, tel: 630-1971. Call for weekend reservations.
**President's Golf Course**
357 West Squantum Street, North Quincy, tel: 328-3444.
**Putterham Meadows Golf Club**
1281 West Roxburgh Parkway, Brookline, tel: 730-2078.
**William J. Devine Golf Course**
1 Circuit Drive, Dorchester, tel: 265-4084.

### Sailing
Sailing small boats on the Charles River Basin is a tradition. Less tranquil, but more exciting, is sailing in the harbor.
**Community Boating Inc.**
21 Embankment Road, tel: 523-1038; dock: 523-9763. Become a temporary member, prove you can sail, and 100 sailboats, windsurfers and kayaks await you. Two-day sailboat fee $100; two-day kayak fee $50. Apr–Oct Mon–Fri 1pm–sunset, Sat–Sun 9am–sunset.
**Jamaica Pond Boathouse**
507 Jamaica Way, tel: 522-6258. Sailboats and rowboats for hire in summer for sailing on pretty lake.

### Other
For public tennis courts, swimming pools and skating rinks, contact the Department of Conservation and Recreation, 251 Causeway St., tel: 626-1250.

# A HANDY SUMMARY OF PRACTICAL INFORMATION, ARRANGED ALPHABETICALLY

## **A** ccidents

In the case of an emergency or serious accident, dial **911**. Your hotel or a taxi driver will be able to direct you to the nearest hotel.

## **B** udgeting for a Visit

Boston is an expensive city, but if you need to economize, there are numerous options. There are many websites devoted to booking lodgings at discount. Among them are: www.travelocity.com; www.hotels.com; www.priceline.com; www.orbitz.com, and www.hotwire .com. Hotel rates fluctuate with the seasons and demand. If your travel time is flexible, call the hotel and ask them when their rates are "off-season". Many colleges and universities in

the area rent rooms in their dormitories during the summer months, when students are not present.

Although the mainstream tourist restaurants can be costly, there are many inexpensive places, including ethnic restaurants in Chinatown and affordable places in Cambridge, particularly the Central Square and Inman Square areas.

### Business Hours

Most offices are open Mon–Fri 9am–5pm, although some offices open at 8am. Banks are open Mon–Fri 9am–3pm and often later. On Thursday they remain open until 5pm or later. Saturday hours are generally 9am–2pm.

## **C** ar Rentals

Drivers must be at least 21 to rent a car; some renters specify 25. Rental agencies have offices throughout the city. Your hotel can help make arrangements, or a listing of agencies is available from the Greater Boston Convention & Visitors Bureau, tel: 536-4100. A valid driver's license and credit card are required.

### Children

There are loads of museums to explore, shops to visit, and activities geared specially to children. The Visitors Bureau's *Kids Love Boston Kit*, available for $4.25 (includes postage and handling), includes a 48-page illustrated guidebook written especially for kids, a Travel Planner, an illustrated kid's map of Massachusetts, and a Boston USA Specials! Card (see Discounts, page 236). It can be ordered online at www.BostonUSA.com or tel: 888-733-2677/international tel: 617-536-4100.

### Child Care
Many hotels offer child care services which charge by the hour. Ask at the front desk.
**Parents in a Pinch, Inc.**, 45 Bartlett Crescent, Brookline, tel: 739-5437/800-688-4697; www.parentsinapinch.com, offers in-room hotel care for children of all ages, with a minimum stay of four hours. Charges: $11/hr for the first child, $1/hr for each additional child, infants up to three months $13/hr.

### Child-Friendly Tours
For a list of organized tours, check out www.BostonKids.net.
**Boston by Little Feet**, tel: 367-2345, www.bostonbyfoot.com. Geared for ages 6–12, the hour-long tour stops at sites along the Freedom Trail. Meets at the Samuel Adams statue on Congress Street. Tour times: Mon 10 am, Sat. 2pm.
**Make Way for Ducklings Tour**, tel: 426-1885, www.historic neighborhoods.org. Guides bring Robert McCloskey's book to life. Among the stops: Boston Common, the Public Garden, and Beacon Hill. Tours in July and Aug Fri and Sat. Call for hours.

### Clothing
Many stores throughout the area cater to children. Among them:
**Baby Gap**, Copley Place, 100 Huntington Avenue, tel: 247-1754. Wide range of clothes.
**Calliope**, 33 Brattle Street, Cambridge, tel: 876-4119. Bright, cheerful togs for infants to age six, and a sensational selection of stuffed animals and puppets.
**Fish Kids**, 1378 Beacon Street, Coolidge Corner, Brookline, tel: 738-1006. Hard-to-find brands for infants to size 10, including a large selection of shoes.

### Activities for Children
Popular places include:
**Boston Children's Theatre**, 647 Boylston Street, tel: 424-6634; www.bostonchildrenstheatre.org. Kids perform for other kids in one of the country's oldest performing arts troupes. Performances are held at venues throughout the city, with free programs for under-fives in Copley Square Wed evenings in summer.
**The Children's Museum**, 300 Congress Street, tel: 426-8855, is packed with interactive exhibits, and will particularly engage those up to 10 years of age. Open daily; Fridays 5-9pm, admission is just $1/person.
**Franklin Park Zoo**, 1 Franklin Park Road, Jamaica Plain, tel: 541-5466 is home to a host of creatures including gorillas, leopards, lions, as well as the more pettable animals in Contact Corral and Franklin Farm. Open daily.
**Museum of Science**, Science Park, tel: 723-2500, has more than 600 interactive exhibits featuring live animal and physical science demonstrations. A visit to the Omni Theater and Planetarium are highlights. Open daily.
**New England Aquarium**, Central Wharf, tel: 973-5200. A four-story ocean tank with sharks, turtles and moral eels is the centerpiece of this state-of-the-art aquarium. The 6-story IMAX screen provides an amazing fish-eye view of the sea. Open daily.
**USS Constitution and Museum**, Charlestown Navy Yard, tel: 426-1812. There's little damage that even the most energetic kid can do to "Old Ironsides", the 1797 warship. Costumed guides are on deck to answer questions. Open Apr–Oct, Tues–Sun; Nov–Mar Thurs–Sun. Free.

## Climate
Part of the magic of Boston is that it is a land of seasons. The first snow may fall in November, and intermittent snow accompanied by cold weather – considerably below freezing – will usually continue well into March. The Charles River usually freezes over. Spring, which can be temperamental, spans March into May. This is when magnolias and lilacs bloom and magic fills the air. Summer (June–Sept) can be very hot and humid with some real dog-days, although most of the time the weather is just pleasantly hot – in the 70° to 80°F (21°–27°C) range.

The fall encroaches gradually, usually with one last splurge of glorious "Indian summer" days. Starting in September and "peaking" in mid-October, resplendent fall colors can be enjoyed in the outskirts of Boston and even more so in the mountains of northern New England. In summary, Boston weather can be described in one word: erratic.

## Clothing
Boston is simultaneously more formal and less so than other parts of the country. The old-guard restaurants and hotels require proper dress, whereas in student enclaves, anything goes. Plan ahead and call if necessary. Remember: it can get very cold in winter and very hot in summer.

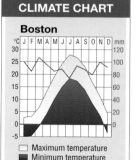

**CLIMATE CHART**

**Boston**

☐ Maximum temperature
■ Minimum temperature
— Rainfall

°C J F M A M J J A S O N D mm

## Consulates

**Australia**: 20 Park Plaza, tel: 542-8655.
**Canada**: 3 Copley Place, #400, tel: 262-3760.
**Ireland**: 535 Boylston Street, tel: 267-9330.
**Israel**: 20 Park Plaza, tel: 535-0200.
**United Kingdom**: 600 Atlantic Avenue, tel: 245-4500.

## **D**entists

**David Brown, DDS**
Tel: 508-963-8383
www.tootheache-dentist.com
Dr. Brown makes hotel and house calls around-the-clock.
**Dental Referral Service** (tel: 800-511-8663) provides free, around-the-clock recommendations .

## Disabled Access

The MBTA (Massachusetts Bay Transit Authority) has an excellent website (www.mbta.com) with information about transportation accessible to disabled travelers. For more information, call the MBTA on 722-5123. The City of Boston's Disabled Person's Commission can be reached on 635-3682.

## Discounts

**Boston Card**. Tel: 742-5950, www.gobostoncard.com. Boston Travel and Tourism's one, three, or five-day pre-paid visitor pass offers unlimited admission to more than 40 attractions and tours, including Beantown Trolley, Boston Duck Tour, Whale Watch, and the Museum of Fine Arts. Cards on sale at Boston Common and The Shops at Prudential visitor information centers.
**Boston CityPass**. Tel: 888-330-5008, www.citypass.com. Save 50 percent on admission to six famous attractions, including: Skywalk Observatory at Prudential Center, Harvard Museum of Natural History, Museum of Fine Arts, Museum of Science, John F.

Kennedy Library and Museum, and the New England Aquarium. The pass ($36.75 adults; $25.50 youths) is good for nine consecutive days, and sold at all the above locations.
**BosTix Ticket Booth**
Faneuil Hall and Copley Square, tel: 482-2849; www.artsboston.org. Boston's official entertainment and cultural information center, providing tickets and information for over 100 attractions. Half-price theater tickets are sold here on day of performance. Faneuil Hall: Tues–Sat 10am–6pm, Sun 11am–4pm. Copley Square: daily, 10am–6pm.
**Boston USA Specials! Card**, Tel:888-733-2677/international tel: 617-536-4100; www.BostonUSA com. Available for free, the pass gives visitors discounts at hotels, attractions, museums, theaters, restaurants, and shops. Locations: Boston Common Visitor Information Center, 147 Tremont Street; Prudential Center Visitor Information Center; and Cambridge Visitor Information Booth, Harvard Square (closed Sunday).
**MBTA Visitor Pass**
Tel: 222-5568 or 800-392-6100; www.mbta.com. A one-day passport costs $7.50; three-day, $18; seven-day, $35. Children's passports (age 5–11) are half the adult price. Passports permit unlimited use on the "T," on MBTA buses up to $1.50 fare (additional fare, if any, payable in cash), commuter rail zones IA and IB, and inner harbor ferries. Passports also earn discounts at some tourist attractions and restaurants. Passports are sold at the airport, the three railway stations; and Visitor Information Center on Boston Common; Faneuil Hall Marketplace Information Center; Harvard subway station; and at some hotels.

## **E** lectricity

Boston homes have "standard" electricity, which is 110 volts. European appliances require an

adapter because European countries use 220–240 volts. Some hotel bathrooms have electrical outlets suitable for use with European appliances (220–240 volts), but it is useful to pack an adapter.

## Emergency Numbers

**Police, Ambulance, Fire** 911
**Credit cards lost or stolen**:
AmEx, tel: 1-800-528-2121;
Diners Club/Carte Blanche, tel: 1-800-234-6377;
MasterCard, tel: 1-800-307-7309;
Visa, 1-800-336-8472.
**Weather info**: tel: 936-1234.

## Entry Regulations

### *Visas & Passports*
For a breakdown of up-to-date US entry regulations, visit http// travel.state.gov/visa/index.html. The Visa Office's mailbox for enquiries is usvisa@state.gov. Tel: 202-663-1225.
### *Customs*
Those over 21 may take into the US: 200 cigarettes, 50 cigars (plus an additional 100, not including Cuban-made, under a gift exemption), or 3 lbs of tobacco; 1 US quart of alcohol; duty-free gifts worth up to $100 (must remain in the US at least 72 hours). Do not bring in meat products, seeds, plants and fruits. Don't even think about bringing in narcotics. Customs agents in the US are very tough and efficient. For information: www.customs.ustreas.gov

The United States allows you to take out anything you wish, but consult the consulate or tourist authority of the country you are visiting next on its customs regulations for entrance.

## **G** overnment

The city is governed by a mayor, who is elected for a four-year term, and by a city council of nine members. The government of the Commonwealth of Massachusetts is based in the State House at the top of Beacon Hill and in other buildings adjacent to the Government Center.

## H ealth

Foreign visitors needing medical attention face a bill of $500-plus for one night in a hospital in a semi-private room. It's worth arranging medical insurance before leaving home.
**Massachusetts General Hospital**, 55 Fruit Street, tel: 726-2000, operates a Medical Walk-In clinic 8:30am–8:30pm for non-emergency situations, and emergency room care for more serious conditions.
● Other facilities with 24-hour care include:
**Brigham & Women's Hospital**, 75 Francis Street, tel: 732-5500;
**Children's Hospital,** 300 Longwood Avenue, tel: 355-6000;
**New England Medical Center**, 750 Washington Street, tel: 636-5000.
● Other medical hotlines:
**Beth Israel Deaconess Hospital**, tel: 667-7000.
**Massachusetts Eye & Ear Infirmary**, tel: 523-7900.
**Tufts Dental School**, 1 Kneeland Street, tel: 636-6828. Emergencies Mon–Fri 9am–10.30am and 1pm–2:30pm. Walk-in clinic with limited admissions.
**Pharmacies open 24 hours**:
CVS, 155 Charles Street, Boston, tel: 227-0437.
CVS, Porter Square, Cambridge, tel: 876-5519.

## I nternet Access

**Boston Public Library**, 700 Boylston Street, tel: 536-5400. Mon–Thur 9am–9pm; Fri–Sat 9am–5pm. Free, 15-minute Express Internet; up to one hour a day free internet use with a complimentary Visitor's Card.
**Harvard University Information Center**, Holyoke Center, Harvard Square, tel: 495-1573. Mon–Sat 9am–5pm. Free access, 10-minute maximum when people are waiting.

**Internet Cafe**, 252 Newbury Street, tel: 267-9716. Open Mon–Fri 9am–8pm; Sat and Sun noon–7pm. $5/hr or $3/15 min.

## M aps

Insight Guides' *FlexiMap Boston* is laminated for durability and easy folding, and contains travel information as well as exceptionally clear cartography.

## Media

### Print

**Boston Globe**, www.boston.com: daily newspaper. Thursday supplement gives events listings for the next seven days.
**Boston Herald**; www.bostonherald.com: daily newspaper. Friday supplement contains listings for following week.
**Christian Science Monitor**; www.csmonitor.com: a prestigious daily newspaper published in Boston on weekdays. Strong on international news.
**Boston Phoenix**; www.bostonphoenix.com: a thick Thursday alternative weekly with intelligent articles plus listings and comments on entertainment events.
**Improper Bostonian**; www.improper.com: a free sophisticated biweekly digest with a strong listings section.
**Boston Magazine**; www.bostonmagazine.com: a slick and informative monthly of local interest.
**Bay Windows**, www.baywindows.com: a weekly publication catering to the gay, lesbian and transgender community.
The kiosk in the middle of Harvard Square (tel: 354-7777) sells a wide range of national and international publications.

### Radio Stations

Radio stations in the area include:
**WEEI** on 850 AM for sports;
**WRKO** on 680 AM for talk;
**WBZ** on 1030 AM for news;
**WILD** on 1090 for contemporary music;

**WCRB** on 102.5 FM for classical music;
**WBCN** on 104.1 FM for rock music;
**WJIB** on 96.9 FM for country music;
**WGBH** (Public Radio – classical music) on 89.7 FM;
**WBUR** (Public Radio – news and information) 90.9 FM;
**WZLX** on 100.7 for classic rock.

### Television Stations

These include:
**PBS** on channel 2 (WGBH);
**CBS** on channel 4 (WBZ);
**ABC** on channel 5 (WCVB);
**NBC** on channel 7 (WNEV);
**Fox** on channel 25 (WXNE);
**UPN** on channel 38 (WSBK);
**WB** on channel 56 (WLVI).

## Money

The safest way to carry large sums of money is traveler's checks, the most widely accepted being American Express, Visa, and MasterCard. Discover is also widely accepted; Diners Club less so. If in doubt, be sure to double-check before you order dinner or have your purchases tallied up.

## P arking

Public parking facilities are found at Government Center; Post Office Square; the Public Garden; the Prudential Center; on Clarendon Street near the John Hancock Tower; and elsewhere. There are various private lots.
Parking garages close to Harvard Square in Cambridge include: Charles Square Garage, 1 Bennett Street; Church Street Parking Lot, Church Street; Harvard Square Garage, JFK and Eliot streets; and Holyoke Center Garage, access via Dunster and Holyoke streets.

## Postal Services

The main Post Office is at 25 Dorchester Avenue (tel: 654-5302), behind South Station. Hours are Mon–Fri 6am–midnight; Sat 8am–7pm; and Sun noon–7pm. If you do not know where you will be staying, mail can be addressed to: General Delivery, Main Post Office, 25 Dorchester Avenue, Boston 02101.

The Post Office at Logan Airport is open until midnight. Stamps are available in vending machines in airports, hotels, stores, bus and train stations.

## Public Holidays

All government offices, bank and post offices are closed on public holidays. Public transportation doesn't run as often on these days, but most shops, museums, and other attractions are open.

● **January** New Year's Day; Martin Luther King Day (third Mon)
● **February** President's Day (third Mon)
● **March/April** Easter Sun
● **May** Memorial Day (last Mon)
● **July** Independence Day (4th)
● **September** Labor Day (first Mon)
● **October** Columbus Day
● **November** Thanksgiving Day (last Thursday) and following day
● **December** Christmas Day (25).

## T elephone codes

Area codes for Boston and its environs are **617** and **857**. When dialing a phone number, you must include the area code along with the seven-digit number. Area codes for Cape Cod, Martha's Vineyard and Nantucket are **508** and **774**. The North Shore, including Cape Ann, use **978** and **351**. Towns to the south of Boston use **781** and **339**. Western Massachusetts is **413**.

## Time Zones

Boston runs on Eastern Standard Time. Every spring the clock is turned one hour ahead, and every fall one hour back. Boston is three hours ahead of Los Angeles, one hour ahead of Chicago, five hours behind London and 15 hours behind Tokyo.

## Tipping

Tipping is voluntary. Gratuities are not automatically tallied into the bill. Some guidelines:
● Waiters are usually given 15 percent of the bill. For above-average service, or in a better restaurant, tip 20 percent.
● Taxi cab drivers usually get 15 percent of the fare.
● Doormen, skycabs and porters receive one dollar a bag.
● Hairdressers, manicurists and masseurs usually receive 10–15 percent of the total charge.

## Tourist Information

**Boston National Historical Park** 15 State Street, opposite Old State House, tel: 242-5642; www.nps.gov/bost. Starting point for free Freedom Trail walks. The Center services include information, displays and sales on historic Boston and Massachusetts; book store; rest rooms; telephones, and disabled accessibility. Daily 9am–5pm.
**Cambridge Visitor Information Booth.** Located at booth in the center of Harvard Square, tel: 497-1630. Source of comprehensive Cambridge-specific information, including tours. Closed Sun.
**Harvard University Information Office.** Holyoke Centre in Harvard Square, tel: 495-1573. Source of Harvard-specific information. Sept–May, Mon–Sat 9am–5pm; June, July, Aug Mon–Sat 9am–7pm, Sun noon–5pm.
**Faneuil Hall Marketplace Information Center.** South side of Quincy Market; tel: 523-1300; www.faneuilhallmarketplace.com Mon–Sat 10am–9pm, Sun 2–6pm.
**Greater Boston Convention & Visitors Bureau.** Two Copley Place; tel: 536-4100/888-733-2678; www.bostonusa.com Offers phone information for visitors, and maintains the Prudential Visitor Center on the west side of the Prudential Plaza, open Mon–Sat 9am–5pm, Sun 1–5pm; and the Boston Common Visitor

Information Center, 147 Tremont Street. The booth here marks the start of the Freedom Trail, and is open daily, 9am–5pm.
**Massport International Information Booth.** Logan International Airport (terminal E). Provides assistance to international visitors. Summer, noon–8pm; winter, noon–6pm.
**Massachusetts Office of Travel & Tourism.** 10 Park Plaza, Suite 4510, tel: 727-3201/800-227-6277; www.massvacation.com. "MOTT" can supply details on the state and day trip information. Mon–Fri 9am–5pm.
**Travelers Aid Society.** Offices at 17 E Street, tel: 542-7286. Booths at Greyhound Bus depot at South Station and at Logan Airport, Terminals A and E.

## W ebsites

**www.BostonUSA.com.** Greater Boston Convention & Visitors Bureau's official site.
**www.massvacation.com** Massachusetts Office of Tavel & Tourism's site provides information for the entire state.
**www.goboston.com** Boston's all-inclusive visitor pass.
**www.mbta .com.** For up-to-date information about the transportation system.
**www.massport.com** All you need to know about Logan Airport.
**www.capecodchamber.org** Cape Cod Chamber of Commerce information.
**www.visitNew England.com** For information about the region.
**www.northofboston.org** Details of places to the north of the city.

## Weights & Measures

The US uses the Imperial system, and metric is rarely used. Some useful conversions:
1 inch = 2.54 centimeters
1 foot = 30.48 centimeters
1 mile = 1.609 kilometers
1 quart = 1.136 liters
1 ounce = 28.4 grams
1 pound = 0.453 kilograms
1 yard = 0.9144 meters

# FURTHER READING

## Non-Fiction

*About Boston*, by David McCord, (Little, Brown, 1973).
*Bibles, Brahmins, and Bosses*, by Thomas H. O'Connor, (Public Library, Boston, 1991).
*Boston: A Topographical History*, by Walter Muir Whitehall, (Belknap Press of Harvard University Press, 1968).
*Boston's North Shore*, by Joseph Garland, (Little, Brown, 1978).
*Boston Sites and Insights*, by Susan Wilson, (Beacon Press, 1994).
*The Charles – The People's River*, by Max Hall, (Godine, 1986).
*Cityscapes of Boston*, by Robert Campbell and Peter Vanderwarker, (Houghton Mifflin, 1992).
*Common Ground: A Turbulent Decade in the Lives of Three American Families*, (about busing crisis), by Anthony J. Lukas, (Alfred A. Knopf, 1985).
*Dead Certainties*, (about 1849 Parkman-Webster murder case), by Simon Schama, (Knopf, 1990).
*Freedom By the Bay*, by William Schofield, (Branden Publishing Company, 1988).
*The Houses of Boston's Back Bay*, by Bainbridge Bunting, (Harvard University Press, 1967).
*Imagining Boston: A Literary Landscape*, by Shaun O'Connell's, (Beacon Press, 1990).
*The Islands of Boston Harbor*, by Edward Rowe Snow, (Dodd, Mead, 1971).
*Lost Boston*, by Jane Holtz Kay and Pauline Chase-Herrell, (Houghton Mifflin, 1980).
*The Massachusetts Historical Society: A Bicentennial History, 1791–1991*, by Louis Leonard Tucker, (Massachusetts Historical Society, 1996).

*The Nature of Massachusetts*, by Christopher Leary, *et al*, (Audubon Society/Addison-Wesley 1996).
*Paul Revere and the World He Lived In*, by Esther Forbes, (Houghton Mifflin, 1942).
*The Proper Bostonians*, by Cleveland Amory, (Dutton, 1947).

## Fiction

*The Blithedale Romance*, by Nathaniel Hawthorne, (Oxford University Press, 1991).
*Boston Adventure*, by Jean Stafford, (Harcourt, Brace, 1986).
*The Bostonians*, by Henry James, (Knopf, 1993).
*The Europeans*, by Henry James, (Viking Penguin, 1985).
*Faithful Are the Wounds*, by May Sarton, (Norton, 1986).
*The Friends of Eddie Coyle*, by George Higgins, (Viking Penguin, 1987). Also several other mysteries such as *Cogan's Trade, Impostors, Outlaws, Penance for Jerry Kennedy* in an ongoing series based in Boston.
*Godwulf Manuscript, Promised Land* and other Spenser mystery novels, by Robert B. Parker, (No Exit Press).
*The Good Mother*, by Sue Miller, (Dell, 1987).
*Johnny Tremain*, by Esther Forbes, (Dell, 1987).
*The Last Hurrah*, by Edwin O'Connor, (Little, Brown, 1985).
*The Last Puritan*, by George Santayana, (Macmillan, 1981).
*The Late George Apley*, by John P. Marquand, (Little, Brown, 1965).
*Little Women*, by Louisa May Alcott, (Simon & Schuster, 1988).
*Memorial Hall Murder*, by Jane

Langton, (Gollancz, 1990).
*A Modern Instance*, by William Dean Howells, (Penguin, 1984).
*Mystic River*, by Dennis Lehane, (Morrow, 2001).
*The Rise of Silas Lapham*, by William Dean Howells, (Random House, 1991).
*The Scarlet Letter*, by Nathaniel Hawthorne, (Knopf, 1992).

## For Children

*Make Way for Ducklings*, by Robert McCloskey, (Penguin, 1976).
*Trumpet of the Swan*, by E.B. White, (Harper Collins, 1973).

## Other Insight Guides

More than 180 **Insight Guides** and **Insight City Guides** cover every continent. In addition, a companion series of more than 120 **Insight Pocket Guides** provides selected, carefully timed itineraries for the traveler with little time to spare and include a full-size fold-out map. And more than 130 **Insight Compact Guides** provide ideal on-the-spot companions, with text, maps and pictures all carefully cross-referenced.
Titles which highlight destinations in this region include:
● *Insight Guide: New England*
● *Insight Pocket Guide: Boston*
● *Insight Pocket Guide: New England*
● *Insight Compact Guide: Boston*
● *Insight City Guide: New York*
● Boston is one title in the comprehensive range of **Insight Flexi-Maps**, laminated for ease of use and durability.

## ART & PHOTO CREDITS

**Map Production:** Stephen Ramsay and Dave Priestley
©2006 Apa Publications GmbH & Co. Verlag KG, Singapore Branch

# BOSTON STREET ATLAS

The key map shows the area of Boston covered by the atlas section. An index of street names and places of interest shown on the maps can be found on the following pages. For each entry there is a page number and grid reference.

## Map Legend

| | | | | | | |
|---|---|---|---|---|---|---|
| Freeway with Junction | | ✈ Airport | Freeway | Ⓜ | Subway |
| Freeway (under construction) | | ✝ Church (ruins) | Divided Highway | 🚌 | Bus Station |
| Divided Highway | | ✝ Monastery | Main Roads | ❶ | Tourist Information |
| Main Road | | 🏰 Castle (ruins) | | ✉ | Post Office |
| Secondary Road | | ∴ Archaeological Site | Minor Roads | ✝ | Cathedral/Church |
| Minor road | | ∩ Cave | | ☪ | Mosque |
| Track | | ★ Place of Interest | Footpath | ✡ | Synagogue |
| International Boundary | | ⌂ Mansion/Stately Home | Railroad | ⚲ | Statue/Monument |
| State Boundary | | ☀ Viewpoint | Pedestrian Area | ◻ | Tower |
| National Park/Reserve | | ⚑ Beach | Important Building | 🗼 | Lighthouse |
| Ferry Route | | | Park | | |

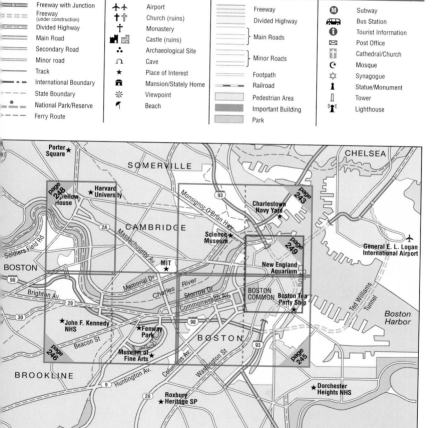

A   B

2nd Av.
Crabbe Hill Rd
Charles St
2nd Av.
Poplar St
Joy St
Linwood St
3rd Av.
Beth
Inner
3rd Av.
93

1

Fitchburg St

SOMERVILLE

Rutherford
Essex St
Main St
South Eden
Mead

PHIPPS
BURYING GROUND

Community
College

Bunker H
Commun
College

Gore St
Rindge Rd
Stevens Ct
Winter St
Monsignor O'Brien Highway
Linehan

Gilmore Bridge
Charlestown Av.

Otis St
Gore St
Gore
5th
Otis St
Otis Hospital
Lechmere
Cambridge St
Lechmere Square
2nd St
1st St
Otis St

2

Fulkerson St
8th
7th
Spring St
Thorndike St
Holy Cross
Polish Church
Middlesex Country
Courthouse
Bulfinch
Place

EAST CAMBRIDGE

John J
Ahern Field
Spring
Pl
Hurley St
4th St Pl
Sciarappa
Lopez St
Spring
Hurley St
2nd St
1st St
Cambridgeside
Galleria

Museum of
Science

Charles River Dam

Mugar
Omni
Theater

Hayden
Planetarium

Charles St
Bent
Charles St
St
3rd St
2nd St
Charles St
1st St
Charlesgate
Yacht Club

3

Rogers St
6th
5th
St
Rogers St
Land Boulevard
Charles River

Binney St
Binney St
2nd St
1st St

Munroe
St
Cambridge Parkway
CHARLESBANK
PLAYGROUND

Charles St
Blosso
Massa
Genera

Potter St
Athenaeum St

Mass
Ear I
Fruit St

Broadway
3rd St
Charles
Street Jail
Charles (MGH

Kendall/MIT
Main St
Longfellow Bridge
Charles
Camb

4

Carleton St
Hayward St
Wadsworth St
Amherst St
Memorial Drive

Community
Boating

West Hill
Pl
Charles
River Sq.
Revere St

W. Cedar St
Phillips
St
Charles St

0        400 yards
0        400 m

BEACON H

A   B

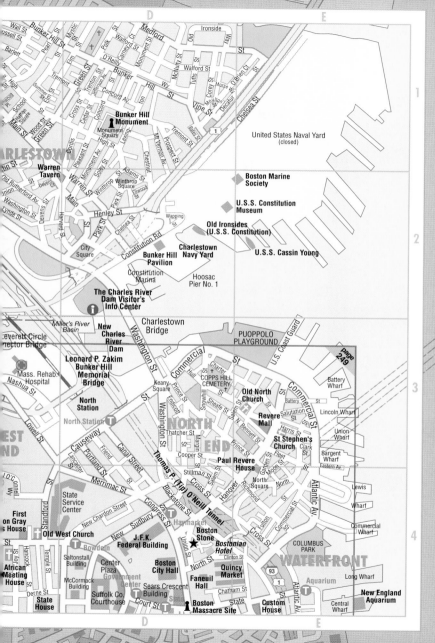

**Charlestown**
- Bunker Hill Monument
- Warren Tavern
- Bunker Hill Pavilion
- City Square
- Constitution Marina
- Boston Marine Society
- U.S.S. Constitution Museum
- Old Ironsides (U.S.S. Constitution)
- Charlestown Navy Yard
- U.S.S. Cassin Young
- Hoosac Pier No. 1
- The Charles River Dam Visitor's Info Center
- Charlestown Bridge
- New Charles River Dam
- Miller's River Basin
- United States Naval Yard (closed)
- PUOPPOLO PLAYGROUND
- U.S. Coast Guard

**North End**
- Leonard P. Zakim Bunker Hill Memorial Bridge
- Thomas P. (Tip) O'Neill Tunnel
- COPPS HILL CEMETERY
- Old North Church
- Revere Mall
- St Stephen's Church
- Paul Revere House
- North Station
- Haymarket
- Battery Wharf
- Lincoln Wharf
- Union Wharf
- Sargent Wharf
- Lewis Wharf
- page 249

**West End**
- Mass. Rehab. Hospital
- State Service Center
- First Harrison Gray Otis House
- Old West Church
- African Meeting House
- State House
- J.F.K. Federal Building
- Center Plaza
- Government Center
- Saltonstall Building
- McCormack Building
- Suffolk Co. Courthouse
- Sears Crescent Building
- Boston City Hall
- Everett Circle
- Prison Point Bridge

**Waterfront**
- Boston Stone
- Bostonian Hotel
- Faneuil Hall
- Quincy Market
- Boston Massacre Site
- Custom House
- COLUMBUS PARK
- Aquarium
- New England Aquarium
- Commercial Wharf
- Central Wharf
- Long Wharf

Charles River

Hatch Shell

BEACON

Charles Street Meeting House

Chestn

Pinckney
Louisb'g
Squa

Embankment Rd

Mt Vernon St

Chestnut St

Lime St

River St

Charles St

Byron St

Branch

Beaver Pl

Beaver St

Make Way for Duckli

Emerson College

Beacon St

Arlington St

PUBLIC

Washington Monument

GARDEN

Gibson House Mus.

Lagoon

Back St

Berkeley St

Clarendon St

Storrow

Ritz-Carlton

Fo
Se

Storrow Drive

Back St

Cushing-Endicott House

Marlborough

Commonwealth Av.

Emmanuel Church

Arlington St Church

Arling

Hunnewell Mansion

St

Beacon St

Exeter St

Marlborough St

Dartmouth St

Newbury St

First Baptist Church

Boylston St

Berkeley St

Av.

BAY

VILLAG

Fairfield

Gloucester

Ames-Webster House

Algonquin Club

BACK BAY

New Old South Church

Copley

Trinity Church

Providence

Columbus Av.

Piedmont

Winchester

John F. Andrew House

Hereford

Commonwealth Av.

Dalton St

St James

Hancock Tower

Stuart

Plaza Castle

Isabella St

Burrage Mansion

Newbury St

Lenox Hotel

Boston Public Library

Blagden St

Copley Square

Westin

St James

Fairmont Copley Plaza

Stanhope

Cortes St

Mass.

Boston Architectural Center

Lord & Taylor

Exeter St

Stuart St

Hynes/ICA

Institute of Contemporary Art

Saks

Huntington Av.

Copley Place

Copley Place

Back Bay/ South End

Buckingham St

Berkeley St

Boylston St

Cambria St

Prudential Center

Hynes Auditorium

Visitor Center

Harcourt

Chandler

Appleton

Warren Av.

E. Ber

Berklee Performance Center

Scotia St

Sheraton Boston Hotel

Lawrence

Gray St

Clarendon St

Boston Center for the Arts (Cyclorama Bldg.)

Hilton Back Bay

Belvidere St

Prudential

St Germain St

Clearway

Prudential

Yarmouth

Sycamore

Carleton

Braddock Pk

Canton St

Holyoke St

Appleton

Dartmouth Pl

Montgomery St

Hanson St

Milford St

Mapparium

Publishing Soc. Bldg.

Colonnade

Newton St

Columbus Av.

Warren Av.

Dartmouth St

Tremont St

Upton St

Christian Science Complex

W. Rutland St

W. Canton St

Pembroke

W. Brookline St

W. Dedham St

Holy Cross Cathedral

Union

Westland Av.

Horticultural Hall

Cumberland St

W. Newton St

Rutland Sq.

Concord Sq.

W. Newton St

SOUTH END

Mons. Reynol

Symphony Hall

St Stephen St

Botolph St

Claremont

Greenwich

W. Haven St

Rutland

Tremont St

BLACKSTONE SQUARE

Brad

Symphony

Huntington

Massachusetts Av.

Clarendon

Aguadilla

W. Concord St

Nelland St

Washington St

FRANKLIN SQUARE

St George St

Brookline St

New England Conservatory of Music

Matthews Arena

Columbus Av.

Wellington St

Tremont St

W. Springfield St

Newton St

Y.M.C.A.

Camden St

Northampton St

Worcester St

Newland St

Sterns

Mystic St

WM. E. CARTER PLAYGROUND

400 yards

Northampton St

Washington St

0

400 m

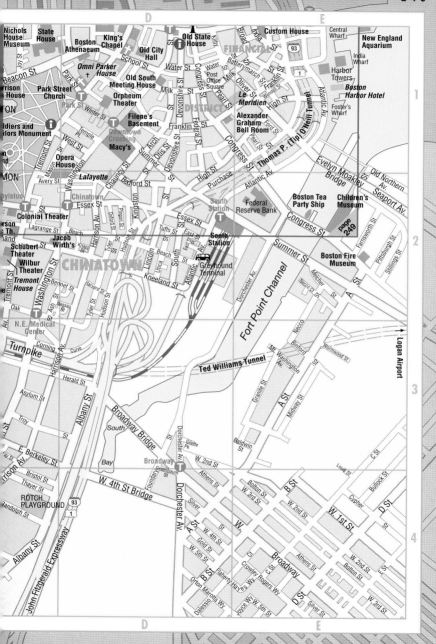

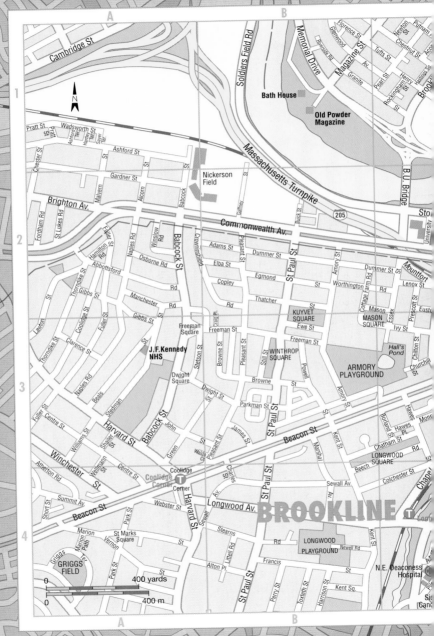

**D** **E**

**MIT Chapel**

Memorial Drive

Vassar St

Memorial Drive

**Charles River**

Harvard Bridge

Storrow Drive

**University**

Back St

Bay State Rd

Back St

Commonwealth Av.

Back St

Bay State Rd

Marlborough

Beacon St

**Massachusetts**

Kenmore

Kenmore Square

Newbury St

Newbury St

Emerson College (Ames Mansion)

Turnpike **205**

Ipswich St

Hynes/Ica

Park Drive

Beacon St

Landsdowne St

Ipswich St

Boylston St

Haviland St

Audubon Circle

Brookline Av.

**Fenway Park**

St

Fenway

Hemenway St

Norway St

**Fenway**

Van Ness

St

**BACK BAY FENS**

Burbank St

Boylston

Peterborough St

Park Drive

**Westland Av.**

Riverway

Peterborough St

Queensberry St

Agassiz Rd

Symphony Rd

Gainsborough St

Pilgrim Rd

Queensberry St

Jarvis St

Fenway

St Stephen St

Brookline Av.

Fenway

**BACK BAY FENS**

Fenway

Forsyth Wy

Hemenway St

Northeastern

**Beth Israel Hospital**

Park Drive

**Museum of Fine Arts**

Forsyth

**Massachusetts College of Art**

Av. Louis Pasteur

**Isabella Gardner Museum**

Museum Rd

Art Museum

Huntington Av.

Greenleaf St

**Northeastern University**

wood Av.

Palace Rd

Evans Wy

Louis Prang St

Ruggles St

Parker St

**D** **E**

A B C

1

2

3

4

Concord Av.
Craigie St
Chauncy St
Berkley
Berkley Pl.
St Johns Rd
Phillips Pl.
Longfellow House
Brattle St
Episcopalian Theological School
Manson
Henry Vassal House
LONG-FELLOW PARK
Hawthorn St
Willard
Acacia St
Ash
Brattle
Radcliffe Yard
Loeb Drama Center
Appian Wy St
Farwell Pl.
Mt. Auburn St
Hilliard St
Story St
Church
Palmer
7 Waterhouse
Garden St
Waterhouse St
Sheraton Commander
CAMBRIDGE COMMON
FLAGSTAFF PARK
OLD BURYING GROUND
Holden Chapel
University Hall
Harvard St
Harvard Square
Harvard
Massachusetts Hall
Brattle Square
Bennet St
Winthrop
Dunster
The Charles
J.F. Kennedy School of Government
JOHN F. KENNEDY PARK
Eliot House
Kirkland House
Lowell House
Newell Boathouse
Charles River
Memorial Drive
Soldiers Field Rd
J. F. Kennedy St
Larz Anderson Bridge
South St
Mill
Plympton
Weld Boathouse
Memorial Drive
Leverett House
Soldiers Field Athletic Area
Harvard Stadium
North Harvard St
Harvard University Graduate School of Business Administration
Harvard University
Kresge
McCollum
Soldiers Field Rd
John W. Weeks Footbridge
Dunster House
Mather House
Flagg
Banks
Cowperthwaite St
Surrey St
Fallon Pl.
Hague
Rotterdam St
Windom St
Seattle St
Seattle St
Western Av.
Western Av. Bridge
Western Av.
Field Rd
ALLSTON
Cambridge St
River St Bridge
Soldiers Field Rd
Memorial Drive
Oxford St
W. Sorento St
Eatonia St
Almy St

Massachusetts Av.
Harvard Law School
Langdell Hall
Austin Hall
University Museum of Natural History
Oxford St
Peabody Museum
Harvard-Yenching Library
Jefferson Physical Labs
Busch-Reisinger Building
William James Hall
Science Center
Memorial Hall
Gund Hall
Oxford St
Harvard University
Memorial Church
Coolidge Hall
Irving Ter
Cambridge St
Harvard Yard
Sever Hall
A.M. Sackler Museum
Cambridge Rind & Latin High Sc
Fogg Museum
Widener Library
Houghton Library
Carpenter Center for the Visual Arts
Lamont
Broadway
War M
Cambridge Public Library
Massachusetts Av.
Adams House
Mt. Auburn St
Arrow St
Linden St
Bow St
Plympton St
Holyoke St
Quincy House
Lowell House
Athens St
Wolf St
Grant St
Putnam Circle
Prescott
Ware St
Dana St
Harvard St
Cleveland St
Trowbridge St
Remington
Ellery
Massachusetts Av.
Green St
Franklin St
Kinnaird St
Putnam Av.
Magee
Akron St
Elmer St
Hingham St
Hayes St
Callender St
Hews St
Dodge St
Jay St
Howard St
Western Av.
Blackstone St
Putnam Av.
Ballord Pl.
RUSSELL E. HOY FIELD
River St
Fairmont St
Rockwell St
Andrew St
Allston St
Prince St
Kelly St
Kenwood St
Pleasant St
Whitney St
Chestnut St
Putnam Av.
Ma

University Museum of Natural History
Peabody Museum
Harvard-Yenching Library
Busch-Reisinger Building
William James Hall
Harvard University
A.M. Sackler Museum
Fogg Museum
Carpenter Center for the Visual Arts

Francis
Bryant St
Irving St
Scott
Farrar St
Kirkland St
Trowbridge St
Sumner Rd
Irving Ter
Divinity Av.
Oxford St

0 — 400 yards
0 — 400 m

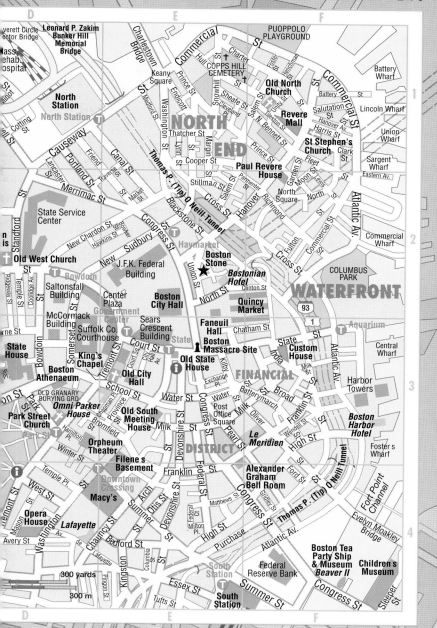

# STREET INDEX

# GENERAL INDEX

# Boston Subway

**B Line**

Boston College · Greycliff Rd · South St · Chestnut Hill Av. · Chiswick Rd · Sutherland Rd · Mount Hood Rd · Washington St · Summit Av. · Warren St · Griggs St · Allston St · Harvard Av. · Packards Corner · Babcock St · Pleasant St · St Paul St · BU West · BU Central · BU East · Blandford St · Kenmore · Hynes/ICA · Copley · Arlington · Boylston · Park Street

**C Line**

Cleveland Circle · Englewood Av. · Dean Road · Tappan St · Washington Sq · Fairbanks St · Brandon Hall · Summit Av. · St Paul St · Coolidge Corner · Kent St · St Mary's St

**D Line**

Riverside · Woodland · Waban · Eliot · Newton Highlands · Newton Centre · Chestnut Hill · Reservoir · Beaconsfield · Brookline Hills · Brookline Village · Longwood · Fenway · Kenmore

Hawes St · Summit Av. · St Mary's St

**E Line**

Heath · Back of the Hill · Riverway · Mission Park · Fenwood Road · Brigham Circle · Longwood Av. · Museum · Northeastern · Symphony · Prudential · Copley

Davis · Porter · Harvard · Central · Kendal/MIT · Charles/MGH · Park Street

Alewife

Lechmere · Science Park · Bowdoin · Government Center

Oak Grove · Malden Center · Wellington · Sullivan Square · Community College · North Station · Haymarket · State · Downtown Crossing · Chinatown · NE Medical Center · Back Bay/South End · Massachusetts Avenue · Ruggles · Roxbury Crossing · Jackson Square · Stony Brook · Green Street · Forest Hills

Wonderland · Revere Beach · Beachmont · Suffolk Downs · Orient Heights · Wood Island · Airport ✈ · Maverick · Aquarium · State

South Station · Broadway · Andrew · JFK/UMass

North Quincy · Wollaston · Quincy Center · Quincy Adams · Braintree

Savin Hill · Fields Corner · Shawmut · Ashmont · Cedar Grove · Butler · Milton · Central Avenue · Valley Road · Capen Street · Mattapan

### Legend

| Station |
| ⊕ Interchange station |
| ✈ Airport |

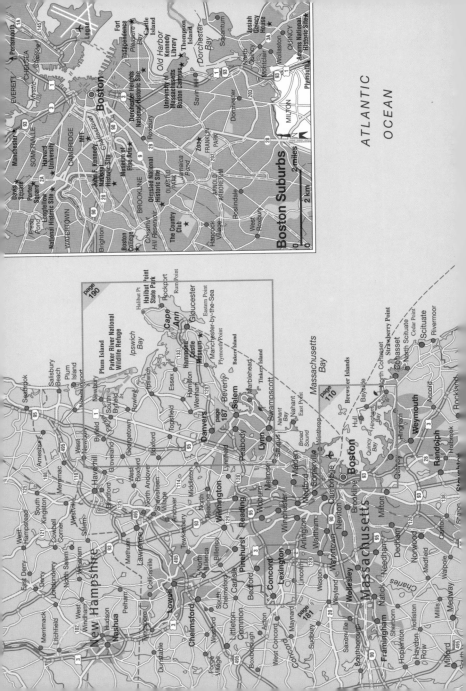

ATLANTIC
OCEAN

**Boston Suburbs**

0   1   2 miles
0   1   2 km

Massachusetts Bay

Massachusetts

New Hampshire

page 190

page 181

page 187

page 110

ATLANTIC OCEAN